THE JACOBEAN DRAMA

An Interpretation

by

UNA ELLIS-FERMOR

" *While we look up to Heaven we confound
Knowledge with knowledge.*"

" *Look you, the stars shine still.*"

SECOND EDITION, REVISED

METHUEN & CO. LTD. LONDON
36 *Essex Street, W.C.*

First Published   .   .   .   *February 20th, 1936*
Second Edition, Revised .   *1947*

To C. F. E. S.

PREFACE TO FIRST EDITION

THIS book is an attempt to interpret some aspects of the major Jacobean drama.

The time has passed, as a recent critic has said, for estimates of the Elizabethan and Jacobean dramatists, and it would be equally unnecessary, perhaps even ill-advised, to attempt surveys of either of those periods of dramatic history. The individual studies of the nineteenth-century critics culminated in Swinburne's and have led on, in our own day, to those of Rupert Brooke, Herford and Simpson, Lucas, Eliot and others ; the surveys, begun in the same century by Ward and Symonds, have been carried forward in the twentieth century by Schelling, Tucker Brooke, Boas, Reed, the authors of the *Cambridge History of English Literature* (vols. V and VI) and others working on specialized aspects of dramatic history. In the twentieth century a scientific foundation for historical and critical writing has been laid by the biographical and bibliographical researches of such scholars as Greg and Pollard, followed more recently by Alexander, Eccles, Hotson, Sisson and Wilson. All this being so, it is with some degree of hesitation that a modern reader adds a comment.

All that is attempted in the present book is a consideration of the outstanding work of less than a dozen playwrights, chiefly in regard to certain dominant lines of thought and habits of dramatic technique, which are indicated in the first two chapters. The individual studies which follow suggest, in more detail, how each of the playwrights stood in relation to these prevailing characteristics and attempt to give at the same time, for the reader who is not familiar with it, some indication of the individual quality of the work of each. For the benefit of those who wish to refer to them, a brief summary of our biographical knowledge, in the light of the most recently published research, is added under the heading ' Biographical Notes ', and for the same reason there is also given a note on the Jacobean stage and audience and a list of the most important publications in the field since the year 1923, where Sir Edmund Chambers' bibliographies in *The Elizabethan Stage* necessarily end.

Any attempt to survey the drama of the Jacobean age is met at the outset by two problems, both concerned with the defining of the material to be used. The first may be stated briefly as a problem of selection, the second is that of distinguishing individual work (within the material selected) in an age which was equally prone to aggressive individualism and to promiscuous collaboration.

I have selected as my limits in time a period beginning approximately in 1598 and ending rather before 1625, because I consider that this covers, if not precisely the reign of James I, at least the range of moods which characterized the drama of that reign ; the mood of unease and disillusionment which culminated in or about 1606 is already setting in, here and there, by anticipation, before the actual death of Elizabeth but when the probable consequences of that death were becoming plain. In view also of the gap in major dramatic output, apart from Shakespeare, that occurs between the early years of the 'nineties and the first plays of Ben Jonson, it seemed unavoidable to view the new dramatic age as a growth dating from or about the year 1598, after the cessation of the work of Marlowe, Peele, Greene, Kyd and at the beginning of that of Chapman, Marston and Ben Jonson. The upper date, chosen somewhat arbitrarily as being approximately that of the death of Fletcher, the end of the career of Middleton and the last of the reign, has been disregarded

in the case of Ford ; because of his clear connexion
in tone with the Middleton-Rowley tragi-comedies and
his obvious extension and completion of the tragic
theories of Webster, of Beaumont and Fletcher and of
Shakespeare, he belongs, in 1628–34, as essentially to
the Jacobean age which has passed as Ben Jonson in
1597–8 belonged to a Jacobean age which had not yet
begun.

The limits of material are far harder to determine
and must indeed be left, to some extent, to determine
themselves. I have included the work only of the
major dramatists. To have done otherwise would have
been, in a book of this size, to give incomplete consideration to certain outstanding ideas of the age which I
believe the drama to reveal more clearly perhaps than
any other of its activities. I hope at some future date
to treat, perhaps, separately, the so-called ' minor '
Jacobean drama and to include the names omitted here.
Inevitably there are some included whom another
author would have omitted and equally of course the
opposite comment will be made. This is inevitable
in any selection of material from so great a mass of
extant plays and so many authors. I cannot justify
my omission of Heywood and Shirley and my inclusion
of Fulke Greville otherwise than by saying that tor the
purposes of this interpretation the one, for all his isolation, seemed nearer the heart of the experience I am
concerned to describe, the others, all question of standing or achievement apart, to be less clearly indicative
of certain lines of thought which I believe, on the
whole, to represent the dominant mood of the major
drama.

One omission of even more substance must be separately justified—that of Massinger. I have not included
his separate work nor the work done in collaboration
with Fletcher otherwise than as a part of the Beaumont
and Fletcher group. The reason for this is that only
a very little of his work was certainly done before the

end of the period with which I am here concerned and
that the greater part of it belonged, in date and in spirit,
to a later age ; to have followed him into that later
period would have been to enter a domain other than
that of the dramatists included here, and to bisect him
appeared disrespectful. My reasons for including Ford
(otherwise in a very similar position) I have already
given.

The question of boundaries defined (or, at worst,
begged), there remains the far more teasing problem of
collaboration. In an age which produced, beside the
matchless individualism of the major plays of Shakespeare, Tourneur, Ben Jonson, Webster, Middleton and
Ford, products of almost indistinguishable collaboration
between Beaumont and Fletcher, Middleton and Rowley
and a shifting kaleidoscope of the work of Dekker,
Marston, Chapman, Ben Jonson, Middleton, Fletcher,
Massinger, Webster, Rowley and Ford, in which almost
every combination compatible with date can be found,
any attempt to group the drama under the authors
seems at once essential and impossible. It was the age
that left us not only the problems of the Beaumont-
Fletcher and the Middleton-Rowley canons, but the
individual cases of *Eastward Ho* and *The Witch of
Edmonton* and the problem, never laid to rest, of *The
Two Noble Kinsmen*.

Ideally, or perhaps it would be more accurate to say,
arithmetically, there should be no problem here at all,
and many generations of scholars have worked upon
the assumption that the two partners to a collaboration
can be recognized with reasonable sureness and
separated ; of course to a large extent this has been
and can be done. But the differences of conclusion
reached by the authorities in these special areas warn
us that it is not a simple problem of identification and
subtraction ; that some further law operates in the process of collaboration than those governing a plain mixture of parts. Doubtless in the case of hasty stop-gap

work like that recorded in the accounts of *Keep the Widow Waking*, it would, had the play survived, have been possible to pick out with reasonable certainty the parts Dekker wrote himself from those he farmed out to Webster, Ford and Rowley. But this is hardly collaboration in the strict sense ; it might more suitably be classed as stage joinery. In collaboration proper the difficulty remains a formidable one.

It is tempting in the case of Dekker, for instance, to adopt some such plan as the following : estimate Dekker's characteristics from the five plays which are reasonably likely to be from his hand only and call the result x, take the highest common factor of the twelve or so plays in which he is generally agreed to have had a hand and call it y, subtract from these plays again the ascertained qualities of Middleton, Massinger, Webster, Ford, Rowley, etc., and call the residuum z. Ideally, of course, x, y and z should prove of identical quality and we should be in a position to give a reliable estimate of Dekker's work as a whole. This excellent design is unfortunately frustrated by that curious law (of undeniable operation in Jacobean drama) by which the result of collaboration of any two or three men is not the summation of their qualities, but often some rather different product. The quality of *The Witch of Edmonton* could not be estimated by adding together Dekker, Rowley and Ford (so far as we know them), nor *Eastward Ho* by a stirring together, however thorough, of the individuals known as Marston, Chapman and Jonson. The relation between the characteristic work of two individual dramatists and that produced in collaboration is much more like that between two elements and the chemical compound they combine to form ; some attributes of both parents may indeed be traced, but it will almost certainly show other properties which are entirely its own. Were this not so the literature on the group loosely known as ' Beaumont and Fletcher ', for example, would have been reduced by at least half its bulk and the controversies on Jacobean canons laid long to rest.

I have followed therefore a procedure which has at least simplicity to recommend it though I myself am the first to admit its relative inadequacy. Using as basis those plays whose authenticity for one reason or another is confirmed, I have, in my estimates of the individual qualities of the authors, relied mainly upon these and upon obviously kindred parts (if there be any such) in the products of collaboration. General conclusions upon the quality or technical characteristics of Jacobean drama as a whole have of course been drawn from any of the extant body of significant plays, irrespective of problems of authorship.

It remains for me to express as much as is possible of my debt to those who have helped with this work. The debt to my predecessors cannot be stated here ; I hope it is indicated in the bibliographical references in the appendix and footnotes. I have to thank Miss E. Carrick and Miss M. Treadgold for help in checking and proof reading and for part of the substance of the biographical notes on Fulke Greville and Chapman ; in the same way, I have to thank Dr. R. E. Brettle for allowing me to consult him on the biography of Marston. For discussion of the whole book, chapter by chapter, I am deeply indebted to Dr. D. Tarrant and for conversations and discussions on dramatic imagery, for many years past, to Professor Caroline Spurgeon. For criticism and discussion of individual points I have to thank Dr. V. M. Jeffery, Dr. G. B. Harrison, Mr. J. Butt and Mr. R. Abercrombie. I wish to acknowledge the kind permission accorded by Mr. W. H. Godfrey and the Clarendon Press, Oxford, to reproduce the design for the Fortune Theatre, used to illustrate Chapter XIV, and finally, as always, I have to thank the officials of the British Museum Library for their unfailing help and courtesy.

U. M. E.-F.

December 1935
LONDON

PREFACE TO SECOND EDITION

RELATIVELY little alteration has been made, in this edition, to the main part of the volume. Extensive changes are not practicable under present conditions and the main differences between this edition and its predecessor are those made necessary by certain important biographical discoveries and deductions made between 1936 and 1946. These have not affected the critical estimates which constitute the body of the volume, but they have involved (for instance, in the case of R. C. Bald's work on Middleton) some serious modifications of our views on the lives of certain dramatists and the canons or chronology of their work. There are also considerable additions to the book lists in Appendix II, which, in the first edition, covered the period between the publication of E. K. Chambers' *The Elizabethan Stage* (1923) and the year 1936, and were designed to serve as a supplement to certain parts of the bibliographies in that work. Appendix II has now been extended to include a certain number of books and articles written between 1936 and 1946. For all general purposes E. K. Chambers' bibliographies remain, of course, the authoritative sources of information.

Certain errors that escaped my notice in correcting the first proofs have, I hope, been corrected and emended here.

Other changes, that might perhaps have been made in ordinary circumstances have been impossible under present conditions. No changes in the critical content have been attempted, even in cases where (as in the dating of *Troilus and Cressida*) an alternative interpretation has since commended itself. I have taken a slightly different view of the problem of *Troilus and Cressida* in my volume *The Frontiers of Drama*, just as I have, in that volume, extended the discussion on certain aspects of dramatic technique which form parts of Chapter II.

I hope, however, that enough of the fruit of recent research has been included in the appendices to make them as nearly representative of the position in 1946 as the earlier lists were for 1936, and that any necessary inferences from these have been indicated in the foot-notes to the body of the text.

My thanks are due to various friends who have detected and mentioned obscurities or misprints and, in especial, to Mrs. Walter Bullock for valuable help in re-organizing the biographical and bibliographical material at the end of the volume.

UNA ELLIS-FERMOR

LONDON
    1946

CONTENTS

ABBREVIATIONS

C.H.E.L.	Cambridge History of English Literature.
C.U.P.	Cambridge University Press.
Eng. Ass.	English Association.
Eng. Stud.	Englische Studien.
H.L.B.	Huntington Library Bulletin.
J.E.G.P.	Journal of English and Germanic Philology.
J.W.C.I.	Journal of the Warburg and Courtauld Institutes.
M.L.N.	Modern Language Notes.
M.L.R.	Modern Language Review.
Mal. Soc.	Malone Society.
Mod. Phil.	Modern Philology.
N. and Q.	Notes and Queries.
O.U.P.	Oxford University Press.
P.M.L.A.	Publications of the Modern Language Association of America.
P.Q.	Philological Quarterly.
Rev. Ang.-Amér.	Revue Anglo-Américaine.
Rev. Ang.-Germ.	Revue Anglo-Germanique.
Rev. de Litt. Comp.	Revue de la Littérature Comparée.
R.E.S.	Review of English Studies.
S.T.S.	Scottish Texts Society.
S. in Ph.	Studies in Philology.
T.L.S.	Times Literary Supplement.

CHAPTER I

THE JACOBEAN DRAMA

I

THE mood of the drama from the early Elizabethan to the late Jacobean period appears to pass through three phases, each reflecting with some precision the characteristic thought, preoccupation or attitude to the problems of man's being of the period to which it belongs.[1] That of the Elizabethan age proper, the drama of Greene, Kyd, Peele, Marlowe and the early work of Shakespeare, is characterized by its faith in vitality, its worship of the glorious processes of life, an expansion and elation of mind which corresponds directly to the upward movement of a prosperous and expanding society. This robust gusto appears directly in the comedies of Shakespeare and only less directly in *Romeo and Juliet*, instinct with the sense of the nobleness of life ; it is there in the vigour of the *Spanish Tragedy* no less than in the tenderness of Greene or Peele's tremulous response to loveliness. But already within this age another movement sets in, paradoxically, it might seem, were it not that one age always overlaps another and thought is for ever anticipated in germ. Marlowe, the leader of the earlier age in tragic thought, already points it towards the sense of defeat that was so marked a characteristic of the Jacobeans. For all his strength, for all the desperate valour of his aspiration, the final position of each play in turn is an intimate defeat of aspiration itself. This runs through a protean series of forms, as might be supposed of an Elizabethan thinker, to culminate in the quiescence of *Edward II*. Marlowe's keen spiritual sense sees through the delusion of prosperity that intoxicates his contemporaries as a whole and anticipates

---

[1] I regard these phases as covering roughly the periods from the beginning of the Elizabethan drama to about 1598, from about 1598 to 1610 or 1611, and from about 1610 or 1611 to near the end of the reign of James I.

that mood of spiritual despair which is its necessary result and becomes the centre of the later tragic mood. And this position is reached by Marlowe through one section of his experience which is, in its turn, an epitome of the experience that touched a large number of the Jacobean dramatists after him, his exploration of the system of Machiavelli.

The impact of this system came obliquely to the Elizabethans, through the preposterous stage figure of the pseudo-Machiavellian villain, which presented truly neither Machiavelli's individual precepts nor the balance of his thought as a whole. Yet, because of the perversions suffered by his thought in transmission, what was received by the Elizabethan drama brought with it not only the withering breath of matter-of-fact materialism proper to his method, but a more bitterly cynical individualism than he had ever implied. This, touching some of the playwrights immediately (while others it almost missed), spread gradually over the habit of tragic thought, reinforced by the tradition of Marlowe's study of spiritual defeat.

It was reinforced still more effectively after the turn of the century by the apprehensions and the disillusionment that spread through political and social life with the death of Elizabeth, the accession of James, the influence of his court and the instability of the first years of his reign. This mood, culminating as it did in and about the year 1605, took the form for public and private men alike of a sense of impending fate, of a state of affairs so unstable that great or sustained effort was suspended for a time and a sense of the futility of man's achievement set in. One immediate corollary of this is a preoccupation with death where the Elizabethan had been in love with life. Even when the actual threat was removed, those who survived found the great age gone and themselves the inheritors of poverty of spirit.[1]

[1] This period of despondency or anxiety appears to last, in one form or another, from some four or five years before the death of Elizabeth, to some five or six years after the accession of James ; the causes were similar though not identical throughout the period. The sense of instability in the latter years of the reign of Elizabeth came mainly from the memory of the crises of the past three accessions and of the series of plots to assassinate the Queen throughout her reign combined with the knowledge that there was no obvious heir to the throne at her death. The threats of invasion by the Catholic power of Spain culminating in 1588 were still fresh in men's memories, as

These things then were the heritage of the Jacobean drama on the threshold of its growth : spiritual uncertainty springing in part from the spreading of Machiavellian materialism emphasized by Marlowe's tragic thought and in still greater degree from the cause which has reproduced it to-day for us, fear of the impending destruction of a great civilization. The greatest plays of the years 1600–12 form a group reflecting this mood in one form or another : *Troilus and Cressida, Hamlet, The Malcontent, All's Well that Ends Well, Measure for Measure, Volpone, Lear, Macbeth, Timon of Athens, The Revenger's Tragedy, The Tragedy of Byron, The Alchemist, The Atheist's*

was the knowledge that Pius V had exempted Elizabeth's Catholic subjects from their oath of allegiance in 1570. The larger the number of her possible successors (James of Scotland, Lady Arabella Stuart, certain English nobles of royal blood, various foreign princes—particularly the Infanta of Spain—and, latterly, Essex himself) and the more level their claims, the more likelihood was there of civil war breaking out at her death and of the intervention of foreign power. The situation reached its crisis in the rebellion of Essex on February 7, 1601, and was to some degree alleviated by his defeat and execution. But the shock of the fall of so great and brilliant a figure had in itself an effect second only to the relief at the collapse of the political menace. By the following year (1602) it was generally recognized that James was the probable heir.

The short period of relief that followed his accession in 1603 gave way almost at once to a feeling of uncertainty and danger even greater than that of the last years of Elizabeth. His personal unpopularity as a sovereign went some way to bring this about. The lowering of standards in the court was immediate ; slackness of discipline, loss of dignity and increase of expense combined to produce at once dissatisfaction and a feeling of unsteadiness. Plots to depose him broke out again almost at once ; Cobham's in November 1603 involved Ralegh, a man who still represented the Elizabethans in the eyes of some of his contemporaries, and the Gunpowder plot in November 1605, which only just missed its mark, would have left the country deprived at one blow of all its leaders, temporal and ecclesiastical, and all the machinery of state. The constant plotting of the Jesuits against James went on for some time after the failure of the plot in 1605.

These are of course only a few of the political reasons which help to account on that side for the mood of misgiving, apprehension and uncertainty which spread through the thinking world, and is reflected with particular clearness in the drama, during ten or twelve years. (One of the most easily available recent summaries of the situation in England between 1598 and 1606 will be found in Mr. G. B. Harrison's chapter *The National Background* in *A Companion to Shakespeare Studies*, pp. 163–86. Cambridge, 1934.)

Tragedy, The Chaste Maid in Cheapside, The White Devil.
Through all these runs, besides the sense of spiritual emptiness
or fear, a growing tendency to hold more closely to the evidence
of the senses and of practical experience, to limit knowledge
to a non-spiritual world of man and his relations with man.
Comedy thus, with Marston, Ben Jonson, Middleton, Chapman,
becomes increasingly immediate and concentrated upon the
manners, habits and morals of man as a primarily social, non-
poetic and non-spiritual animal.   Tragi-comedy with Beaumont,
Fletcher and Massinger escapes into romance.   Most significant
of all, tragedy, the form of drama responsible for interpreting
to man the conditions of his own being, becomes satanic,
revealing a world-order of evil power or, if it attempt excursions
beyond man's immediate experience, bewildered and confused.
This, passing through the work indicated above, finds its fullest
expression in the unremitting satanism of Tourneur and,
belatedly, in the scientific detachment of Middleton.

After the spiritual nadir of the middle years of the period
a slow return to equilibrium sets in.   The great age has gone,
but so has the age of brooding, Senecan apprehension.   ' O nos
dura sorte creatos ', that phrase which epitomizes (for the
early Jacobeans, as for Seneca or for us) the inexplicable fate
of a generation born for destruction, is no longer the instinctive
expression of their perplexity.   Satanism and a revived Sene-
canism go hand in hand for a time, but gradually they give
place to a mood that is sometimes serenity, sometimes indifference, but, in either case, that of an age that has ceased to live
in touch with catastrophe.   The resolution is complete in Shakespeare's latest plays, it breaks through imperfectly in incidental
touches in the *Duchess of Malfi*, more strongly in the later plays
of the Middleton-Rowley group, and is supreme in Ford.   ' Look
you, the stars shine still.'   They do, indeed ; but the whole
gamut of tragic experience lies between Greene or Peele at the
beginning and Ford at the end of the period, like as their moods
and cadences sometimes are, and the severity, the increasingly
undramatic continence which is the most marked feature of
Ford's development, shows that a phase is closing, that he is
the last spokesman of a dramatic period that, from the first
plays of the early Elizabethans to his latest work, had been one
continuous sequence in three clearly defined movements.   It
is with the last two of these that this study is primarily concerned,

but something must be said first of the earlier, from which the later originated.

II

The double life of the age, the outer life of event and action and the inner of reflection and thought, stored in the drama, finding a high imaginative interpretation in theme, in commentary and, perhaps most fruitfully, in incidental and revealing imagery, is markedly different in the first two phases of the period, the Elizabethan proper and the early Jacobean. The notable changes that came with the turn of the century and the last years of Elizabeth form, in poetry as in social and political life, a division between the world of the 'nineties now past and the age we call Jacobean, setting in before the actual accession of James. In drama especially, the second grew out of the first, was in fact so directly fathered by it that the relationship between them forms the most fitting introduction to the later growth.

In the earlier drama, the Elizabethan, the qualities most marked are clarity and exhilaration, the material chosen the tumultuous event of war and conquest or the romance of fairy-tale, myth or love. It reflects, as great poetic drama must, rather the desires of its audience than their normal lives, gathering together the moments of heightened experience in which they have lived most swiftly rather than the normal alternating of rapid event and inertia. The imperishable instinct for horrors that chill the blood and raise the hair is satisfied simply, lustily, childishly (almost, in the case of Kyd, gaily), with a gusto as healthy as high winds in spring ; *The Spanish Tragedy*, *The Battle of Alcazar*, *Titus Andronicus*, *The Massacre at Paris*, *The Jew of Malta*, even *Arden of Feversham* and *The Yorkshire Tragedy*, do not so much represent the average effect of Elizabethan daily life as reveal a hearty, credulous love of straightforward bloodshed, murder and mutilation uncontaminated by sophisticated skill of setting. Equally robust and rude is the new patriotism, the sudden realization of nationalism which runs a whole gamut, from jingoism in Peele's *Edward I* through Gaunt and his compeers to the gravity of *Henry V*, the bright exhilaration of the last scene of the *Arraignment of Paris* or the chivalry of Greene. The average man's eager preoccupation with politics foreign and domestic finds its account in a whole world of historical plays, Shakespeare's, Greene's, Marlowe's, Peele's and a host of chronicles given over wholly or in part to the exploration of problems of government, of the nature of kingship, the king-becoming virtues, the evolution of the common Elizabethan's idea of a state. And beside this vivid mirroring of event are the plays of fantasy and romance, the delicate myths of Lyly, the diaphanous joy and humour of Peele's *Arraignment* and *Old Wives' Tale*, the straightforward tenderness of Greene's romantic scenes, their descendants in the early romantic plays of Shakespeare. Scattered throughout this drama are reflections of speculative thought carried out in the same mood of bold exploration, more amply revealed in the prose and metaphysical verse, but never with more depth of implication than in *Tamburlaine* and *Faustus*. All this, most noticeably, is not a literature of escape from, but a road to life ; a way into reality by imaginative experience strictly related to, though no mere reproduction of, the experience of every day. Above all it is a literature of radiant comedy and of tragedy (and it produced very little genuine tragedy outside *Faustus* and *Romeo and Juliet*) [1] still breathless from its first contemplation of the magnitude of fate.

But already Marlowe's decisive genius had made a significant modification in the field of experience to be drawn on by the drama, had defined the underlying mood that was to be a main factor in the development of English tragedy and in so doing had delimited indirectly the mood and field of its comedy.[2] The full effect of his emphatic decision does not show itself immediately and might indeed never have done so had not much else in the fortunes and experience of the Jacobean age been propitious, but, coming when he does, the first explorer of tragic thought in English drama, he imposes something of his inter-

---

[1] Of the five or six plays of major interest in the tragic form, some (*Edward II, Richard III, Richard II*) are primarily histories with their main interest in problems of state, government and kingship, while others (*The Spanish Tragedy, The Jew of Malta*, &c.), though they end in catastrophe, have not the mood of poetic tragedy that is present in *Faustus, Romeo and Juliet* and their Jacobean successors.

[2] This can, as I have suggested later (see *post*, p. 17), only be realized when the whole body of comedy is considered, the individual comedy being far freer in its choice of mood and treatment than is tragedy which must either fulfil its function of interpretation or visibly repudiate it.

pretation, contributes at least to the force and direction of its progress. For in Marlowe we find, earlier than in any of his contemporaries, the significant schism between the ideal or spiritual world and the world pragmatically estimated by everyday observation, which seems, in one form or another, to be an essential part of any tragic conception of the universe. The cleavage is anticipated in *Tamburlaine* and presented in its full operation in *Faustus*, where the possibility of reconciling the course of man's life with the aspiration of his spiritual instincts is rejected. ' Belike we must sin and so consequently die. Aye, we must die an everlasting death.' The separation between the two worlds is complete and the total of man's experience for him is thereafter no true universe but a battleground, a dual presentation of mutually contradictory experiences. Rejecting, then, the medieval Church's conclusion upon this conflict, Marlowe, a true pragmatic Elizabethan in this, accepts the immediate and actual world as real and arrives, through the series of historical plays, at some kind of synthetic interpretation of the half he has chosen to retain. But the invisible world he has rejected troubles him, though the Church's anathemas do not, and nearly to the end a·note of ·defiance betrays his insecurity : ' Of this am I assured, that death ends all.' He is not assured, and, what is more important, he transmits to the succeeding dramatic tradition a limited interpretation, a deliberately truncated universe, a world that is self-contained in its actualism, seeking its synthesis and its elucidation within its own bounds, rejecting that wider universe of the soul of which the writers outside the drama still for a while remain free.

Marlowe in this is less an innovator than a thinker coming at the climax of a movement, defining what has long been implicit and, in so defining, giving to it a fresh direction, a modified or intensified significance. The beginnings of this movement may be traced in the separation of drama from the medieval Church and the slow process of secularization has occupied some three hundred years. But because of this act of separation, in spite of the retention of doctrinal and traditional themes, the drama seems to have grown beneath the surface during that interval into the least ecclesiastical—if not an anti-ecclesiastical —art. It was at the hands of Marlowe that the Church finally lost the drama but his attitude of religious atheism would not have been enough alone to separate the world of the drama from the complete universe still contemplated by many of his contemporaries if it had not been for the part played by Church and drama in their mutual misinterpretations of each other and of that universal whole.[1]

For, partly through the accident of Marlowe's leadership, but partly also through conscious or unconscious anti-ecclesiasticism, the dramatists [2] arrive earlier than the body of their contemporaries at a uniform rejection of the element of religion which habitually plays so large a part in the evolution of drama and so small a part in its full development. For outside the drama we can still meet in Marlowe's contemporaries of the late sixteenth century either a simple piety or a philosophic interpretation capable of beholding the apparent conflict as two aspects of a single world, capable of dwelling in this single world, this true universe where the seen is only an image of the unseen, of passing easily and without anxiety from contemplation of one aspect to that of the other. Whether in Sidney's sonnets, in Nashe's verses on the plague, in the description of the death of Sir Humphrey Gilbert, in Hooker's survey of the nature of Law, in Bacon's pseudo-Aristotelian interpretation of First and Second Causes, there is, in all these, no doubt as to the relations of the spiritual world and the world of observed fact, nor as to the validity of man's judgment in supposing the seen to be the image and instrument of the unseen.

This still characteristic attitude, this unrestricted citizenship in two worlds simultaneously, this power of transfusing the world of affairs suddenly with irradiation from a spiritual universe at once circumambient and interpenetrating, this rhythm of which Marlowe's hard, clear thought had helped to denude the drama, is never better seen than in the man who seems himself an epitome of his age, Sir Walter Ralegh. In him is laid bare more clearly than perhaps in any other one man the process by which the best of both these worlds is achieved. In his letters and the records of his life we find an explorer associated with

[1] The significance of this separation is brought out clearly by Mr. Granville Barker in his chapter on *Shakespeare's Dramatic Art* in *A Companion to Shakespeare Studies*, pp. 46–87.

[2] It is, of course, understood that this applies only to dramatic work. The non-dramatic work of any given poet may retain the very qualities which are significantly absent from his plays.

every major expedition of the last fifteen years of Elizabeth's reign, a leader of great practical acumen and an almost matchless power of controlling men, a soldier of some distinction and an able captain ; a courtier and adventurer who had made his way by studying the whims of the Queen and made himself hated by forcing others in turn to study his ; a statesman who achieved eminence, in Ireland if not in England ; an historian and chronicler second to none in his age ; a scientist among the first and no mean mathematician ; a bold, adventurous man whose instinct for intrigue was only checked by his impatience of the processes of intriguing ; a worldling—but such a one as reminds us there are worse things than a good worldling. And out of this medley of intrigue and adventure, extravagance and violence, comes a voice of grave assurance :

> Blood must be my bodies balmer,
> No other balme will there be given
> Whilst my soule like a white Palmer
> Travels to the land of heaven.

Nor is this a paradox. Ralegh, bred up as so many of his generation to ' hold the world but as the world ', pursued it whole-heartedly in the half-conscious assurance that the other was at hand the moment he chose to withdraw into it. It was indeed about them on every side, and though they did not necessarily mingle the two, they did not forget which claimed precedence. Indeed, the mind of Ralegh (and of not a few contemporaries of like habit) has a double motion like the planets of Faustus's system, and while the daily revolution is concerned only with worldly business, the *primum mobile* is ever exerting, unseen, the quiet and irresistible pressure of its heavenly sway.

Such things as these are not the momentary indications of a passing mood, but rather the decantation of his thought, clear, simple and quintessential, so closely related to the sum of precedent experience as to be alone capable of completing and containing it. This apparent paradox—in truth the simplest of conditions—is the characteristic approach to life of Ralegh and of many of his contemporaries.

It is, then, this unity, whether in terms of Bacon's immense lucidity or Hooker's, or of Ralegh's snipe-like flight, threading from world to world, it is this acceptance of both the outer and the inner world, the seen and the unseen, the evidence of observed fact and the intuition of a spiritual universe, which

Marlowe rejects and the drama after him is for a time powerless to recover, though here and there an individual such as Dekker makes a faint attempt. The denial of dogmatic theology gives a momentary freedom to the range of thought, a sudden and immense increase of stature and dignity to the figure of man who thus becomes the significant deity, at once priest and victim, of his own universe. For a time with Marlowe himself the stirring of this freedom, like a dark wind of thought, moves him to an exultation higher than the contemplations of his contemporaries whether in poetry or in drama. But even in him the mood dies down and the gigantic figure of Faustus, archtype of man's defiance in defeat, shrinks in Mortimer ' to a little point, A kind of nothing '.

III

The sinking of the clear exaltation of Elizabethan dramatic poetry into the sophisticated, satirical, conflicting mood, deeply divided, of the Jacobean drama has many concurrent causes other than Marlowe's rejection, after *Faustus*, of that ' wonder which is broken knowledge '. There were far-reaching political and social changes consequent upon the death of Elizabeth and the changing of the dynasty and these were felt by anticipation some years before that death actually happened. The apprehension, regret and disillusionment inevitable to the conscious passing of a long period of high civilization were not in this case unfounded, and those who had known the great age, even those who had only grown to manhood during its latest years, were touched by them, often (like the generation that succeeded the Great War) without being able to define their loss in what had passed. Moreover, the literature, and especially the drama, had reached a stage of its development in which some transition from wonder and discovery to assessment and criticism was inevitable ; this would have happened had Elizabeth been immortal. As it was, the phase, within the drama itself, of testing and questioning the findings and methods of the earlier age coincided with a period of disillusionment and apprehension in the world from which that drama drew its themes and this, combined with the still living tradition of Marlowe's thought, set up a mood which resembles on one side that of English poetry in the second and third decades of the twentieth century and on another that of Seneca and his public in the first.

This was especially emphasized in the dramatic tradition by a factor which, though partly accidental, is of overwhelming importance, the impact upon the poetic universe of the Elizabethans of the thought of Machiavelli. Nothing could have been more alien to Elizabethan dramatic poetry, as it appears in the early work of Marlowe, Peele, Greene and Shakespeare, than Machiavelli's cold, scientific appraisal of the poverty of man's spirit. Although, in their utter inability to grasp the essentials of his system, they at first twisted his thought into some likeness to their own healthy love of melodramatic villainy, enough of his clear, withering honesty survives the perversion to drive the drama with irresistible force towards the acceptance of a materialist universe. For (and it is there that one accidental element occurs) through Gentillet's perversion of the system in the *Contre-Machiavel*,[1] a figure so suitable for drama was evolved from Machiavelli's essentially undramatic philosophy that the Machiavellian villain became one of the most popular stage figures for twenty years and nearly every tragic dramatist from Marlowe to Webster adds his share. Again it is Marlowe who is responsible for the acclimatizing of Machiavellianism in England,[2] and so again it is in Marlowe's own career that the trend of the later drama is anticipated. While the Machiavellian villain appealed to Kyd and to many of his public only as a theatrical figure apt for promiscuous villainy (which would have had relatively little lasting effect), Marlowe was concerned with the real system that lay behind this farrago of preposterous melodrama, came to a limited understanding of Machiavelli himself and so transmitted to his successors the results of his exploration of a materialist and approximately satanic interpretation of life. His own discovery of Machiavelli came hard upon the heels of the negative conclusions of *Faustus* and confirmed in him the rejection of the spiritual universe by offering him a systematic, logical, self-contained and severe interpretation of the world of facts which might else have been left disparate and inconclusive. The ardour of Marlowe's early Machiavellianism in the *Jew of Malta* and the *Massacre at Paris*

[1] Innocent Gentillet: *Discours . . . Contre Nicholas Machiavel*: (1576.)

[2] Kyd's study of Lorenzo is actually both earlier and more complete than any one of Marlowe's figures, with the possible exception of the Guise, but it is Marlowe who first invests the figure with tragic intensity.

is only matched by the pressure it exerted upon the subsequent tradition.

For Machiavelli, although easily misrepresented, was no mean force. One of the greatest, in some ways the most independent of assessors of human values, deeply civilized, trained to the highest point of sagacity and scientific precision, honest as few men are honest, Machiavelli offered to the mind that could grasp him with any completeness a compact, unshakeable interpretation of civilization based frankly upon the assumption of weakness, ingratitude and ill-will as essential elements of human character and society, upon the acceptance of religion only as the means of making a people docile to their governors, upon the open admission of cruelty, parsimony and betrayal of faith as necessary (if regrettable) instruments. It is the sublime honesty of thus setting down what many men assumed in action but denied in profession that caught Marlowe's imagination ; it was Marlowe's exploration of the system that imposed upon a drama already the inheritor of spiritual bewilderment a tradition by which it proceeded to a deeper and deeper confusion. Moreover, the Machiavellian theory of society, in the hands of its more serious students such as Marlowe, reached English drama in a peculiarly vicious form, again partly as the result of an accident. Lacking the background of Machiavelli's experience (a country invaded by foreigners, given over to civil conflict between State and State for which there seemed no remedy in the ordinary course of political event), they missed the motive upon which the writing of *The Prince* [1] at least depends : ' justum enim est bellum quibus necessarium, et pia arma ubi nulla nisi in armis spes '.[2] The dramatists, without a single exception, pass by without perceiving it the burning vision of the twenty-sixth chapter of *The Prince*, the great sixteenth-century vision of Italia Redenta—redeemed by the one thing that could unite it, the dominance of a just, firm, ruthless leader.

Nè posso esprimere con quale amore e' fussi ricevuto in tutte quelle provincie che hanno patito per queste illuvioni esterne ; con che sete

---

[1] It was, until recently, supposed that *Il Principe* was not available in English until the middle of the seventeenth century, but Hardin Craig, in his edition of 1944 (University of North Carolina Press) finds reason to believe that one existed in MS. before 1585.

[2] *Il Principe*, XXVI.

di vendetta, con che ostinata fede, con che pietà, con che lacrime.
Quali porte se gli serrerebbano ? quali populi gli negherebbano la
obedienzia ? quale invidia se gli opporrebbe, quale italiano gli
negherebbe l'ossequio ? [1]

By omitting the corner-stone of his thought, this vision of national
union and liberation, by isolating from their context the most
startling of his individual statements on religion, war and
government and by appealing directly and indirectly to current
sixteenth-century superstition and sentiment, it was easy for
the popular purveyors of the tradition to display his books as
the grammar of a diabolic creed, inculcating a policy of self-
seeking and cynical aggression.   So easy was it to spread this
impression that even Marlowe, who seems to have read Machiavelli himself, appears to have read him partly by the light of
this prejudice and to produce a materialist interpretation tinged
with satanism which is certainly not Machiavelli's, though the
process by which it is derived is an easy one :

> Mi è parso più conveniente andare drieto alla verità effettuale della
> cosa, che alla imaginazione di essa . . . perchè egli è tanto discosto
> da come si vive a come si doverrebbe vivere, che colui che lascia quello
> che si fa per quello che si doverrebbe fare impara piuttosto la ruina
> che la preservazione sua.[2]
> Si vorrebbe essere l'uno e l'altro [amato e temuto] ; ma perchè
> egli è difficile accozzarli insieme, è molto più sicuro essere temuto
> che amato, quando si abbia a mancare dell' uno de' dua.[3]
> Si vede, per esperienzia ne' nostri tempi, quelli principi avere fatto

---

[1] I cannot describe the love with which he would be received in
all those provinces that have suffered from these foreign invasions ;
with what thirst for vengeance, with what dogged faith, with what
religious reverence, with what tears.   What doors would be shut
against him ?   What people would refuse him obedience ?   What
envy would oppose him ?   What Italian would refuse him allegiance ?
(*Il Principe*, XXVI.)
[2] I have thought it better to investigate the actual truth of the
matter than what we imagine it to be . . . because how we live is
so far away from how we ought to live that he who leaves what is
done for the sake of what ought to be done brings about his own
ruin rather than his own preservation. (*Il Principe*, XV.   The text
used is that of Guido Mazzoni and Mario Casella : *Tutte le Opere
storiche e letterarie di Niccolò Machiavelli*.   Firenze, 1929.)
[3] One would prefer to be both [loved and feared] ; but since it is
difficult to manage both at once, it is much safer to be feared than
loved, when one has to let go one or the other. (*Il Principe*, XVII.)

gran cose, che della fede hanno tenuto poco conto, e che hanno saputo con l'astuzia aggirare e' cervelli degli uomini ; e alla fine hanno superato quelli che si sono fondati in sulla lealtà. . . . E se gli uomini fussino tutti buoni, questo precetto non sarebbe buono ; ma perchè sono tristi, e non la [la fede] osservarebbono a te, tu etiam non l'hai ad osservare a loro. . . . Anzi ardirò di dire questo, che, avendole e osservandole sempre, sono dannose ; e parendo di averle, sono utili ; come parere pietoso, fedele, umano, intero, religioso, ed essere ; ma stare in modo edificato con l'animo, che, bisognando non essere, tu possa e sappi mutare el contrario.[1]

Come dimostrano tutti coloro che ragionano del vivere civile, e come ne è piena di esempli ogni istoria, è necessario a chi dispone una republica, ed ordina leggi in quella, presupporre tutti gli uomini essere cattivi,[2] e che gli abbiano sempre a usare la malignità dello animo loro, qualunque volta ne abbiano libera occasione ; e quando alcuna malignità sta occulta un tempo, procede da una occulta cagione, che, per non si essere veduta esperienza del contrario, non si conosce. . . . Gli uomini non operono mai nulla bene, se non per necessità.[3]

Pensando dunque donde possa nascere, che, in quegli tempi antichi, i popoli fossero più amatori della libertà che in questi ; credo nasca da quella medesima cagione che fa ora gli uomini manco forti : la quale credo sia la diversità della educazione nostra dall'antica, fondata nella diversità della religione nostra dalla antica. . . . La nostra religione ha glorificato più gli uomini umili e contemplativi, che gli attivi. Ha dipoi posto il sommo bene nella umiltà, abiezione, e nel dispregio delle cose umane : quell' altra lo poneva nella grandezza dello animo, nella fortezza del corpo, ed in tutte le altre cose atte a

---

[1] From the evidence of our own times it can be seen that those princes have achieved greatly who have taken little count of good faith and have known how to mislead men with their astuteness and in the end they have overcome those who have relied on loyalty. . . . Now if men were all good this precept would not be good ; but since men are bad and will not observe it [faith] with you, you also need not observe it with them. . . . I will go so far as to say this, that if you have them [virtues] and always practise them they are dangerous ; but they are useful if you appear to have them : as, to appear compassionate, faithful, humane, upright and religious—and to be such, but to have a mind so constituted that, when it is necessary to be the opposite you may be able to change to it. (*Il Principe*, XVIII.)

[2] I have departed from the text of Mazzoni and Casella here. They adopt the reading ' rei '.

[3] As all writers point out who treat of the organization of society and as every history illustrates, he who organizes a republic and appoints its laws, must of necessity assume all men to be bad and that they will try to exercise their evil instincts whenever a favourable opportunity offers. If this evil remains quiescent for a time, there is a hidden reason for it, which, from our having no contrary experience, is not recognized. . . . Men do not work in the direction of good unless forced by necessity. (*Discorsi*, I, iii.)

fare gli uomini fortissimi.   E se la religione nostra richiede che tu
abbi in te fortezza, vuole che tu sia atto a patire più che a fare una
cosa forte.   Questo modo di vivere, adunque, pare che abbi renduto
il mondo debole, e datolo in preda agli uomini scelerati ; i quali
sicuramente lo possono maneggiare, veggendo come l'università degli
uomini, per andarne in Paradiso, pensa più a sopportare le sue
battiture che a vendicarle.[1]

The figure of the self-seeking ' politician ', with no object
beyond his own supremacy, though full of melodramatic promise
is actually unrealizable, and Marlowe himself perceived its
insufficiency as soon as he examined it closely.[2]   But the unreal
and fantastic figure of the Machiavellian continued to attract,
with a curious, sinister fascination, both dramatists and public
until well into the second decade of the seventeenth century.
Always it contained the elements of its own destruction, always
it operated in a world in which there was ' no place to mount '
to any significant height, and it transmitted also something of
the real pragmatical estimate of Machiavelli, resulting in an
uneasy attempt to limit their reading of life, even in tragedy to,
' la verità effettuale della cosa ', edged with the unspoken fear
that ' losing this world we lose all '.   Shakespeare alone of all
the major dramatists appears to escape ; he followed Marlowe's
conclusion (after working over the same ground in his double
picture of Richard of Gloucester) and rejected the pseudo-
Machiavellian villain as a figure psychologically contradictory

[1] When I consider how it happens that the men of antiquity were
fiercer lovers of liberty than those of to-day I am inclined to believe
that it comes from the same cause as our lack of robustness, and that
cause is the difference in upbringing then and now, arising from the
difference of religions. . . .   Our religion has glorified men of humble
and contemplative mind more than men of action.   It has in fact
declared man's highest good to stand in humility and abjection, in
contempt of human things : where the other placed it rather in greatness of soul, in strength of body and in all those other things that tend
to make men valiant.   And if our religion ever recommends strength,
it demands rather that you should be strong in suffering than that you
should achieve a valiant deed.   This way of life seems to have weakened
the world and given it over as a prey to evil men.   They are secure
in their control of it, knowing that the majority of mankind, having
in mind their places in paradise, think more of supporting injuries
than of avenging them. (*Discorsi*, II, ii.)

[2] The tragedy of Mortimer (such tragedy as there is in that
denuded figure) is not that he falls, but that ' there was no place to
mount up higher '.

and so, ultimately, dramatically valueless.[1] But he does not seem to accept, either directly or indirectly, the Machiavellian scale of values whose oppressive influence can be traced, to greater or less degree, in most of the succeeding tragedy. Marlowe remains, then, the main channel by which this interpretation of life entered the Jacobean drama ; Kyd it is true anticipates him, but the others derive from him. Greene's [2] study is a childish repudiation of his ; Shakespeare and Tourneur [3] take over his findings with their own elaboration ; Chapman's [4] picture (far more superficial than it appears at first glance) is a reasonable enough reaction against Marlowe's ; Marston's [5] though partly original is often a confused and incompletely synthesized acceptance of his deductions, and Webster,[6] who makes the most deeply original studies after Marlowe's, is caught immediately into the world of Machiavellian values that the later work of Marlowe had bequeathed.

[1] I do not find in Shakespeare what is so noticeable in Marlowe, the attempt to identify himself imaginatively with the system in the hope of finding there an answer to his political curiosity.

[2] The study of Ateukin in *James IV* is slight and shows little more than an acquaintance with the terminology transfused with the same revulsion that dictates the references to 'pestilent Machiavellian policy' in the *Groatsworth* and elsewhere.

[3] Vindice has tricks of the politician about him, but very little of Machiavelli's spirit and he is primarily an avenger, a character of Seneca's not Machiavelli's fathering. D'Amville is a better Machiavellian in mood and conduct, but often where he appears to owe most to him, in his stoicism and his nature-worship, he seems on closer study to go behind him to his source, Livy, and probably also to Lucretius (through Montaigne).

[4] This consists chiefly in the use of the terms 'politician' and 'policy' by Byron and Bussy, both of whom, but especially Byron, are in their main qualities incompatible with either the cunning or the secrecy of the true Machiavellian.

[5] Piero is an interesting cross of Machiavellian with Senecan tyrant, Mendoza and Malevole sound studies in the tradition of Marlowe's Guise.

[6] In Flamineo and Bosola he studies the flaws by which normal humanity almost inevitably destroys the perfect flowering of the complete politician ; in the Cardinal (*Duchess of Malfi*) he makes the only surviving attempt to present dramatically a figure derived directly from Machiavelli's Prince.

IV

> While we look up to Heaven we confound
> Knowledge with knowledge.

Webster's words, then, not only sum up the content of his own great tragedies, but are the most nearly universal comment that was made upon the world of chaotic thought behind the Jacobean drama.   The outer and the inner worlds have become two ; Bacon's First Cause working through Second Causes has vanished, at least from the world the drama presents, and their philosophy,

> that leaned on heaven before
> Shrinks to a second cause and is no more.

The visible is no longer either the image or the instrument of an invisible world, but exists *in* and *per se* as an alternative truth in conflict with the other and offering a rival interpretation of phenomena. So marked is this divergence that there is hardly a dramatist who can bring the two together.   In comedy this is not necessarily noticed because it is a prerogative of comedy to select its material from a wide range of possibilities, farce, satire, romance, fairy-tale and others, so that no individual play suggests limitation and only the consideration of the whole body of comedy reveals that after about 1600 there is something lacking, that there is an emphasis on the immediate and a rejection of the remote, a habit of accurate satiric observation rather than poetic or romantic idealization.[1]   But in tragedy, whose function is different from that of comedy and not merely complemental to it, which must by its very nature try to evaluate all the known issues of life and attempt an estimate of that total validity, this is apparent at once in the whole body and in nearly all individual specimens.   There is hardly a tragedian of standing in whom the basis, implicit or explicit, of his tragic conception

---

[1] This, as has been suggested (*ante*, p. 6), is a necessary corollary of the development of Jacobean tragedy. Of romantic idealization there is, of course, plenty after the year 1600, but it is not usually intimately mingled with the normal comedy, appearing rather as an accidental aside (with Middleton's earliest work) or as frank escape into a non-real world (with Beaumont and Fletcher) ; the difference between the final effect of these plays and of, say, *Twelfth Night, As You Like It, Much Ado* indicates the extent to which the separation has gone since the Elizabethan age proper.

2

is not this sense of the loss of a spiritual significance from within the revealed world of fact and event.   And as the world has become two, of which the dramatists have chosen for their province the immediate, so knowledge has become dual and what is valid in the one is meaningless in the other ; to pass from one to the other is no longer as with Sidney, Hooker, Bacon, even Ralegh, to look through the manifestation to the thing manifested but to ' confound knowledge with knowledge '. In that vast range of drama very few characters (except those officially concerned, priests, friars and the like) ever attempt this glance out from the world in which their fortunes move to the circumambient reality which assigns at once its proportions and its rhythm.   In the world of Marston, Chapman, Middleton, Tourneur, Webster, Beaumont, Fletcher, Ford, there is crime and suffering, often of Aeschylean depth, but no hint of the Aeschylean resolution of evil through the education that suffering brings.[1] If there is any comment (and often enough the tragedy ends in a crash of hardy and unmoved defiance) it is at most a thin, wavering doubt, a wandering scent blown for a moment on the tempest across the dark action of the final catastrophe. ' I limned this night-piece and it was my best ' is the typical, unbending summing up of the first, and, of the last, d'Amville's repudiation of Nature (' Sure there is some power above Her that controls her force '), a belated reaching out to another world of knowledge which he cannot grip and which only confounds that to which he is committed. With Shakespeare, in the corresponding phase of his thought, though perhaps only in *Lear*, this other illumination penetrates the ' deep pit of dark-ness ' in which ' womanish and fearful mankind dwell(s) ' and there is a momentary indication of what may lie beyond, the realization ' I have thought too little of this ' with the sequent education by suffering of the people that share the central experience.   Stronger, or at least more explicit, is the Duchess of Malfi's confident piety, but it is obliterated and washed over by subsequent event as though the dramatist himself renounced it, except as a will-o'-the-wisp of thought, of no permanence or stability.   Only Dekker, who never grappled hard enough with

[1] There is, of course, the isolated and belated instance of Chapman's *Caesar and Pompey*, but the explicit speeches of Cato and of Pompey suggest rather direct importations from the stoic philosophers than a re-discovery of the Aeschylean principle.

the material of his themes to produce coherent tragedy, carried into the drama that capacity for sudden and swift withdrawal into a world quite other, a simple and explicit piety which recalls the earlier serene transitions of the Elizabethans.

For the most part the tragedy, outside certain of Shakespeare's, accepts with protesting wonder or with stoical resolution the ' wearisome Condition of Humanity ', its insecure progress through vicissitude and confusion to an unjust and ineluctable fate.   It is the argument of *Faustus* now expanded into terms embracing all common experience : ' We have seen the best of our time : machinations, hollowness, treachery, and all ruinous disorders, follow us disquietly to our graves.'

> Alone, forsaken, frindless onn the shore
> with many wounds, with deaths cold pangs imbrased
> writes in the dust as onn that could no more
> whom love, and tyme, and fortune had defaced.
> of things so great, so longe, so manefolde
> with meanes so weake, the sowle yeven then departing
> the weale, the wo, the passages of olde
> and worlds of thoughts discribde by onn last sythinge.
> as if when after phebus is dissended
> and leves a light rich like the past dayes dawninge,
> and every toyle and labor wholly ended
> each livinge creature draweth to his restinge
> wee should beginn by such a partinge light
> to write the story of all ages past
> and end the same before th'aprochinge night.[1]

The sense of the lateness of time, the weariness of spirit, the burden of fruitless experience is heavy upon these lines as it is upon *Measure for Measure*, *Troilus*, *Lear* and *Timon*, as it is intermittently through *Hamlet*, *Cymbeline*, *Philaster*, *The Maid's Tragedy*, *The Duchess of Malfi*, as it remains in *Tis Pity* and

---

[1] ' The 11 : th and last booke of the Ocean to Scinthia ' (ll. 89–103), *MS. Hatfield* (Cecil Papers, 144), ed. A. M. C. Latham : *The Poems of Sir Walter Ralegh*, p. 80, 1929.   Though I accept Miss Latham's ruling (op. cit., p. 179) as to the date, 1592, for this poem, I avail myself of (what many editors of Ralegh have admitted) the curiously prophetic note of much of his early work, to illustrate the Jacobean mood out of lines which, though they are not the outcome of that mood, sum up one of its aspects with fidelity and penetration.

(In l. 90, I adopt the spelling ' imbrased ' which Miss Latham admits as possible (p. 172, fn.), though she herself prints the alternative ' inebrased '.)

The Broken Heart. It is indeed an Embassy of Death [1] at which we assist in this drama, not continuously, except in a few plays such as *Philaster* and *The Broken Heart*, but recurrently, knowing that at any moment a character may fall suddenly in love with his own death.

And that love of death grows, as much as from anything, from the inexplicableness of the world to which the drama has delimited its thought. Paradoxically, it has narrowed down the issue, abandoning the metaphysical universe to limit itself to the palpable and actual that can be pragmatically assessed, only to find itself the inheritor of a host of obstinate questionings, not only the ' blank misgivings of a creature Moving about in worlds not realized ' but the half-fretful, insistent, monotonous questionings of destiny, conduct, motive, even his very nature itself. ' Since no man knows aught of what he leaves, what is it to leave betimes ? '

> Now in this twilight of Deliberation,
> Where man is darke, because he will not see :
> Must he not trust to his self-constellation ?
> Or else grow confident, he cannot be ?
> Assuming this, hee makes himselfe his end,
> And what he understands, that takes to friend.[2]

But, and Greville himself was the first to admit it, man's understanding is imperfect, his immediate environment rather bewilders than befriends him and the ' twilight of Deliberation ' which obscures all conclusion in the tragic period of Shakespeare, Tourneur and Webster, only gives place to a frivolity of debate, an endless questioning and requestioning in Beaumont and Fletcher.

It is indeed in this stoic endurance that they come, if at all, to rest. In those parts of their plays that hint a solution, define in any way a tragic conception, the dramatists seem to assume a dual world, sometimes (as with Webster) near to Euripides' view of man doomed to destruction by the gods which, less noble than he, are yet stronger, sometimes, as in Marston, Tourneur, one phase of Chapman and another mood of Webster, even in Shakespeare, and in one side of Ford, to that obstinacy

---

[1] To borrow the phrase adopted by Mr. Wilson Knight to describe a similar manifestation in *Hamlet*. (*The Wheel of Fire* (1930), Chap. III.)

[2] Fulke Greville : *An Inquisition upon Fame and Honour* (stanza 11), 1633.

of defeat which grew from their growing sense of the futility of man's endeavour, of the doom which waited not upon him only, but upon the civilization he had built. Small wonder that the dramatists, shaken by the impact of the Machiavellian disillusionment and the fading of glory and disintegration of faith and tradition that so amply bore it out, fell back upon an older, over-shadowing influence, the Seneca of their childhood. The Elizabethans had rifled Seneca with glee as great as that with which they had earlier appropriated the pseudo-Machiavellian villain ; they looked upon him as a store-house of theatrical themes and tricks, but outside the Senecan play proper [1] they paid little attention to his sentiments or his poetry. The Jacobeans, when his resources in this line had been assimilated or transformed by forty years of use, remembered him not as the source which ' let blood line by line ', ' will afford you whole . . . handfulls of tragical speeches ', but as the moralist whose ' sententiae ' and images had fixed themselves in their minds from the pages of their schoolbooks. That the Stoic generalizations they reproduced were not necessarily his, were at least equally those of Cicero, Epictetus, Marcus Aurelius and later European borrowers, was beside the point. Except for a scholar like Ben Jonson the source of the thought was immaterial ; it was its aptness to their present need that mattered. Moreover, in this it was, I fancy, Seneca who came nearest to them ; his disillusionment was the greater, his rhetoric the more specious ; he lived too far from any golden age to have even their fading memory of its glory, but he shared their vision of a decaying civilization, he opened to them the language of undefeated despair. Tourneur with his enveloping atmosphere of evil, Webster with his juxtaposition of keen pathos and horror, Shakespeare in *Lear* or Timon's vision of the falling hierarchy

---

[1] It would be convenient, perhaps, to revive (though with a modified meaning) the term ' Senecal ' for the classical imitations of Seneca's plays, especially those influenced by the French imitators, such as the Countess of Pembroke's and Kyd's translations of Garnier and Daniel's imitations, all in the nineties, and Alexander's and Greville's imitations in the first decade of the seventeenth century. The more common ' Senecan ' could then be used for the popular adaptations from the *Spanish Tragedy* onwards. On the distinction between the two types, see the clear and exhaustive study in Kastner and Charlton : *The Poetical Works of Sir William Alexander, Earl of Stirling* (*S.T.S.* II, 1921), vol. I. *Introduction*, section V.A.

of civilization from which ' degree ' has been taken away, Greville with his sense of the weary paradoxes of man's life, all touch Seneca's most characteristic thought and touch it intimately. Some if not all of their plays have for setting that City of Dreadful Night which meets us in *Thyestes*, but more potent than the survival of his sense of horror is the affinity of experience that echoes his vision, sometimes accompanied by that very cosmic imagery with which he himself sought to universalize it.[1]

> . . . Nondum
> Nocte parata non succedunt
> Astra, nec ullo micat igne polus.
> Nec Luna graves digerit umbras.
> Sed quidquid id est, utinam nox sit.
> Trepidant, trepidant pectora magno
> Percussa metu, ne fatali
> Cuncta ruina quassata labent,
> Iterumque deos, hominesque premat
> Deforme chaos : iterum terras,
> Et mare et ignes, et vaga picti
> Sidera mundi Natura tegat.
> Non aeternae facis exortu
> Dux astrorum secula ducens
> Dabit aestatis Brumaeque notas.
> Non Phoebeis obvia flammis
> Demet nocti Luna timores,
> Vincetque sui fratris habenas
> Curvo brevius limite currens.
> Ibit in unum congesta sinum
> Turba deorum.
> Nos e tanto visi populo
> Digni, premeret quos everso
> Cardine mundus.
> In nos aetas ultima venit,
> O nos dura sorte creatos,
> Seu perdidimus solem miseri,
> Sivi expulimus ! abeant questus.
> Discede timor. Vitae est avidus,

---

[1] It may perhaps be remarked that Marlowe's star imagery derives equally from Seneca and that he too in some degree universalizes his poetic experience by referring it to the eternal criterion of the heavens. But Marlowe's mood meets another side of Seneca ; the bold resolution with which he endows his characters in action. And the star imagery in consequence tends to be more akin to that of the *Hippolytus* (*Phaedra*) or the opening choruses of the *Hercules Furens* than to that of the *Thyestes* or the later passages of the first Hercules play.

Quisquis non vult, mundo secum
Pereunte, mori.[1]

Everything in this passage can be paralleled, not as mere imitation but.as proof of an analogous experience, of a participated mood, in one part or another of the Jacobean drama. The dark beauty of the opening description (like that of Hercules' descent to hell or that, still more deeply imagined, of the House of Atreus) has the very quality of Tourneur's massive gloom, the unrelenting evil, sustained and cumulative ; the pathos that Seneca touches with unfaltering sureness when he speaks of peace, children, the obscure life, woods and mountains is not unworthy of comparison with Shakespeare's and with Webster's ; Seneca the stoic watching the dying civilization about him crumbling to its destruction anticipates Shakespeare's vision ' We have seen the best of our time ' no less than he does the only comfort Shakespeare himself can offer in that phase, ' The meeting it is all '. Small wonder the Jacobeans turn back to their memories of Seneca like children to a schoolmaster.

> Piety, and Feare,
> Religion to the Gods, Peace, Justice, Truth,
> Domesticke awe, Night-rest and Neighbour-hood,
> Instruction, Manners, Mysteries and Trades,
> Degrees, Observances, Customes and Lawes,
> Decline to your confounding contraries,
> And let Confusion live.[2]

---

[1] *Thyestes*, 828–48, 880–89. (Chorus IV.) Jasper Heywood's translation (1560) of the last ten lines, in spite of occasional inadequacy (ll. 884, 885–6), preserves the mood as the Jacobeans also preserved it and as some later ages do not :

> ' We are thought meete of all men whom agayn
> Should hugy heape of Chaos overly.
> And would oppresse with overturned masse.
> The latest age now falleth us uppon.
> With evil hap we are begot alas.
> If wretches we have lost the sight of sonne,
> Or him by fraught enforced have to flye
> Let our complayntes yet goe and feare be past :
> He greedy is of life, that will not die
> When all the world shall end with him at last.'

The whole of this Chorus, particularly the astronomical imagery of the middle, recalls the magnificent threnody on the death of a civilization, where ' Art after art goes out and all is night ', in the concluding lines of the fourth book of the *Dunciad*.

[2] *Timon of Athens*, IV, i, 15–21.

The revulsion from this spectacle of universal decay and corruption, if it be not always so intense as in *Timon, Lear, The Revenger's Tragedy* is almost invariably like Seneca's own : ' O nos dura sorte creatos ', the acceptance of the bitter fate, the sense that there is ' No safe place on the ridge of the world ', the stoic acceptance of death, with or without the stoic fortitude, and the true stoic repudiation of wealth, power and high place. This repudiation occupies with the Jacobean dramatists approximately the same position as in Seneca's drama : it is freely professed, in the form of wistful comments, but only very rarely practised by the characters as portrayed dramatically :

> Stet quicunque volet, potens
> Aulae culmine lubrico :
> Me dulcis saturet quies,
> Obscuro positus loco,
> Leni perfruar otio.
> Nullis nota Quiritibus
> Aetas per tacitum fluat.
> Sic cum transierint mei
> Nullo cum strepitu dies,
> Plebeius moriar senex.
> Illi mors gravis incubat,
> Qui notus nimis omnibus,
> Ignotus moritur sibi.[1]

---

[1] *Thyestes*, 391–403. Andrew Marvell, one of the few translators who can render Seneca without expanding or diluting him and in a metre akin to his own, turns these lines as follows :

> ' Climb, at Court, for me that will,
> Tottering favour's pinnacle ;
> All I seek is to lie still :
> Settled in some secret nest,
> In calm leisure let me rest,
> And far off the public stage,
> Pass away my silent age.

> Thus, when, without noise, unknown,
> I have lived out all my span,
> I shall die, without a groan,
> An old honest countryman.
> Who, exposed to others' eyes,
> Into his own heart ne'er pries
> Death to him's a strange surprise.'

This is the very mood of Webster at Vittoria's death :

> ' O happy they that never saw the court,
> Nor ever knew great men but by report.'

but it is noticeable that the thought does not occur to him until this moment. The whole question is, of course, laid open in *Cymbeline*, III, iii.

And once the drama has fixed this mood, leading the way, by reason of the conjunction of factors noted at the beginning of this chapter, into the non-spiritual universe by which it was so straitly bound, we begin to recognize signs of the same process at work at last outside it. The violent contrast between the two worlds of Ralegh's mind, though he himself seems to have had no apprehension of it, are now seen to be indicative of the same schism that was growing to open conflict elsewhere. The break is complete in the case of Donne and the contrast between his secular and his divine poems is the measure of the extremity in which so many men could only preserve the spiritual world at all by relinquishing the material, could only reject that interpretation represented by Machiavelli's system by repudiating wholesale the world of observed fact and everyday experience from which that system drew its evidence. Thus the Jacobean drama, leading, as might be expected, the thought of the nation, arrives first at that point of view which spread later through popular thought—poetry, philosophy, science—separating each in turn from religion. The division is first obvious in the early eighteenth century (though discernible in the sixteenth- and seventeenth-century deists) when side by side with deism we find Pope's lament over the downfall of a civilization. But the Jacobean dramatists had long before this seen the same vision as he, often a vision of almost infinite despair, the withdrawal of the light of the spirit from within a world that it had once inhabited entire.

V

As the political dangers of the first half of the reign died away and the Stuart dynasty seemed to be settled upon the throne securely enough to avoid civil war, invasion and economic ruin, the tension of the first decade began to relax. Men no longer lived under the shadow of a half-unknown horror or seemed to move upon the very rim of eternity itself. Gradually there passes that sense of living at the world's end : ' In nos aetas ultima venit.' Imperceptibly at first, a more normal rhythm of mind comes back ; everyday life resumes its course. Nowhere is this more clearly seen than in the romantic tragicomedy of Beaumont and Fletcher, where, though the issues touched are serious enough, there is no sense of bitterness, horror or despair. The horror is resolutely put aside, the great questions rest untouched except as debating topics, the world is becoming a cloud-cuckoo-land of pathos, tender or poignant sentiment, noble reflexions and fairy-tale adventures. The end is saved from catastrophe by a mood that gave us clearly to know from the outset that catastrophe was never really imminent. It is the same world as that of Almanzor some fifty years later and its significance, for the purpose of this interpretation, lies in just that quality of evasion, the fact that horror and catastrophe have now become things that can be played with, that the dark world of tragedy can be skirted without that tightening of the nerves, that sickening sense of impending doom, inseparable from the major drama of the first decade. It is the emotional irresponsibleness of Beaumont and Fletcher (whatever be their intentions as academic homilists) that marks the beginning of a new phase, a phase when soldiering is again remote enough to become a nursery game.

Different, but equally significant is the corresponding modulation in the poetry of Shakespeare's last plays and of the Middleton-Rowley tragi-comedies. With Shakespeare the mood is of solution rather than indifference : *Pericles, Cymbeline, The Winter's Tale*, and *The Tempest* succeed a tragic period in which Shakespeare has been immersed as deeply as Webster, Tourneur, Marston or Chapman in the dismay and foreboding of the Jacobean age, and he arrives at serenity by resolving, not by discarding the earlier experience. Middleton's position is much more like that of Beaumont and Fletcher, for, though he had more dramatic experience behind him at the period of *A Fair Quarrel* and the succeeding tragi-comedies of the second decade, it was of comedy only, romantic or realistic or both. But in Middleton it is again the mood of an older man who has lived through the tragic age, though, with the sardonic detachment characteristic of one side of him, he has taken no part in its imaginative explorations. The reflexions in Middleton's later plays indicate an equanimity as clear and undisturbed as Shakespeare's, but, like Shakespeare's again, they are comments fully aware of the nature of the darker world upon which they reflect and side by side with which, in the case of Middleton, they cohabit. The essential difference between his late tragi-comedies and Shakespeare's late plays is, in fact, in this indication of two minds in Middleton's work, where there is one in Shakespeare's. In the later Middleton the sardonic commentary on the fertile culture of human baseness (characteristic of the mood of such plays as *A Chaste Maid*) went side by side with a steady equanimity in which, as truly as for Webster, ' the stars shine still ' ; but they went side by side and the one never wholly absorbed the other. In Shakespeare there is no opposition ; evil is resolved and converted, as later with Ford, ' A Touch more rare, Subdues all pangs, all feares '.

With Ford, who in this as in much else forms the fitting conclusion to the great Jacobean dramatic period (though his best work falls within the reign of Charles I), the steady serenity reaches its final phase. The clear piety of his early work (those phrases that carry us back to Dekker's intermittent illumination) and the gradually increasing compactness and reticence of his later work rest alike upon a foundation of security. Horror, in spite of the often absurd concessions of his plots, never touches his final conclusion : the soul of goodness in things evil was never more clearly revealed than by the clear sureness of the thought that illuminates the nightmare of event. This is not the evasion of Beaumont and Fletcher nor the divided mind of Middleton, but a secure and accustomed conversion of evil resting upon the assumptions implicit in Shakespeare's latest solutions. The cycle has been completed since the first tragedy of Marlowe. With Ford, to look up to heaven leads not to the fear that we shall ' confound knowledge with knowledge ' but to the assurance ' Look you, the stars shine still '.

CHAPTER II

JACOBEAN DRAMATIC TECHNIQUE

I

THE technique by which the Jacobeans developed their
theatre is as peculiar to them as is their choice of theme
and their mood, and in many cases of as high a degree of originality. For the modern reader it is sometimes necessary to begin
by dismissing from our minds what most of us have imperceptibly acquired in childhood, a prepossession in favour of a
drama which, by a kind of protective mimicry, endeavours to
reproduce the situations, the events, the speech and the tempo
of everyday life, to win its way into our minds, to suspend
disbelief and to convince us precisely by not allowing us to
realize that this is drama. In the hands of a major dramatist,
like Ibsen, and at the expense of sleepless skill, this convention
of actuality is served without violation of the fundamental
necessities of dramatic experience. In *The Wild Duck* and still
more in *Rosmersholm* this stupendous juggling feat is achieved ;
in the latter masterpiece, indeed, by a supreme concentration
of the artist's faculties, the essential drama is not only unharmed
but in the end empowered by it. The process is such that,
with the lifting of veil behind veil, we penetrate gradually to a
knowledge of the preliminary facts upon which the dramatic
events we are watching have their base and so feel ourselves
almost in the presence of actual experience, with its imperfect
and irregular progression towards the knowledge in which the
events are illuminated, often after they have taken place. Not
until the fall of the curtain do we know all the relevant facts
that preceded its rising. This, like Pirandello's *Henry IV* or
Six Characters in our own day, carries structural verisimilitude
to its highest pitch and a host of dramatists between the two
have consciously or unconsciously accepted Ibsen's plan and
trained their audiences in the tradition.[1]

[1] This, of course, only indicates one of the multifarious forms of
modern dramatic structure, but it is that in which English drama until

But this is not the only excellent way and the Jacobeans, for the most part, like the Greeks, have none of it.

Broadly speaking, there is one other way, with which it contrasts sharply, and the distinction derives from a different estimate of the relation between the art of drama and the material of experience from which it is formed. Those dramatists who seem boldly to accept an essential distinction between art and the material furnished by experience are for the most part unafraid of making the superficial distinction equally clear. They accept conventions, different in different races and periods, which while being much more recognizable as conventions impose no such clogging restraints upon the free movement of dramatic poetry ; they do not consent to this deadly servitude to actuality and in their habit of risking the illusion at intervals to reveal quickly some essential fact or thought (the fundamental difficulty of working dramatists from Aeschylus to Mr. O'Neill) they tend to slash their way through the obstacles to conviction instead of, at the expenditure of enormous patience and skill, trying to convince us that these obstacles do not really exist.[1] The Jacobean prologue, soliloquy, rhetoric, formalized presentation of ritual or procedure as it never did and never could occur,[2] all these succeed, paradoxically, in bringing us nearer to reality than the careful elimination of everything which does not tally with the audience's impression of actual speech, event, tempo and relations of character to circumstance. So magnificent is the indifference of the Jacobean dramatists and their audiences, particularly in the

the last decade was mainly fostered. I have chosen Pirandello's technique as a point of comparison in our own day both because it is familiar to all English readers and because its relations with that of Ibsen are often of peculiar interest.

[1] They would never dream, for instance, of attaching so much importance to the illusion of actuality as to jeopardize for its sake the understanding of the story. In many of his plays, most notably perhaps in *Six Characters*, Pirandello concentrates on producing in his audience the effect of having stumbled into a patch of life on which it is, and remains, imperfectly informed.

[2] As, for example, in the trial scenes of *The White Devil*, *The Devil's Law Case*, *Appius and Virginia*, *The Atheist's Tragedy*, where the playwrights are obviously more concerned with indicating the principles and problems of justice than with mirroring contemporary procedure as Chapman does in *Chabot*.

tragedies, to this unessential modern convention that they are often accused of failing in some part of their task. We have outgrown the eighteenth century's habit—indeed we speak of it with kind indulgence—of assuming the task of the Elizabethans and Jacobeans to be that of Aeschylus, Sophocles and Euripides. We have not necessarily escaped the slightly less reputable error of assuming it to have been that of Ibsen, of Galsworthy, of Pirandello.

Setting aside prejudice one way or the other and assuming only that form to be good which fulfils the purpose its maker proposed, thinking always in terms, moreover, of the playhouse for which the Jacobeans worked and not in terms of theatrical conditions which were not part of their concern, what, as a matter of fact, are the characteristics of their dramatic structure ? And can we say that they have in common any such character-istics as to distinguish them as a body from the more or less homogeneous surviving Greek drama on the one hand or the specific post-Ibsen tradition of our own day upon the other ?

In examining the form of Jacobean tragedy—for it is mainly in tragedy that the question arises—we notice two things. First that each of the major dramatists, if he reach maturity of work at all, tends to make for himself a form which mirrors his thought, his comment upon events or people and their relations, rather than to select primarily a chronological sequence of events to make a pattern ; thus, Webster's notorious neglect of events in *The Duchess of Malfi* (a neglect which does not even trouble to make the action plausible by readjusting a few confusing references) is balanced by the surprising shapeliness which appears when we look at the play as a two-dimensional map of moods and personalities in their relations to each other rather than as a single-dimensional line of progression from event to event. Second, that, while these plays may seem to have little relation to the forms which other dramatists or groups of dramatists have chosen for their expression, their formal excellence sometimes becomes much clearer when we compare it with that developed by artists working in other mediums ; thus there are sometimes clearer resemblances in fundamental form between the structure of Ben Jonson or Ford or Webster and a painting or a musical composition of similar magnitude than there are between these artists and other dramatists. It has, of course, been pointed out [1] that the Jacobean audience, and apparently the dramatist, preferred to experience a succession of striking situations and to carry away a number of such separate images, rather than the memory of a unified and integrated aesthetic experience—that it had, in short, neither use nor capacity for the Aristotelian ' whole '. This is probably true of the audience and consequently of the dramatists as men of business. But the artist, particularly the Jacobean artist, is notoriously good at serving two masters provided one be the public and the other his own instinct. He sometimes serves the first in the apparent form, the chronological sequence of event, and the second in the real, underlying form which maps the territory as an area of human experience. The omission of a few essential links in what we like to call the ' plot ' of the *Duchess of Malfi* is thus seen to offer no difficulty in either world.

This becomes clearer when we examine certain individual pieces of work or parts of certain plays ; considerable light is thrown by the induction or exposition scenes of the major dramas of the period (for it is there that the demands of verisimilitude are hardest to meet), by the whole form of one or two plays of outstanding interest and by consideration of their method of circumventing certain ineradicable difficulties such as the revelation in drama of unspoken thought.

Exposition is a somewhat arbitrary term : all that I mean by it here is that part of a play which serves to introduce us to the chief characters, to let us grasp the main facts upon which their relations and the subsequent action depend and see that action set going. It will be obvious at once that this allows of considerable variety also in the order in which these things are achieved. In the Greek form for instance the important facts which precede the play are all accounted for by a prologue either frankly external to the play or incorporated in the opening dialogue ; so, as a rule, are the relations between the main characters, in so far as it is proper for the audience to be reminded of them ; we might bear in mind as representative of this method, the opening of the *Phoenissae* with Jocasta's eighty-seven lines of virtual prologue after which she goes out and the

---

[1] In recent criticism we may recall the comments of Mr. F. L. Lucas on the structure of Webster's tragedies. (See especially the Introduction to his edition, vol. I, pp. 17–22.)

play begins.[1] In the characteristic plays of Shakespeare's
maturity on the other hand these three needs, together with
the brief preliminary setting of the mood which is Shakespeare's
individual contribution to the opening, are satisfied simultaneously, though with a free use of conventions which serve as
short cuts to knowledge for the reader.   In the modern post-
Ibsen drama or tragedy at least as much energy and ingenuity
is spent in avoiding these short cuts as in the main business of
the drama ; and while the author is equally concerned with the
Jacobeans to introduce his chief characters and their positions,
to tell us what has happened before the play and to start the
action, he has wantonly taken upon himself a fourth task, far
more difficult than Shakespeare's ringing of the keynote, a
task moreover which pulls across the direction of his main
effort, and has entered a conspiracy to conceal, what after all
need never be concealed, the fact that we are in a playhouse
listening to a play.   Only an audience which had lost the power
of exercising poetic imagination would need the help of such
specious immediacy ; only the inheriting an audience so imaginatively debased could have led a poet of Ibsen's stature to give
it habitually that help.   Consequently we have that supreme
tour de force of modern dramatic structure, the first act of the
Wild Duck, with its flawless faithfulness to everyday event
through which the necessary knowledge of highly complicated
situations and character is yet transmitted to the audience in
the minimum of time.   But it reveals reality no quicker than
the superficially far more improbable opening scenes of *Peer
Gynt*.[2]

[1] This kind of exposition (with or without the help of an opening
chorus) represents pretty generally the method of Aeschylus and of
Euripides.   (It seems to be used by Aeschylus in all but the *Septem*
and by Euripides in all but the *Rhesus* and *Iphigeneia in Aulis*.)
Sophocles, of course, proceeds rather differently and, except for the
Electra, in which the first fifteen lines serve the whole purpose of a
prologue, incorporates the prologue material in the first part of the
opening dialogue, which thus serves as a chorus-dialogue standing a
little apart from the onset of the action.
[2] In the case of *Rosmersholm* we hardly feel that the fourth wall
convention modifies the form ; the material in this case called for
that structure, just as *Oedipus Tyrannus* called for a corresponding
structure in terms of the Greek theatre.

II

If we now turn back to the Jacobean tragic writers, the full measure of the structural freedom of their expositions can be appreciated. Perhaps the most remarkable instances of this non-realistic opening, which serves its poetic purpose directly and economically, often through abandoning verisimilitude altogether, are to be found in the plays written between about 1603 and 1613 and in a few of Middleton's and Ford's plays which fall ten or fifteen years later.[1] Perhaps the most notable are *Measure for Measure*, *The Honest Whore*, *Bussy d'Ambois*, *Volpone*, *Revenger's Tragedy*, *Timon of Athens*, *Byron's Tragedy*, *Cymbeline*, *Atheist's Tragedy*, *Tempest*, *White Devil*, *Duchess of Malfi*, *Two Noble Kinsmen*, *The Changeling*, *Spanish Gipsey*, *'Tis Pity* . . . and *Perkin Warbeck*. All of these are highly individual in method and there is very little resemblance between them.

The four Shakespeare plays all depart from his usual method, seen, perhaps, at its best in *Hamlet*, *All's Well*, *Macbeth*, *Lear* and *Antony and Cleopatra* (and by no means rigidly even there), by which he chooses for the immediate opening a passage which, whether or no it advance the action, gives us an indication of the terms on which we must follow the rest of the play, thus setting our mood by prompting an emotion strictly relevant to that of the main characters and to the theme and strictly related also to the emotion and thought which will, at the end, determine our response to the whole play,[2] and then proceeding to intro-

---

[1] For a partial explanation of the relative decline of this form of experimentation after the middle of the second decade, see Chap. XIV, *Jacobean Theatres and Audiences*.

[2] Thus in *Hamlet* he sets the mood of apprehension and uneasiness by the appearance of the ghost and the response of the characters to it, then introduces, very plausibly, a prologue speech in Horatio's reply to Marcellus and so, with another prologue speech from Claudius in the next scene, and a soliloquy from Hamlet, puts us in possession of characters and situation and starts the action. In *All's Well* there is a bold though partly concealed use of straightforward explanation, a short cut by soliloquy, a digression which sets the tone and another soliloquy. In *Macbeth* the brief witch scene sets the mood of evil, and in the second scene the prologue work is done openly by the dialogue and the Captain's speech. In *Lear* the mood is set still more subtly by putting the crude shallowness of Gloucester beside Edmund's brooding and the rest covered in a long scene practically without

duce characters, situation and action by the general use of what we may call the fourth wall method freely mixed with characteristically Jacobean short cuts. *Measure for Measure*, on the other hand, opens with a fairly long dialogue that contributes little to the audience's knowledge and is mainly a general comment on the nature of government and public service. It is longer than any of the normal Shakespearian opening scenes and is not used as they are to set the mood of the audience, though it undoubtedly turns their thoughts into a suitable channel. Not until the next scene is the mood thus set, the rest of the action started and some other necessary information given. *Timon*, which is still more revolutionary in form, spends a whole act in presenting the initial situation and the characters before the action starts, and of this the first scene is partly occupied by a brief prophetic survey in semi-symbolic form that balances the situation rather than sets the mood.[1] In *Cymbeline* and *The Tempest* the latitude and ease of a highly experienced structural artist reach what is perhaps their fullest expression. Verisimilitude is entirely abandoned at times, without the slightest detriment to the compulsive power of the reality Shakespeare is concerned to reveal. *Cymbeline* opens with a prologue dialogue which is a frank and rapid survey of preliminary facts, of situation and of characters. All this being dispatched in sixty-six lines, the action of the play starts without shock or noticeable change of tone. In *The Tempest*, the first scene, of medium length, tells us nothing which we should not have gathered from the second scene ; its sole function appears to be that of setting a mood, whose predominant tone is, somewhat surprisingly, one of humour and gusto, a tone related fundamentally but not obviously to the main theme ; the second scene opens with a frank prologue-dialogue, even less conventionally justified than that of *Cymbeline*. After this, the action starts.

The only drama of Ben Jonson which shows great freedom

devices. In *Antony and Cleopatra* the mood is set briefly in thirteen lines which also serve as a partial prologue and the rest achieved without short cuts.

[1] This, at first glance, resembles the use made of Vittoria's dream in *The White Devil*. But the later passage has a far more powerful emotional content, achieved through the imagery, and has none of the structural and emotional detachment of the earlier passage from the main body.

of method in its opening is *Volpone*, though this, for sheer simplicity and economy of structure, stands apart. It opens without subterfuge upon the keynote and with the main character revealed in a long soliloquy.[1] This merges into a dialogue still concentrated on the limited theme of the main character and his personality ; this is followed again by soliloquy, a bare-faced and quite undramatic statement of the necessary preliminary information for which we have hitherto waited. At this point the action, which in any case has hardly begun, is quietly set aside by the mask of the dwarf, hermaphrodite and eunuch, whose function seems to be to make explicit the background of abnormality implicit in the opening passages. Then we strike suddenly into the action and are thereafter caught into that gradual increase of tempo which is a familiar characteristic of the structure of Ben Jonson's major dramas. So slow is this opening, so spellbound the mood and so close the atmosphere that it seems that nothing short of a violent effort from the dramatist has broken the enchantment to let in the outside world and action. But how powerful is the domination of the mood thus instilled into the audience and how powerful the theatrical effect of the change, when it does come, to hurrying movement, spinning ever faster and faster ! In Ben Jonson's other plays the method is in general that of Shakespeare's characteristic plays (shorn, of course, of his peculiar tonic openings) but slowed down, by general reflexions in *Epicœne*, by dialogue of pure invective in the *Alchemist*, to emphasize the acceleration of the acts that follow.[2]

The two plays of Tourneur and the two of Webster again show the supreme audacity of an experienced artist. The *Revenger's Tragedy* begins with a virtual dumb show of great theatrical effectiveness and passes immediately into a long soliloquy, partly frank prologue, partly lyrical self-revelation

[1] Mosca is actually present, but the effect of the speech is that of soliloquy as Volpone never considers his presence. Only two other major Jacobean plays, the *Revenger's Tragedy* and *Bussy d'Ambois*, open thus with a soliloquy by the main character.

[2] In *Sejanus* and *Cataline* this slow exposition is not justified, as in the three major dramas, and the scenes, especially in *Sejanus*, are clogged with material which is equally non-theatrical and non-poetic, disquisitions on the state of Rome, ' characters ' of Romans living and dead, comments on the central figure. *Cataline* is of course varied by the comic scenes which set one part of the intrigue in motion.

by the central figure. Vindice hovers between a chorus and a participant in the play. There is no pretence at verisimilitude in this, yet it takes us to the heart of the play's mood and purpose with unparalleled rapidity. As often with Tourneur, it is boldly theatrical but it is also finely dramatic.[1] *The Atheist's Tragedy* opens in the opposite way, with a close but abstract discussion of the ideas that lie at the base of D'Amville's conduct. This, after some time, is followed by a Shakespearian exposition, but the tax on the audience is, in the meantime, a severe one and the scene is less theatrically effective. There is no question, however, of the artistic soundness of the scene ; it directs our attitude to the play, not, as Shakespeare usually does, by setting our mood, but rather, as he does in *Measure for Measure* (only more definitely), by setting to work a train of thought which will guide us in selecting and holding the main theme of the play.

Webster's two plays offer a similar contrast. *The White Devil* has one of the most memorable and theatrical openings of the period, with the crash of the single word ' banished ' that sums up a mood and a situation.[2] The general comments that follow, interlaced with specific references, drop into our minds most of the necessary information without any noticeable loss of verisimilitude and, with the help of the imagery, set an atmosphere of virile evil that never lifts from the play. The next scene takes us straight to the two chief characters and here there is a free use of speeches that obviously do the work of a prologue and of others that are as obviously ' characters '.[3]

---

[1] I do not wish to make an arbitrary distinction between the theatrical and the dramatic ; but it can be observed, in the work, for instance, of such a dramatist as Marston (see *post*, Chap. IV), that some situations, characters or speeches have considerable theatrical plausibility and little fundamental dramatic value, while others may have both simultaneously.

[2] The mood set here is that of vindictive brooding and the figure of Ludovico has little other function in the play than that of representative and agent of this passion. To an audience accustomed to the train of thought of the revenge plays this would be received as a kind of shorthand formula, whereas a modern audience, untrained in this type of play, is liable to confuse itself by attaching too much importance to the character of Ludovico himself and to mistake his function.

[3] Less like the brief ' characters ' in the long Introduction to Marston's *Antonio and Mellida* or ' The Characters of the Persons ' which Ben Jonson added to *Every Man Out of His Humour* in the 1616 folio

The change of pace here shows the highest skill and after the rapid opening the action moves on slowly, pausing to include comment, reflexion, even the prophetic symbolism of Vittoria's dream. *The Duchess of Malfi*, in complete contrast, opens with a frank prologue dialogue, a discourse on statecraft, that, like a colour-wash, modifies what is added later and draws it into its own scale of tones. The later is more thickly scattered than the earlier play with brief ' characters ' which at times concentrate to exclude everything else and at times are interspersed with dialogue that serves little purpose but to focus our attention on one of the characters, allow a pause between the sketches and a preparation for a fuller comment that follows.[1] The whole forms an entirely unconventional exposition which is technically more like that of the novelist ; not until about 250 lines have been spoken does the action start.

Of the remaining plays instanced, *The Honest Whore* has for its first scene a triumphant theatrical effect, but it takes relatively fewer liberties with convention than those already considered ; Chapman's four tragedies make free use, as we should expect, of reflective soliloquies or monologues (generally effective in setting the tone of thought) and long dialogues on the evils of court life or the moral effects of war and peace, and he tends to introduce at once the main character or a long discussion of him ; Ford gives us quiet, sober, naturalistic openings in *The Lover's Melancholy*, *Love's Sacrifice* and the *Broken Heart*,[2] but in *'Tis Pity she's a Whore* he opens with a discussion, involving one of the two chief characters, that simultaneously sets the mood and the thought and introduces the main theme and the necessary explanation ; the distinguishing characteristic of this opening is, as we should expect from Ford, its utter economy.[3]

than like those of *Cynthia's Revels*. Webster's character sketches differ even from these latter, however, in being genuinely embedded in the play, whereas even those of Crites and Asotus are complete, detachable essays.

[1] As, for example, the dialogue between Ferdinand and Castruccio in the middle of the first scene.

[2] In *Perkin Warbeck* this takes the form of a frank prologue dialogue. Ford, a consummate artist, is at no pains to pretend that he is not doing what both he and his audience know must be done and agree had better be done quickly.

[3] Beaumont and Fletcher, with one major exception of *A King and no King*, use in general what we may call the Shakespearian method

The exposition scenes of the major Jacobean dramatists are, then, free in form and closely adapted to the purposes of the thought. They may depart from the representation of the actual in any one of half a dozen directions, but they all share in common a freedom from that convention which, in its special twentieth-century modification, came to be associated with the fourth wall set. They seldom try to persuade us that we are assisting at a cross-section of life. They are concerned rather, as narrative, lyric or epic poetry might be, to put us in tune with certain emotions, to set us thinking along certain lines ; invariably they take the most direct way to present this reality (whether of emotion or thought) without undue concern about maintaining at the same time a strict correspondence with the surface of life.

III

But the originality of the Jacobean dramatists' technique is not limited to their first scenes. In fact the Jacobeans, better than most other poetic dramatists, afford us instances of another highly interesting structural characteristic, that of a play which contains two types of experience simultaneously throughout its extent and thus offers its form to be considered simultaneously in two aspects. One type of experience is primarily concerned with the subject-matter as a chronological record of event and proceeding from this we arrive at an aspect of form described most naturally in terms of plot, story and the causal connexion of event. The other experience is spatial instead of temporal and it regards the play as a grouping of moods, characters, forms of diction or of prosody and looks for form in the interrelations of these. The first may be, and indeed generally is, affected by extra-aesthetic knowledge,[1] the second is an entirely aesthetic experience having reference solely to the individual drama under consideration. Obviously the two experiences may either fuse

without, of course, the brief preliminary passage that sets the mood. They present character, situation and start of action simultaneously and with less use of short-cuts and non-dramatic presentation than he. Massinger, with the exception of the doubtful *Believe as You List*, follows what we may call the Beaumont and Fletcher method and Middleton, except in *Changeling* and *Spanish Gipsey*, approximates to it also. By the second half of the reign of James I it had, apparently, become automatic. Ford's plays are the main later modifications.

[1] As in the case of *The White Devil* mentioned above   (See p. 36, fn. 2.)

into a single aesthetic experience or remain in some degree dissociated. For the moment, the point I should like to make is that drama does in certain cases, and they are relatively frequent in the Jacobean period, afford this second form, which can be considered apart from that composed of the series of events that make the plot.[1]

This can perhaps be made clearer by reference to the art in which the distinction is habitually made, that of painting. There the two experiences derived from what are often spoken of as the subject-matter and the ' body ' or plastic, are habitually distinguished in criticism whether or not they co-operate in the actual picture discussed. We can think, that is, of what the picture represents, illustrates or means, we can think alternatively of the form which grows out of the relation of the masses, and we may, if we are able and when we are familiar with the picture, have an aesthetic experience which fuses the two. In the case of pictures or of plays which are able to do this, the experience derived from extra-aesthetic knowledge tends to drop out, and in a completely realized work of art such as the *Duchess of Malfi* it will, I think, have been transmuted so that the ' story ' gradually ceases to have importance, very much as does the element of illustration in a picture. It would be absurd to suggest that in a play there is naturally a complete divorce of these two elements. ' Of course,' as Mr. L. A. Reid says, ' the painter is interested in the expressiveness of visual *forms*. But he is interested in their *expressiveness*. The forms are " significant ". And what does a human face express more definitely than human character.' [2] That is very nearly the position of character in drama. An examination of *The Duchess of Malfi* (as a privately read drama, for the moment, rather than as a theatre production) will, I think, illustrate this point, and will serve to suggest, as Mr. Wilson Knight for instance has led us to deduce in the case of Shakespeare, that in drama of certain kinds an aesthetic experience akin to that of the plastic in painting can be recognized. As he himself says, however, of his own somewhat different distinction between the spatial and temporal aspects of the play, ' It is evident that my two principles

---

[1] As has been pointed out, in the case of Shakespeare, by Mr. Wilson Knight. See especially *The Wheel of Fire* (1930), Chap. I.
[2] L. A. Reid : *A Study in Aesthetics* (1931), Chap. XII, *Competition and its Types* (p. 321).

thus firmly divided in analysis are no more than provisional abstractions from the poetic unity.' [1]

But because literature, like music, must be revealed in time, there will be a definite succession in time of these effects just as the outward form is revealed by a definite recounting in time of the events. It would be enough in considering some plays to map these spatial relations statically and in the less highly developed cases this probably marks fairly their achievement in the direction of inner form.[2] But for the highly evolved works of art this is not enough and the inner form only reveals itself fully when it is perceived as a progression of such relations.

In drawing together our impressions of the *Duchess of Malfi* we probably notice first of all certain related rhythms of the characters, such as would be given by our first impression of the potentially moving masses of a picture. The eye is carried first to the figure of the Duchess because of the clear luminous quality with which it is invested (mainly through the imagery connected with her) and next but almost simultaneously to the group made of Ferdinand and Bosola, the tension and implied rapidity and confusion of movement in Ferdinand contrasting and throwing up the ease and limpidity of the portrayal of the area occupied by the Duchess, in which we next notice the subsidiary figures of Antonio and Delio. Midway between the two, drawn a little back, but constituting a point of balance to which the eye tends more and more to return, is the Cardinal, whose function in the play seems like that of some centre of immobility in a picture ; his stillness throws up the movements, whether disjointed or co-ordinated, of the other figures of the drama ; the hardness and impenetrableness of his texture emphasizes the sentient life in them and is emphasized by it.

But this mapping of the static relations of the figures cannot be carried further without under-estimating the subtlety of the play, for that depends rather upon something like the sequence of relations in a musical composition. Not only are the characters so grouped that the mind passes with increasing aesthetic satisfaction from one figure or group of figures to another,

[1] Wilson Knight : *The Wheel of Fire* (1930), Chap. I, p. 5. See also the subsequent argument and the volume, *passim*.

[2] It is often the case in straightforward comedy of character combined with intrigue, for example. I think, to choose a few instances at random, that it will be found true of *Gammer Gurton's Needle, A Mad World, my Masters, The Good-Natured Man* and similar cases.

always led by the contrasts and re-affirmations which the play-wright himself has indicated, the masculine toughness of Julia against the more slender but no less enduring quality of the Duchess, each emphasized in a death speech which is, as it were, a point of light bringing out the contrast while yet emphasizing the fundamental community of colour in both minds. It is not only in this delicate relating of mood and quality, a relating which spreads over the whole play and whose effect could be analysed in immense detail, it is not only in this that Webster shows his supreme understanding of such form as was germane to his purpose, such form as, without slavery to verisimilitude, could mirror immediately his thought. The whole of this subtly articulated group produces also in the course of the play an ordered progression of moods as though the lighting of a picture should be replaced by another lighting and that again by a third, while all the time the value of the relations between the masses and of the relations between the colours remained un-diminished or even increased in strength while they themselves and the very relations between them changed and were trans-muted. Thus neither the characters, nor the mood which each calls up in the reader, nor the relations between the groups, are the same at the end of the play as they were at the beginning. What is perhaps more important, from somewhere in the fifth act (about the opening of the third scene) these things cease to be in themselves significant ; the figures remain and the play continues apparently in order that some final aesthetic deduction as to the values in the preceding parts may be drawn in the course of the experience of that act. What is the nature of this detached and relatively abstract aesthetic experience I am not yet sure, though it is clear that it occurs in the same way in both of Webster's last acts and in a similar way in some of Ford's. As to the way in which it appears or the process by which it is brought about, we may, I think, say a little more. The action, after the murder of Julia and the final re-grouping of Bosola and the Cardinal, is practically predetermined ; each of the deaths that follow is intended by one character or another capable of carrying out his intention, and, though the event does not fall precisely as it was planned, the result corresponds with our expectation. This, combined with the brooding, prophetic cloud in which the moods of one after another of the characters is wrapt, serves to free us from speculation as to what will happen and simultaneously the increasing concentration of Webster's interest in the reflexions of the characters and their imagery withdraws a great part of our attention from the question of how it will happen.   From that moment the playwright is free to develop the concluding movement of his play mainly in terms of the inner form, leaving the outer form to wind itself off mechanically.   From the entry, therefore, of Ferdinand in Scene iv, ' Strangling is a very quiet death ', we find our inter-est concentrated more and more on the speech rhythms not only in individual lines, but in increasingly long related passages which now take over the interpretation of the material of event and character and add in this way our final understanding of the relations which gave it its inner form.   Imagery, therefore, and reflective comment, Webster's usual means of suggesting the existence of this inner form throughout the play, now fall into subsidiary relation to this dominating factor of verbal music, which thus becomes the final and most significant mode of expression.   The rhythms become more and more packed with Webster's characteristic qualities ; the thick groupings of double-stressed feet, the heavy, slow movements of the lines which seem to gather into themselves and roll back again rhythms like the intoxicating beat of a tom-tom, beyond the everyday experience of human speech ; these characteristics so divert and dominate the lines that, without violent resistance, they could not be spoken naturalistically and nothing remains for the reader but to submit to this increasing volume of significant sound and for the actor but to accept an intonation which often runs across the apparent meaning of the words or the necessities of the story.   After the crash and turmoil of the fighting in which Ferdinand is killed, there is a sudden silence which can only be fitly rendered as such a pause would be by the conductor of an orchestra.   It is broken slowly by the voice of the dying Cardinal, ' Thou hast thy payment too ? ' and upon Bosola's reply come in again the hurrying lords, the impetuousness half-hushed now in horror.   From this moment the musical move-ment transcends everything else.   From the clear, long-drawn tonic of Bosola's ' Revenge for the Duchess of Malfi murdered ' it is a compact sequence, broken for a moment by Pescara's everyday tones, but lifted immediately after to its climax.   In the hush before the great final passage Malatesta's question comes slow and still :

> . . . Thou wretched thing of blood,
> How came *Antonio* by his death?

and then—we can almost see the conductor's baton—the long-drawn pause and the slow, almost inaudible beginnings of Bosola's last speech, gradually gathering volume until it sinks again on the last line. Hard upon this comes the almost matter-of-fact, realist movement of Delio's epilogue, which ends, as only the great artists dare to end, upon the simplest of major harmonies.

Mal. O sir, you come too late.
Delio. I heard so, and
Was arm'd for 't ere I came : Let us make noble use
Of this great ruine ; and joyne all our force
To establish this yong hopefull Gentleman
In 's mother's right. These wretched eminent things
Leave no more fame behind 'em than should one
Fall in a frost, and leave his print in snow—
As soone as the sun shines, it ever melts,
Both forme and matter : I have ever thought
Nature doth nothing so great, for great men
As when she's pleased to make them Lords of truth ·
Integrity of life, is fame's best friend,
Which noblely beyond Death, shall crowne the end.

And this interpretation—concerning which the rhythm of the lines appears to give no choice—is utterly alien to any plausible stage representation. Considered from the point of view of psychological probability, Malatesta's question could not, as the movement demands, drop slowly into the silence ; it would come quickly, promptly, the voice of a soldier taking charge of the position. In fact, it would not be the inefficient Malatesta who would ask the question at all ; it is quite alien to his character. He happens to be the only performer free at the moment. Nor could Bosola's speech be spoken (in an English theatre of Webster's day or ours [1]) with that almost inaudible faintness which the implied musical notation demands. These things Webster left to his producer to solve and it was enough for a practical theatre-man that he left a more or less naturalistic

---

[1] This would, I think, be possible in a French theatre, especially a *théâtre intime* of small proportions and in certain of the Little theatres of England, America and Germany. But it seems, as far as it is possible to judge, impossible to produce in a large public theatre without disregarding the prosodic indications I have suggested above.

presentation possible as well. But behind, indeed in contradiction to, the stage effects, he gave us the unmistakable indications of his own interpretation of the values of the play.   These,
by the end of the play, have almost completely separated from
and transcended the chronological record of events or plot.

We may suggest more briefly how this same capacity for the
simultaneous structure of an inner and an outer form appears
in another and totally different piece of Jacobean dramatic structure, the *Alchemist*.   Any of Ben Jonson's major dramas could
be chosen, but I think it appears most clearly in this one.   And
again we might use, to clear our view of the inner form, an
analogy with the art of painting.

If we choose as our starting-point a picture that consists of
spirals and related curves forming one design and, underlying
them or superimposed, two-dimensional blocks of colour forming
another and apparently independent design (as in one manner of
Picasso), we have a convenient starting-point for describing
some of the characteristics of the structure of the *Alchemist*.
The play is outwardly [1] a comedy of character and event, so
that the intrigue and interactions of the plot have one set of
relations, analogous to the rhythmic design expressed in the
painting by the lines.   But the inner form of the play is one
which is hardly representational at all of this interaction of event
in everyday life, for the characters, and consequently the moods
they impress upon our minds, exist independently also as something more than the means to this first design : they have a
relation with each other somewhat like that of the related blocks
of colour in the picture, no more co-terminous with the lines
of the intrigue than the colour-groups were with the line design.

Let us take first what we may call the line design of the
Alchemist and it will appear, I think, that the description of the
intrigue has a quality of pure movement which can most suitably
be described graphically in terms of a line or a related group of
lines.   In fact, the steadily increasing tempo of the play suggests
to many readers nothing so much as the increasing concentration

---

[1] It is not necessary, of course, to refer to these different aspects of
the structure as the outer and the inner form.   It would be at least
as reasonable, perhaps more so, to call them the primary and secondary
designs.   I have kept the terms ' outer ' and ' inner ' only because the
first, which is concerned with the story and the obvious relating of
events, meets us first, at our approach to the study of the play, and the
second not until we have ' entered in ' in some degree to its significance.

and tension of a series of helical spirals described by moving bodies where each curve of the helix is not only more closely wound than the last but more rapidly described. The action, like that of *Volpone*, begins in a leisurely way, the development being deliberately retarded by comic rhetoric, one section of the intrigue being set in motion at a time. This is of course intentional and is, in fact, inevitable in all comedies which approximate to a vortical movement, as it serves both to give contrast to this movement with which the climax is approached and to fix in the audience's mind that necessary knowledge without which the final revolutions would become unintelligible. Not until the second act, when the first two plots of Subtle and Face have been set on foot, is there any perceptible quickening. The third and fourth intrigues, brought about by their next two pieces of plotting, have joined the general movement by the middle of the act, the fifth enters in the second half and at the end we prepare for a sixth and a seventh.[1] In the third act the complications begin and it is about this point that we realize, I think, how nearly symbolic or decorative and non-representative is the design we are following. The progress of the first intrigue in this act, the proximity of the path of the second, with its dependents, the sixth and seventh, give us clearly enough the sense of increasing pace, which is emphasized towards the end by the threat of collision between the first and third. Since it is of the essence of Subtle and Face's plots that the different intrigues they set on foot should be kept apart, it is equally of the essence of the whole design that we should continually anticipate collisions followed by collapse, that these should be avoided by a progressively narrow margin and that implicit in this should be the anticipation at each evasion of a subsequent still closer approach which will require a proportionally greater inventive effort on the part of the plotters if catastrophe is again to be avoided. It is this which, by the end of the third act, has made

[1] The summary of the action which I have tried to give here as briefly as possible, is, I think, as clear without description of the individual intrigues as it would be with such descriptions and is more quickly set down. For the sake of this brevity I have given each intrigue a number in order of its appearance and used this number to refer to it in the text. Thus the plot set up against Dapper is the first, that against Drugger the second, Sir Epicure Mammon's the third, Surly's the fourth, Ananias' the fifth, Mistress Pliant's the sixth, Kastril's the seventh.

the helical action clear. In the fourth act a marked reversal of movement sets in and we begin to anticipate disaster rather than the success we have so far assumed. An eighth intrigue, actually only the inversion of the fourth, is forced upon the plotters, they shift its direction and its movement is made to combine without disaster with that of the seventh, there is a resolution of the third intrigue and a momentary postponement of the catastrophe which seemed imminent there ; Subtle and Face are left, at the end of the third scene of this act, in possession of the money without risk of exposure, which is, of course, the type of resolution proper to all seven intrigues. But we are shown clearly that this resolution is merely a check in the progress towards collision and catastrophe when we find that the reversing movement introduced into the action by the eighth intrigue has now invaded the fourth and seventh which are also reversing themselves. The plotters make a brilliant momentary recovery by working together two more plots (the fourth and the sixth) that they manage again to combine without collision. In the fifth act the pace becomes formidable. The impediment of Lovewit's arrival gives a separate though similar impetus to the helical movement of each intrigue, which, combined with the threat of catastrophe that each already carried within it, gives us a fifth act which is a rapid succession of episodes representing each intrigue in turn, impinging more and more nearly upon it and recurring at briefer and briefer intervals until nothing but the superhuman dexterity of the plotters serves to fend off, one after another, the successively approaching catastrophes. As if this was not enough, the double-crossing of Face by Subtle and Doll introduces two fresh lines of intrigue at the last moment and the action resolves itself into a race between Subtle and Face not only to save from collision and catastrophe as many of their ventures as possible but to snatch the results of success from the partner who has now become a rival. The honours fall to Face, who, by a last effort of highly imaginative plotting, contrives to possess himself of all the findings and simultaneously to escape all the penalties.

As a piece of almost geometrical form, this play appears to be without a companion in the drama with which I am acquainted. The flawless art with which the action is maintained through the steadily increasing tempo of the last two acts and the exquisite proportioning of that acceleration, where the slightest misjudgement would have ruined the subtly articulated balance of movements, must be an unfailing source of aesthetic delight.

But this is only one part of the ' plastic ' form of the *Alchemist*. As early as the beginning of the second act we find ourselves pondering the speeches of Sir Epicure Mammon (those speeches which anticipate about equally the *Pseudodoxia Epidemica* and some of the less easily assimilated portions of the *Golden Bough*). What is their part in the structural scheme ? Not to introduce or even confirm the character of Sir Epicure, whom we already know well enough for all purposes of the story. Are they then an impediment to the action ? We hardly have that impression. Perhaps, then, they are merely outside it. Knowing Ben Jonson's habit of deliberately slowing the earlier movements of his vortical plays, we probably remind ourselves that this is, after all, only the second act, and pass on. But a similar thing happens later, where it cannot be explained in this way, in the third act, after the action has begun to move. Is the long speech of Tribulation Wholesome (III, i) dramatically relevant ? Does it serve any purpose in furthering the plot, in revelation of character, which could not equally be served by something far briefer ? It provides us, of course, with a significant and arresting contrast of mood which, upon inspection, proves to be of great value in emphasizing the colour correspondences or contrasts in the dominant moods of the play. Can it be then that Ben Jonson has been unable to reject a passage of description good in itself and bearing some interesting relations to other portions of the play, to prevent its interfering with the form of the whole ? [1] No reader, I think, who has already noticed the supreme skill with which the intrigue has been conducted would assume imperfect control of his material here. The fact is that throughout the play there are passages, the dialogue of Subtle and Face in Act I, the speeches of Sir Epicure Mammon in Act II, those of Tribulation in Act III, the semi-Miltonic, semi-Burtonian ravings of Dol in Act IV, which scarcely or not at all affect the plot, but are deliberately introduced parts of a colour design, related and balancing against

---

[1] This is, of course, admittedly a habit of his early work and it recurs to some extent in the later plays from *Bartholomew Fair* onward. But, so far as I can judge, the three great middle comedies are free from structural flaws of any kind.

each other like slabs of pure colour standing apart from and independent of the line pattern in a picture.

Nor is this all. In the *Duchess of Malfi* the non-representational part of the design separated, as we have noticed, particularly as the end of the play approached, from that aspect of form which coincided with the representation of the subject-matter. In Ben Jonson's play, however, there is a correspondence, entitled, I think, to be called ' fusion ', between the play regarded as subject-matter and the play regarded as a plastic design. So much is this so that we are continually liable, as will have been noticed, to describe the one in terms of the other.

The examination of these two plays is perhaps enough to indicate what I mean when I claim for the major Jacobean dramas not only the highest aesthetic originality and freedom from deadening conventions whether of the theatre or of the naturalistic obsession, but also a formal excellence which has often, quite needlessly, I think, been disputed.[1] There are at least a dozen other plays which yield an equally fruitful analysis, and among them one may instance one considerably later play which, though it has had due praise for its psychological insight, has not always been estimated fairly on aesthetic grounds—*The Broken Heart*. To say that the recurrence of theme, mood and verbal rhythm in this play is of a calculated formal exquisiteness is to say what most of its readers will, of course, have acknowledged. But the formal exquisiteness in this case is perhaps more easily isolated from the content and examined if it be compared with a form it naturally resembles, that of a major musical composition. To those readers who apprehend the peculiar quality of Ford's work, it is, again, little more than a commonplace to suggest the obvious resemblance in artistic demeanour between his dramatic structure and the music of Sibelius. A prolonged analysis could in fact be made of *The Broken Heart*, that supreme reach of Ford's compositional power, by which its inner structure, the spatial grouping of values (in this case the clear patterns of mood or emotional condition derived from the characters and the subtle patterns of metrical rhythm), could be shown to be more nearly that of a musician's grouping of his material than of a painter's. The distinction between the outer and the inner form can be made even clearer here than in Webster's case, for the subject-matter,

[1] Not, of course, in the case of Ben Jonson's major plays.

the themes of many of his plays are so melodramatic as to have given him, among certain critics, a reputation for abnormality, violence and sensationalism. This is of course almost unintelligible to any reader who is concerned with the aesthetic content of the plays of Ford rather than with the raw material by transmutation of which the work of art is shaped. But the source of the error is never so clearly revealed as when, guided by the aesthetic of the art of painting, we attempt the perfectly legitimate momentary separation of subject-matter and artistic form.

IV

It remains only to corroborate our impression of the high originality of the great Jacobean dramatists by indicating their practice in face of some of the difficulties peculiar to their form of art, difficulties that present themselves to every poet who tries to express in dramatic form his interpretation of the material offered by his actual experience. Just as the painter's eternal difficulty is that of presenting the experience of a three dimensional world on a two dimensional canvas, so perhaps the major difficulty inherent in drama as a specialized form of literature is the revelation of unspoken thought. This, which the descriptive or lyric poet and the novelist can give us in his capacity of commentator, the strict dramatist is debarred from narrating in his own person. By what devices does he at one time circumvent the difficulty or by what reaches of creative imagination does he at another make for himself those formulas which, though they may become (and are often called) conventions, are at their finest and most independent rather inspired and unobtrusive short-cuts through chaos, bridging the gap between what drama can present directly and what, without a momentary breaking down of the strict dramatic attitude, it cannot present except by implication ? The distinction between the cumbersome and doubtfully effective method of implication and the method which, in one way or another, prefers a bold and imaginative suspension of the dramatic semblance, serves effectively to separate the modern prosaic drama from the great poetic drama of the Greeks and the Elizabethans. The modern dramatist of the school of Ibsen conveys this knowledge (with the highest skill) in different ways, some of which, like stage directions, are not really solutions at all but departures into the province of the novelist, some of which (comments by other characters,

4

theatrical juxtapositions of mood or of situation, careful distinction of diction, even the introduction of passages of dialogue which serve little other purpose) are actually an even more pernicious convention and weaken the essential drama. And in so conveying it he gradually chokes his play, if not its action, then certainly its poetic vitality. For this purpose the great ideal dramatists, the Greeks and the Jacobeans, use variously the prologue, the chorus, the monologue and the soliloquy. And they use them boldly, succeeding in preserving an unbroken dramatic effect in their plays by knowing intuitively when to depart from a strictly dramatic method. There is no middle way, apparently. A dramatist either risks his illusion from time to time by the frank use of an inspired convention or he chokes the essential dramatic power in an effort to preserve the illusion.

The drama of Aeschylus rests, of course, upon a foundation of direct or lyric expression ; monologue and soliloquy enter as freely as though the actor were, for the time being, himself a narrative or lyric poet speaking directly to the audience. This is true, with modifications, of Sophocles too, and here, in addition, we sometimes feel the chorus guiding our interpretation of the thought that was implicit in a monologue.[1] It goes, I think, a step further with Euripides, where at times the chorus clearly reflects and extends the thought of the principal characters.[2] With the Jacobeans this task of revealing thought that the audience needs for its guidance, but that would not normally be spoken aloud, is thrown entirely upon the soliloquy which thus becomes recognized by audience, dramatist and actor as an agreement, a ' convention ', to suspend for a moment the dramatic form. No one is in the least disturbed then when Vindice in the opening speech to his mistress's skull passes from the denunciation of the ' dry ' duke, the ' parched and juiceless luxur ' (which is quite plausible), through an apostrophe to the skull and a ' reminiscential evocation ' of its former beauty to what is not plausible at all as a reflection of normal self-communing, the purely narrative lines,

> Thee when thou wert apparelled in thy flesh,
> The old duke poisoned, &c.,

---

[1] For example, in *Oed. Col.*, 1211–48 and 1556–78, where the choric ode is still certainly a comment, but may, I think, be regarded as simultaneously a reflexion of the thought of Oedipus.

[2] As in *Hipp.*, 525–63 and 732–73.

For a profound and detailed discussion of this question, see H. D. F. Kitto, *Greek Tragedy*.

lines which are indispensable to the audience if they are to follow the play but for whose likeness to the language not only of everyday life but of life in heightened terms, no case can be made out. The point is that neither Tourneur nor a dozen other of his contemporaries attempt to make one.[1]

It is as a drama, then, which preserves resemblance to the life its audiences knew, or imagined they knew, only so far as is necessary to the suspension of disbelief for that particular race, age and group of society that we had better approach the Jacobean. As soon as this irreducible minimum is satisfied (and it is, probably, for any work or group of works of art, in indirect ratio to the completeness of the artistic experience presented by the work or works) the poet is concerned only with the expression of his artistic experience, of his apprehension of sense impressions in imagery and metre and of his mixed moral, intellectual and aesthetic experiences and judgements in terms of character and comment.

---

[1] The most notable present-day attempt to tackle this inherent difficulty, the revelation of thought which would not normally be spoken, comes naturally to mind at this point. Mr. Eugene O'Neill's sporting attempt (to say the least of it) in *Strange Interlude*, serves, if it does nothing more, to set apart, yet again, the almost infallible rightness of judgement in dramatic essentials of the Greeks and the Jacobeans. The technique which Mr. O'Neill has evolved for this play (a technique which could never, I think, have a numerous progeny) appears to attain at once the immediacy of drama and the completeness of narrative, by its continuous unconscious soliloquies inaudible to the other characters. Upon inspection, of course, this is seen to retard the action to little more than the pace of a psychological novel, so that the play, by trying to tell us more than the nature of drama permits, ends by removing the whole thing to a curiously illuminated distance, whereas the Greeks and Jacobeans who momentarily shattered their dramatic illusion with a bold hand kept, throughout their plays, the maximum effect of immediacy. In his two later plays, *Mourning Becomes Electra* and *Days without End*, fresh experiments in tackling this problem are made, though neither is technically so remarkable as that of *Strange Interlude*. In *Mourning Becomes Electra* the modern, naturalistic chorus has a function which is partly that of the Greek chorus, while in the later play, the presentation of both halves of the hero's divided mind simultaneously upon the stage (as if Jekyll and Hyde were both present at once with Hyde invisible to but audible to the other characters) is a more manageable but a correspondingly less suggestive device.

[For a more detailed examination of several of the points discussed here the reader is referred to M. C. Bradbrook's subsequent *Themes and*

Conventions of Elizabethan Tragedy (C.U.P., 1935). H. D. F. Kitto's invaluable work, *Greek Tragedy* (Meth., 1939), goes in great detail into certain aspects of Greek dramatic structure only touched on here. Certain of the ideas I put forward in the above chapter are developed or modified in my *Frontiers of Drama* (1946).]

CHAPTER III

GEORGE CHAPMAN

I

CHAPMAN, whose comedy was written between 1596 and
1606 and his tragedy between 1603 and 1613 (or later),
who was thus contemporary with Marston from 1599 to 1606,
with the whole of the latter part of Shakespeare's work from
middle comedy and history through tragedy to late comedy,
with Middleton's early work and middle comedy, with Tourneur's short career and with the beginning of Webster's, with
the whole of the first part of Dekker's, with the collaboration of
Beaumont and Fletcher and with the main work of Ben Jonson,
is in a position to represent the period as hardly any other playwright can do who touched equally tragedy and comedy. And,
in a way peculiar to himself, this is precisely what he does. He
was a man of maturity, some forty years old, when he began to
write drama, and his mind seems to have been formed by the
Elizabethan age to which in many ways he belonged. So that
he carried into the Jacobean period many of the ideals and aspira-
tions of the Elizabethans, particularly of the group of men about
Thomas Walsingham (Ralegh, Harriot and Marlowe), some of
whose influences, particularly that of Marlowe, he preserves
to the end But the material he used as subject-matter for his
plays and the problems he discussed were essentially those of
the age for which he wrote, though he is more often in rebellion
against it than in accord with it.

Both his comedy and his tragedy reflect something of the two
ages he represented ; his Jonsonian comedy mirrors its society
satirically (without comment), his romantic comedy attempts,
after the Elizabethan habit, to relate it with the wider universe
beyond, while his tragedy simultaneously resists, escapes from
and reflects the mood of spiritual uncertainty that bewilders his
contemporaries. The resistance is conscious and explicit and is
to be found principally in the long moral or philosophic argu-

ments that he imposes on all his tragedies, culminating in *The Revenge of Bussy d'Ambois*.

There is no doubt of the tenacity of this resistance : Chapman's desire to believe in a world order of harmony and goodness is genuine, he seems to have carried over from Elizabethan society the realization that to ' go with sway of all the world together ' is the only sane relation beween man and his universe. But more potent than this Epictetan mood that he endeavours to impose upon it is the rising tide of despondency and spiritual negation in the drama as a whole, and the very influence of Marlowe among the Elizabethans is, ultimately, at work in the same direction. Chapman, prompted by his own instincts and reinforced by Epictetus, may stand like a rock against it, but he does not stem the current. Indeed, as his fight against the spiritual uncertainty of the age goes on, his attitude becomes more and more defiant, less and less secure, and the noble speeches on the soul in *The Revenge of Bussy d'Ambois*, the passages on immortality in *Caesar and Pompey*, become more and more detached from their setting and seem more and more the strained emphatic speech of a man arguing to convince himself.[1] Simultaneous with this there is the tendency to escape from spiritual issues into social and political reform, to substitute history for tragedy, political theory for poetry, most clearly, perhaps, in the second Byron play, in *Chabot* and in *Caesar and Pompey*. The reflection of the mood of his age, finally, is mainly unconscious, it is to be found in momentary flashes of bitter criticism and in brief statements that echo the reflections of his contemporaries in contradiction to his own avowed beliefs (' Our knowledges do light us but to err '). Most of all, since Chapman was primarily a poet, it is the chaos and obscurity of his imagery which reveals, now by its themes, now by its form, the presence within and about his mind of the very tendencies his conscious principles opposed.

II

Certain difficulties lie in the path of the reader who approaches Chapman's plays for the first time, for he sometimes wrote with a haughty defiance of dramatic necessity, especially in his

[1] They contrast sharply, for instance, with the natural confidence of Strozza's mysticism in the romantic comedy of *The Gentleman Usher*, to which most authorities give the relatively early date 1601 or 1602.

tragedies, that would have ruined the impetus of any play created with less fire and passionate thought than were his. He is likely at all times to treat his minor characters like a row of pawns, distinguished by position and function rather than by individuality, and in tragedy this sometimes spreads to all but a few of the major characters. He is likely, in the speeches of these major characters themselves, to make undramatic and even inappropriate digressions to expound a theory or weight a sentiment, and this, side by side with passages of penetrating revelation, gives not only a sense of confusion, but, at first reading, an impression of complexity of character which Chapman does not necessarily intend.[1] The intrusion of these long passages of reflexion and argument, moreover, even where they are germane to the character (or even, as in Clermont d'Ambois, essential to it), is undramatic, digressing from the action of the play rather than commenting on it, as in Shakespeare's less frequent use. The style of his tragedies is often difficult, sometimes deliberately so, and though this does not take from the dramatic significance of the imagery, it does, I think, diminish the corresponding value of the reflective passages. Finally, Chapman's prejudices, which were as emphatic as his loyalties and his beliefs, prevent him as a rule from identifying himself dramatically with women, with lovers,[2] with timid or low-spirited natures—indeed with any but men of action or of that blend of thought and action glorified by Cicero, Seneca, Epictetus, Marcus Aurelius and the stoics generally. But these are readily overcome if we approach him first through his earlier work, the comedies ; indeed, the chronological order is important for this dramatist, as the plays which lie nearer the great Elizabethan age have a fuller and more undisturbed possession of the Elizabethan spirit than those which fall five or ten years later and

---

[1] To cite only one of many instances, the speech on religion and the state at the beginning of *Byron's Tragedy*, III, i, is for the most part entirely inappropriate to Byron's character, though an admirable summary of Chapman's views. When this is laid beside the entirely different speeches of the same character in Act V (where Chapman's penetration is beyond praise) our first impression may well be that Chapman is intentionally offering us a character made up of a surprising number of contradictory elements.

[2] Except for the characters of Cynanche and Margaret in the *Gentleman Usher* and the relations between Vincentio and Margaret (see esp. IV, ii).

certain important modifications in his mood can best be followed in this way.

His comedies are, after Middleton's (some critics might put them ahead of his in this respect), the most entertaining of the early Jacobean group. They vary considerably in tone, but they all [1] share to some extent the same excellence of comic action, characters, dialogue and flexible blank verse. The most significant of these indeed fall into an interesting companionship with the early mixed romantic and humour comedies of Middleton. There is some satire on wives and husbands and an excellent satirical portrait of the Puritan Florilla in *An Humourous Day's Mirth* (which actually anticipates every essential characteristic [2] of the humour play as it was produced in the following years by Ben Jonson), but it is good-humoured in tone and has none of the almost Gallic detachment of Ben Jonson's analysis. Chapman's sensitive adaptation of two Terentian plots in *All Fools* seems to have imbued him with something of Terence's quality, for that and its two most interesting successors all have something of the exquisite Terentian balance of mischievous intrigue with poignant or pathetic romance, completely blended in action and character, and treated with limpid simplicity of dialogue and graceful economy of action.[3] Side by side with this, though, and amply accounting for the fact that Chapman does not quite preserve the delicate Terentian poise, is something which is nearer to the Elizabethans, a fine comic gusto, whether for situation, character, pure dialogue or inset passages of

[1] The comedies accepted by the authoritative edition (that of Professor T. M. Parrott, 1914) are *The Blind Beggar of Alexandria* (1595–6), *An Humourous Day's Mirth* (1597), *All Fools* (1598–9), *May Day* (1600–2), *Sir Giles Goosecap* (1601–3), *The Gentleman Usher* (1602), *Monsieur d'Olive* (1604), *The Widow's Tears* (? 1605) and his share in *Eastward Ho* (1605). Parrott does not accept Chapman's authorship of *The Ball*, though he includes it in the volume. Of these, the most interesting are *An Humourous Day's Mirth*, *All Fools*, *The Gentleman Usher*, *Monsieur d'Olive* and *Eastward Ho*.

[2] The isolation of the humour within the character, the choice of characters primarily for the possession of this quality, the humour parade which often sacrifices the intrigue, the crowded stage which, though not an essential of humour comedy, seems to have been almost an inseparable condition with Jonson's early plays also.

[3] No English playwright has perhaps ever achieved completely this Terentian balance of moods, but it is interesting to notice how near to it come Chapman's *All Fools* and *Gentleman Usher* and Middleton's *Phoenix*.

description and comic rhetoric. There is as a rule a rapid and essentially amusing intrigue [1] from which certain individual scenes emerge as peaks of the action, led up to by the foregoing events, such as the application of the principle of double-bluff so neatly made by Valentino in IV, i, of *All Fools*, where nobody but the audience realizes fully to what extent he is inducing Gostanzo to commit himself—and even the audience is by then a little out of breath. There are, however much the minors are neglected, excellent central figures in every play, vital, engaging individuals, never purely types, Lemot, La Besha, Dowsecir, Moren, Labervele, Florilla [2]; Cornelio, Valerio,[3] Bassiolo, Margaret, Cynanche, Strozza [4]; D'Olive and Eurione, and Vandome in the earlier part of the same play.[5] Some of these, Florilla, Strozza and D'Olive, are studies of such originality and subtlety as to deserve to be named beside the most notable Jacobean figures. There is a like infectious gusto in purely extraneous passages of rhetoric, chiefly of course those of D'Olive himself whose character is largely compounded of them (such as his speech on tobacco in II, i, or his description of his ambassadorial train in III, ii), but equally liable to fall to almost any character high-spirited enough to carry them ; Valerio's description of the rout of the bailiffs in the law-courts (*All Fools*, II, i, 319–35), almost reading like an episode from *The Unfortunate Traveller*, or the fanfaronade of nonsensical comic rhetoric in the concluding speech on horns.

But the romantic element, already there in the fantasy of *The Blind Beggar*, growing successively stronger and more serious in *All Fools* and *The Gentleman Usher*, and lingering still in *Monsieur d'Olive*, is of at least equal weight with the comic. It involves only a few characters and a part of the action in *All Fools*, but in the next play it takes possession of the main action and gives rise to characters such as Margaret, serious, frank and courageous, Cynanche, a light but beautiful study of a wife, Strozza, the Elizabethan gentleman with the underlying gift of Christian mysticism. *Monsieur d'Olive* begins with an action

---

[1] The actual intrigue is a little too intricate in *An Humourous Day's Mirth*, excellent in *All Fools*, neglected at the beginning of *Gentleman Usher* and at the end of the romantic plot of *Monsieur d'Olive*, but there are excellent parts in all.
[2] All in *An Humourous Day's Mirth*.   [3] *All Fools*.
[4] *Gentleman Usher*.   [5] *Monsieur d'Olive*.

even more solemn, and the characters of Vaumont, Vandome and Eurione are only displaced from mastery over the play by Chapman's neglect of the romantic action at the instigation of that uncontrollable comic figure, D'Olive. There are scenes of grave, romantic dignity in the first play between Margaret and Vincentio and between Cynanche and Strozza,[1] but Chapman never burdens his comedies, even in the serious romantic action, with the disquisitions that later on delay and obstruct the tragedies. Some serious reflection there is, comments on love and marriage and the mystical speeches of Strozza, but it never becomes a debate and it is always firmly woven into the play, natural to the character and necessary to the action or at least to the expression of that side of the character which is in control of the action. All this brings us much nearer to his Elizabethan predecessors than to his Jacobean successors in the not dissimilar form of tragi-comedy. In these plays he is still in the main an Elizabethan, with the characteristic blending of serious romance and comic gusto and, what is highly significant, with the Elizabethan sense of a wider universe of spiritual existence surrounding even comedy.

His technique, however, has in one or two respects developed beyond his predecessors. Just as in *An Humourous Day's Mirth* he assembled the elements of the humour comedy which Ben Jonson developed so rapidly after him, as in the intimate blending of serious and comic his *Gentleman Usher* stands between, say, *Much Ado* and the tragi-comedy of Beaumont and Fletcher, so, his development of dialogue and of comic blank verse make valuable contributions to the medium of later comedy. His blank verse, as has been pointed out,[2] reveals in his earliest comedy, *The Blind Beggar*, a strong though by no means slavish likeness to Marlowe's, and throughout the other comedies there is a continuous modification of Marlowe's line towards the variety that comedy and tragi-comedy need. In *An Humourous Day's Mirth* it has simplicity, lightness and ease, in *All Fools* an even greater increase of variety, and in *The Gentleman Usher* it has a range capable of all themes from comic to tragic ; indeed, in this play the variableness and adaptability of his verse ranges from the suppleness of quick comic dialogue to some-

---

[1] *Gentleman Usher*, IV, ii, and IV, i, and iii.
[2] See *Comedies of George Chapman*, ed. T. M. Parrott (1914), notes on pp. 676, 690, 760-1, 781.

thing a little nearer (in the serious scenes [1]) the toughness of his
own tragic verse in the succeeding group of Bussy and Byron
plays. He thus anticipates the easy flexibility of Fletcher's
tragi-comic blank verse and the apt and unobtrusive instrument
of Middleton. Conversational dialogue, in the same way,
shows a remarkable development of subtle inflections and implications ; the scene (*Gentleman Usher*, III, ii) where Vincentio
gulls the complacent Bassiolo or that (*Monsieur d'Olive*, II, i)
where Vandome teases the love-sick Eurione are full of close
and delicate suggestion.[2] The dialogue in both these scenes
follows so flexibly the intimate interplay of the minds that it
acts itself from the written page ; we cannot fail to see the
gestures, the expressions that cross the faces of the speakers
and to hear the very tones of the voices. At his best, as thus,
Chapman reaches a point which leaves very little even for
Fletcher to add.

In the passage, for instance, in which Vincentio sets to work
to convert Bassiolo into the messenger between him and Margaret, there is an exquisite revelation, not only of both characters, but of Prince Vincentio's subtle understanding of the
foibles of the man he is gulling. Delicately and neatly he
plays upon the self-conceit, the officiousness, the innate but
relatively harmless snobbishness and the simultaneous slow-
wittedness of the gentleman usher ; his professions of friend-

[1] As, for instance, IV, i, especially 40–6, 59–68, &c.
[2] And the passage in which Eurione betrays to Margaret the love
for St. Anne, of which she is hardly conscious yet herself, is more like
Shakespeare's treatment of such a situation than anything we should
expect (or, indeed, find again) in Chapman's habitual contemptuous
comments on the tricks and devices of women :

> You thinke belike I love the Noble man :
> Heaven is my Judge if I : indeede his love
> And honour to his Wife so after death :
> Would make a Fayry love him, yet not love.
> But thinke the better of him, and sometimes,
> Talke of his love or so ; But you know Maddam
> I cald her sister, and if I love him,
> It is but as my Brother I protest. (*M. d'O.*, II, i, 42–9.)

In the succeeding dialogue with Vandome, Chapman has touched in
most delicately the trick of her mind which ever and again draws
references to St. Anne into apparently quite irrelevant passages of
conversation and as quickly follows them up by plausible explanations
—explanations which deceive no one but herself.

ship, his insistence on intimacy go to Bassiolo's head like wine.
From the moment he has induced him to call him by a nick-
name, he has him in his hand and casually begins to introduce
the name of Margaret.   It is the naturalness and flexibility
both of the language and of the blank verse, the minute detail
of personality that it implies or reveals that gives this passage
at once its virtue as pure comedy of character and its technical
excellence :

Vin.   . . . well sir, you shall have none ;
          You are as coy a peece as your Lords daughter.
Bass.   Who, my mistris ?
Vin.   Indeede, Is she your Mistris ?
Bass.   Ifaith sweet *Vince*, since she was three yeare old.
Vin.   And are not wee too friends ?
Bass.   Who doubts of that ?
Vin.   And are not two friends one ?
Bass.   Even man and wife.
Vin.   Then what to you she is, to me she should be.
Bass.   Why *Vince*, thou wouldst not have her ?
Vin.   O not I : I doe not fancie any thing like you.
Bass.   Nay but I pray thee tell me.
Vin.   You do not meane to marry her your self ?
Bass.   Not I by heaven.
Vin.   Take heede now, do not gull me.
Bass.   No by that candle.
Vin.   Then will I be plaine.
          Thinke you she dotes not too much on my father ?
Bass.   O yes, no doubt on't.
Vin.   Nay, I pray you speak.
Bass.   You seely man you, she cannot abide him.
Vin.   Why sweete friend pardon me, alas I knew not.
Bass.   But I doe note you are in some things simple,
          And wrong your selfe too much.
Vin.   Thanke you good friend,
          For your playne dealing, I doe meane so well.
Bass.   But who saw ever summer mixt with winter ?
          There must be equall yeares where firme love is.
          Could we two love so well so soddainely
          Were we not some thing equaller in yeares
          Than he and shee are ?
Vin.   I cry ye mercy sir, I know we could not, but yet be not too bitter,
          Considering love is fearefull.   And sweete friend,
          I have a letter t'intreate her kindnesse
          Which if you would convay.
Bass.   I, if I would sir ?
Vin.   Why fayth, deare friend, I would not die requitelesse.
Bass.   Would you not so sir ?
          By heaven a little thing would make me boxe you,

Which if you would convaie ? why not I pray ?
Which (friend) thou shalt convaie.
Vin.   Which friend, you shall then.
Bass.   Well friend, and I will then.
Vin.   And use some kinde persuasive wordes for me ?
Bass.   The best I sweare that my poore toung can forge.
Vin.   I, wel said, poore toung   O tis rich in meekenesse ;
You are not knowne to speake well ?   You have wonne
Direction of the Earle and all his house,
The favour of his daughter, and all Dames
That ever I sawe, come within your sight,
With a poore tongue ?   A plague a your sweete lippes.[1]

As in his comedies Chapman seems to follow directly from
Shakespeare's blend of comic and romantic, perhaps most
nearly from that of *Much Ado About Nothing*, and to associate
himself, among his contemporaries, most nearly with the earliest
work of Middleton and, in less degree, with the humour comedy
of Ben Jonson, so in his tragedy it is again to an Elizabethan
that he carries us back, to Marlowe   In certain fundamental
qualities he is, as has been said, nearer to his Elizabethan predecessors than to his contemporaries.   His tragedy sometimes
lacks, indeed, the Elizabethan clarity of emotion, music and
image, but it is free, at the same time, from certain prevailing
habits of his contemporaries, from their pervasive sense of the
theatre that sometimes directs not only episode and situation,
but, with Marston, Tourneur, Webster, Beaumont and Fletcher,
emotion also.   He shares with Sidney, Marlowe and other
Elizabethan poet-critics an exalted sense of the infinite virtue of
poetry, of nobility of thought and expression.   Again and again
in his tragedies the revelation of character is interrupted or
confused by passages of bold, abstract thought which again takes
us back to Marlowe ; he has indeed the same tendency to the
poetic and often undramatic expression of reflection as we find
in Tamburlaine's speeches on beauty and the nature of the soul.
And side by side with this goes a similar fundamentally subjective approach to character in tragedy, a similar projection of
the author's own personality and beliefs into certain of the
characters, together with a tendency to treat perfunctorily
those not immediately concerned with the expression of the
central ideas.   Often, indeed, his figures break down into an
undramatic exposition of the particular doctrines (Senecan,
Ciceronian, Epictetan) that were uppermost in Chapman's mind

[1] *Gentleman Usher*, III, ii, 130–72.

and we see the native ardour of the Elizabethan obscured by the characteristic cast of Jacobean uncertainty.

> Then thou most strangely-intellectuall fire,
> That, proper to my soule, hast power t'inspire,
> Her burning faculties, and with the wings
> Of thy unspheared flame visitst the springs
> Of spirits immortall; Now (as swift as Time
> Doth follow Motion) finde th' eternall Clime
> Of his free soule, whose living subject stood
> Up to the chin in the Pyerean flood,
> And drunke to me halfe this Musean storie,
> Inscribing it to deathles Memorie . . .[1]

It is not for nothing that this invocation to that poet whose ' genius was all air and fire ' stands at the beginning of Chapman's serious dramatic work. It does not need the tenderness of the concluding lines,[2] surprising and almost without parallel as they are in the rest of Chapman's work, to assure us of the affinity of spirit between the two. The ten lines quoted here are perhaps the most penetrating and illuminating comment ever made on the quality that these two minds possessed in common, the ' strangely intellectual fire ' that distinguished each in turn from his contemporaries, whether Elizabethan or Jacobean. So that it is not surprising that, from one aspect at least, Chapman appears to continue his task of completing Marlowe's work, not for four sestiads but for the rest of his life. In spite of the wide differences in taste, opinion, ethics and mood which must have divided them, this innate aspiration, this burning intellectual clarity bound them together.

The definite reminiscences of Marlowe's work are the least significant part of this curiously lingering association, lingering as persistently as did the memory of Sidney in Fulke Greville's equally tenacious mind. When we have noted the intrusions of Marlovian cadence and imagery in the somewhat unexpected settings of The Blind Beggar of Alexandria and An Humourous

---

[1] Chapman's continuation of Marlowe's Hero and Leander (1598). Sestiad, III, 183–92.
  [2] Confer with it and make my pledge as deepe,
  That neither's draught be consecrate to sleepe.
  Tell it how much his late desires I tender,
  (If yet it know not) and to light surrender
  My soules darke offspring, willing it should die
  To loves, to passions, and societie.
                                                    (Ibid., ll. 193–8.)

Day's Mirth (and they are, I think, distinctly more frequent than Swinburne implied [1]), when we have allowed also for reminiscences of theme, such as that of *Faustus* in the conjuring scene of *Bussy d'Ambois* (IV, 2) or even of another man's apt reference,[2] we have, after all, only the evidence of admiration and affection shared by many of his contemporaries.

But the impression of Marlowe's characteristic mood is stronger than this and outlasts the turn of the century, growing more marked in the French history plays which were not begun until some ten years after his death and culminating in the study of Byron made in or about the year 1608. The figures of Bussy, of Guise and of Byron all look back in one way or another to the heroic figures of Tamburlaine, Guise or Mortimer and catch, carry forward and modulate into surprising and often exquisite extensions the aspiration of Marlowe's early plays, developing also, as was natural to a Jacobean, the element of defeatism already anticipated in Marlowe's thought. Essentially it is the mood which is preserved, and preserved in such vitality as to change under our eyes into some such later growth as Marlowe's own might have afforded had he lived. Sometimes it is so close to Marlowe's thought that it is associated with imagery like his and with a metre which equally derives from his at a little distance.

> O thou King of flames,
> That with thy Musique-footed horse dost strike
> The cleere light out of crystall, on darke earth ;
> And hurlst instructive fire about the world : [3]

These lines of Bussy's are, but for the last line (and perhaps even that but for the word ' instructive ' in that setting), lines that we feel Marlowe meant to write but overlooked. But sometimes, as when Byron says ' Tis immortality to die aspiring ', we know that Marlowe, up to the stage at which he ceased to

---

[1] T. M. Parrott, however, states it more decisively and works it out more fully : *The Comedies of George Chapman* (1914) : *The Blind Beggar of Alexandria. Introduction*, p. 675. See also the comments on the development of Chapman's blank verse in comedy in the earlier part of this chapter.

[2] The echo of Peele's ' Fit to write passions for the souls below ' (*The Honour of the Garter. Ad Maecenatem Prologus* : 1. 64) is curiously unexpected in Montsurry's mouth (*B. d'A.*, V, i, 47), but there is no mistaking it.

[3] *B. d'A.*, V, 3, 41–4.

write, could not have said it, because it was too explicit a statement of the instinctive principle of his own poetry, though it is also probable that, had he lived to look back from the Jacobean age upon the aspiration of his early poetry and to rationalize not the poetry but the guiding principle of the thought, he might have said something like it. But sometimes the full and final development of Marlowe's thought has gone beyond his own hard-edged certainty and has correspondingly lost its clarity of image and music. At such times, a passage, though we believe it to derive ultimately from Marlowe and to embody much of his passion, is filled with the crowded and huddled imagery, the verse which sways and thunders into a multitudinous, or to use his own work, a ' numerous ' rhythm, that is Chapman's only. In no circumstances could Marlowe, I think, have written Byron's magnificent manifesto of aspiration (at the end of the third act of the *Conspiracy*). Here Chapman has been carried a step further and his statement of what Marlowe's later thought might well have been is revealed in language which, though it lacks the smoky convolutions of his most characteristic imagery, is yet peculiar to him and improbable to Marlowe :

> you have height enough,
> Beneath this steepe heaven to use all your reaches,
> 'Tis too farre off, to let you, or respect you.
> Give me a spirit that on this lifes rough sea,
> Loves t'have his sailes fild with a lustie winde,
> Even till his Sayle-yeards tremble ; his Masts crack,
> And his rapt ship runne on her side so lowe
> That she drinkes water, and her keele plowes ayre ;
> There is no danger to a man, that knowes
> What life and death is : there's not any law,
> Exceeds his knowledge ; neither is it lawfull
> That he should stoope to any other lawe.[1]

This is far from being Chapman's final or indeed his essential view of individualism and aspiration, but it is the finest epitome of the spirit of Marlowe's plays that has ever been made, while at the same time the undertone of defiance and tension gives the measure of Chapman's resistance to the fatalism more common in his age.

The same growth in Chapman's revelation of that aspect of experience that he seems to hold in trust for Marlowe can be

[1] *Byr. Con.*, III, iii, 132-43.

traced in his characters. Bussy, ' at all parts buckled in [his] fate ', is still, in the earlier play, essentially a Tamburlaine in aspiration and confidence ; he ' holds the fates fast bound in iron chains ', until the moment of mortality comes. But the superimposition of Suetonius, Seneca, Horace and perhaps Epictetus and Marcus Aurelius tends not unnaturally to obscure this, and there is beginning a sense of dislocation and uncertainty of spiritual values, impossible to the unmoral Tamburlaine and his creator.[1] Here again, then, Chapman is at work on a Jacobean extension of Marlowe's idea, not on a mere rigid retention of it.[2] This becomes clearer still in Byron, who is at first introduced by Roncas (*Byron's Conspiracy*, I, i, 61–9) in terms that would suit excellently with that pattern of heroic figures Almanzor of *The Conquest of Granada*. But now the source of the aspiration is no longer living.[3] Chapman begins to explain to us, as Marlowe might have done had he lived to look back, what were the seeds of disintegration latent all along in this glory. He shows us Byron, no longer, like Tamburlaine, a poet unconquerable because of the foundation of poetry on which his aspiration rests, but a practical soldier boasting of his unflawed career ; no brilliant figure of fairy-tale chivalry like Almanzor, but a man crumbling and falling to pieces under our eyes in weakness that is strictly relevant to and the proper nemesis of his arrogance. He, like all such figures, Chapman would tell us in his mature shrewdness, ' hath ever but slenderly known himself ', and even as he approaches ever nearer to the figure of the fairy-tale Almanzor, his irresponsible individualism is broken by the poet who, though he alone understood fully the spring and source of Marlowe's mood, understood also the significance of government, of stability, of the patient, responsible service involved in kingship and leadership and could not see this glorious histrionic tilter at windmills without seeing simultaneously the wrack and ruin of civil war that he and his like had spread through sixteenth-century Europe. And so Byron goes down before Chapman's stern sense of public responsi-

[1] This, of course, develops still more clearly in the Heroic play of the late seventeenth century.

[2] And it is developing, I believe, in the only direction it can logically take, towards that incredible, unreal, absurd and yet paradoxically attractive figure, Almanzor.

[3] Even Marlowe could not repeat the mood of *Tamburlain*, Part I ; it is impossible, in fact, to preserve it beyond the initial play.

5

bility and knowledge of the instability of human fortune.[1]
Byron, boasting like Tamburlaine or his Guise, but with an echo
of the hubris of Seneca's tyrants, flings himself upon his fate,
not with his earlier *Amor Fati*, but with an ever-mounting frenzy
in which Chapman exposes the unstable, loose-knit elements on
which their glory was built.   The penetration and judgement
of these last scenes of *Byron's Tragedy*, where the madness
appears to range through every convulsion possible to a man
caught by fate in ignorance of himself, comes of a more specific
disillusionment than Marlowe's, and again it is to Seneca that
we turn for the familiar summary :

> Illi mors gravis incubat,
> Qui notus nimis omnibus,
> Ignotus moritur sibi.

With inflexible sternness, characteristic at once of his moral
rectitude and of his dramatic art when he chose to exercise it,
Chapman follows the last stages of the ' glorious ' man through
its characteristic hysteria.   Like Richard II and Edward II
when their insolence is gone and their fortunes are beyond
recovery, Byron flies into the compensating insolence of claiming
sainthood.   For a man who has so far had little regard for ' the
immaculate justice of the Highest ' he is curiously ready to
speak with assurance of its processes, especially on his own
behalf.   Marlowe, Chapman and Shakespeare all knew that,
just as any war can be called a ' holy ' war, so any execution
can be made to appear a martyrdom.   They all understood that
form of hysteria which, clutching at a kind of delirious trans-
cendentalism, claims for itself first place in the Kingdom of
Heaven for little other apparent reason than that it has lost the
corresponding place in the kingdoms of this world.   And Chapman, in addition, indicates in his study of religiosity the fundamental ignorance of spiritual law, the lack of valid spiritual
experience characteristic of the world about him.   It is a fine

---

[1] This might also have been the ultimate comment of Marlowe
(that fine Machiavellian scholar), on the romance of conquest, just
as it was, though far otherwise expressed, of Shakespeare.   All three
of these came to reject not only the irresponsible glory of Tamburlaine, Hotspur and Byron, but the element of self-seeking in the
less irresponsible ideal of Machiavelli : Marlowe by exploring Barabbas,
the Guise and Mortimer, Shakespeare in the double study of Gloucester,
afterwards Richard III, and Chapman (who was never really seduced
by it) in Lafin.

and discriminating study of individualism becoming egotism, egotism becoming megalomania and megalomania breaking down into hysteria.   And in its psychological essentials Marlowe himself—who could set Mycetes over against Tamburlaine— might ultimately have derived it from his own original position.

Consciously or unconsciously, Chapman in 1598 took into his custody far more than the first two sestiads of *Hero and Leander*.   Throughout the first decade of the succeeding century he continues to give expression, not only to the ideas that Marlowe had left unexpressed but even, it would almost seem, to those that he had not yet reached in his own progress.[1]

III

What, as has already been suggested, lies outside Marlowe's province is the fine, constructive political idealism of Chapman. This, itself perhaps a form of escape from spiritual uncertainty into the domain of practical, constructive politics, is conspicuous in the two plays in which Byron, the individualist adventurer, the Hotspur-Tamburlaine-Essex figure, so notable a feature of the drama and of the history of the late sixteenth century, is set against Chapman's slowly evolved idea of a king in the figure of Henry IV,[2] and, again, in the figure of Cato in *Caesar and Pompey* (again an individualist, but this time at odds with a society in which Chapman found no redeeming feature), who sums up the poet's philosophy on the dignity of the spirit of man as nobly as Henry IV does that of the responsibilities of kingship.[3]

[1] It might be suggested that certain of his preoccupations or prejudices Chapman also shared with Marlowe. The relative indifference to women and the inability to enter their minds, shown throughout the plays (with the exception of the *Gentleman Usher*) and culminating in Clermont's denial of ' love in marriage ' in *The Revenge of Bussy d'Ambois* (IV, i, 169–88), and the interest in what was, roughly, materialistic philosophy (deriving perhaps, in both, originally from Lucretius), most conspicuous in *Bussy*, V, 2, and *Byron's Conspiracy*, III, 3, are clearly reconcilable with Marlowe's declared or implied views.

[2] See especially the following passages : *Byr. Trag.*, I, i, 99–107, 134–40 ; III, i, 10–48 (a singularly inappropriate speech for Byron), III, ii, 31–54 ; IV, ii, 39–47, 63–85 ; V, i, 49–65 (an idea which Webster uses at the beginning of the *Duchess of Malfi*).

[3] See, for a close and admirably clear analysis of Chapman's ideas on kingship and government, T. M. Parrott's introductions to the relevant tragedies, particularly pp. 595–8 and 636–7.

In the earlier of the two Byron plays, the figure of Henry is only noticeable among Jacobean monarchs for a certain simple, unassuming candour (perhaps best seen in his patient tolerance of Byron's insolence in V, i) ; he is a good-humoured democrat, whose democracy goes deeper than that of Shakespeare's Henry V but who is no more infirm of purpose or of intellect than his Shakespearian predecessor. In the later play Chapman himself speaks through the mouth of Henry, more and more clearly enunciating his conception of kingship, that divinely ordained and inescapable office, sacred, by reason of its place in the hierarchy [1] that ascends from the lowest of mankind to God and by reason that it symbolizes on earth the law of God, but— and this is where Shakespeare and Chapman separate from the average Elizabethan or Jacobean statement of the divine right of kings—conferring upon the individual who occupies the office few privileges (and those only as compensation), no scope for the growth or exercise of his individuality, but only endless responsibility. The position is further defined by the portraits of intriguing or lawless kings or rulers in *The Revenge of Bussy d'Ambois*, *Chabot* and *Caesar and Pompey*, and the evil wrought by an irresponsible or individualistic king is as clearly analysed in *Chabot* as it had been memorably revealed by Shakespeare in *Henry VI*, *Richard II* or *Lear*. In two speeches in *Byron's Tragedy*, Chapman sums up, with the admirable clarity characteristic of his expository rather than his impassioned poetry, the thought that is illustrated throughout his plays by the relations of kings to their subjects, to the laws and to God.

> But God, who knowes kings are not made by art,
> But right of Nature, nor by trechery propt,
> But simple vertue, once let fall from Heaven,
> A branch of that greene tree, whose root is yet,
> Fast fixt above the starrs . . .
> Religion is a branch, first set and blest
> By heavens highe finger in the hearts of kings,
> Which whilelome grew into a goodly tree,
> Bright Angels sat and sung upon the twigs,
> And royale branches for the heads of Kings,
> Were twisted of them but since squint-ey'd envye :
> And pale suspicion, dasht the heads of kingdomes,
> One gainst another : two abhorred twins,

---

[1] Much of this part of the play can be compared with the similar ideas in *Troilus and Cressida*, I, iii, 85–134.

With two foule tayles : sterne Warre and Libertie,
Entred the world. The tree that grew from heaven
Is overrunne with mosse ; the cheerfull musique
That heeretofore hath sounded out of it,
Beginnes to cease ; and as she casts her leaves,
(By small degrees) the kingdomes of the earth
Decline and wither : and looke whensoever
That the pure sap in her, is dried up quite ;
The lamp of all authoritie goes out,
And all the blaze of Princes is extinkt ; [1]

O thou that governst the keene swords of Kings,
Direct my arme in this important stroke,
Or hold it being advanct ; the weight of blood,
Even in the basest subject, doth exact
Deepe consultation, in the highest King ;
For in one subject, deaths uniust affrights,
Passions, and paines, (though he be nere so poore)
Aske more remorsee, then the voluptuous spleenes
Of all Kings in the world, deserve respect ;
Hee should be borne grey-headed that will beare
The sword of Empire ; Judgment of the life,
Free state, and reputation of a man, .
(If it be just and worthy) dwells so darke
That it denies accesse to Sunne and Moone ;
The soules eye sharpned with that sacred light,
Of whome the Sunne it selfe is but a beame,
Must onely give that judgment.[2]

In *The Revenge of Bussy d'Ambois* and *Caesar and Pompey* a
different but related order of reflexion takes first place in Chapman's mind. He is concerned in these later plays rather with
the individual, the philosopher who holds the ' only use of
learning to live well ', the ideal man, which for Chapman was the
' Senecal man '. Of these two stoics, Clermont and Cato, the
later is at once the finer figure and the more complete statement
of Chapman's ideal. Clermont combines the lingering traces
of the chivalric warrior (Tamburlaine-Bussy-Byron) with the
stoic who is indifferent alike to so-called good and evil. Chapman has brought him into the plot to fulfil an act of vengeance
which no sixteenth-century gentleman could have neglected but
no stoic would have considered worth performing. The inconsistency runs throughout the figure, and the Epictetan philosophy
upon which the Senecal side of his character is based suffers
strangely in this company, and ever and again he comes forth

[1] *Byr. Trag.*, III, i, 10–42 *pass.*   [2] *Ibid.*, IV, ii, 63–79.

an unregenerate prig.   But this means less with Chapman than
with most dramatists, and provided that we do not try to make
the two sides square into a coherent character [1] we can accept
the noble sentiments, apart from their setting, as Chapman's
own.   The ideas on vengeance, on law, on the virtue of self-
knowledge, the magnificent lines (III, iv, 47–75 ; IV, i, 131–57)
on the individual and his rhythmic union with the universe, the
unexpected passage of highly imaginative Christian theology
put into the mouth of the ghost (V, i, 82–91),[2] all these, culminating as they do in the devoted suicide which is the sequel
to Clermont's love for Guise, are beyond reach of cavil.   It is
in his infallibility that Clermont becomes insipid, and in the
brutality of his sentiments on love and marriage [3] that he becomes
a prig of that peculiar puritanical dye that Chapman himself was
the first man to denounce (as in Florilla) when he recognized it
in the world about him.

But such inconsistency as this is gone from the figure of Cato,
who is free at once from the contradictions of Clermont and the
roughness of the original from whom he was drawn, and nearer,
at least in the death scenes, to the Socrates of the *Apology*.
Through his mouth Chapman speaks, nominally it is true as a
dramatist, but in effect mainly as a firm, grave moralist whose
ethics are still lighted by that rarest of all things in Jacobean
drama, a steady illumination from a source beyond reason,
proof or observation :

> For we shall know each other ; and past death
> Retaine those formes of knowledge learn'd in life ; . . .

---

[1] There is always, as has been suggested, a danger of confusing
negligence and inconsistency in Chapman's drawing of a figure with
intentional contradictions within the character, regarding as puzzling
and intricate a character which is only a mixture of dramatic portraiture
and intrusions of the dramatist in person.

[2] This passage, which was obviously isolated from its setting in
Chapman's mind, appears, by juxtaposition of what precedes and
follows, little short of blasphemous.

[3] See Act V, Scene i, ll. 156–end ; especially the well-known lines
186–8 :

> But what excites the beds desire in bloud,
> By no meanes justly can be construed love ;
> For when love kindles any knowing spirit,
> It ends in vertue and effects divine ;
> And is in friendship chaste, and masculine.

And that our soules in reason are immortall,
Their naturall and proper objects prove ;
Which immortallity and knowledge are.
For to that object ever is referr'd
The nature of the soule, in which the acts
Of her high faculties are still employde.[1]

There is, though, recognizable in these lines, as in many others
in which Chapman opposes his faith to the rising tide of doubt
and disillusionment about him, a tension which reminds us
again of the aspiration of the later Tamburlaine, where the author,
passionately longing to believe his own profession, is beginning
to affirm it to convince not only his hearers but himself.   The
idea though clear in his mind depends upon the will of the poet
to support it ; it is not based on a serene enough conviction to
support him.   His resistance to the surrounding spiritual uncertainty is firmer here than in corresponding speeches of
Strozza in *The Gentleman Usher,* and the increase in definition
is the measure, not only of the increasing rigidity of the thought,
but of the increasing weight with which the pressure of the
time bore down upon him.

Yet of Chapman, the last of the Elizabethans, we may say
that he is the only dramatist of the Jacobean age to emerge with
any kind of explicit statement from the wilderness in which ' our
knowledges do light us but to err ' and in which to look up
to Heaven is to confound knowledge with knowledge.   Like
Faustus before him, he melts his pagan wisdom and his Christian
theology so utterly together that neither can be wholly separated again from the other, but, unlike Marlowe, it is not to
' confound Hell in Elizium ' but to employ Aristotle's concept of
the harmony between form and matter to prove the resurrection
of the body through the immortality of the soul.[2]   Possibly
because his was not a readily adaptable mind, he seems never
to have entered into the final phase of the Elizabethan-Jacobean

---

[1] *Caes. and Pom.,* V, ii, 137–46 *pass.*
[2] And yet at the close is again a line that Marlowe might have
written and behind Cato's last words there is a sense still of the presence
of his original inspiration :

Now wing thee, deare soule, and receive her heaven.
The earth, and ayre, and seas I know, and all
The ioyes, and horrors of their peace and warres,
And now will see the gods state, and the starres.
(*Caes. and Pom.,* V, ii, 158–61.)

drama, into the serenity of Shakespeare, the disregard of the bulk of the tragi-comedy writers or the security of Ford. He resisted the mood of intense despondency into which Shakespeare passed in the first decade and was, perhaps in consequence of this, unable to enter into anything like Shakespeare's resolution of that mood. To the end he is assailed by ' the joys and horrors of their peace and wars ' and is never entirely certain that ' the stars shine still '.

IV

These dominant characteristics of Chapman's thought and emotion are reflected in his dramatic imagery. In this, though it is of many kinds, two may chiefly be distinguished, the relatively clear, descriptive image by which, as in his clearer music, he is close to the Elizabethans and the more confused and clouded imagery by which he is more commonly known, that brings him nearer to the Jacobean dramatists of the first decade. The first is the imagery of a man who watched the sky day and night and knew like a shepherd the habits of stars and moon, clouds and mist, birds and trees. Moving waters, seas and rivers, animals at large and wild, all are alive in these passages, which suspend for the moment of description our consciousness of the play.

> As when the Moone hath comforted the Night,
> And set the world in silver of her light,
> The Planets, Asterisims and whole state of Heaven,
> In beames of gold desending ; all the windes,
> Bound up in caves, chargd not to drive abrode,
> Their cloudy heads an universall peace,
> Proclaimd in scilence of the quiet earth.
> Soone as her hot and dry fumes are let loose,
> Stormes and cloudes mixing ; sodainley put out
> The eyes of all those glories : The creation,
> Turnd in to *Chaos*, and we then desire,
> For all our joye of life, the death of sleepe.[1] . . .

The second is cloudy, fuliginous and obscure, but of immense compulsive power, and in the confusion of picture or the relation between picture and thought is mirrored something of the deep division of Chapman's mind. The chaos and conflict in the imagery helps to reveal his underlying sense of a similar chaos

---

[1] *Byr. Con.*, III, i, 6–17.

in the universe about him, the poet thus reflecting the spirit of
the age which has invaded him against his conscious purpose
and is revealing itself, also unconsciously, through his poetry.

> Now is it true, earth mooves, and heaven stands still ;
> Even Heaven it selfe, must see and suffer ill :
> The too huge bias of the world hath swai'd
> Her backe-part upwards, and with that she braves
> This Hemisphere, that long her mouth hath mockt :
> The gravitie of her religious face :
> (Now growne too waighty with her sacriledge
> And here discernd sophisticate enough)
> Turnes to th' Antipodes : and all the formes
> That her illusions have imprest in her,
> Have eaten through her backe : and now all see,
> How she is riveted with hypocrisie.[1]

Significant as is this imagery in the revelation of Chapman's
thought, it is not without, simultaneously, a well-marked
dramatic function. Unlike the long passages of argument and
disquisition, it is not digressive nor does it hinder or damage the
dramatic content of the scene. What in effect his imagery does
is somewhat akin to the function of Webster's, otherwise utterly
unlike it. It assumes the interpretation not of the outward body
of the play, action event or even character, but of the mood in
which the often sketchily drawn characters are as it were
enveloped as though in drapery. The long, weighty passages
of imagery fold themselves about their limbs so that they go
forth clothed, not indeed in their own virtue or personality,
but in pictures which, though they bear often little relation to
their wearers, are found, when the scene or play is regarded
spatially, to form part of a pattern, to create with others a sustained harmony of colour and mood which runs through the
play almost as a plot within the plot.[2]

The magnificence of Chapman's crowded imagery seems at
first glance to be of the same order not only as Fulke Greville's

---

[1] *B. d'A.*, V, i, 161–73.
[2] The question of Chapman's imagery demands, of course, far fuller
treatment than can be attempted here. All I have attempted to do
is to indicate its significance for our understanding of his dramatic
technique and for certain aspects of his thought. For a thorough
study of the imagery itself reference should be made to Miss Elizabeth
Holmes : *Aspects of Elizabethan Imagery* (1929), and the two articles
by Mr. James Smith in *Scrutiny*, March and June, 1935.

but also as Donne's. But it hardly ever resolves itself into
felicity as Donne's does by the mastery of passion over intellect.
Rather, I think, the clarifying comes, with Chapman, when the
intellect escapes from or outgrows passion or when the passion
is recollected, not in tranquillity (for that mood is almost unknown to him as a dramatist) but at a distance that softens or
mutes it, as in the lines to the memory of Marlowe. It is seldom
that passion leads, as with Webster and many other of his contemporaries, to inevitable words ; Chapman's lines do not
memorize themselves ; individual words continually elude the
reader and, once slipped, are not easy to restore. Still further
is his tragic imagery from the graceful facility of the tragi-comedy
writers or Middleton ; ease and slightness of imagery is no more
a part of his mental process than ease of character diagnosis and
analysis. What we find in him and in no other contemporary
except in part Fulke Greville is, in a single image, in a group
of lines, in a long sustained passage, a sudden glow through the
smoulder, a wide, crimson illumination in which the shape of
thought and vision stand out black and urgent with significance.

V

Among contemporary dramatists there are few whose preoccupation or purpose is closely akin to his. With two only
does he seem to share any part of his intention or of his major
interests. Like Ben Jonson, he believed in the moral function
of his work, though he does not show the same consciousness of
aesthetic dictatorship. But his idealism, and it is with Chapman
rather a matter of idealism than of moral criticism, found a
natural expression in his tragedies, partly because he was able
to use contemporary French history, types, both individuals and
political groups, that would serve as vehicles for the expression
of his theory of society. And since the interest of his audiences
was highly stimulated by such closely contemporary material, his
task was easier than that self-appointed one of Ben Jonson, of
embodying a stern moral and aesthetic creed in classical comedy.
But in the great Jonsonian Roman tragedies and in Chapman's
French plays (and particularly in his one Roman play), the fundamental dignity of purpose and of personal integrity is revealed
as clearly as it is in their letters, their dedications and their
prefaces. Both men when they wrote their prefaces were concerned not solely or even mainly with the treatment the play

had received at the hands of its audience, publisher or players,[1] with the nature of theatrical effectiveness, of action or of diction,[2] but with the true conduct of ' autentical tragedy', ' the elegant and sententious excitation to virtue and deflection from her contrary ', the ' truth of argument, dignity of persons, gravity and height of elocution, fulness and frequency of sentence '.[3] But Chapman is still primarily a poet, where Ben Jonson is primarily a conscious moralist and artist ; the conscious idealist often intrudes, with Chapman, upon the poet, but there is no consistent subjugation of poetry to moral or artistic theory : the two go side by side, and if they conflict, the conflict is obvious. Thus Chapman's work is at bottom more akin to Shakespeare's, Webster's, Tourneur's, in spite of superficial divergence ; he is no homogeneous theorist but at best a poet, and at worst a contradictory mixture of poet and propagandist. And in this very inconsistency he reflects, in spite of himself, the doubts and spiritual uncertainties of the Jacobean age.

With one other dramatist, Fulke Greville, he has affinities on another side. With him he shares his absorbing interest in statecraft and government (an interest only equalled else by Shakespeare, in very different kind, at the period of the history plays, and by Marlowe) and in the various problems of the relation between the temporal and the eternal state. Some, moreover, of their philosophic positions are the same.[4] Both poets, too, have the same difficulty in subordinating language to thought or, more properly, in charging language with the weight of their thought. A habit of obscurity makes almost unintelligible some of the reflective passages with which they

---

[1] Compare, for example, Marston's address To the Reader (Malc., Q. 1604), Fletcher's Address to the Reader (The Faithful Shepherdess, Q. 1609), Webster To the Juditious Reader (The Devil's Law Case, Q. 1623). (This does not apply, of course, to a prologue, such as that to All Fools, written directly for the theatre.)

[2] Compare, for example, Marston's remarks on the publishing of plays written solely for the Theatre, To the Reader (Fawne, Q. 1606.)

[3] See Chapman's Dedication to The Revenge of Bussy d'Ambois (Q. 1613) and Jonson's prefatory note To the Readers (Sejanus, Q. 1605). And compare Chapman's comments on the function of the stage in the Revenge of Bussy d'Ambois, I, i, 319–55.

[4] But by no means all. Chapman's comments on atheism must have shocked Greville (if he met them) as much as Greville's revolutionary socialism would have shocked the creator of Henry IV and Chabot.

fill their scenes, though in both there is, simultaneously, the same power of illuminating the obscurity with imagery which is in turn magnified and extended by it.

What follows us, then, throughout Chapman's greatest work, never entirely deserting any tragic utterance of his and present to a large degree in his romantic comedy, is the aspiration, the spontaneous heroic mood of his early contemporaries, especially of Marlowe.   To the later part of his dramatic career belongs the growth of his mature genius, the coherent, constructive thought on the nature of the state and the function of statesmanship, with the representative figures of two rival theories in Byron and Henry IV.   With these, but mainly revealed in the tragedies, goes his distinctive gift of building up the very substance of the play, often through long speeches, out of voluminous epic imagery on a scale seldom attempted and seldomer maintained by his contemporaries.

CHAPTER IV

JOHN MARSTON

I

COMING at the opening of the Jacobean period, Marston is a dramatist of greater originality and significance than is always admitted. His early work was experimental, ill-disciplined and irregular, but it was at least original and fertile in invention. His comedy, even in the comic sub-plots of his early tragedies, is sure and appears, paradoxically, more serious than his early tragedies, if only because it can be taken seriously. In his maturity he was the fit companion of Middleton, Ben Jonson and Dekker in comedy, and in tragi-comedy or tragedy a poet of no mean order, an eager experimenter and a keen critic. Dramatic theory and practice seem to have grown side by side with him, at first (it would seem) to the detriment of the practice, and in his earliest work the burden of his somewhat inchoate thought hinders both character drawing and language, leading to the inconsistencies of the first and the notorious and much abused eccentricity of the second.

But Marston, though at first a little clumsy in handling the technique of tragedy, knew as well what he was about as any of his immediate successors. Being almost the first man to break the ground, he was more erratic and wildly experimental than those who had the benefit of his experience behind them. But the chaos of his thought is but a symptom of the boiling confusion of idea that surrounded the tragedians of the first decade and its eager contradictions are themselves an index to certain dominant themes. The most significant perhaps of his early experiments is his attempt to draw the figure of a satanic man (Piero, Mendoza, Malevole), now Machiavellian, now Senecan tyrant, suddenly become immense upon a background which has surrendered its implication of infinity. The uncertainty of his drawing and his lack of control is due partly to the luxuriance of his material, but mainly to

77

that bewilderment to which the whole of his generation was subject.

In comedy he is similarly representative of the age, concentrating like Ben Jonson and Middleton on a limited world and delineating it, though not without grave implications of social satire, without reference to any larger universe. He makes his own contributions, too, to the development of the technique of portraying manners, bringing his considerable experience as a theatre man to the service of his attempt to give a closer and closer impression of immediacy in the details of dialogue. With his shrewd sense of the theatre to guide him in comedy and his natural instinct for passionate thought to intensify and widen his tragic themes, Marston developed rapidly, during the seven years of his theatre career, from a mainly undramatic social satirist to a dramatist whose potentialities, though never fulfilled, contained the germ of much that formed the base of his successors' achievements.

Finally he did notable service to the subsequent drama in the very department in which at first he made himself most notorious, his diction. For it is Marston who, when the spasmodic and undisciplined hyperbole of his early vocabulary is reduced (whether by the ministrations of Ben Jonson or by the milder operations of time and natural development), maintains by the strength and daring of his imagery the tragic tradition of Marlowe and of Shakespeare's early work, confirming imagery as a vital and integral part of dramatic expression, conferring upon it a function which no major dramatist of the succeeding decade disregarded, that of supplying the essential indications of mood and underlying thought without which neither plot, character nor the true aesthetic values of the play could be rightly apprehended.

II

Marston's genius then was not primarily dramatic and it is doubtful whether it ever wholly became so. His early poems are a battle-ground between moralist and poet and his early plays between satiric character writer and dramatist. These two, the persistent, aggressive and exacerbated moralist and the suddenly mellifluous poet, fairly divide his work, from whichever angle we approach it. The speculative moralist led him into undramatically expressed explorations of the Stoic and Machiavellian ideals, while the instinct of the character writer took him into equally undramatic experiments in type-studies of Senecan villains and Machiavellian politicians. The poet led him to the discovery of Seneca's nature descriptions, to flashes of fine phrasing and sweet cadences ; also, less fortunately, to number-less abortions, fine phrasing miscarried. Even in that notorious style for which he was so heartily abused the same conflict is at work giving him in his early days more than a touch of Nashe's quality—a haughty dominion over vocabulary. He had from the first a rough, driving force which sometimes exploded into a fulminous splendour though far more often, driven askew, it collapsed into incoherent splutterings easy to hold up to mockery. It was this erratic force and the language which is the clue to it that so disgusted Jonson, who added to an even greater force the discipline that made it formidable. Yet it is Marston with his incoherence and the tumultuous con-fusion of thought and passion who flashes illumination, as it were of lightning upon a distant hillside, upon roads we are to travel later with Shakespeare, with Webster or with Ford.

The earlier poems, *Pygmalion*, *The Satyres* and the *Scourge of Villainy*, serve mainly to show us the portrait of a young man who chose to begin his career by satirizing what he can least have known, man and society. In this he did merely what others were doing about him and the satirical works have nearly all that irritating quality which we associate with a young man trying to make a noise in the world. The *Pygmalion* is a descend-ant of the family of *Hero and Leander*, but with the puritan-satirist already about his work of corruption. The *Satyres* have vigour—Marston had always this—and now and again a vivid, brief portrait that anticipates the excellent and wholly undramatic 'characters' in he plays. There are musical lines in abundance and now and again the shadowing of a more comprehensive interpretation of life, but still always satiric and still, as always, shadowy rather than coherent. At its best it is clever portraiture, imaginative speculation after the manner of Chapman and Tourneur or intimate journalistic riposte with other satirists such as Hall ; at its worst, it leaves us to echo Hamlet : 'words, words, words . . .'

The three satirical plays with which his dramatic career opened at the end of the sixteenth and beginning of the seventeenth century (*Histriomastix* which he probably revised, *Jack Drum's Entertainment* of which he probably wrote the whole or the larger part,[1] and *What You Will*) show little more than the same great natural indignation accidentally determined in now one now another specific direction.[2] Not until he discovered the Malcontent figure did he find a coherent expression for his early satiric denunciation, though already in these plays the absurd and grotesque violence of image and vocabulary is polarized, from time to time, by romance or by a mood of genuine melancholy, into something nearer the gloomy solidity of the imagery of Seneca.[3] In these passages the smoothness of metre which had appeared erratically in the satiric poems returns more fittingly, and, though there is no consistency of mood for any length of time, there is at least a promise here and there of continuity.

The interest of these plays lies chiefly in their somewhat puzzling satire upon contemporary dramatists and the irregular promise of Marston's later poetry and character drawing, but it is hard to find any clear statement of his notorious quarrel with Ben Jonson.[4] (Half of it—and by far the most important half—must have been prompted by meetings, conversation and gossip, things whose records not only have not survived, but probably never found their way into print at all.) Certainly if we rely upon these three plays for evidence of Marston's contributions they seem inoffensive or indefinite enough.

What, however, is of interest in these plays is the increasing depth of tone which becomes especially noticeable in the latest, *What You Will*. This, uneven though it is, has remarkable

[1] See Dr. R. E. Brettle, *John Marston* (Univ. of Oxford. *Abstracts of Dissertations*, Vol. I. 1928).

[2] This, though true of the general effect of *What You Will*, must be qualified by reference to the remarkable imaginative passages noticed later in the chapter.

[3] This is particularly noticeable in the romantic passages between Pasquil and Katherine in Act III of *Jack Drum* and the speeches of Brabant Junior after the supposed death of Planet in the fifth Act of the same play. Nor is it fantastic perhaps to suggest that his real knowledge of Seneca dates from a period between these early plays (where he is already attuned to it but shows little close memory of it) and the first of his characteristic dramas, *Antonio and Mellida*, where he has entered into it as into a heritage.

[4] For a note on the Theatre War between Ben Jonson, Marston and Dekker, see *post*, Appendix I.

passages which anticipate Marston's finest writing in the *Malcontent* or the satire of the later comedies. There is sometimes a bitter, penetrating quality in which the irregular, irascible mood of the early satirical poems and plays has given place to a mature, sardonic comment on the folly and futility of men's ways. Lampatho Doria's scholar (II, i), in process of transforming himself into a man of the world and embittering rapidly in the process, recalls far more the biting comments of Marlowe in *Hero and Leander* or *Edward II* [1] than the reverence Chapman offered to Dowsecir or Ben Jonson to Horace : [2]

> I was a scholar : seaven use-full springs
> Did I defloure in quotations
> Of crossed oppinions boute the soule of man . . .
> Delight my spaniell slept, whilst I baus'd leaves, . . .
> And still I held converse with *Zabarell*,
> *Aquinas*, *Scotus*, and the musty *sawe*
> Of antick *Donate*, still my spaniell slept.
> Still on went I ; first *an sit anima*,
> Then, and it were mortall . . . still my spaniell slept.
> Then whether twere Corporeall, Locall, Fixt,
> Extraduce ; but whether't had free will
> Or no, ho Philosophers
> Stood bandying factions, all so strongly propt,
> I staggerd, knew not which was firmer part ;
> But thought, quoted, reade, observ'd, and pryed,
> Stufft noting Bookes, and still my spaniell slept.
> At length he wakt, and yawned, and by yon skie,
> For aught I know he knew as much as I. [3]

But it is not upon the poems nor upon the plays of the Theatre War that we depend for our estimate of Marston. That is far better served by the early tragedies and by the comedies and tragedies of his maturity, the two parts of *Antonio and Mellida*, *What You Will*, *The Dutch Courtesan*, *The Malcontent*, *The Fawne*, *Sophonisba*, his share in *Eastward Ho* and the unfinished *Insatiate Countess*.

One of our first impressions in these plays is again of a composite artist, this time part theatre-man, part playwright. The

---

[1] *Hero and Leander*, I, 441–84 ; *Edward II*, 751–65 (Oxford ed.).
[2] In *An Humourous Day's Mirth* and *Poetaster*.
[3] *What You Will*, II, i. This is a passage which presents several textual difficulties. I have made no attempt to emend, beyond adopting Brereton's ' bandying ' for ' banding ' in the thirteenth line quoted.

6

hand of the producer,[1] of the man accustomed to think in terms of production, is visible no less in the elaborate stage directions than in the constant references to playhouse affairs and in the still more significant mistrust of a play's ability to take care of itself as reading matter. ' Enter *Forobosco* ', he tells us near the beginning of Act II of *Antonio and Mellida*, ' with two torches : *Castilio* singing fantastically ; *Rossaline* running a Caranto pase, and *Balurdo* : *Feliche* following, wondring at them all '. Or again in the *Malcontent* (I, iv) ' *Bilioso* entering, *Malevole* shifteth his speech '. (That is, his manner of speaking ; the ' speech ', in the other sense, goes on continuously.) These stage directions are homogeneous with the text ; they explain it and give such directions on the inter-pretation of character as we should expect from the man who spoke apologetically upon another occasion of ' a Comedie, whose life rests much in the Actors voice . . . writ to be spoken, not read . . . the life of these things consists in action '.[2]

More fundamental is the sense of the stage that seldom or never deserts him in the treatment of his material, and this, though it damages the dramatic merit of the early tragedies, is of great importance in the years 1599–1600 when both audience and dramatists were far less experienced in tragedy than they were in comedy and history plays. Time and again, when char-acter, continuity of plot and probability of situation or utterance have all been violated, he imposes on us by some preposterous turn of theatrical brilliance which all but hides the dramatic weakness. In that otherwise unbelievable scene *Antonio and Mellida*, I, i, how effective in performance would be the latter part with the long silence of Mellida as she hears the supposed news of Antonio's death. Again, take the last scene of the same play. A vizored figure enters offering to deliver to Piero the

---

[1] For some interesting comments on the producer-dramatist in the private theatre, see Mr. J. Isaacs' *Production and Stage-Management at the Blackfriars Theatre* (Shakespeare Association), 1933.

[2] *The Fawne*. Prefatory notice, ' To my equall Reader '. Other stage directions, moreover, are notable for their fullness of description. Some are as long as those in Ben Jonson's masks, though they generally describe action rather than scenery. Comments on individual actors, playhouse customs and theatre history are interchanged as briskly as the corresponding references in a modern revue, especially in the Inductions to *Antonio and Mellida* and the *Malcontent*.

head of his enemy Andrugio, in consideration of certain promised rewards. The promise is readily given, the helmet removed and, behold—there is the head in question ! Dramatically, how preposterous ; but theatrically, how splendid a situation ! There is colour, surprise, emphasis and an admirable rhetorical speech in which an audience that only heard it spoken would have no time to notice the lack of normal motivation. Perhaps, after all, there is reason in Marston's objection to delivering his plays into the hands of readers.[1] . . .

But by far the most interesting effect of this theatrical experience upon Marston's art as a dramatist lies in the experiments in diction into which it led him. Most readers of his plays come to them already familiar with the diction of the satires which, though sometimes undeniably effective, more often wastes itself and destroys the meaning of a passage by its clumsy, ramshackle violence. In the plays, especially in the earliest, the same flavour of vocabulary lingers, but the originality which once sought mainly that outlet is now taking other directions as well. Imagery, not on the whole a feature of the satires, and, particularly, sustained imagery which is hardly to be found there at all, becomes one of the most startling features of the tragic parts, obtruding itself so aggressively that it must be part of a self-conscious theatrical intention, infelicitous though it often is, crabbed and contorted with thought. At the same time in the comic dialogue there are a series of attempts to present actual speech naturally, even naturalistically, and to include in the very writing of the dialogue those variations and modifications usually left to the imagination of actor and producer to supply. In some of the speeches that read most fantastically, the broken sentences of Balurdo, the stammering of Piero, he appears on second glance to be but attempting to catch the manners living,

[1] The device in this case is practically redoubled by the entry of Antonio still more effectively concealed in his own coffin ; he also springs to life the moment he has caught Piero in the presence of witnesses. It is hard to decide whether the repetition must, even for Jacobeans, have blundered into farce or whether, with the right panache in the production and with an audience trained in melodramatic moods, it would not have resulted in the increasing tension that raises the experience to a climax. I think, in fact, that Marston must often have miscarried of a scene or situation through not having a clear enough perception of this distinction, but the experiment is the significant thing.

or with more life in them than his contemporaries were concerned to define. Often again this miscarries, but often,
prompted by a sound stage instinct, he succeeds in setting
down minute flexions of speech such as even a modern leaves
as a rule to his actor to work out.[1]   There is no great matter to
be achieved by it when it is brought to perfection, no doubt,
but it gives flexibility to dialogue, a flexibility which finds its
reward in the natural, rapid speeches of later comedies such as
The Fawne.[2]

The part played by diction generally and imagery in particular
in the early plays is naturally far greater and is connected at
least as much with his instinct as an artist as with his experience
as a theatre-man.   Moreover, it is of the highest importance
for the succeeding drama that the function of imagery should
thus early be thus emphatically confirmed.   In this, as in other
departments of art and thought, Marston had a theory ; and
here, as perhaps in the others, he was at his best when he forgot
it.   *Antonio and Mellida* is ushered in by a Prologue lamenting
the ' heathy drynesse of her braine ' and then proceeding to
implore heaven for

> Abstruse and synowy faculties,
> That, with a straine of fresh invention,
> She might presse out the rarity of Art,
> The pur'st elixed joyce of rich conceipt.

---

[1] Take the scene (*Antonio and Mellida*, III) in which the maid holds
the glass for her mistress to set her face and Rossaline talks as she paints
her lips :

Flavia. ' By my troth, you looke as like the princess, now—'

Ros. ' —I, but her lip is lip—is a little—redder, a very little redder :
but by the helpe of Art, or Nature, ere I change my perewigge, mine
shall be as red.'

I adopt the emendation of J. le G. Brereton, in his *Notes on the Text
of Marston*, *Engl. Stud.*, 33, 1904, and give the latter part of the speech
to Rossaline.

[2] See, for example, Tiberio's speech (II, i–end).   Marston has now
outgrown his early desire to lay down for actor and producer the
minutiae of their tasks and has contented himself with a good, rapid
stage speech ;   isolated single words, broken sentences and repeti-
tions bring it so near the immediacy of actual conversation that one
understands the earlier efforts and even wonders whether some of
his other infelicities and extravagances were only abortions in the
samĕ kind.

Concerning the operation of this celestial cyder-press we are more than doubtful and indeed we are met from the first by such a torrent of ' pur'st elixed juice ' that it is obvious that the ' abstruse and synowy faculties ' are well at work :

> If a breast,
> Nail'd to the earth with griefe : if any heart
> Pierc't through with anguish, pant within this ring :
> If there be any blood, whose heate is choakt
> And stifled with true sense of misery
> If ought to these straines fill this consort up,
> Th' arrive most welcome.[1]

Just so.

But it is nevertheless in the early plays that the imagery is most interesting and that single lines or images of great beauty from time to time appear. This happens with Marston, as with Donne, when the strong emotion has entirely had its way and the intellect's attempt to wrest terms into harsh and abnormal associations gives way to a movement that suggests Webster, who carries his weight of thought without distress :

> Have I outliv'd the death of all these hopes ?
> > *(Ant. Mel.*, I, i.)
> > There's nothing left
> Unto *Andrugio*, but *Andrugio* :
> > *(Ant. Mel.*, III, i.)
> Lord, in two houres what a toplesse mount
> Of unpeer'd mischiefe have these hands cast up !
> > *(Ant. Rev.*, I, i.)
> > I am great in blood
> Unequald in revenge.
> > *(Ant. Rev.*, I, i.)

Upon all of these there is the stamp of the great Jacobean coinage ; the shock and stir of fine and sudden images, the majestic march of the music. Upon a far greater proportion, of course, an obscurity rests as yet, only too like the mists and fogs (which themselves form a considerable source of his imagery) in which he envelops his characters at the crises of their fortunes. Such is this obscurity sometimes that it is impossible to see what picture he had in mind ; sometimes a vague indication is felt rather than seen, but the passage, suffused by inspissated gloom

---

[1] *Antonio's Revenge*, Prologue, 21–7.

as it generally is, does not finally lose by this indefiniteness.[1] Sometimes again his picture is clear enough, but its connexion with its subject is not so clear, sometimes because of mere clumsiness on Marston's part, sometimes because the completed image is a genuine case of heterogeneous ideas yoked by violence together. They are, then, original and startling rather than illuminating (we may contrast Shakespeare's which are generally the second and Webster's which are often both) and their originality lies not so much in Marston's discovery of a given source as in the more amazing discovery that that particular source could be called in aid to illustrate that subject.[2]

In the later plays the imagery diminishes not only in quantity but in violence. There are instances of crabbed passages (generally passages of close psychological self-analysis as in the *Fawne*), but already in the *Malcontent* the climate of the mind has changed, the predominant imagery is drawn from outdoor

---

[1]   Poore soule, wanting apt instruments
   To speake or see, stands dumbe and blinde, sad spirit,
   Roul'd up in gloomie clouds as black as ayer,
   Through which the rustie coach of Night is drawne.
                                        (I *Ant. Mel.*, IV, i.)

Now I suggest that this is a fine image, that it does specifically deepen the effect of impalpable gloom in the speech. But with what definite picture, unless of a feather bed (which would be obviously indecorous), is one to associate it ? This would seem to be the very antithesis of Shakespeare's (or Tourneur's) images which welcome concrete, solid and definite pictures.

[2] In all, in the earlier plays, there appear to be three main streams of imagery ; one which is drawn, though at one or two removes, from the beautiful star and nature imagery of Seneca's plays and is itself brilliant with azure, silver and light, one drawn more directly from the Tartarian imagery of Seneca, grisly with darkness and blood, with wounds, destruction and mangled limbs, and one which I think springs from deeper in Marston's nature, from the more mature satiric bitterness of his own temper. This third kind is deliberately ugly and naturalistic. It might be called, to borrow a phrase from M. Lenormand, anti-poetic ; it belittles and degrades its subject like Webster's anti-poetic later diction, but without the added grimness which ever and again transforms Webster's into the poetry of horror. There proves, upon analysis, to be an almost overwhelming preponderance of images from the body and its functions, sometimes normal but more often images of disease, deformation or maiming ; these make up more than a third of the total imagery of one play (I *Antonio and Mellida*) and give a clue, if not to Marston's conscious thought, at least to his unconscious preoccupations.

life,[1] and, while a little of the grim early type remains, there is far less of the Marston who, like his master Seneca, could irradiate a scene of horror with the words ' Look, Lucio, 'tis bright day '.[2] By the time we reach the later plays, *Sophonisba* and *The Insatiate Countess* (in so far as she pertains to Marston), imagery has become rare and diction on the whole unobtrusive ; the absurdities have gone, but so unfortunately have the gallant vitality and the restless originality. Like our contemporary, Pegeen, we feel a vague discontent with this later stage, the man with ' No savagery or fine words in him at all ', and the greater artistic coherence of plays in which diction and imagery are subordinated to larger effects hardly compensates us.[3] Like Marlowe before him, he gains, in his brief career, a mastery over the technique of playwriting which, since it eliminates in him the undramatic irregularities, enterprises and intrusive theories of his youth, leaves us wondering whether, after all, it is not the technique which has mastered him.

It must be admitted that it is by his undigested ideas that he is most trammelled in the early days—whether it is a theory of how to raise ' the freshest blooms of purest eloquence ' or an attempt to rifle and appropriate the ' humour ' theory of Ben Jonson or the 'character ' of the prose writers, whether it leads him to produce abortive Senecals and Machiavellians instead of natural men in tragic circumstance or to make a character the mere mouthpiece of an idea, the stoical ideal or the ideal of the anti-stoic. The fact remains that the operation of that most delicate faculty of the dramatist, the perception and revelation

[1] The bulk of it, rather unexpectedly, from village and farming life.

[2] Or of that Marston who could pause in the midst of a satiric denunciation to cry :

Oh hidden depth of that dread secrecie,
Which I do trembling touch in poetry.
(*Scourge of Villainy*, I, iv.)

[3] There is, of course, the famous Lucanesque grave-yard scene in the fourth act of *Sophonisba*, but that, though it contains what is probably the best sustained instance in Jacobean drama of unmitigatedly horrible description, contains surprisingly few images and those ineffectual. As a well-articulated string of ghoulish detail it makes all contemporary charnel-house literature that I have come upon look anaemic and polite ; even the mighty father of all such descriptions, even had he weighed into the balance his ' Thyestean feast ', would probably have confessed himself outweighted. But the fact remains that the significant part of it is not imagery.

of character, suffers at first most severely.   The plotting is less harmed by it, even in the tragedies (such violence as it suffers arising from Marston's general desire to inflate everything within reach, diction, emotion and action), and the comic plots (even the comic sub-plots in the tragedies) are good from the first and grow, with the *Dutch Courtesan* and *The Fawne*, to excellence. But character is a more delicate plant and Marston has to free himself from the habit of writing at the same time with the explicitness of a satirist and the implicitness of a dramatist before he offers us, in Malevole, a character who stands solid and compact.   As it is, he appears to find his way to consistency of character mainly through the understanding of unity of poetic atmosphere.

His development over the short period 1599–1606 is indeed remarkable.   Unassimilated philosophic debate (from Lampatho Doria's fine anatomy of the scholar,[1] through the endless three-sided discussion of Stoicism by Andrugio, Antonio and Pandulpho,[2] to the pure Jacobean conversion of the stoic,[3] the debate on the antagonism between lust and love),[4] all these, which step out of their context, so vividly and so eagerly are they felt, give place gradually to something far more dramatically appropriate, a growing interest in psychological analysis, particularly self-analysis ;   Freevill's mistrust of his own motives,[5]   Mendoza's astute comments on Ferneze and his

[1] *What You Will*, II, i.

[2] *Antonio and Mellida* and *Antonio's Revenge*.

[3] Pandulpho in *Antonio's Revenge*.   It is perhaps worth noticing that Marston's battle is not precisely the Senecan one between self-possession and self-indulgence, but the more specifically Jacobean one, between continence and over-expression. In the conversion of his stoic, therefore, he plays, as does Shakespeare in *Macbeth*, upon the two conceptions of ' manliness ', the feeling and the unfeeling man. At the end of all his heroic defiance of fate and misfortune, his pose of Roman father, Pandulpho speaks the lines which save him from the mechanical inhumanity of the other characters :

> I spake more than a god ;
> Yet am lesse than a man.
> I am the miserablest sowle that breathes.
> (*Ant. Rev.*, IV, v.)

Or, as Marston sums it up later (*Dutch Courtesan*, II, i):

> Not he that's passionless, but he 'bove passion's wise.

[4] *Dutch Courtesan*, especially II, i (where, assuredly, he knows what he is talking about).

[5] Ibid., i.

self-deceiving lust [1] ; the speech of the disguised Duke Hercules of Ferrara on the effects of flattery,[2] these are shrewd pieces of insight, the characters at last have the ' sinking thought ' that Feliche sought so long and so vainly.

Hercules. By him by whome we are, I thinke a Prince,
Whose tender sufferance never felt a gust
Of boulder breathings, but stil liv'd gently fann'd
With the soft gales of his owne flatterers lippes
Shal never know his owne complection.
Deere sleepe and lust I thanke you, but for you
Mortall till now, I scarce had knowne my selfe
Thou gratefull poyson, sleeke mischiefe *Flatery,*
Thou dreamefull slumber (that doth fall on kings
As soft and soone as their first holy oyle,)
Be thou for ever dam'd I now repent
Severe indictions to some sharpe stiles,
Freenes, so't grow not to licentiousnesse,
Is gratfull to just states . . . But since our rancke
Hath ever been afflicted with these flyes
(That blow corruption on the sweetest vertues)
I will revenge us all upon you all
With the same stratagem, we still are caught.[3]

At last the synthesis of thought and passion is complete, opinion and character no longer cohabit uneasily together and the single good speech in *Sophonisba* [4] (the last play of his certain authorship) has a clear beauty, made up of many simple lines ; no one of them stands out by its music, its imagery or that finding of inevitable words which is the stamp of early Jacobean dramatic diction ; each phase succeeds the other naturally and calmly and the effect is cumulative, having something of the still calm of Ford's great scenes. Indeed, it is to Ford at the end of the period and to the late tragi-comedy of Middleton and Rowley that this passage points, rather than to Webster or to Shake-

[1] *Malcontent*, II, i.   [2] *Fawne*, last speech of I, ii.
[3] *Fawne*, I, ii—end. The resemblances between the thought here and in parts of Middleton's *Phoenix* (especially I, i, 59–78 and 113–123, and I, iv, 225–7) are, of course, unmistakable, but they do not in any case affect the question of Marston's dramatic handling of the sentiment, which, in this passage, can stand comparison with that of the *Phoenix.* (The question of priority is difficult to decide. *The Phoenix* was published in 1607 but probably written in 1603–4, while *The Fawne* was published in 1606 and probably written between 1604–6. See *post, Biographical Notes : Marston* and *Middleton.*)
[4] *Soph.*, V, ii, the death speech of Sophonisba.

speare. We remember the corresponding mellowing mood of Marston's latest comedy : ' Never grieve or wonder,' says Hercules at the end of the *Fawne*, ' all things sweetely fit.' Who, having known only the turbulence and conflict of *Antonio and Mellida*, would have supposed it possible ?

Soph.   How neere was I unto the curse of man, Ioye,
       How like was I yet once to have beene glad :
       He that neere laught may with a constant face,
       Contemne *Ioves* frowne. Happinesse makes us base.
       [*She takes a bole, into which* MASSINISSA *puts poison.*]
       Behold me *Massinissa*, like thy selfe,
       A king and souldier, and I pree thee keepe,
       My last command.
Mass.   Speake sweet.
Soph.   Deere doe not weep
       And now with undismaid resolve behold,
       To save *You, you,* (for honour and iust faith.
       Are most true *Gods*, which we should much adore)
       With even disdainefull vigour I give up,
       An abhord life. [*She drinks.*] You have beene good to me,
       And I doe thanke thee heaven, O my stars,
       I blesse your goodnes, that with breast unstaind,
       Faith pure : a Virgin wife, try'de to my glory,
       I die, of female faith the long liv'de story. . . . [1]

In the same way plot, character, diction, atmosphere and mood, jarringly at variance in his early work, fall gradually into an ordered relation in his later. His earliest conception of dramatic episode has been summed up by Marston himself :

    Give them a scene may force their struggling blood
    Rise up on tiptoe in attention,
    And fill their intellect with pure elixed wit.[2]

We might indeed have deduced something of the sort from a close inspection of the two *Antonio and Mellida* plays, where the general lines of the plots are weakened by unnecessary complications and confusions devised to fill out the action with dismal episodes. Though there is no lack of originality and vigour, the plays are strained to breaking-point with borrowed episodes and situations. As a concentrated endeavour to ' presse out

---

[1] *Soph.*, V, ii.
[2] *What You Will*, V, i. It is only just to remind ourselves of the concluding lines of the Epilogue to *Antonio's Revenge*, where a finer idea is implied.

the raretie of Arte ' this pair has few parallels.[1] ' Never more
woe in lesser plot was found,' Marston declares with gusto at
the end—and we may grant him it.   But the beginnings of irony
in the second part (Maria's joyful preparations to meet her
husband whom we know to be already dead or Piero tenderly
sending for the child we have just seen killed) are a step in the
right direction.   In the comedies that follow his plotting grows
apace and in the *Malcontent* there is a good, rapid conduct of a
close-wound action, something like that of the fifth act of *Volpone*
extended to fill a whole play.   Marston is still liable to give us a
good situation not firmly set into the plot, such as the dancing
scenes;[2] which Ford was to re-handle later and far otherwise,
but on the whole the tragic action is a well-compacted plot,
close and clearly drawn, while the comic under-plot is a froth
and foam of ' humours ' made macabre and at times sinister
by the dark shadow that falls upon it from the main plot.

Marston's characters show much the same progression, from
the sporadically alive Lampatho Doria,[3] through those Senecan
and Machiavellian robots, Antonio, Andrugio, Feliche and
Piero,[4] straining like rival street singers to higher and higher
pitches of emotion, to the more consistent Atreus figure of the
later Piero [5] with his strange turmoil of blood-lust and poetry.
(Even this Piero falters at times when the vaulting ambition of
revenge o'erleaps itself and leaves us face to face with a figure
bearing a disturbing but irresistible resemblance to a later
tyrant, who dealt not so much in ' the steam of recking gore '
as in ' something with boiling oil in it '. . .)   But with Malevole of the *Malcontent*, Marston comes into his own, achieving
for the first (and perhaps the last) time a living central figure in a

[1] Characteristic of the absurdity of his treatment of the crucial
situations are the sudden lapses into Italian in Piero's speeches, and,
more fatally, in the dialogue between Antonio and Mellida themselves
in the third act.   It is a mistake to reveal the climax of the play in a
foreign tongue especially when the usage of it is as childish as it is
here.   In spite of his own Italian ancestry, it is a little hard to see why,
at the crises of their fortunes, the characters of Marston suffer a like
fate with the builders of Babel and fall to discoursing strange tongues.

[2] *Malc*, IV, ii, and V, iii.

[3] *What You Will.*   [4] *Antonio and Mellida.*

[5] *Antonio's Revenge.*   I am not sure that Marston has not here a
better imaginative understanding of the passion for revenge than any,
except Webster and Tourneur, of the many writers who used it as a
dramatic motive.

serious play. The variableness, the quick-witted consciousness of himself, the sudden moments of weariness and disgust, the incisive wit and the steadily growing hardness of purpose are real and convincing things. He has some of the exquisiteness of Hamlet, something too of the macabre jesting, with its implications of obscenity and blasphemy as the undertones of pain. Mendoza, too, in the same play, is a good study of a Machiavellian, neither forced nor superficial ; the root of the matter is there in his quick adjustment to situation without dismay, pity or fear.[1] Pietro, too, is convincing, even to his conversion. It is not hard to see why Dyce accepted the title-page and attributed the play to Webster. To write like this ' it is at least necessary to read and to think '. The lines spoken by Pietro, when, convinced at last of his wife's infidelity, he comes, supported by the other lords, to surprise her with her lover, are a simple and at times a pregnant expression of the agony in his mind. There is nothing melodramatic or merely theatrical here. The emotions revealed are chaotic—as indeed they should be—but their conflict has a precise, flexible expression.

Pietro. My Lords : The heavy action we intend,
Is death and shame, two of the ugliest shapes
That can confound a soule, thinke, thinke of it ;
I strike but yet like him that gainst stone walles
Directs his shafts, reboundes in his owne face,
My Ladies shame is mine, O God tis mine.
Therefore I doe conjure all secrecie,
Let it be as very little as may be ; pray yee, as may be !
Make frightlesse entrance, salute her with soft eyes,
Staine naught with blood—onely *Fernezе* dies,
But not before her browes : O Gentlemen,
God knowes I love her, nothing els, but this,
I am not well ; . . . o that I might die,
Before her shames displaide, would I were forst
To burne my fathers Tombe, unheale his boanes,
And dash them in the durt, rather than this :
This both the living and the dead offends . . .[2]

The comic characters meanwhile, like the comic plots, have escaped from the nursery sooner. Already in the two early plays, Balurdo is worth watching even though he be mainly a transposition of Sir Andrew Aguecheek. Mrs. Mulligrub of

[1] His tactics, of course, suggest that he is left-handedly descended from Lorenzo of *The Spanish Tragedy*.
[2] *Malc.*, II, iii–end.

the *Dutch Courtesan* may owe something to Dekker to start with, but by the end she lives in her own right. The unforgettable groups of *Eastward Ho* may be the property of his collaborators, even Touchstone and Gertrude (the romantic citizeness who surpasses Chloe of the *Poetaster*), but nothing can take from Marston the achievement of the characters in the *Fawne* ; Gonzago, that eminently actable nobleman, that exquisite study of fatuous pomp and delicately flattered self-esteem, Herod, Zuccone, Amoroso, Granuffo and all those who meet their deserts in the brilliantly conducted final mask. The speeches of Gonzago in especial are written with faultless comic tact that bestows upon him a double portion of bland self-congratulation at the very moment when his daughter, having completely hood-winked him, is either just about to use him as a tool in her for-bidden love-affair with Prince Tiberio or has just, by the same process, induced him to achieve her purpose for her. Modesty compels him, upon both occasions, to disclaim credit for the astuteness with which he has handled the affair :

Gon. Alas daughter, heaven gives every man his talent, indeed vertue & wisedom are not fortunes giftes . . . for our owne part wee acknowledge heavens goodnes, and if it were possible, to bee as wise againe as wee are, wee would neare impute it to our selves : for as wee bee flesh and bloud, alas we are fooles, but as wee are Princes, Schollars, and have reade *Cicero de Oratore*, I must confesse there is another matter int, what of the Prince deere daughter ? [1]

Gon. Of all creatures breathing I doe hate those things that struggle to seeme wise, and yet are indeed very fooles, I remember when I was a young man in my fathers dayes, there were fower gallant spirites for resolution, as proper for body, as witty in discourse, as any were in Europe, nay Europe had not such, I was one of them ; Wee fowre did all love one lady, a modest chaste virgin shee was, wee all injoyde her, I well remember, and so injoyde her, that despight the strictest guard was set upon her, wee had her at our pleasure, I speake it for her honour and my credite : where shall you finde such witty fellowes now a daies : Alas how easie it is in these weaker times to crosse love trickes, Ha ha ha alas, I smile to think I must confesse with som glory to mine own wisedom, to thinke how I found out and crossed, and curbd, and jerkt, and firkte, and in the end made desperate *Tiberios* hope, Alas good sillie youth, that dares to cope with age, and such a beard : I speake it without glory.[2]

This rapid development of facility and proportion, this sudden advance into independent maturity, is never more

[1] *Fawne*, IV. [2] *Ibid.*, V.

noticeable than in his relation to the dramatists who preceded and followed him. Indeed the whole story of Marston's artistic progress and position might be written in terms of this relation.

One of the most delightful entertainments for a reader of the early plays is that of tracing to their sources and assigning to their original makers the elements out of which those plays are assembled. In the first four, *Jack Drum*, the two *Antonio* plays and *What You Will*, it is possible to trace situations and persons (or at least scattered limbs) from *The Spanish Tragedy*, *Merry Wives*, *As You Like It*, *Twelfth Night*, *Much Ado*, *Every Man in his Humour* and, especially, *Love's Labour's Lost*. In the same plays there are verbal echoes or subdued and exasperating (but quite recognizable) paraphrases from all of these and in addition from *Faustus*, *Richard II*, *John*, *Henry IV*, Part I, *Henry V*, *Henry VI*, Part III, and the comedies of Lyly generally. Marston has indeed ' been at a great feast of languages ' and his stealing has hardly stopped at the ' scraps '. His debts to Seneca alone (acknowledged and unacknowledged) would fill a small pamphlet, showing a marked fondness for *Thyestes*, *Hippolytus* and *Hercules Furens*.[1]

But as soon as we reach the later stage of his work this disappears ; with the exception of the pervasive and less analysable suggestion of Dekker that hangs about Marston's portraits of citizens, he is himself alone.

And yet he is, disturbingly, more than himself. Already in *Antonio and Mellida*, side by side with the echoes from earlier plays there were faint but seemingly unmistakable anticipations

---

[1] The passages most fully drawn upon are *Thyestes*, Act I (generally and ll. 23–30 specially), Chorus II, Act II, especially 214–17, 195–6, Act V. *Hipp.*, IV (the storm), where I suspect that Studley's translation was at least as well known to Marston as Seneca's original and *Hercules Furens*, the approaches to Hell and the Tartarian imagery generally. There is a late recrudescence in *The Insatiate Countess*, where he paraphrases the familiar *Hipp.*, II, 715 seq., and blends it with the corresponding passage on ' great Neptune's ocean ' (*Macbeth*, II, ii, 61–4). There are also, of course, as J. W. Cunliffe pointed out, about a dozen quotations from the Latin of the *Hippolytus*, *Thyestes*, *Agamemnon*, *Octavia*, *Thebais* and *Oedipus* in *Antonio and Mellida*, *The Malcontent* and *The Fawne* (see J. W. Cunliffe, *The Influence of Seneca on Elizabethan Tragedy* under *Marston*). Other passages, particularly from *De Providentia*, are noticed by F. L. Lucas, *Seneca and Elizabethan Tragedy* (1922), pp. 123–5. See also J. O. Eidson in *M.L.N.*, March, 1937.

of *Hamlet* and of *Macbeth*.[1]   Again, as in the cases of obvious borrowing, it is not a matter of character and situation only ; it extends simultaneously to phrases, and the very cadences of Hamlet himself start up from time to time in scenes which already turn upon the situation of a woman about to marry her husband's murderer, whose son feigns madness to her and her betrothed husband, or in which the ghost of that father describes to his son the manner of his death, securing the promise of that son's vengeance.   If we do not wish to think that Shakespeare and Marston interchangeably lent and borrowed, we are at some pains to dismiss this and a host of other likenesses to *Hamlet* and to *Macbeth* in the Antonio plays and the *Malcontent*.

But once we pass out of the somewhat hypnotizing influence of Shakespeare's honoured name the case is clear beyond dispute. Mr. Lucas has given us a lead in showing [2] how Webster borrowed from Marston now an image, now a phrase, transmuting them, as he did so, from material that held the promise of poetry into the essence of poetry itself.   We may add to the name of Webster those of Tourneur and of Ford and, I should suggest, of Shakespeare, and in each case, in the differing spheres of imagery, character and situation, the same or a similar transmutation may be observed.   Webster's debt is the subtlest ; it is a matter of the delicate adjustment of image and background, the sense of significant and momentary detail, the touch of the one transforming point of colour, the silvery brightness that betrays us again to the darkness we had else grown inured to : ' By heaven,' exclaims Piero when the murder of Andrugio and Feliche is safely achieved,

> By heaven, I thinke
> I ha said my prayers, within this month at least :
> I am so boundlesse happie.

Webster never, I think, uses this form of words, nor anything outwardly like them, but how often and how closely does he reproduce the shuddering illumination shed by the momentary vision, in a nightmare hallucination, of what is cool, sweet and

---

[1] This problem has been discussed fully by Dr. F. Radebrecht : *Shakespeares Abhängigkeit von John Marston* (1918).   For later discussions, especially with regard to *The Malcontent* and Shakespeare, see the work of Walley, Stoll and McGinn. (App. II, under ' Marston '.)

[2] See especially his note on *Webster's Imitation* in his edition of the *Works*, Vol. I, pp. 57–63.

serene. There are, of course, other less impalpable debts; perhaps the dirge for Feliche gives something to Cornelia's dirge for Marcello, the echo scenes to his echoes. With Tourneur there is again this matter of situation and setting but there passes on also something of that misplaced semi-philosophic reflection, which in the hands of the later poet becomes more firmly jointed into the frame of the play. Something of the startling yet irrelevant *virtù* of these passages reminds one of the similarly sudden, excellent and to a point undramatic analyses of motivation or reflexion in Tourneur's plays. With Ford the case is again different, but no less illuminating. The dance scenes in the *Malcontent* are, as so often with Marston, a fine situation relatively ill-set; with Ford the hint is developed to its full tragic growth and built solidly into the plot with an architectural splendour upon which the end of the play rests. But there is more than this. For in that last imperfect and otherwise negligible play of *Sophonisba* the death speech of Sophonisba and the last speech of Massinissa contain the germs, the one of the central mood, the other of one of the main doctrines of Ford's art.[1] Nor is it for nothing that this play, upon whose last scene, with its momentary recovery, the spirit of Ford seems by anticipation to rest, ends in fact upon the note most characteristic of Ford's own drama.

> O thou for whom I drinke
> So deepe of greefe, that he must onely thinke,
> Not dare to speake, that would expresse my woe.

Standing then at the threshold of the Jacobean period and renouncing the stage for the Church just as his power as a dramatist had matured, Marston presents us at first with a confused and ill-assorted assemblage of Elizabethan melodramatic themes treated in Jacobean moods. But the show of violence was not native to him or permanent. As a poet his real virtue lay (aside from his comic genius) like Ford's in a sweet stillness that he rarely permitted to himself, or like Webster's in grim, macabre and pregnant imagery and reflexion. But he entered his career as a theatre-man, rifling and contending with his contemporaries, and it was not till half-way through it that he fully transformed the theatrical into the dramatic, the spectacular into the poetic. Having done this, he did no more

[1] *Soph.*, V, ii, and see p. 90.

than look into the promised land before the end of his career.
Or, rather, perhaps, he did a rare and exceptional thing and
pointed the way to it to men whose names have lived while his
has been undervalued. For it is hard to find another instance
of a man thus suffered to pass on to the hands of masters the
vision he himself could not express, transmitting to them
images, phrases, situations which just fail in his hands of
becoming poetry and with them become inevitable and immortal. Truly, as the witch said to Banquo, ' Thou shalt get
kings though thou be none ', and that itself is no slight boon.

CHAPTER V

BEN JONSON

A MAN should study other things, not to covet, not to feare, not to repent him : To make his Base such, as no Tempest shall shake him : to be secure of all opinion ; and pleasing to himselfe, even for that, wherein he displeaseth others. For the worst opinion gotten for doing well, should delight us : would'st not thou be just, but for fame ; thou ought'st to be it with infamy : Hee that would have his vertue published, is not the servant of vertue, but glory.[1]

It is in such passages in *Discoveries*, the Dedications and the Letters. that the moral basis of Ben Jonson's drama is most clearly summed. For in the authoritative plays, the ' Works ', we meet a realist by principle, while in the direct statements of his belief we find the principles themselves from which were derived not only his criticisms of contemporary society and literature, but the attitude to his material which sets him apart from his contemporaries.[2] The deliberate schooling in objectivity, the persistent subjection of the imagination to the evidence of the actual, the irradiation by that ' lumen siccum ' honoured so highly by Bacon whom he also honoured, these habits of his mind are the counterpart in the domain of art of that thorough

[1] *Timber : or, Discoveries ; Made upon Men and Matter. . .*, by Ben Johnson, p. 111. London, 1641.

[2] No specific references to *Discoveries* can be given : the whole of that brief work is indispensable to a study of Ben Jonson, though it may be indicated that the earlier jottings are chiefly on moral themes, while most of the aesthetic and literary criticism comes in the longer essays towards the end of the collection. Of the dedications (with which should be taken the Inductions and Prologues to the plays), perhaps the most significant are (*a*) Dedications, to *Every Man Out of His Humour* (F. 1616), *Every Man In His Humour* (F. 1616), *Alchemist*, *Cataline* and, pre-eminently, *Sejanus* and *Volpone*. (*b*) Inductions, to *E.M.O.H.*, *Cynthia's Revels*, *Staple of News*, *Magnetic Lady*. (*c*) Prologues, to *Poetaster*, *Volpone*, *Epicoene*, *E.M.I.H.* (F. 1616). To these should be added the 1602 Epilogue (in Dialogue form) to *Poetaster* and its *Apologetical Dialogue* and the *Ode to Himself* written after the reception of the *New Inn*. Of the letters perhaps the best known and most characteristic are those to the Earl of Salisbury in 1605 (see *Herford* and *Simpson*, I, 194–6) and to Dr. Donne (ibid., 203–4).

and conscious principling which permeated his life.   Theory and criticism play as large a part in the growth of his dramatic art as they did in the early attempts of Marston and naturalistic portraiture came as inevitably to him as it did to Middleton ; but the tenacity of Ben Jonson's principles welded theory and practice together in his comedy and the dominance of a clear intellect prevented the severance and conflict of elements that we find in Marston's work, while his evident conscious purpose sets his realism at once apart from that of the unselfconscious comedy of Middleton.   From the rest of his contemporaries he is even more clearly separated, for he seldom enters the domain of imaginative tragedy or of romance in which the conflict of thought of the first decade finds its inevitable expression and he never condescends, as do most of them, to mingle with his purposed art the popular theatre attractions of sensation or sentiment.

Yet even he, independent and self-sufficient as he is, reflects unconsciously the limitations imposed on comedy by the tendency of the age.   In his own province, he concentrates as closely as does the comedy of Middleton upon what is immediately before his eyes, limiting its scope to the domain of morals and manners within society, with no reference to any but ethical law.   Already in his comedy, to a less degree only than in that of Middleton, we can feel setting in that deliberate absorption in the immediate surroundings of man in society, that striving for ever closer precision in detail, that culminates in the highly specialized social comedy of Etherege and his successors.

This is entirely a matter of accepting certain terms of reference, of limiting the background against which the comedy is played to a self-contained universe made up of just those elements freed from all further or undefined implications.   The relative seriousness or lightness of the tone is not the basis of distinction ; Shakespeare's three late comedies and some of Middleton's latest tragi-comedies have far less earnestness than Ben Jonson's social satire at its severest, but the scope of Ben Jonson's most representative comedy is limited, in comparison with them, to a narrow, sharp focussing on an immediate area of experience. Ben Jonson's treatment of his material may, moreover, be called scientific for its endeavour to present moral and psychological truth more and more nearly in terms of actuality and to eliminate more and more thoroughly the subjective.   It follows by implication that, as an artist and as a man, Ben Jonson was originally non-dramatic ; at no time did he dramatize himself [1] and it was only with some difficulty that he dramatized anything else.   In an age in which many writers were forced into drama who would now find their way into some other form of literature, Ben Jonson still stands out as one whose effort to convey his thought in that form was more serious and more prolonged than those of most of his contemporaries.   There is, as it were, a deeply inherent non-dramatic principle in him, and this offers at least one way of approach to the multifarious aesthetic problems of his work.

II

For the truth is that, with Ben Jonson, we must choose a way of approach ; his scope is too wide for some of us to include in one continuous movement of the mind, and his conscious and determined reference to principle introduces inconsistencies and conflicts that are not to be found in most of his contemporaries. Though we may explore his work, perhaps justly estimating the parts, may subject our imagination to each mood in turn, may, in fact, be comprehended by it, we cannot readily comprehend it. The poet of the gay humour comedies, *Every Man In His Humour* and *Epicoene*, of the jovial and virile observation of *Bartholomew Fair*, *The New Inn*, *The Staple of News*, *The Magnetic Lady*, is not the same man as the humour theorist of *Every Man Out of His Humour*, of the sharper prologues and inductions nor the satirist of *Cynthia's Revels*, *Poetaster* and the *Apologetical Dialogue* ; still less is he the poet of the epitaphs on Lady Sidney and Salathiel Pavy or of the Donne-like and unexpected love-songs.[2]   Nor is any of these the man in whom a *saeva indignatio*, disciplined by that same subjection to fact into the true *virtù ordinata*, made of the satirist simultaneously a Roman after the heart of Juvenal and an Italian after the heart of Machiavelli.

---

[1] Unless perhaps in the speeches recorded in Drummond's *Conversations*.   And there the mind of Ben Jonson has, as one of his editors suggests, ' suffered a double refraction in the unlike media of his own vinous ardour and his hearer's unsympathetic sobriety '.   (C. H. Herford, *Introduction* to the Mermaid Edition of Ben Jonson's plays, Vol. I, p. lx.)

[2] Especially of the *Underwoods* poems : ' By those bright eyes ', ' Fair friend tis true, your beauties move ', and equally significant, but more like the Ben Jonson of the letters and the *Discoveries*, ' I now think, Love is rather deaf than blind ', and ' Wretched and foolish Jealousy '.

In *Sejanus*, a drama built out of scorn and indignation and little emotion else, in *Catiline*, an unexpected descendant from a less usually imitated part of Seneca's work, in the more voluminously moving and more nearly tragic *Volpone*, a play that stands as utterly alone as any in the age, it is the massiveness of Jonson's imaginative grip on fact that amazes us.   And yet this Jonson, again, is not at all points identical with the poet of the most nearly perfect marriage of form and material in this or any age of English comedy, *The Alchemist*.   Nor is this, nor any of these, the proud, blunt talker of *Discoveries* and the *Conversations*, who ' would not flatter though he saw Death', disillusioned about man but not about Nature or Nature's God, paying to the two men he honoured tributes as enduring, though brief, as were ever made by any contemporary,[1] and curiously anticipating in mood and manner his great namesake ; nor is it again the poet of the masks and of the *Sad Shepherd*, of the tribute to Virgil [2] and of Edward Knowell's defence of poetry.[3]

If we lay side by side, without comment, a group of passages from a few of these, something of the range of his work and of the variations of his personality will be indicated, and at the same time (what is equally significant) the essential simplicity, the freedom from complexity of his emotions :

> Or, living, I could stampe
> Their foreheads with those deepe and publike brands,
> That the whole company of *Barber-Surgeons*
> Should not take off, with all their art, and playsters.
> And these my prints should last, still to be read
> In their pale fronts : when, what they write 'gainst me,
> Shall like a figure, drawne in water, fleete,
> And the poore wretched papers be employ'd
> To cloth *tobacco*, or some cheaper drug.
> This I could doe, and make them infamous.
> But, to what end ?   When their owne deedes have marked 'hem :
> And, that I know, within his guilty breast

---

[1] See the passages on Bacon in *Discoveries : Dominus Verulamius* (ed. 1641, pp. 101–2), Lord S. *Albane* (ibid., p. 102), and on Shakespeare, *De Shakespeare Nostrat.* (ibid., pp. 97–8), and the lines ' To the Memory of my beloved Master William Shakespeare, and what he hath left us ' (F. 1623).

[2] *Poetaster*, V, i.   Following, with some relief, the clearly argued conclusion of the editors of the Oxford Jonson, I assume these lines to be a reasonable tribute to Virgil and not an improbable tribute to Shakespeare or an uncritical estimate of Chapman.

[3] *Every Man In His Humour* (Q. 1601), V, iii, 313–43.

> Each slanderer beares a whip, that shall torment him,
> Worse, than a million of these temporall plagues : . . .
> . . . Leave me. There's something come into my thought,
> That must, and shall be sung, high, and aloof,
> Safe from the wolves black jaw, and the dull ass's hoofe.[1]

Over against this we may set the clear, almost lyrical eulogy of poetry in the first form of *Every Man In his Humour*, as straightforward a statement of poetic faith as any in *Discoveries* and equally free from anger, satire or irony.

> If it may stand with your most wisht content,
> I can refell opinion and approve
> The state of poesie, such as it is,
> Blessed, aeternall, and most true devine : . . .
> . . . But view her in her glorious ornaments,
> Attired in the maiestie of arte,
> Set high in spirite with the precious taste
> Of sweete philosophie, and which is most,
> Crownd with the rich traditions of a soule,
> That hates to have her dignitie prophand,
> With any relish of an earthly thought :
> O then how proud a presence doth she beare.
> Then is she like her selfe, fit to be seene
> Of none but grave and consecrated eyes.[2]

As the furthest reach, perhaps, of his fanciful description we might offer any of several passages from *The Sad Shepherd*, perhaps best of all that description of the witch that recalls rather the Thessalian magic of Theocritus than any contemporary :

> Where you shall find her sitting in her fourme,
> As fearfull, and melancholique, as that
> Shee is about ; with Caterpillers kells,
> And knottie Cobwebs, rounded in with spells ;
> Thence shee steales forth to releif, in the foggs,
> And rotten Mistes, upon the fens, and boggs,
> Downe to the drowned Lands of *Lincolneshire* ; . . .
> . . . the shreikes of lucklesse Owles,
> Wee heare ! and croaking Night-Crowes in the aire !
> Greene-bellied Snakes blew fire-drakes in the skie !
> And giddie Flitter-mice, with lether wings !
> The scalie Beetles, with their habergeons,
> That make a humming Murmur as they flie !
> There, in the stocks of trees, white Faies doe dwell,
> And span-long Elves, that dance about a poole ![3]

---

[1] *Poetaster : An Apologetical Dialogue (passim).*
[2] *E.M.I.H.* (Q. 1601), V, iii, 313–43 *passim.*
[3] *Sad Shepherd*, II, viii–end.

I strongly doubt whether Jonson wrote this ' first in prose ' no matter what ' his master Camden had taught him '.

Distinct again from this by its tenderness and, like Edward Knowell's lines,[1] in the vein of serious poetry, stands such a poem as the epitaph for the Countess of Pembroke :

> Underneath this sable herse
> Lies the subject of all verse,
> Sidney's sister, Pembroke's mother ;
> Death ere thou hast slain another,
> Learn'd and fair, and good as she,
> Time shall throw a dart at thee.[2]

While, finally, we may pass rapidly to the opposite extreme of mood and, taking what is perhaps the sharpest piece of his satiric portraiture that can be isolated in brief space, include a few of the speeches of Zeal-of-the-Land-Busy, perhaps the bitterest ironic exposure of puritanical hypocrisy in a drama which includes also the comments of Chapman, Marston and Middleton upon the same theme, whose handling of it also was not gentle. It is at the conclusion of the debate as to whether members of the ' sanctified assembly ' may without offence to the weaker brethren commit the act of eating roast pig in Bartholomew Fair :

Zeal-of-the-Land-Busy . . . It may be eaten, and in the *Fayre*, I take it, in a Booth, the tents of the wicked : the place is not much, not very much, we may be religious in midst of the prophane, so it be eaten with a reformed mouth, with *sobriety*, and humblenesse ; . . . In the way of comfort to the weake, I will goe, and eat. I will eate exceedingly, and prophesie ; there may be a good use made of it, too, now I thinke on't : by the publike eating of Swines flesh, to professe our hate, and loathing of *judaisme*, whereof the brethren stand taxed. I will therefore eate, yea, I will eate exceedingly. . . . And it were a sinne of obstinacy, great obstinacy, high and horrible obstinacy, to decline, or resist the good titillation of the famelick sense, which is the smell. Therefore be bold (huh, huh, huh) follow the sent. Enter the Tents of the uncleane, for once, and satisfie your wives frailty. Let your fraile wife be satisfied : your zealous mother, and my suffering selfe, will also be satisfied.[3]

---

[1] See above, p. 102.

[2] *Underwoods*, xv (Gifford, viii, pp. 324–5). Gifford takes as his authority Whalley's inclusion of this poem in the edition of 1756 and his report that it was ' universally assigned to our author, though it hath never yet been printed with his works '.

[3] *Barth. Fair*, I, vi; III, i.

Yet all these are one man ; scholar, satirist, poet ; strict discipliner of all that 'Sufflaminanda erant ' ; critic of life and letters, driven perhaps into too great severity, both as critic and as poet, in his contempt for sensation and sentiment ; the rough talker with the touch of swagger that so jarred upon Drummond, that fastidious Celtic gentleman ; the man of infinite humility to his God and equal haughtiness to man ; the man who possessed, above all, that virtue of resolution that the Elizabethans justly worshipped, and observed, in the dominion of letters, the *virtù ordinata* that was its Machiavellian forbear ; the man who studied ' not to repent him '. And when this has been said, half at least has not been touched, for it is no more possible to describe Ben Jonson in brief space than it is to imprison Shakespeare.[1]

What, after all, are the passages that come first into the mind when we try to present him ? Not the prologues and commentaries, the Manifestoes and Declarations of Poetic Right ; not, certainly, the theory of Humours ; not necessarily any group of characters, not even the individual and unsurpassed dramatic structure that he evolved ; but, surely, a series, often disconnected, of fragments from *Discoveries*, fragments, nevertheless, which bear the closest relation to the material of the plays or to their aesthetic problems, which, if they do not immediately illustrate his attitude to either of these, illuminate the conflict between conscious principle and fundamental simplicity of emotion from which the aesthetic theory and practice emerges.[2]

---

[1] With this obvious difference, of course, that Ben Jonson can be described at length (as in the endlessly suggestive commentaries of the Oxford editors). He can even, indeed, be summed up in a half-length drawing, as was done by one of these editors in what often seems (upon reading and re-reading) the finest summary of his quality for its length to be found. (See C. H. Herford's *Introduction* to Ben Jonson's plays in the Mermaid Edition.)

[2] ' He knowes not his own strength that hath not met Adversity . . . no ill can happen to a *good* man. . . . Yet, that which happens to any man, may to every man. But it is in his reason what hee accounts it, and will make it.'

' I cannot thinke *Nature* is so spent, and decay'd, that she can bring forth nothing worth her former yeares. She is alwayes the same, like her selfe. . . . Men are decay'd, and *studies* : Shee is not.'

' I will have no man addict himself to mee ; but if I have any thing right, defend it as Truth's, not mine. . . . Stand for *Truth*, and 'tis enough.'

' *Man* is read in his face : *God* in his creatures ; but not as the

The total effect of *Discoveries*, disparate and yet cognate, is perhaps something like the total effect of the works and deeds ; a personality to which indeed the epithet ' masculine ' may justly be assigned. Resolute and self-reliant, with a penetrating judgement, the habit of observing men and manners in a dry light, a prodigious memory for characters, incidents and details so observed, a sense of beauty but no unnecessary (and something less even than the needful) freedom in the expression of that experience, admiration rarely but generously given, a capacity for tenderness but apparently for no passions else except scorn and indignation, such a personality was indeed fundamentally undramatic.

Philosopher, the creature of glory reads him : But, as the *Divine*, the servant of humility.'

' *Truth* is man's proper good ; and the onely *immortall* thing, was given to our mortality to use.'

' . . . I had not told posterity this, but for their ignorance. . . . And to justifie mine owne candor, (for I lov'd the man, and doe honour his memory (on this side Idolatry, as much as any).'

' *I know* no disease of the *Soule*, but *Ignorance.*'

' *Knowledge* is the action of the *Soule* ; and is perfect without the *senses* . . . but not without the service of the *senses* : by those Organs, the *soule workes.*'

' I have, and doe reverence him for the greatnesse, that was onely proper to himselfe, in that hee seem'd to mee ever, by his worke one of the greatest men, and most worthy of admiration, that had beene in many Ages. In his adversity I ever prayed, that *God* would give him strength : for *Greatnesse* hee could not want.'

' That houre, wherein I would repent me to be honest : there were wayes enow open for me to be rich.'

' Pure and neat Language I love, yet plaine and customary.'

' To this perfection of Nature in our *Poet*, wee require Exercise of those parts, and frequent. If his wit will not arrive soddainly at the dignitie of the Ancients, let him not yet fall out with it, quarrell, or be over hastily Angry : offer, to turne it away from Study, in a humor ; but come to it againe upon better cogitation ; try another time, with labour. If then it succeed not, cast not away the Quills, yet : . . . but bring all to the forge, and file, againe ; tourne it anewe. There is no Statute *Law* of the Kingdome bidds you bee a Poet, against your will ; or the first Quarter. If it come, in a yeare, or two, it is well.'

Discoveries (1641), pp. 87, 89, 89, 95, 95, 97–8, 100, 100, 102, 104, 118 and 127.

With the last passage we naturally compare that ominous saying recorded by Drummond, ' his opinion of Verses, that he wrott all his first in prose, for so his master Cambden had Learned him '. (*Conversations*, 15, ed. G. B. Harrison, p. 16.)

III

But, as he himself said to intending poets, ' If it come, in a yeare or two, it is well ', and though there is evidence enough in the first four or five plays that it was more than a year or two before the habit of presenting his material dramatically came to Ben Jonson, the resolution carried it in the end.   In the plays written between 1597 and 1602, *Every Man In His Humour* (Q. 1601), *Every Man Out of His Humour, Cynthia's Revels, Poetaster*, there is a constant tendency to revert to non-dramatic methods or to confuse the action.   The main weaknesses of the first-named play are, indeed, far less noticeable than those of the next three ; a confusion of plot that might befall any inexperienced playwright with a natural love of complicated involutions and without the necessary theatre sense to know when he was displaying these too rapidly for his audience's comfort,[1] and a tendency to reveal character or emotion by rather improbable soliloquy and monologue.[2]   The next two plays, and to some extent *Poetaster*, are overburdened with non-dramatic material which, while attempting to explicate character and plot, actually succeeds only in deadening them.   Work that is done by dialogue in Shakespeare's or Ben Jonson's own later plays is done here by a series of undramatic narrative devices, and ill done.   The people are described in character sketches, as in the Introduction of *E.M.O.H.* or throughout *Cynthia's Revels* (especially in II, i, with the full and justly famous ' characters ' of Asotus and Crites), and even so, are not easily kept clear in the reader's mind when the description has ceased ; even Marston, who began with descriptive satire, learnt the difference between narrative that analyses and dialogue that reveals quicker than this.[3]   Action, again, is often described where it might better have been presented and this not always for the sake of brevity and proportion : in *Poetaster*, I, i, the brief description

[1] We might complain, for instance, that Brainworm's intrigue is not made clear enough when he first hints at it at the end of II, iii, and that by V, i (IV, x, F. 1616), it has become genuinely confusing.

[2] But these are only failures of the attempt at dramatization and the play as a whole has still some of the sound theatre quality of its predecessor, *The Case is Altered*.   It is when, with the next three plays, Ben Jonson begins to practise his art still more consciously that the non-dramatic basis of his position is revealed.

[3] Oddly enough, Jonson too seems to have known it earlier, in *The Case is Altered*, and to have perversely rejected it now.

of the relations of the poets and their mistresses and of the rather bewildering change of names leave us adrift, as an immediate, if brief, presentation of these ladies would not have done ; in *Sejanus*, V, x, the description of the crowd, excellent in itself, is, like the rather similar description in *King John*,[1] a passage of the kind that is naturally replaced by dialogue in the hands of the maturer authors of *Bartholomew Fair* and *Coriolanus*. It must be admitted that, for *Cynthia's Revels*, the constant use of narrative rather than dramatic technique in both these ways seems to have been due to a genuine if temporary inability to work well in dialogue form—the only sustained attempt being Act IV, where it reaches a depth of imbecility almost unrecognizable as Jonson's.[2] The preliminary survey of the plot in the Induction to *Cynthia's Revels* and the Induction and critical commentary of *Every Man Out of His Humour* show an apparently growing unsureness of his control over plot and character, for the running commentary of Mitis and Cordatus is by no means only aesthetic criticism, it is often used to help out the conduct of the plot, intimately connected with the exposition of the theory. Indeed he seems to have realized that his undramatic tendency expressed itself chiefly, on the technical side, in an inability to get his characters introduced both quickly and clearly. In *Every Man Out of His Humour*, for instance, and in *Cynthia's Revels*, the rapid parade of imperfectly realized ' humours ' leaves the reader dazed [3] ; these persons who just then are only responsible for displaying their own personalities are, paradoxically, far more difficult to realize than those of workaday dramatists or of the Ben Jonson of *The Alchemist*, who pushed their people on to the stage to start the action or explain the situation and left them to reveal themselves incidentally. But here, as so often in self-criticism, Jonson has been before us :

Cor. I see not where he could have insisted lesse, and t'have made the humours perspicuous enough.

---

[1] *King John*, IV, 2, 185–202.

[2] What is perhaps more bewildering still is the fact that this very passage is developed and extended in the alterations made some time before the publication of F. 1616.

[3] This would be mitigated to some extent in performance where voice, gesture, shape and clothes would all help to distinguish the figures. But even in performance I believe the Humour parade would seem too rapid.

Mit. True, as his subject lies : but hee might have altered the shape of his argument, and explicated 'hem better in single *Scenes*.

Cor. . . . Why ? be they not the same persons in this, as they would have beene in those ? and is it not an object of more state, to behold the *Scene* full, and reliev'd with varietie of speakers to the end, then to see a vast emptie stage, and the actors come in (one by one) as if they were dropt downe with a feather, into the eye of the spectators ? [1]

To all of which the answer is that the author of *Volpone*, *Epicoene*, *The Alchemist*, *Bartholomew Fair*, etc., not only ' might ' but did ' explicate 'hem better ', and that without diminishing their number, relinquishing one arabesque of his multiform plot or falling into any of the tediousness which the earlier Jonson, with his Elizabethan lust for a crowded scene and a crowded action, at once feared and produced.   In *Volpone* the ' actors come in one by one ' with a vengeance, the exposition of the play is almost like a slow-motion film of a court reception, but we never notice a ' vast empty stage '.

It is an unavoidable conclusion that, as he himself admitted later,[2] ' at first, he scarce could hit the bore ', and this is perhaps the more interesting when we remember how many of his contemporaries—by no means only Shakespeare—' wanted Arte ' in Jonson's censure.   Far more than ' a yeare, or two ' is required before it comes in his own case.   But it may be said with equal certainty that when it comes ' it is well ' and Jonson has not only imposed dramatic form upon his own recalcitrant imagination, but, what was at least an equal part of his original purpose, has rescued the early Jacobean comedy from any danger that may have threatened it of frivolity or slovenliness of thought or form.

IV

By the time of the writing of *Sejanus*, that weighty and impressive play whose intransigent learning would alone have secured it ' Safe from the wolf's black jaw, and the dull ass's hoofe '. the great and massive ' Arte ' that took so much building, that Shakespeare ' wanted ', was won.   And there is something in these greatest plays of his middle period, *Sejanus*, *Volpone*, *Epicoene*, *Alchemist*, *Catiline*, that has come to them, and could only have come, by the conversion of this obstinately resisting

---

[1] *E.M.O.H.*, II, iii, 290–301.
[2] Prologue to the *Sad Shepherd*, l. 3.

material to the purpose of that strong, realist imagination, that conscious and persistent art. When at last, by the heat of the contention between this moralist, denunciatory imagination and the will that forced it to dramatic presentation in accordance with theories derived and shaped in advance of the experience they were to control, when at last the material was thus resolved and re-moulded, there was a massiveness in what resulted, a hard-won control of matter not easily bent, like the achievement of a great foundry, colossal, tough, dense, hard and precise. And so thorough is the process that when the undramatic has at length put on the dramatic, there is nothing to distinguish Ben Jonson from his contemporaries to the manner born, except that his art is solid, all of a piece, defensible at every point, where theirs is casual. He seems to build his theory always a little in advance of his experience, so that the experience is moulded by the theory rather than the other way round, and, true to the same curious habit that led him to write all his verses first in prose, he arrived, in defiance of psychological law and aesthetic practice, where he intended to be.

The two Roman tragedies which begin and end this central period of Ben Jonson's greatest work may perhaps fitly be considered together ; though each is distinct enough from the other in its own peculiar quality, they are, as the Oxford editors point out, indistinguishable as regards development and both might have been written at about the same date. Both are Roman plays in a sense that is true of no other play of this period ; both present the picture not only of a civilization that differed in some notable essentials from Ben Jonson's own but of a race whose mental habit, whose prevailing moods, the very juxtaposition of whose emotions were continually unlike those of Jacobean Englishmen. To these Jonson has again and again in *Sejanus*, and to almost equal extent in *Catiline*, subjected his imagination, and the result is two plays which are not Jacobean London transposed to a foreign setting but Rome itself, the Rome of Tacitus and Sallust not only in fact and historical detail, but in spirit. The Rome of *Julius Caesar*, of *Antony and Cleopatra*, is a world made by imagination ideally true ; that of *Sejanus* and *Catiline* seems, by reproducing the psychological processes of another race and age, to give us a truth whose virtue lies, on the other hand, precisely in its actualness. Small wonder that the plays were failures on the contemporary stage.

It is not only the groups of relatively unfamiliar figures insufficiently distinguished, the complexities of a plot that often depends for its intelligibility upon hints that refer to equally unfamiliar customs,[1] not even the absence of all passion but indignation and anger (though these are formidable enough), that made *Sejanus* a theatre failure while it is an excellent reading play ; it is, I think, something more and deeper, the picture of an alien mind which, however great credit it does Jonson as an imaginative scholar and historian, was fatal to the engendering of the audience's sympathy. For *Catiline*, which is not by half so confusing a story,[2] failed equally, and that though the mood of the play is more akin to Seneca the Celtic provincial than to Tacitus the historian of Tiberius. Both are of that order of art which a later classicist so clearly appraised when he said of his own, ' I shall dine late, but the room will be well lighted and the guests few but select.' Both choose for theme the minute and close-woven intrigues of the corrupt and subtle Court of Tiberius, an atmosphere which the Jacobeans tended to associate rather with its later manifestation in the political writings of Machiavelli than with the glories of Imperial Rome. In both the author deliberately speaks as judge and critic of morals, thus cutting himself off from sympathetic identification with any characters but Silius, Arruntius and Cicero and from any emotion but the

---

[1] This is perhaps most noticeable at the beginning of Act III and throughout Act V.

[2] The confusion that appears in the plot of *Sejanus* is not, I think, the same weakness of technique as has been noticed in the earlier plays, but should be set down to the other causes indicated above. If, at a first reading, we depend upon the play to explain itself, there is some difficulty in distinguishing the people and the action. If, instead of reading the play again at once, we forget it, study Tacitus's record and return to the play again, we find that not only are the action and the people clear enough, but that the play is one of very considerable interest. Ben Jonson's weakness here seems to have lain not in dramatic technique but in forgetting that his audience did not know the details and background of the story as he did. For this is essentially a classical play in which (as in the *Oedipus*) the audience is expected to remember the story. Many of the best effects in the last act—the irony of Sejanus's confidence in his already lost cause—depend on foreknowledge of this kind in the audience and are so presented as to show that Jonson assumed this knowledge. Thus the confusion is essentially different from that of *E.M.I.H.* (Q. 1601), where the background and social customs, at least, were as familiar to the audience as to the author.

righteous indignation, scorn or rebuke which speak through them.[1]

Silius.   Since I have done thee that great service, CAESAR,
        Thou still hast fear'd me ; and in place of grace,
        Return'd me hatred : so soone all best turnes,
        With doubtfule Princes, turne deepe injuries
        In estimation, when they greater rise,
        Than can be answer'd . . .
Cot.   Suffer him speake no more . . .
Sej.   He hath spoke inough to prove him CAESARS foe.
Cot.   His thoughts look through his words.
Sej.   A censure.
Sil.   Stay,
        Stay, most officious Senate, I shall straight
        Delude thy furie. SILIUS hath not plac'd
        His guards within him, against fortune's spight,
        So weakely, but he can escape your gripe
        That are but hands of fortune : Shee herselfe,
        When vertue doth oppose, must lose her threats.
        All that can happen in humanitie,
        The frown of CAESAR, proud SEJANUS hatred,
        Base VARRO's spleene, and AFERS bloudying tongue,
        The Senates servile flatterie, and these
        Mustred to kill, I'am fortified against ;
        And can looke downe upon : they are beneath me.
        It is not life whereof I stand enamour'd :
        Nor shall my ende make me accuse my fate.
        The coward, and the valiant man must fall,
        Only the cause, and manner how, discernes them :
        Which then are gladdest, when they cost us dearest.
        Romanes, if any here be in this Senate,
        Would know to mock TIBERIUS tyrannie,
        Looke upon SILIUS, and so learne to die.   [Stabs himself.] [2]

The gravity and dignity of Sejanus is undeniable ; its peculiar, simple emotions contrast, as in all his masterpieces, with the intellectual duplicity of the characters, the subtle processes of plot construction and the details of observation. And Catiline, though here his judgement in the projecting of the play is not so clear, has a dark beauty of image which is of the very quality of Seneca himself.[3] Solemnity he can assuredly command, if

[1] See especially the death speech of Silius, Sejanus, III, i, and the opening of Cicero's oration in IV, ii, of Catiline.
[2] Sej., III, i, 300–39.
[3] Jonson is not, of course, directly indebted to Seneca for anything in this play except the Thyestean prologue and the choruses, but it is evident that the poetry of Seneca was in his mind throughout, at least,

not tragedy ; we feel the presence of a satirist or a great moralist rather than of a tragic poet even in the magnificent elegy upon Germanicus which, with rather doubtful dramatic propriety, opens *Sejanus*.[1]

Sil. We were his followers, (he would call us friends.)
    He was a man most like to vertue ; In all,
    And every action, neerer to the gods,
    Than men, in nature ; of a body' as fair
    As was his mind ; and no less reverend
    In face, than fame : He could so use his state,
    Temp'ring his greatnesse with his gravitie,
    As it avoyded all selfe-love in him,
    And spight in others . . .
Sab.   . . . All the good, in him [Alexander]
    (His valour and his fortune) he made his ;
    But he had other touches of late *Romanes*,
    That more did speake him : POMPEI's dignitie,
    The innocence of CATO, CAESAR's spirit,
    Wise BRUTUS temperance, and every vertue,
    Which, parted unto others, gave them name,
    Flow'd mixt in him. He was the soule of goodnesse ;
    And all our praises of him are like streames
    Drawn from a spring, that still rise full, and leave
    The part remainyng greatest.[2]

The blank verse here and throughout both plays is, as in *Volpone* and *The Alchemist*, transparent but firm. It hardly ever arrests by its mellifluousness or by any other quality ; we take for granted the fine, clear medium of speech. But they are essentially blank verse plays ; to take away that sensitive rhythm from either would be unimaginable. It is no more vivid than is the imagery of the earlier of the pair (untouched by Seneca's

the early parts of the play. There is, as all lovers of Seneca know, a beauty in some of his imagery which almost invariably eludes translators and imitators. Heywood's translation of the *Thyestes* (1560) is perhaps an exception, and, after nearly fifty years, Jonson in this play reproduces and even surpasses that majestic gloom of imagery which is in the finest of Seneca's poetry.

[1] This may, of course, be compared with the similar eulogies of Virgil, Shakespeare and Bacon already referred to. The very completeness and finish of the two dramatic eulogies (Virgil and Germanicus) makes them essentially undramatic. We have only to contrast for a moment those much more sparing epitaph. that Shakespeare gives his characters to realize how much more deeply the briefer, more dramatic utterance searches the heart.

[2] *Sej.*, I, i, 123-31, 147-57.

spirit), but imagery and music alike are lucid,[1] choice and fit.

In neither of these plays, then, nor indeed in the plays that follow, is there any hesitation in presenting the characters or the action ; the characters reveal themselves, by whatever method suits best with the setting, and the action, if complex, is clear.[2] In *Volpone*, that masterpiece so sublimely simple and homogeneous in its mood of purposed evil, the compact flawlessness of the first four acts is only equalled or surpassed in Jonson's age by his own two succeeding comedies. Moreover, in this play there stirs something that we hardly meet else in Ben Jonson's writings, the promise, continually upon the verge of fulfilment, of that passionate obsession in the author with the figure of his own creating that is familiar to us in nearly all of his contemporaries : in Webster, Dekker, Chapman, Marston, Beaumont and Fletcher, Shakespeare himself and Ford, and is utterly alien to Ben Jonson's detached moralist's art.[3] Ever and again about the figure of Volpone there moves, undefinable and unseizable, this sense of an imagination kindling not to critical denunciation, but to oblivion of critical positions, to identifying of itself with the passion and the power of its own creation. It is impossible to Ben Jonson wholly to allow this, since Volpone was originally begotten of his moral satire, but equally impossible wholly to impoverish him, to strip away a certain magnificence of daring, the high insolence with which, unaware, he has himself fallen in love. When, in the fifth act, the moment comes for the reversal and unmasking of this figure, when like Subtle or Morose he should have been driven into ignominious terms, we realize suddenly what hold this magnificent insolence has laid upon Jonson's imagination. For at the last moment Volpone revolts and, like an equally potent and equally rebellious creation of Shakespeare's, nearly wrecks the play. Mosca (and perhaps Ben Jonson himself) realizes too

[1] The imagery of *Sejanus* is, indeed, not so much lucid as potentially lit. The images need to be isolated and some artificial intellectual light turned upon them ; they lack the fire of surrounding passion that enables Webster's images to draw their illumination from their setting.
[2] For a description of the form of *The Alchemist*, see *ante*, Chap. II, pp. 44–8.
[3] The only Jacobean who shares fully this detachment from emotional preoccupation with his own characters is Middleton (see *post*, Chap. VII), though Tourneur almost achieves it.

8

late that it is no slave-minded craven whom he is blackmailing, but an aristocrat whose high spirit he has failed to gauge. With one last terrific gesture, utterly unbefitting a comedy and all but precipitating it into tragedy, Volpone pulls down disaster upon himself and his enemy alike. ' I limmed this night-piece and it was my best ' ; the pride of Lodovico himself dictates his last free gesture and he withdraws, no way disabled in mind or spirit, a Venetian magnifico still. Never again did Jonson come so near feeling for a character of his own creating an admiration like that he gave to the two great contemporaries whom he reverenced, and the closing scenes of *Volpone* are his comment on the Jacobean ideal of an aristocrat, his characteristic variant of the theme ' I am Duchess of Malfi still '.[1]

Indeed, paradoxically, almost perversely, from the opening lines of Volpone's slow-moving monologue, it is the splendour of the play that haunts us, a splendour that is symbolized superficially by the gold and massive plate of the legacy-hunters and finds its antitype in the depths below depths of evil into which the characters coldly and resolutely plunge. Cruel and ruthless as they are, repulsive and contemptible as they are all intended to appear, the very solidity of the atmosphere of evil lends, as in the otherwise dissimilar *Revenger's Tragedy*, and *Changeling*, a greatness to their tenacity and their resolution. By a supreme act of imagination Ben Jonson has penetrated behind the melodramatic semblances with which tradition had invested the Machiavellian plotter and exposed the cold concentration, the flawless courage which was a major quality—if not the major quality—of the portrait Machiavelli drew. Small wonder then that for posterity this play rivals even *The Alchemist* and, for some of us, seems the supreme reach of Ben Jonson's poetic power.

Volp. Good morning to the day ; and, next, my gold :
   Open the shrine, that I may see my *saint*.
   Haile the worlds soule, and mine. More glad then is
   The teeming earthe to see the long'd-for sunne
   Peepe through the hornes of the celestiall *ram*,

---

[1] The satanic magnificence of this figure carries it into the same class as the great tragic characters of the contemporary drama, and it may be noticed in passing that Volpone is of those figures expanded to a magnitude only possible to man when the spiritual background of his being is dwarfed.

Am I, to view thy splendor, darkening his :
That, lying here, amongst my other hoords,
Shew'st like a flame, by night ; or like the day
Strooke out of *chaos*, when all darknesse fled
Unto the center. O, thou sonne of Sol,
(But brighter then thy father) let me kisse,
With adoration, thee, and every relique
Of sacred treasure, in this blessed roome.
Well did wise Poets, by thy glorious name,
Title that age, which they would have the best ;
Thou being the best of things : and far transcending
All stile of joy, in children, parents, friends,
Or any other waking dreame on earth.
                    . . . Deare *saint*,
Riches, the dumbe god, that giv'st all men tongues :
That canst doe nought, and yet mak'st men doe all things ;
The price of soules ; even hell, with thee to boot,
Is made worth heaven ! Thou art vertue, fame,
Honour, and all things else ! Who can get thee,
He shall be noble, valiant, honest, wise.[1]

In *The Alchemist* the relation of material and form is so nearly perfect as to appear fortuitous. One of the most complex group of plots in English comedy [2] is wound up to its harmonious conclusion without violation of character in the smallest degree. Here as in *Epicoene* the language and mood is that of comedy ; though the light-heartedness of the prose play is gone, the virtuosity of comic imagery, the fantastic invective is richer than ever. Base, contemptible, hypocritical as are its elements, there is no suggestion of tragedy : that indefinable breath of passion that flawed and yet heightened the quality of *Volpone* is gone. The poet is again detached, at ample distance from all the characters, seeing them to the minutest detail, grouping them in the surest proportion. In amazement at the subtly revolving dance he sets the motley chorus to work upon, we forget his almost excursion into the world of poetry and power and give ourselves up to the more truly Jonsonian spectacle, which he forbids us to enter emotionally yet warns us (by the very effect of the blank verse after the prose of *Epicoene*) to regard as a serious and enduring comment upon human frailty.

This is the highest reach of his art, but it is not the end of his development or the last of his comments. Through the later

---

[1] *Volpone*, I, i, 1–27.
[2] For a further comment on the structure of *The Alchemist*, see Chap. II, pp. 44–8.

plays, but especially in the next, *Bartholomew Fair*, the range of
his observation and recording, the easy vividness of his characterization can be seen increasing. Whatever his contemporaries
reported from the life of Jacobean London, Jonson seems to
have noticed and analysed, often a little sooner than they. So
full is this picture of contemporary life, thoughts, habits and
discoveries that comparison immediately suggests itself with the
only two contemporaries fit to compare with him for breadth.
Like Middleton, he comprehends in his picture most of the forms
of life to be found in Jacobean London, distinguishes their habits
and processes, reflects their background, their daily life, their
eccentricities and the peculiarities of their gestures and speech,
but with this difference, that where Middleton records only, he
records and criticizes simultaneously. Like Shakespeare, he
gathers up in his plays the findings of all contemporary exploration, but with this difference, that, where Shakespeare transmutes
all into an eternal and a universal expression, Ben Jonson analyses
all into a no less permanent but far from universal critical record.
And this, in the last event, the material of his plays, unkindled
as it is by passion, must remain. In the form and the structural
technique we recognize a supreme, self-constituted artist ; the
spirit that animates the people whose movements make that
form, remains, except for the single case of *Volpone*, critical and
so undramatic.

It is to the conscious critical purpose of Ben Jonson, then,
that we return as the point of distinction between him and his
contemporaries. All the other major dramatists that we have
considered were artists by instinct, theatre-men by profession
and moralists, if at all, by fits and starts. Their work, when they
outgrew the moralist (which they invariably did, as in the case of
Marston), was that of artists conforming naturally to the popular
and professional demands upon their art, so that they reflect
clearly not only their own individual preoccupations, but the
mood of their times. In Ben Jonson the moralist came first—
if only by a short length. He was a very considerable artist too,
but it was his peculiarity that his ethical principles not only
controlled in part the subject-matter of his art but, transmuted
into aesthetic theories, controlled also its form. We hardly need
the evidence of the poems, the masks, the *Sad Shepherd* and
the early passages on poetry to indicate how much of this considerable artistic instinct was suppressed and disciplined into

other forms by his conscious moral and aesthetic purposes, for
we have the evidence of a rebellion that was nearly successful
in the transformation of his mood in *Volpone*. It is probable that
Ben Jonson crippled himself as an artist by his moral imposition.
Certainly one of the results is a deeply divided mind ; though
it is half concealed by the unified surface of purpose that he
presents to us, it is this fundamental division that is responsible
for our inability to conceive of his work as a whole. But whatever the effect upon his ultimate achievement, one thing is
certain, that the severity of Ben Jonson's aesthetic standard,
coming as early in the Jacobean age as it did, was of immense
value in giving a standard of subject-matter, thought and structure to serious critical comedy. His contemporaries may have
rebelled at first against his theories and the high-handed imposition of classical standards, but the effect of his practice is indubit-
able. It is not that there is any considerable imitation of his
comedy—imitation of Ben Jonson's technique is in any case
unprofitable—but that the strength and severity of hard-knit
comedy had been demonstrated from the beginning of the
century. Natural comedians like Middleton, born with an
instinct for easy, graceful plotting and unencumbered by purposes ethical or aesthetic, evolved their own technique very
much more readily than Jonson, but it is at least arguable that,
without the experience of Jonson's tougher texture, the *Chaste
Maid in Cheapside* and the grimmer comedy of Middleton would
have been less serious stuff, less close-knit and less ironical.

And his greatness therefore is incompletely reflected in the
plays : it is a greatness of character, not only—nor principally—
of imagination. Like many men, he unconsciously characterized
himself when he wrote of the man to whom his reverence most
naturally turned, and what he said of Bacon might be repeated
with some modifications of himself :

> I have, and doe reverence him for the greatnesse, that was onely
> proper to himselfe, in that hee seem'd to mee ever, by his worke one
> of the greatest men, and most worthy of admiration, that had beene
> in many Ages. In his adversity I ever prayed, that *God* would give
> him strength : for *Greatnesse* hee could not want. Neither could I
> condole in a word, or syllable for him ; as knowing no Accident could
> doe harme to vertue ; but rather helpe to make it manifest.

The peculiar virtue that he thought 'onely proper' to Bacon
was shared by Bacon's greatest eulogist.

CHAPTER VI

THOMAS DEKKER

I

DEKKER was a theatre-man whose output, like Middleton's (seeing that play-writing was only one side of his work), appears enormous, easily challenging that of the fluent nineteenth-century dramatists. His work, wherever we can safely trace his hand,[1] bears the marks of this. In the plays written during the first part of his career, at least, there is unevenness of style, carelessness of form and lack of depth in the characters ; all the results of vivid observation rather than of thorough or penetrating study. Wherever, that is, the specifically dramatic power differs from the specifically theatrical, he will generally be found to possess rather the gifts of the theatre—but to possess these abundantly. But were he no more than this, he would not have written at least five fine plays (alone or in collaboration), have written or shared in several more thoroughly serviceable ones, have drawn from Lamb and succeeding critics enthusiastic praise or have impressed upon one of the greatest of his collaborators some of his own essential sweetness and simplicity.[2] He was, indeed, a poet of exceptional sweetness, of the family of Peele, Greene and Daniel ; many songs and exquisite isolated lines show this from the first, no less than his ready apprehension of universal suffering and the deep, underlying happiness of his spirit. The conviction indeed prevails among his biographers and editors that, given more even circumstances or a more ambitious temper, Dekker might have become a considerable artist. As it is, he is at his best in the quick and eager revelation of emotion ; unconscious of art, his attempts to labour a detail

---

[1] Upon this question, see the biographical note on Dekker and the Introduction.

[2] Little is known of his collaboration with Ford beyond two plays, *The Sun's Darling* and *The Witch of Edmonton*, but the results of this partnership are I think traceable in all Ford's earlier plays and to some extent in the later ones. See *post*, Chap. XII.

or even to point a moral consciously are generally inconsistent with the rest of his play, with the sounder and sweeter unconscious morality that springs from his faith and his geniality.

It follows from this, then, that when Dekker reveals the preoccupations of his generation, either in thought or dramatic technique, he will do so, in the main, unconsciously, that he will not, like Chapman or Ben Jonson, offer a reasoned and coherent group of principles either moral or aesthetic in opposition to the trend of contemporary social or literary development. Up to a point, in fact, his work resembles rather that of Middleton in its ready reflection of what came to his notice and the absence if not of satirical humour, at least of the satire which attempts reform. But it is only up to a point that we can find in Dekker's work the clear mirroring of the Jacobean world that Middleton's comedy offers, for Dekker, though he has apparently no artistic creed, has an intermittent moral code which seems to derive rather from a simple, but genuine, though unformulated, mysticism—the very quality, indeed, that Chapman indicates in Strozza in *The Gentleman Usher*. But he is utterly without Chapman's systematic reasoning, that built upon this a coherent body of principles. Dekker's mysticism, though it is as different from the brooding spirit of the age as is Chapman's own, escapes in flashes, moments of bright faith which, since they are entirely spontaneous and never forced, have, paradoxically, a security which Chapman's firm declarations sometimes lack. He has not, therefore, in his response to his material or to the mood of his generation, the consistency of either Chapman or Middleton ; not Chapman's consistent principling, not Middleton's consistent detachment. With Ben Jonson, of course, he offers no comparison (except in his use of somewhat similar material for some of his comedies) ; he never appears to have taken himself or his art seriously enough to have evolved any explicit aesthetic creed, much less to preach. His comedy, then, reflects clearly enough the circumscribed world of immediate events and persons, with momentary escapes never long maintained, but never quite abandoned, into a wider universe of the spirit. But at no time, I think, is there fusion or synthesis of the two.

II

The plays that we turn to as the indices of Dekker's individual quality are, then, those of his sole authorship and those written in collaboration with Chettle, Middleton, Webster, Massinger, Ford and Rowley ; namely, *Old Fortunatus*, *The Shoemaker's Holiday*, *Patient Grissill*, *Sir Thomas Wyat*, *The Honest Whore*, *Westward Ho !*, *Northward Ho !*, *The Roaring Girl*, *Match Me in London*, *The Virgin Martyr*, *The Witch of Edmonton*, *The Sun's Darling* and *The Noble Soldier*, and even these are by no means of the same degree of interest.

Perhaps Nicholas Vavasour in the note from the ' Printer to the Reader ' prefixed to the *Noble Soldier* (Q. 1634) spoke more truly of Dekker than of many of his Jacobean contemporaries when he said, ' The Poet might conceive a compleat satisfaction upon the Stages approbation.'   And indeed it is, as in part with Marston and Middleton, in terms of the ' Stages approbation ' that he works.   We miss in his plays the technical experiments of Marston, the speculative thought of Chapman, the scientific precision of Tourneur, the deep imaginative absorption of Webster, but we seldom or never find miscalculation of a stage effect : everything that he wrote could be played, I believe ; most of it better than it can be read.   We need not instance the startling theatrical opening of the *Honest Whore* (which, in any case, may belong to his collaborator, Middleton), the macabre scene of Hippolito's mourning (IV, i, Part 1),[1] the sudden turns of situation, the verve and vigour of the whole of the comic plot of *The Shoemaker's Holiday*.   There are, besides

---

[1] This passage raises a problem which may perhaps be indicated here.   The situation itself is, of course, no more improbable than Olivia's similar paroxysm of typically Elizabethan grief in *Twelfth Night*, but its relation to similar scenes in *Hamlet* and *The Revenger's Tragedy* is puzzling.   Hamlet in the grave-yard takes up a skull and addresses it in words unmistakably echoed here.   Vindice (*R.T.*) reminds himself of the need for vengeance by carrying with him his murdered mistress's skull and later uses it to effect that vengeance. Hippolito in this scene puts side by side a portrait of his mistress and a skull and at the end of his soliloquy echoes some of the phrases of Vindice in his second skull scene.   Are we to assume then that Dekker (or Middleton) is here borrowing impartially from *Hamlet* and *The Revenger's Tragedy* and thus put the date of production of the latter play prior to that of *Honest Whore*, Part I ?   Or are we, retaining our belief in the later date of the *R.T.*, to assume that Tourneur's terrific phrases in that apocalyptic scene received their instigation from these far feebler and more commonplace ones of Dekker's ?   The more we learn of the ' sources ' of imagery the less inclined are we to be dogmatic.   But this is hard to believe.   For recent discussion of the problems of Dekker's canon and chronology, see App. II, under ' Dekker '.

these, continuous stretches of dialogue, which, like Marston's, increase steadily in naturalness as his skill develops and, like Middleton's or like Beaumont's in a very different class, catch the very manner of living speech, whether it be in the brothel scenes of the *Honest Whore*, fit companions of the similar scenes in the *Dutch Courtesan* or *Your Five Gallants*, or the passage where the Prince in *Patient Grissill* reveals in secret his affection for the children he has publicly disowned. The freshness and directness of all these diverse scenes is perhaps itself a reward of the lusty, journalistic habit of almost simultaneous observation and reproduction which so often damages the balance of Dekker's character and plot.

It is hard to form any clear opinion on Dekker's structural capacity when we know so little of the shares of the collaborators in his plays. If we assume, in the light of Dr. Sisson's findings,[1] that he sometimes led the team and drew up the plot himself, then we must credit him with the relatively good shape of *Honest Whore*, Part I, and *The Witch of Edmonton* as well as with that of his own *Shoemaker's Holiday*. But whether this be or be not true, the one other play in which he appears completely happy is distinguished by its riotous inconsequence of structure, *Old Fortunatus*.[2] Before this most bewildering and in some ways most delightful of all early Jacobean plays we may well wonder whether we have an ancestor of the eighteenth-century pantomime or of Strindberg's *Dream Play* or a mongrel descendant of the Morality, the Bible-history, the Elizabethan mask, the Robin Hood plays and the chronicles.[3] Its fantasy is that of a dream ; it hints, not at a delicate grouping but at a

[1] In the case of *Keep the Widow Waking*, Dekker and Rowley may, as Dr. Sisson suggests from the evidence, ' have worked out the whole plot together, then called Webster and Ford into consultation, and apportioned the acts '. *The Library*, Vol. VIII, Sept. 1927, p. 245.

[2] This is based upon an old play probably in two parts, a fact which might go far to account for certain inconsistencies (notably the parts played by Fortune, Virtue and Vice). But it does not account for the unity of atmosphere which prevails (as in *The Old Wives' Tale* or any other fairy-tale) over the inconsequence of event.

[3] The Morality is, of course, suggested by the abstract figures of Fortune, Virtue and Vice, the Bible History in such a speech as Fortune's denunciations of Andelocia in IV, i (which is generally reminiscent of a Judgement play), the mask in some of the elaborate directions for entries and costumes, the Robin Hood and Chronicle plays in the average deportment of the principal dignitaries.

reason beyond reason in its apparently incongruous episodes and characters.   However it came into being, this blood-relation of *The Old Wives' Tale*, *Jack Drum's Entertainment*, *The Knight of the Burning Pestle* and *The Sun's Darling* (with at least a cousin-ship with *Cambyses* and *Mucedorus*) is one of the happiest and perhaps the most beautiful of Dekker's plays.

Dekker's poetry, then, is to be found in intermittent flashes, not in a sustained interpretation of the tragic or comic theme, in the form of his drama or the depth and penetration of his characters.   It lies in his songs,[1] in single speeches, in single lines, in sudden turns of thought which redeem an uneven scene ; in a certain elementary but sweet music which makes his cadences distinct even from Middleton's or Ford's whose they else most resemble :

> If you remember on my wedding day,
> You sent me with this pitcher to the well,
> And I came empty home because I met
> The gracious Marquesse and his company.
> Now hath he sent you this cup full of tears
> You'll say the comfort's colde, well be it so,
> Yet every little comfort helpes in woe.

In these lines, spoken by Grissill at the lowest point of her fortunes, there is a simplicity of pathos which uses no art at all and yet, like the same note in Wordsworth's poetry, holds the ear because of its very plainness.   Dekker never learnt like Webster and Ford to use this tone to reveal by its stillness the terror or the tension of the rest of a scene, nor, like Middleton, to render it pellucid and sustain it through whole scenes or acts ; it is in fact natural to him and stands out from surrounding weakness or imperfection as something which has been expressed as the rest should indeed have been.   *Old Fortunatus* and even *The Shoemaker's Holiday* are full of lines so beautiful that they

---

[1] Certain of the songs can be assigned to him with some certainty, those for example in *The Shoemaker's Holiday* and some of those in *The Sun's Darling*.   But several of those that were long attributed to him must be reconsidered, in the light of the evidence of Chettle's possible authorship brought by Mr. Harold Jenkins in his *Life and Work of Henry Chettle* (1935).   This, unfortunately from the point of view of those who would have liked to assign them to Dekker, affects particularly the songs (and they are among the best) in *Patient Grissill*, which he wrote in collaboration with Chettle.

seem a momentary emergence of poetry from an unworthy
setting and must be quoted in isolation or not at all.

I am Sorrow's heir and eldest son to Shame.   (*O.F.*, I, i.)
He dies that troubles me ; call me not king.   (*O.F.*, II, i.)
            It cannot be,
Such a bright taper should burne out so soone   (*H.W.*, I, i.)

Side by side with this is the even more characteristic note
which with him and with Middleton may be called the poetry
of gusto. In Dekker's work, apart from these moments of
clear expression, there is a continuous sense of joy, a love of
things, people, sensations, experiences for their own sakes and
in their own essences, that approach to life peculiar to the comic
poet, to the man for whom comedy is instinct with poetry, found
perhaps most constantly in the work of Chaucer, Dekker,
Shakespeare, the middle comedies of Middleton and Gold-
smith. It underlies the tender no less than the robust moods of
Dekker, the gentle constancy of Jane no less than the hearty,
homespun feelings of Eyre, Firk, Margery and Sybil. Andelocia
in *Old Fortunatus* touches it and the placid contentment of the
worthy citizens in *The Honest Whore* is its natural development.
But it finds its supreme expression in *The Shoemaker's Holiday*,
in the brisk workaday-morning mood of healthy, good-hearted
and not over-sensitive people. Here is the London of Beaumont's citizens,[1] but with a full copiousness, a depth of spontaneous laughter, a Homeric richness sustained, for the measure
of this one play, more completely than even Beaumont or
Middleton ever sustain it :

Lord Mayor. Ha, ha, ha, I had rather then a thousand pound,
I had an heart but halfe so light as yours.
Eyre. Why what should I do my lord ? a pound of care paies not
a dram of debt : hum, lets be merry whiles we are yong. . .
By the lorde of Ludgate, its a madde life to be a lorde Mayor, its
a stirring life, a fine life, a velvet life, a carefull life. Well Simon
Eyre, yet set a good face on it, in the honor of sainct Hugh.[2]

---

[1] It runs, of course, all through *The Knight of the Burning Pestle*,
being especially vested in the citizen and his wife, but it occurs again
in the crowd scenes of *King and No King* and *Cupid's Revenge*, indeed,
in any passage where Beaumont's hand has touched the London citizen
or his equivalent.
[2] *The Shoemaker's Holiday*, III, v, and V, ii.

The pitch of excitement rises in the last act to a continuous rhythmic incantation whose pace leaves behind even the opening scenes of the same play. Through the steady crescendo of the third scene, the rhythm of the Shrove Tuesday bell rings above the shouts of the crowding apprentices, heightening the noise, tightening the emotion until, at the end, the sources of Dekker's laughter are found, paradoxically, to lie as near tears as his pathos commonly trembles on the edge of laughter, resolving themselves into that boisterous Tudor loyalty so thoroughly understood alike by Elizabeth and by her dramatists.

But with all this, or perhaps because of this, Dekker was seldom a subtle student of character. A ready observer, with a copious memory of men and manners and a quick sympathy for the suffering that makes men kin, he lacked insight into the individual desires, moods, processes of mind that make them dissimilar.[1] Indeed, his strength lies chiefly in these two qualities, in his power of recording the outward characteristics of his racy, bluff, hearty contemporaries (whether bawds, whores and sharpers or jovial and reputable citizens), and in his understanding of those moments of suffering when the sense of generic humanity wipes out the distinctions between man and man. How excellent are the rapid portraits of Sybil, Firk, Margery, Eyre or of Fustigo, George, Roger, Bots, Fingerlock and Horseleech ; how equally excellent, in its very different tempo, the scene (*Shoemaker's Holiday*, III, iv) where Ralph returns wounded from the war to learn of the disappearance of his wife at the lips of the good-naturedly callous Margery, entirely preoccupied with her new dignities as sheriff's wife. How simply and yet how effectively he lays tragedy and comedy alongside each other here, the stunned silence of Ralph's slow nature beside the babble of the unconscious Margery : ' Alas, poore soule, hees overcome with sorrowe, he does but as I doe, weepe for the losse of any good thing.' His understanding here is unassailable, the understanding of that common humanity that underlies sex, class or nationality, that community of

---

[1] It is this limitation which, among others, helps to distinguish him sharply from Middleton, who had the same ready observation and voluminous memory, but was able to perceive not only superficial differences of manner but fundamental differences of mental process.

suffering the knowledge and practical experience of which has
brought him his peculiar illumination.[1]

The limitations of Dekker's perception of character are most
clearly revealed perhaps in his portraits of virtuous women.
He can differentiate a Candido, a Hippolito, a Mattheo sharply
and well, he can create in Orlando Friscobaldo or Simon Eyre
or Cuddy Banks an unforgettable and living figure. But Grissill
and Bellafront, even sometimes Jane, Susan and Winnifred, are
drawn entirely from without and from a standpoint so purely
masculine as to be sometimes unimaginative and to send our
sympathies veering round to the husbands who wrong them, far
as it is from Dekker's intention that we should do so. Jane (of
Shoemaker's Holiday) is indeed an exception to this, but Bellafront, convincing enough as a whore, priggish as a convert and
spineless as a respectable matron, is actually a piece of sentimental and cheap idealism that cannot bear a moment's comparison with Ford's Spinella, Shakespeare's Imogen or Middleton's Clara or Francisca. Grissill, with her helpless, patient
submissiveness, recalls now Amelia, now Nellie Denver, now
Esther Eccles, but seldom or never the sane, self-respecting
women that Dekker's contemporaries, Shakespeare, Middleton
and, later, Ford, knew so well. At first glance his women
recall Greene's, but the distinction is obvious between the
courageous, creative understanding that Greene's Margaret and
Dorothea give to the men they love and the slavish meekness, the
limp, automaton-like submissiveness of Dekker's. The patience
of Dekker's women exasperates where that of Greene's wins us
utterly. It would seem that Dekker partly knew this (even if
he did not see how to mend it), for he lets that sane, sound-
hearted gentleman, Orlando Friscobaldo, sum up for himself
and us the very pith of our own opinions :

Doest thou beg for him, thou precious mans meat, thou ? has he
not beaten thee, kickt thee, trod on thee and doest thou fawne on him
like his Spanniell ? has hee not pawnd thee to thy Petticoate, sold thee
to thy smock, made yee leape at a crust, yet woldst have me save him ? [2]

---

[1] Here, again, Middleton (in *Women Beware Women*) makes use of
a somewhat similar contrast between Bianca and her mother-in-law,
but draws from it undertones of pitiless irony with never a hint of pathos,
sympathy or poignancy. Few things emphasize the terrible aloofness
of Middleton more clearly than when he and Dekker use in turn the
same material.

[2] *Hon. Whore*, Part II, V, ii.

But the sentimental channel is too deeply formed in Dekker's mind and the moment of sane good sense is lost in a recantation leaving the balance where Robertson might have left it or Henry Arthur Jones, but never Shakespeare, Webster, Tourneur, Middleton or Ford.

The characters of the *Witch of Edmonton* stand a little apart in their greater maturity and in the quality that they undoubtedly received from Ford's and Rowley's collaboration. Susan and Winnifred are less abject than his earlier women ; what they say, though it is often paradoxical in its devotedness—and always, of course, to men unworthy of it,—is never actually impossible to a sane woman in love. Winnifred indeed comes a little nearer to the quality of Imogen or the Duchess of Malfi. But the things that hold us are the portrait of the old witch, the pene-trating understanding of the processes by which her mind has been formed, and the unforgettable Cuddy. Mother Sawyer shows, I confess, a sympathy with abnormal humanity that seems to me the true index of Ford's imagination. But the natural, Cuddy, is pure Dekker, with his endearing and innate English love of dogs, so strong that it prevails over the diabolic element in the Familiar. So strong is his innocence indeed that, like the same quality in the ' youngest son ' of the fairy tales, it carries him through dangers in which the other characters founder, making the devil himself harmless in return. Gifford is never more maladroit than when he solemnly condemns the ' idle buffoonery ' [1] of this almost Shakespearian character. Cuddy is, like Dekker himself, at best a child who cannot bear the thought that even the Devil should be left out of heaven :

Cuddy. Were it not possible for thee to become an honest Dog yet ? 'tis a base life that you lead, *Tom*, to serve Witches, to kill inno-cent Children, to kill harmless Cattle, to stroy Corn and Fruit &c., 'twere better yet to be a Butcher, and kill for your self. . . . Or *Tom*, if you could give your minde to ducking, I know you can swim, fetch and carry, some Shop-keeper in *London* would take great delight in you, and be a tender master over you.[2]

This commendable attempt to provide even the Devil with a good home suggests not buffoonery so much as a blood-relation-ship with Til Eulenspiegel.

Above all, he is master of a peculiar form of sweet and sudden

---

[1] See his edition of *The Works of Ford*, Vol. II, p. 544, fn.
[2] *Witch of Ed.*, V, i.

paradox such as few other dramatists ever touch. Tourneur
gives us the shock of crisp juxtaposition, Webster the sudden,
poignant illumination, Ford the pervading beauty and implicit
gentleness, but only Shakespeare, and he only in rare moods,
gives us the sudden turn of thought,—simultaneously a turn of
mood, of cadence, of image and an illumination upwards, as it
were, from the abyss—which is Dekker's peculiar gift.

> *Mattheo.* Is't possible to be impossible ! an honest whoore ! I
> have heard many honest Wenches turne Strumpets with a wet finger,
> but for a Harlot to turne honest, is one of *Hercules* Labours. It was
> more easie for him in one night to make fifty queanes then to make
> one of them honest againe in fifty yeares. Come, I hope thou dost
> but jest.
> *Bellafront.* Tis time to leave off jesting, I had almost
> Jested away salvation.[1]

It is a gift he shares rather with the religious poets of the middle
of his own century than with the dramatists of the earlier part,
with Herbert, Traherne, Vaughan than with Marston, Chapman,
Tourneur or Webster ; most of all perhaps with a modern
who in simplicity and in confident illumination is most like
him, Francis Thompson. For with Dekker we are ever in the
presence of a mind which sees

> the traffic of Jacob's ladder
> Pitched betwixt Heaven and Charing Cross.

Even, with a stronger, Jacobean paradox, between Heaven and
the brothel or the debtors' prison.

[1] *Hon. Whore*, Part I, III, iii.

CHAPTER VII
THOMAS MIDDLETON

I

'A GREAT observer of human nature, without fear, without sentiment, without prejudice, without personality.' This estimate by a contemporary [1] sums up a quality that most modern readers of Middleton are aware of sooner or later, a quality inseparable from the rapid, unselfconscious sureness of his work. A wide and keen observer, he covered a range of mood and material only equalled by Shakespeare among his contemporaries and, like him again, could so identify himself with any given mood or matter as to make it his own and proper to him. No one ever explains a failure of Middleton's on the ground that the theme was uncongenial ; few of us would care to guarantee any theme impossible to him. In this, as in much else, he had no prejudice and much quick, though mainly intellectual, sympathy. God's plenty was as rich a heritage to him as to Chaucer (whose range of mood he more nearly parallels, in the first half of his career, than does any other Jacobean). It is not easy to find limits for the imagination that ranges with equal ease from the coarse, vulgar garrulity of the gossips at the Cheapside christening to the courteous chivalry of the central figures of *A Fair Quarrel*, from the mock sick-bed of Gullman in *A Mad World*, or the barber scene in *Anything for a Quiet Life*, to the grave nobility and romance of *The Old Law* and *The Phoenix*, from the incantations of Hecate to the tenderness of the White Queen's Pawn, the bright, midsummer gaiety of *The Spanish Gipsey* or the implacable tragedies of Bianca and Beatrice. It is essential to this quickly evoked and rapidly moving sympathy that it should operate without conscious preference and that the art that springs from it should be equally free of conscious theory. And so Middleton's comedies do not preach ; what is, on the whole, more remarkable, neither do his

[1] T. S. Eliot, *Elizabethan Essays*.

128

tragedies. And as he appears to have no rigid moral theory, so has he few theories, rigid or otherwise, of art.[1] He appears to work by that instinctive process which is thrown instantly out of gear by self-criticism or awareness of itself. Some such principle as this he seems indeed to have perceived himself and one of his most surprising utterances (and he is continually surprising us by the utterance of some thought we had supposed beyond his range) occurs when, in his last play, he defines it in passing :

> We doe not alwayes feele our faith we live by
> Nor ever see our grouth, yet both worke upward.[2]

He seems to have recognized instinctively the principle that growth and creation, whether artistic or spiritual or both, proceed the more surely when these processes are invisible and unaware of themselves.

These very qualities in Middleton help to provide us with some of the most teasing problems of his work. Because he was, in his early work at least, without opinions and throughout his career without prejudice, because of the adaptation of his mind to his material, reflecting and reproducing it, it becomes increasingly difficult to disentangle his work from that of a collaborator or even a reviser.[3] This ease of adaptation, resulting as it does in a Shakespearian breadth and liberality, in marked contrast to the specialized sympathies of Webster, Tourneur and Ford, is enough in itself to make judgement difficult ; we cannot even determine with any certainty the canon of his plays.[4] We

---

[1] His comments in such prefaces as touch on his methods as a playwright are generally, as in *The Roaring Girl*, confined to a few journalistic comments on contemporary fashions in art and the requirements of the public.

[2] *A Game at Chess*; III, i, 338–9.

[3] We have only to recall the varying opinions that have been held (from the time of Dyce's edition downwards) on the question of his share in *The Roaring Girl* and *The Honest Whore* on one side and *The Changeling*, *Anything for a Quiet Life* and *The Spanish Gipsey* upon the other, to realize that he is no more easily separable from Dekker than from Rowley, from Rowley than from Webster, from Webster than from Ford.

[4] I am obliged to make, for the purposes of this essay, certain assumptions which though they are the best I can arrive at in the present state of knowledge are, I am well aware, liable to be invalidated at any moment by further research. But there is a block of early comedy

can at best describe not a personality but a wide range of aptitudes and imaginative experience. The situation is further complicated by the effect of the journalistic rapidity with which he worked. This, while it simultaneously springs from and ensures a certain frankness and spontaneity of workmanship, unfortunately also sometimes results in writing so scamped and roughly sketched in that we cannot safely judge whether it is his or another man's, nor whether or not we may draw upon it in the total estimate of his work. This carelessness only occasionally touches his plots ; they, as a rule, come off clean, no matter under what conditions he writes—he is like a sharp-shooter so experienced that he can still hit the bull's-eye when almost too drunk to hold the rifle. But his characters suffer more severely ; minor or middle-distance characters most, sometimes springing into actions for which we have hardly been prepared or having speeches foisted on to them which do not belong to their parts, but must be spoken by some one ; there is thus even more than the conventional amount of conversion and psychological adjustment at the ends of the comedies.[1] Sometimes, even, a major character, like Livia in *Women Beware Women*, changes abruptly after the middle of the play, losing the rich and original personality which gave it its value and becoming merely a factor in a catastrophe. All this and more than we can attempt to estimate in other ways—the absence of pregnant phrasing, of strong thought or feeling in all but the few great plays—can be largely attributed to the amount of work Middleton covered between 1602 and the end of his dramatic career.[2]

The comedies form a homogeneous group running continuously from about 1602 to 1613, but though homogeneous, they admit of great variety of tone, character and episode. Though Middleton sometimes reproduces a situation or an episode or reverts to one he had touched-in slightly and develops it more fully, his fertility is too great for this to amount to repetition

(see the note on the canon) which can be assigned to him with enough certainty to give us a very fair impression of the range of his opinion and taste at that period, and in the block of plays by him and Rowley, I assume to be his work those parts or elements which harmonize reasonably with this, or with the later serious work from his hand only.

[1] But see note, p. 133, on Middleton's comedy structure, especially in the last scenes.

[2] For some account of this, see the biographical note.

and he is never monotonous.   The very early plays are varied
and experimental, but Middleton gradually settles to his own
method and material.   Doubts have been thrown on his share of
Blurt, Master Constable,[1] and they are confirmed by the fact
that the treatment seems too mature for a playwright of twenty-
two.   But it is hard to resign to Dekker the figure of Blurt himself who belongs (whatever he may owe to Dogberry) with the
great group of eccentric originals, Lucre, Hoard, Falso, Quomodo and Bounteous Progress, Middleton's chief delight in his
early comic period.   Nor are the occasional poetic passages (of
a delicate quietness that often recalls Peele's) inconsistent with
the corresponding passages in *The Phoenix* (nor indeed with the
later manifestations of the same quality in *The Spanish Gipsey*,
The Old Law and *A Game at Chess*).[2]   The play is, in fact,
very like its successors ;   it is a piece of rapid action and bustling
movement, set up chiefly by the group of young men at the
centre of the plot.   A genius so fertile and so easy as Middleton's
may well have ripened early.[3]

    The Phoenix[4] is a play with a serious—in parts, a romantic
frame, allowing of broad and vigorous comedy side by side
with pathos and sentiment of great dignity.   *The Phoenix*,
excellently constructed and grouped, is, on the comic side, a
close relative of Middleton's three best early comedies, *A Trick*,
The Michaelmas Term and *A Mad World*.   Were all its excellence

---

[1] See App. II, section B. ii, under ' Middleton', especially the work
of Eccles and Bald.

[2] As, for instance, Camillo's lines in the third act :

            . . . he that truely loves
Burnes out the day in idle fantasies,
And when the Lambe, bleating, doth bid Go'dnight
Unto the closing day ; then teares begin . . .
. . . The earlie Larke is wakened from her bed,
Being onelie by Loves plaintes disquieted,
And singing in the mornings eare, she weepes . . .
                         (III, i, 100–09.)

[3] In spite of Bullen's remarks (I, xxi–ii) I still agree with Ward that
one scene at least (V, ii) is confused.   In truth the action is a little too
rapid to be quite intelligible when read casually—a fault that does not
recur with Middleton.   Even in this case I am not sure that it would
not be clearer in the theatre than in the study, but, for what it is worth,
this may be a sign of a relatively inexperienced hand.

[4] It was long the custom to group *The Old Law* closely with *The
Phoenix*. But Bald has recently adduced strong evidence for dating
the former as late as 1616.

of plot and of ironic or satiric situation removed, it would still
live by virtue of the character of Falso.   Fielding himself would
not have been ashamed of this Justice of the Peace, who could
step, with hardly a pause for adjustment, straight into the
eleventh chapter of *Joseph Andrews*.   His very perversions of
justice and morality, regrettable though they doubtless are,
endear him to us and when he falls into a vein of tender reminiscence, looking back with sentiment upon the days when he too
was a young and lusty highway-robber, what hard heart would
refuse him the gang of robbers that he keeps, in the guise of
servants, in his own household ?

> *Falso.*   I have beene a youth my selfe, . . . I remember now betimes
> in a morning I would have peept through the greene boughs, & have
> had the partie presently, and then to ride away finelye, in feare, twas
> e'en Venerie to me y' faith, the pleasantst course of life, one would thinke
> every Woodcok a Constable, and every Owl, an officer, but those dayes
> are past with mee : and a my troth I thinke I am a greater thefe now,
> and in no danger : I can take my ease, sit in my Chaire, look in your
> faces now, and rob you, make you bring your money by authoritie
> put off your hat, and thanke me for robbing of you, O there is nothing to
> a thefe under Covert Barne.[1]

And then, to ride away finely in fear ! '—Middleton's
genial sympathy, the essence of his early comic mood, has the
secret of making the figure individual—not typical—in its
eccentricity.

From this point the group of Middleton's most characteristic
comedies begins, and so close is the kinship in mood and material
between *A Trick to Catch the Old-One*, *A Mad World, My
Masters*, *The Michaelmas Term* and the best scenes in *The
Family of Love*, *Your Five Gallants* and *The Roaring Girl*, linked
to the somewhat later, but clearly related *Chaste Maid in Cheapside* and *The Widow*, that they are best considered together as an
organic growth.

At their worst these comedies have first-rate plots and a skill
in using episodes and incidental material so smooth and mature
as to pass unrecognized in current reading, their dialogue is quick
and supple and the characters at least adequate to the plot and
solid enough to have their own virtue.   At their best, as in the
three mentioned first, they are gay and brilliant, filled with prose
dialogue of almost incredible flexibility and verse dialogue already

[1] *Phoenix*, III, i, 64–75.

passing from his thin and obvious early verse to a style like that of his later plays, simple and pellucid. The plays move with neat rapidity, yet the essential twists of the intrigues stand out by just enough of emphasis or isolation to make the whole thing from point to point perfectly clear to any audience with its wits about it.[1] These are no stupendous engineering feats, like Ben Jonson's intricately constructed and cunningly accelerated intrigues. Middleton's easy manipulation of his plots, with its faultless but unconscious skill, is more like a delicate feat of horsemanship in the ring. Without detriment to the outline of the plot, Middleton extends its necessary parts into gratuitous arabesques ; unexpected turns, ludicrous or comically ironic situations are evolved, dwelt on for a moment and gathered into the continuous action, whose proportions they never disturb. The supposed death of Quomodo in *The Michaelmas Term* and the trap by which he is finally caught (V, i, 100–20), the acrobatic twistings of the plotters in *The Widow* or *A Mad World*, the preposterous and almost farcical interweaving of the constable in the impromptu play at the end, the way in which the intrigue is now and again led to a climax in hilarious and sustained comic situations, like the bedroom scene in *A Mad World* (III, ii), all these are incidental to and perfectly controlled by a smooth and neatly running intrigue.

The same gusto is there in Middleton's treatment of comic characters. His range is like Chaucer's in the Canterbury Tales and he has the same sense of the relations of the comic and the pathetic and, latterly, of the comic and the grim. In several of these plays the central figure is a rogue, a villain or a mixture of fool and rogue whose eccentric individuality warmed the author's heart ; Blurt the blundering constable, Falso the corrupt Justice, Quomodo the cheating linen-draper, Lucre and Hoard the avaricious merchants, Sir Bounteous Progress whose

---

[1] The last acts, it is true, are usually taken at a gallop so that a certain amount is left inconclusive. This is due not so much to carelessness on the part of the author as to an understanding of the psychological condition of an audience at the end of a comedy intrigue. Once they have foreseen the end they only want it sketched, not expounded. So that a kind of short-hand technique, understood alike by audience and dramatist, comes into use and settles into different conventions at different periods. The development of this technique from the early comedies of Shakespeare to the end of the Jacobean period forms a very interesting study.

charity begins abroad and ends at home, all alike are soundly
over-reached by the young men whose marriages they had for-
bidden, whose lands they had stolen or whose allowances they
had refused.   One thing they have in common, they are all as
shrewd as old badgers and as full of devices.   But they are outwitted by the young men, the Witgoods, the Easys and Follywits
who hunt in groups, or at least in couples ably seconded by a
courtesan or a servant, and match the experience of the older men
with the gaiety of their wit and the fertility of their plots.   This
is inevitable in comedy, for the purposes of the old usurers and
cheats are too grim to be allowed free rein, but while they are at
liberty they offer that kind of comedy that Chaucer loved, even
more than Shakespeare [1] ; a world in which roguery, Rabelaisian-
ism, broad gusto, poetry and tenderness meet.   Look at Quomodo's touching soliloquy on the beauty of his newly won lands
—those lands out of which he has cheated Easy by as neat a piece
of coney-catching (I[r]., iii) as ever came out of Greene, Audeley
and Harman :

> *Quomodo.*   Oh that sweete, neate, comely, proper, delicate parcell of
> land, like a fine Gentlewoman 'ith waste not so great as prettie, prettie :
> the Trees in Summer whistling, the silver waters by the Banks har-
> moniouslye gliding, I should have beene a Scholler, an excellent place
> for a student. . . .[2]   Now come my golden daies in :—whither is the
> worshipfull master Quomodo, and his faire Bed fellow rid forth,   To
> his land in Essex ? whence comes those goodly loades of Logs ? from
> his land in Essex ? where growes this pleasant fruit, sayes one Citizens
> wife in the rowe ; at maister Quomodos Orchard in Essex. . . .[3]   A
> fine journey in the Whitsun-holydayes yfaith, to ride downe with a
> number of Citizens, and their wives, some upon pillions, some upon
> Side-saddles, I, and little Tomazin ith middle, our sonne and heire
> Sim Quomodo in a peach colour Taffata jacket, some hors-length, or
> a long yard before us. . . .   To see how the very thought of greene
> fieldes puts a man into sweete inventions.[4]

All these figures move upon a background of strong colour.
The setting is generally in London, in the open streets, in front
or inside the houses of gentry or citizens, in taverns, brothels,
pawnshops, in front of or inside citizens' shops, in the middle

---

[1] Isolated comments are not safe evidence in so uncertain a canon
as Middleton's but his kinship with Chaucer is supported by such a
reference to him as : ' As old Chaucer was wont to say, that broad,
famous English poet.' (*More Dissemblers* I, iv, 36.)

[2] *Michaelmas Term*, II, iii, 91–6.

[3] Ibid., III, iv, 13–18.　　　　　[4] Ibid., IV, i, 74–85 *passim.*

aisle of St. Paul's—anywhere where groups of people may meet, dissolve and reassemble with the free access to and fro that the Elizabethan stage allowed.   But more important than the setting is the group of background figures that serve to indicate it and, in nearly every play of this group, keep the undercurrent of Jacobean London before our minds ; the Rearage, Salewood, Shortyard and Falselight of the *Michaelmas Term* and the corresponding figures in the other plays ; card-sharpers, pickpockets, highwaymen, mountebanks ; bawds, whores, promoters, coneycatchers ; decayed knights and captains living on their wives (or, more usually, on other men's) ; gamblers who have lost their lands and are living by their wits ; everything in the Jacobean underworld that cadged or cheated or informed or bullied its way to a livelihood.[1]   Their talk is rich not only in its individuality, but in the dialects of its various trades.   Middleton, though he did not, like Dekker, run mad at the prospect of a foreign tongue, had a sharp sense of the comic possibilities of specialized branches of English.   Except in *The Roaring Girl* (where one may perhaps suspect Dekker's hand at this point) it is, like all other elements in Middleton's comic writing, kept in its proper place in relation to the intrigue.   But the comic possibility of lawyers' jargon, medical phraseology, ' roaring ' or thieves' cant [2] was no less obvious to him than that of alchemy was to Ben Jonson and was as adroitly if not as impressively used.

The *Chaste Maid in Cheapside*, though it shares much with these plays, stands a little apart.   It is indeed in point of structure, depth and variety of character and ease of dialogue the finest of all Middleton's comedies.   But there are already developing qualities which make it something more than the merry comedies of the earlier years.   It is as though we had passed from the world of the Chanoun Yeoman's Tale to that of the Pardoner's Tale.

[1] See especially the coney-catching scenes in *Michaelmas Term*, II, i, II, iii ; the brothel scenes in the same play and in *Five Gallants*, II, i, &c. (cf. the similar scenes in Dekker's *Honest Whore* and Marston's *Dutch Courtesan*) ; the pawnshop in *F.G.*, I, i, and the tavern in III, ii ; the highway scenes in *F.G.*, III, ii (cf. *Widow*, III, i) ; the city sets in *Michaelmas Term*, *Roaring Girl*, *Chaste Maid*, *Anything for a Quiet Life* (cf., again, *Honest Whore*).

[2] See, respectively, for examples, *Michaelmas Term* (I, iv ; II, iii ; V, i), *A Mad World* (III, ii), *A Fair Quarrel* (IV, i and iv) and *The Roaring Girl* (V, i).

Dicing, whoring, cheating and trickery are accepted parts of both and not, in the one, taken too seriously ; but the shadow of unsanctified death is upon the other and the real grimness of Middleton's tragic commentary begins to be anticipated.   There is thus within one comedy a microcosm of that immense range that characterizes Middleton's dramas.   The result is not a merry play.   Superficially the characters are entertaining enough but the affection with which Middleton condoned the villainies of Blurt, Falso, Lucre, Hoard, Quomodo and Sir Bounteous is gone.   No one condones the prosperous, lecherous, well-fed magnate, Sir Walter Whorehound, nor his intolerable relations with the complaisant cuckold Allwit.   There is no gusto here, but there is an almost superhuman vigilance of observation and economy of drawing.   Throughout the play the varieties of meanness, hypocrisy and corruption jostle and yet balance each other.   It is a world made up, but for the two young lovers (who are tossed about between the rest and barely save themselves), of baseness without relief except in a variant of itself.   At its strongest it never quite rises to the vigour and earnestness of crime ; at its mildest it runs into the vulgar, sentimental prudish-ness, the hypocrisy, that Dickens later saw in lower middle-class society in Victorian London.   Middleton's mood, under its Rabelaisian comedy, is as serious as Shakespeare's in *Measure for Measure* or Chaucer's in The Pardoner's Prologue.   Devoid of sentimentality, utterly matter-of-fact, he compresses into a few acts, sometimes into a single scene, a concentrated exposure of the Jacobean citizen world.   Later by at least six or seven years than *Eastward Ho*, it carries on the sub-sardonic comment of that play on the citizen virtues of thrift and patience.   The satires on citizen vices, the pretentiousness that Marston and Jonson took perhaps a little too seriously there and in their other plays, have given place to cold statements without any comment except that implicit in their juxtaposition ; to things that are real, that are deep-rooted and ominous ; to the smug hypocrisy of the growing Puritan element [1] with its glib, overbearing vulgarity ; to the thrift and patience that accepts cuckoldry with gratitude while

---

[1] Jonson seems to have seen this with the same clearness about the same time—assuming the date of the *Chaste Maid* to be 1611–13, which brings it within a year of *Bartholomew Fair*.   But Jonson's Zeal-of-the-Land-Busy is angrily drawn, Middleton's puritans (here, and in the *Familie of Love*) with a cold, ironic disgust.

there is money in it, and supervises the christening feast with unction :

Allwit. I'le goe bid Gossips presently my selfe,
    That's all the worke I'le doe, nor need I stirre,
    But that it is my pleasure to walke forth
    And ayre my selfe a little, I am ty'd to nothing
    In this businesse, what I doe
    Is meerely recreation not constraint. . . .
    Fye, what a trouble have I rid my Hands on,
    It makes me sweat to thinke on't.[1]

The climax comes in the christening feast, where Middleton, as in his earlier plays, makes one scene the meeting-place of all the intrigues and most of the characters ; here, however, the comedy is no longer mainly a matter of situation, rather of ironic juxtaposition of mood, characters and relations that doubles the virtue of nearly every speech. As we watch the guests assemble, the gossips, the puritan women, the midwife, the real father, the nominal father, Lady Kix the godmother and ultimately the unfortunate Tim and his tutor, as the wine and the conversation grow free together, we find ourselves attending a ceremony that Aristophanes or Chaucer might have described with equal freedom and that either might have passed on direct to Hogarth for illustration. We await from moment to moment the entry of Sarah Gamp and Betsy Prig and wonder by what accident they are uninvited. Clear of the indignation that disturbs and narrows the satire of Ben Jonson, Middleton's has become broad and free as the enveloping air ; it is a liberal and comprehensive exposure. So wide are its implications, though in the narrow limits of a five-act play, that we begin to discern here a capacity for satire on a larger scale, for comic epic not unlike, perhaps, the design and scope of *Tom Jones*. Indeed, in this later comic period of Middleton's, bordering on tragi-comedy and tragedy, it is of Fielding's satire that his work continually reminds us. The creator of Bridget Allworthy and of Lady Bellaston, of Square, of Blifil, of Parson Trulliber and Mistress Western, the man who could forgive all things but hypocrisy, is not far removed in mood (though his own vein of irony was looser and more dithyrambic) from the man who wrote the parting between Sir Walter and Allwit. Sir Walter is borne in wounded and, with the sudden fear of death upon him, undergoes one of those con-

---

[1] *A Chaste Maid*, II, ii, 1–10.

vulsions of mind, so startling and yet so psychologically accurate, in which Middleton shows the sudden, shocked awakening of a heedless or headlong nature :

Sir Walter.   None knew the deere account my soule stood charg'd with
So well as thou, yet like Hels flattering Angel,
Would'st never tell me an't, let'st me goe on,
And joyne with Death in sleepe, that if I had not
Wak'd now by chance, even by a strangers pittie,
I had everlastingly slept out all hope
Of grace and mercie.[1]

While there is yet hope of inheriting his money, Allwit's conciliatory speeches flow as steadily as ever, but when the will is made against him and upon the heels of that the officers of the law are seen approaching to arrest Sir Walter, he passes, without changing a line of his face or a note of his voice, to implacable vindictiveness masked with hypocritical unction :

Allwit (*to officers*).   I pray depart Sirs,
And take your Murtherer along with you,
Good he were apprehended ere he goe,
H'as kild some honest Gentleman, send for Officers.
(*to Sir Walter*).   . . . I must tell you Sir,
You have been some-what boulder in my House,
Then I could well like of, I suffred you
Till it stucke here at my Heart, I tell you truly
I thought you had beene familiar with my Wife once.[2]

II

When Middleton, perhaps as a result of association with Rowley, turned to tragedy through the intermediate stages of such tragi-comedies as *A Fair Quarrel*, the experience of a long period of comedy writing remained with him. The peculiar quality of Middleton's tragedy, the grimness, the plainness, the absence alike of romance, pathos, passion or heroism, derives thus directly from the long training in matter-of-fact and unemotional observation, culminating as it does in the wide but precise satire of *A Chaste Maid*. It is not merely, then, that his range of character and episode has been widened, that his theatre technique has become familiar to the point of oblivion, though both of these advantages undoubtedly came to him, as to Shakespeare, through a long period of successful comedy preceding his

[1] V, i.   [2] V, i.

tragic work ; above all, he understands, in the later half of his career, that those very elements that at one time seemed to point only to a comic universe may now be present in the midst of tragic events, not in detached and significant contrast only, but intimately associated, not only as parts of the plot, but as indispensable constituents of the total mood.   Some of his contemporaries (Chapman, for example, and Ben Jonson) [1] demonstrate in alternate plays their capacity for tragic and for comic work. Some, the tragi-comedy writers, Fletcher, Beaumont and Massinger (occasionally also Chapman), blend the comic with the near-tragic so closely that though ' it wants deaths, 'which is enough to make it no tragedy, yet it brings some near it, which is enough to make it no comedy '.[2]   But Middleton's process, like Shakespeare's, goes as far beyond the second as the second goes beyond the first.   He shows the sternest tragic issues intimately blended with comic ones, with characters that are themselves hardly capable of tragic passion, that yet play an indispensable part, not only in the direct disposal of events, but indirectly through their effect upon the central characters, and contribute vitally to the colouring of the final impression.   The countryman who brings the asps to Cleopatra, the porter of Macbeth's castle, Emilia in *Othello*, the grave-diggers and Osric in *Hamlet*, not only come from a comic world, but bring it with them, unsubdued, when they enter tragedy and modify thereby the mood, the conduct, even, it may be, the very nature of the tragic figures.   This principle of extending and modifying tragedy by the intimate association of comedy, Middleton carried, I think, perhaps further than Shakespeare.   For in Middleton's tragedies, the levelling effect of the one mood upon the other goes so far as to obscure the tragic effect at first glance. The constant, not the occasional, presence of the coarse, the impercipient, the shallow and the callous renders the whole more cynical, diminishes, not the sufferings of the main figures, but

[1] It must be admitted that Ben Jonson once, at least, introduced both into one play, in the excellent comic scenes in the first two acts of *Catiline*. But he himself has disavowed these scenes and poured contempt on the audience that appreciated them too highly.   He can, therefore, hardly be credited with perceiving, like Middleton, the innate union of the tragic and the comic in human circumstance. (See prefatory note to *Catiline*, ' To the Reader in Ordinary '.)

[2] Fletcher, *Address to the Reader*, prefixed to first ed. *Faithful Shepherdess*, 1609.

the dignity of the sufferings. Had *Troilus and Cressida* been focussed upon the death of the two lovers it would have achieved something like the balance of tragic and comic mood in Middleton, though not, even so, Middleton's synthesis. The significant thing is that, even had it been so altered, Thersites' summary would still be valid : ' All the argument is a cuckold and a whore.' A grey light results from this even balancing of tragic and comic ; the colours subdue each other and the mood is neither heroic nor genial, pathetic nor gay, but something in which each impulse strives with its opposite and comes to equilibrium in frustrated denial. But the resulting atmosphere has a stillness and clarity in which we see with startling sharpness the details of the processes at work upon the minds.

This appears clearly in the only tragedy of his sole workmanship, *Women Beware Women*, and hardly less clearly in his and Rowley's joint work, *The Changeling*, and we touch it in the serious elements of *The Witch*, *A Fair Quarrel* and *The Spanish Gipsey*. In *Women Beware Women* much of the tragic effect is derived from the relating of the tragic action with a figure as broadly based and as surely drawn as anything in his best comic work. The character of Livia, as original in conception as that of the Roaring Girl and of far more mature and economical workmanship, plays in the first half of the play a part such as even Shakespeare would hardly have given her in tragedy. Her astuteness and her impercipience, her bluff comradely affection for her brother and her accompanying coarse moral obliquity, her level-headed business sense and her equally business-like sensuality are just such a blend of qualities as make us exclaim at sight upon the truth of the portrait. We might have met her in Augustan Rome or modern London. But it is a genius of liberal comprehension which can set such a character at the centre of Bianca's tragedy, can not only make her the agent of the younger woman's seduction but make these very qualities in her an enveloping atmosphere which infects with moral perversion (from which she herself is free) a nature at once finer and more capable of degradation than herself. This is a true and intimate blending of the tragic and the comic elements of both of which Middleton was master, a perception of the complex interplay of environment on character like those which gave Emilia to Desdemona for counsellor and companion or Pandare to Crisseyde.

Fabricio. Th'art a sweet Lady, Sister, and a witty—
Livia.   A witty ! Oh the bud of commendation
             Fit for a Girl of sixteen ; I am blown, man,
             I should be wise by this time ; and for instance,
             I have buried my two husbands in good fashion,
             And never mean more to marry . . .
             Because the third shall never bury me :
             I think I'm more then witty ; how think you Sir ?
Fabricio. I have paid often fees to a Counsellor
             Has had a weaker brain.[1]

In the next act the two worlds meet, not only in the juxtaposition of events, but in simultaneous production of the two
parts of the action on the stage. Livia holds Bianca's guardian
in play at a game of chess on the stage below, while above (and
conventionally out of earshot) Bianca struggles with her seducer
the Duke to whom she has been betrayed by Livia's contrivance :

Bianca.   . . . great lord,
             Make me not bold with death and deeds of ruine,
             Because they fear not you ; me they must fright ;
             Then am I best in health : Should thunder speak,
             And none regard it, it had lost the name,
             And were as good be still. I'm not like those
             That take their soundest sleeps in greatest tempests,
             Then wake I most, the weather fearfullest,
             And call for strength to vertue

                .   .   .   .   .   .

Livia.   Did not I say my Duke [2] would fetch you over (Widow) ?
Mother. I think you spoke in earnest when you said it (Madam).
Livia.   And my black King makes all the haste he can too.
Mother. Well (Madam) we may meet with him in time yet.
Livia.   I have given thee blinde mate twice.[3]

---

[1] I, ii, 46–56.

[2] The Jacobeans generally (and Middleton consistently) use the term
' duke ' where modern chess-players use ' castle ' or ' rook ' (cf. *Game
at Chess, Induction,* 54 : ' Dukes ? They are called rooks by some ').

[3] The introduction of the terminology of a game which carries
simultaneously its own and a secondary significance, occurs at intervals
through at least English literature and several times in Jacobean drama.
But Middleton's political play *A Game at Chess* (of which this scene
appears to be the germ) is, I think, unique in English drama as a
sustained dramatic allegory in terms of a game. One, moreover, in
which (as in *Alice Through the Looking Glass*) the author contrives a
plot which is at once both a description of a reasonably probable game
and a consistent narrative or dramatic story. (Though how an expert
would regard the running conversation that goes on between Middleton's
players, I dare not contemplate.)

Mother. You may see (Madam)
         My eyes begin to fail.
Livia. I'll swear they do, Wench.

    .   .   .   .   .   .

Livia. The game's ev'n at the best now ; you may see Widow
         How all things draw to an end. . . .
         Has not my Duke bestir'd himself ?
Mother. Yes faith Madam ;
         H'as done me all the mischief in this Game.
Livia. H'as shew'd himself in's kinde.[1]

In what follows Middleton shows that knowledge of the hardening of the spirit under certain forms of shock or misery that is his peculiar province in tragedy and that Ford after him shows also in his treatment of Giovanni (though he develops it to rather different ends, in all his subsequent plays). Middleton in the *Changeling* and in *Women Beware Women* (and, to the extent at least of the figure of Francisca, in *The Witch*) reveals in some three or four unforgettable studies the process by which a nature may be dislocated by a sudden jar or shock of evil fate or contaminated and poisoned by a slow chemical process of infiltration. Leantio, Bianca and Francisca are cases of the first and Beatrice of the second. In every case there is enough indication that the nature is drawn on a generous scale ; it is the promise of a fine flowering that is destroyed. Middleton seems to have grasped the principle (as did few of his contemporaries) that the more generously a nature is endowed, especially perhaps a woman's, the more bitter is its corruption if it is thwarted or maimed in the full course of its development. Not that he cannot imagine also those more placid and limited beings who accept with patience the cutting off of their natural mode of expression.[2] But he knew as only Shakespeare else, and studied at a length which Shakespeare never attempted, the destruction of a nature by the simple process of administering the shock or poison of fate and leaving it to work out its own disintegration.

Bianca.   . . . I saw that now,
         Fearful for any womans eye to look on :
         Infectious mists, and milldews hang at's eyes :

---

[1] II, ii, 355–422 *passim*.
[2] And he has drawn them as exquisitely, again, as Chaucer, in Jane (*A Fair Quarrel*) and Clara—if she be his (*The Spanish Gipsey*). Their situations, it may be observed, roughly duplicate those of Francisca (or Beatrice) and Bianca respectively.

> The weather of a doomsday dwells upon him . . .
>   . . . I'm made bold now,
> I thank thy treachery ; sin and I'm acquainted,
> No couple greater. . . .

[After a few more sentences Bianca rejoins Livia and her mother-in-law, who, in a preoccupied way (being still mainly interested in her chess-board), asks whether she has enjoyed the pictures in the gallery she has been shown.]

Bianca.   . . . I'm so beholding
> To this kinde, honest, curteous Gentleman,
> You'ld little think it (Mother) show'd me all,
> Had me from place to place, so fashionably ;
> The kindness of some people, how't exceeds ?
> 'Faith, I have seen that I little thought to see,
> I' th' morning when I rose.[1]

The rest of the play is a lucid but rapid exposition of the descent of both characters, Leantio and Bianca. In the quick action of a five-act play the contrast is sharpened bitterly between the opening scene and the final clash between husband and wife in the beginning of the fourth act. The same experiment is applied to both and both follow the same broad lines of reaction. Bianca passes from a still, brooding, almost an enchanted meekness of devotion, through the shock of her betrayal, into an awakening which (as Middleton indicates also in *The Changeling*), though more accurately aware of the actual world, may be less clear-sighted in ultimate reality, and is certainly less happy. Her love for the Duke redeems her at the end, but the taunts she gives the husband she has cuckolded almost take us unawares unless we have followed closely the hardening and coarsening of her spirit. Leantio follows a similar course, from the blind, intoxicated devotion of the first act, a mood that hints disaster in the breathlessness of its passion, to the shock of Livia's proof that his idol is a whore.

> As if a punishment of after-life
> Were faln upon man here ; so new it is
> To flesh and blood, so strange, so insupportable.[2]

When the shock has passed it is an easy step to the cynical acceptance of Livia's patronage and the flaunting in Bianca's face of a prosperity as great as her similar relation with the Duke has brought to her. The sureness of Middleton's touch on Leantio's mood here is beyond comment ; it is a mixture of

[1] II, ii, 425–62 *passim.*   [2] III, ii, 246–8.

lingering passion, jealousy and the flaunting vanity with which Leantio tries to cover the simultaneous injuries to his affection, to his manhood and to his self-esteem :

> there read,
> Vex, gnaw, thou shalt finde there I am not love-starv'd.
> The world was never yet so cold, or pitiless,
> But there was ever still more charity found out,
> Than at one proud fools door ; and 'twere hard 'faith,
> If I could not pass that : Read to thy shame there ;
> A cheerful and a beauteous Benefactor too,
> As ev'r erected the good works of love.[1]

It is, finally, essential to the mood of this play that irony, a sense of the bitter repercussions of event, of the fantastic hypocrisy of society's pretensions and the rotten absurdity of its codes, should run through the commentary, touched in at intervals by a single line or phrase or by the relation of scene and scene. Hippolito, whom she knows to be guilty of incest, presents himself before Livia, having killed her lover in redemption of her honour. To his amazement, the sound common sense of Livia will have none of this prattle of honour nor listen to his excellent reasons. ' The reason ! ' she cries. ' That's a jest hell falls a-laughing at ! ' The later ' jests ' of Middleton, particularly those deep, underlying tricks of fortune that tangle the blind agents and bring their spirits to disintegration, are indeed such—the jests ' hell falls a-laughing at '. Certainly, in these later plays, the reader feels no temptation to join the laughter.

The Changeling, although this is joint work with Rowley, has something of the same balance of qualities and a corresponding central theme. The avowedly comic sub-plot could, as with the plays of Ford a little later, be detached without much damage and the resulting tragedy would stand as one of the most compact and pitiless in this drama. The tragic material of Middleton contains, unlike that of Marston and Tourneur, elements of great beauty and the subsequent action, unlike that of Webster, Shakespeare or Ford, disintegrates these elements by the spiritual evil set at work within them.[2] The first scene of

[1] IV, i, 66–73.
[2] The likeness between the themes of *Macbeth* and *The Changeling* is often noted. But *Macbeth* is the only play in which Shakespeare makes a study of spiritual degeneration in any degree similar to Middleton's.

The Changeling sets the atmosphere and defines the nature of the beauty which is in hazard, a beauty of a kind which is indicated in slighter or greater degree in nearly all his later plays, *A Fair Quarrel*, *The Spanish Gipsey*, *The Witch*, *The Game at Chess*. Alsemero, coming out of the temple in which he has seen Beatrice, fittingly defines it in his first speech, and suggests at the same time, the sense, equally essential to Middleton's tragic characters, of ' the unwar wo or harm that comth bihinde ' :

Als. Twas in the Temple where I first beheld her,
    And now agen the same, what *Omen* yet
    Follows of that ? none but imaginary,
    Why should my hopes or fate be timerous ?
    The place is holy, so is my intent :
    I love her beauties to the holy purpose,
    And that (methinks) admits comparison
    With man's first creation, the place blest
    And is his right home back (if he atchieve it).[1]

From this point the play plunges headlong to its action : Beatrice's equally instantaneous love for Alsemero, her father's insistence on the marriage with Alonzo, her insane alliance with the hated De Flores in order to break out of the net and her entanglement in an association far more fatal alike to her fortunes and to her spirit. Middleton wastes no time, as indeed he could not, having so vast a track of experience to cover. His power over plain, brief statements, the records of swiftly succeeding phases of experience and perception, is never more continuously revealed than in Beatrice's speeches throughout the play :

           . . . For five dayes past
    To be recal'd ; sure, mine eyes were mistaken,
    This was the man was meant me, that he should come
    So neer his time, and miss it.[2]

Slowly this sense of contaminated beauty thickens the atmosphere [3] and at the same time, by swiftly moving indications, the

----

[1] I, i, 1–9.   [2] I, i, 85–8.

[3] The frustration of happiness which is the outward form of the contamination of the principle of beauty in this play is, at first glance, like that which besieges the characters in *A Broken Heart*. But suffering in Ford's plays ennobles and matures the mind, in Middleton's it, as often as not, degrades it.

10

mind of the reader is drawn unconsciously to focus on Beatrice
and De Flores, bringing them together in ominous isolation
before the second act is over :

Beatrice. I never see this fellow, but I think
        Of some harm towards me, danger's in my mind still ?
        . . . The next good mood I find my father in,
        I'le get him quite discarded : [1]

And in the course of the next scene the acceleration is completed.
It opens with a brief passage between her and Alsemero where
she passes from mournful regret that Alonso stands between
them, to horror at his offer to challenge him, from that to a half-
unconscious acknowledgement that Alonso's removal is indeed
what she desires, from that again to a sudden realization that
De Flores' proffered service can well be used for this purpose.
It is in the very suddenness of these snipe-like darts of her mind
that Middleton reveals its weakness.   Beatrice has a process of
thought like that of Othello, whose judgements are rather pictures
suddenly presented to it and, once presented, blocking out all
other views.   She rebukes Alsemero for offering to venture his
own life and then, aside :

            Here was a course
    Found to bring sorrow on her way to death ;
    The tears would ne're a dried, till dust had choak'd 'em.
    Blood-guiltiness becomes a fouler visage—
    And now I think on one. I was too blame,
    I ha mar'd so good a market with my scorn :
    'T had been done, questionless. The ugliest creature
    Creation fram'd for some use. . . .
    Why, men of Art make much of poyson ;
    Keep one to expell another ; where was my Art ? [2]

It is the ' art ' of a clever child that has learnt a rule out of a book
and the pert self-satisfaction is a child's too.   When De Flores
enters she is still a child playing with a complicated machine of
whose mechanism or capacities she knows nothing, concerned
only to release the catch that will start it working and delighted
when, in accordance with the text-book's instructions, it begins
to move.   Only when De Flores speaks do we realize that she is

---

[1] II, i 89–92.
[2] I have punctuated this speech in accordance with modern convention to indicate clearly the content.

not a child, but a woman sleep-walking. Without a sign of
realizing what she is doing, she accepts his offer to kill Alonzo.
His most sharply-pointed references to his reward slip past her
consciousness, serving only to measure the depth of her sleep.
Indeed, in De Flores himself, the delirium of love (as in his
earlier dialogue, II, i) invests his figure too with the movements
of a sleep-walker so that he believes he can read her mind and
prophesy its capitulation.   And so both figures move through
the scene, she without sense of the reality about her or within
her, he crippled by his blindness to her nature and to her
unawareness.

From this the main action moves swiftly to the next meeting
after the murder has been done, prefixed only by the brief
speech of terrible irony in which Beatrice's love for Alsemero
builds happily on the assumption of Alonzo's death.   There is
an essential innocence in this ; the quality of her limitation is to
realize nothing that is not pictured in her mind.   The moment
De Flores shows her the dead man's finger she sees the murder
as an actual thing.   From that moment uneasiness stirs her.
The sinister undertones of De Flores' speeches as they skirt the
question of reward for his deed are not clear to her as they are
to the audience, but she knows her danger subconsciously
before she can define it :

> I'me in a labyrinth,
> What will content him ? would I fain be rid of him.
> I'le double the sum, sir.[1]

It is in vain that she attempts to persuade herself that if she does
not see, hear, remember or admit it, it will virtually cease to
exist (and how profound is Middleton's knowledge of this kind
of woman) ; De Flores pushes her resolutely to the realization
from which her life of a spoilt child has hitherto shielded her.
From this point onward every line of De Flores is an immovable
logical statement, each statement revealing a merciless fact in
that world of reality she has wandered into, sleep-walking.
Every line in her part is now the simple utterance of reality ;
the plain speech that is all a swiftly travelling mind can spare
for recording the landmarks in its new and changing observation.
The lines themselves harden and grow metallic as the strokes
of logic harden her mind.

[1] III, iv, 73-5

Beatrice. Why 'tis impossible thou canst be so wicked,
          To make his death the murderer of my honor.
          Thy language is so bold and vitious,
          I cannot see which way I can forgive it
          With any modesty.
De F.   Push, you forget yourselfe,
          A woman dipt in blood, and talk of modesty.
Beatrice. O misery of sin ! would I had been bound
          Perpetually unto my living hate
          In that *Piracquo*, then to hear these words.
          Think but upon the distance that Creation
          Set 'twixt thy blood and mine, and keep thee there.
De F.   Look but into your conscience, read me there,
          'Tis a true Book, you'l find me there your equall :
          Push, flye not to your birth, but settle you
          In what the act has made you, y'are no more now,
          You must forget your parentage to me,
          Y' are the deeds creature, by that name
          You lost your first condition, and I challenge you,
          As peace and innocency has turn'd you out,
          And made you one with me.[1]

' Settle you in what the act has made you. . . . You are the deed's creature.' It is the business of the rest of the play to show the stages by which her hold upon Alsemero and a life of sane happiness is prized away by her complicity with De Flores and its series of unforeseen but inevitable consequences. Step by step she is driven further from Alsemero and identified more and more completely with De Flores, who becomes ' a wondrous necessary man '. In the central scene (III, iv) Middleton has carried Beatrice, as he does Bianca in the corresponding scenes of *Women Beware Women*, from ignorance to experience, from a romantic sleep-walking to an awakening in the midst of horrors. The poison that she had used ' to expel another ' has proved too strong for her ' art ', which proves in its turn to be no art at all, but the dream of a precocious child. Between the pert cleverness of those early lines and the end of this scene a world of reality has intervened and the experience of years has been lived through with a rapidity that leaves the mind stupid, terrified and a prey to its own guilt :

Beatrice. Let me go poor unto my bed with honor,
          And I am rich in all things . .
De Flores Can you weep Fate from its determin'd purpose ?
          So soon may [you] weep me.[2]

---

[1] III, iv, 121–41.   [2] III, iv, 157–63.

She does not see to the end at once and, indeed, until the end, fights with tenacity and strategy to save something of her happiness. Her mind has toughened. Even in becoming coarser in fibre it has become more enduring, more energetic. Only as she moves step by step among the events her deeds have raised does she realize their control and only at the end does she perceive something of their effect upon her :

> Beneath the starres, upon yon Meteor
> Ever hung my fate, 'mongst things corruptible,
> I ne're could pluck it from him, my loathing,
> Was Prophet to the rest, but ne're belev'd. . . .[1]

From the direction inevitably taken by these analyses it will be seen that Middleton's capacity for tragedy is inseparable from his other supreme gift, his discernment of the minds of women ; in this no dramatist of the period except Shakespeare is his equal at once for variety and for penetration. Webster is sure in his intuition within a narrow range of tragic types, Isabella and the Duchess, Vittoria, Julia and Leonora ; Tourneur with a still more limited range of a different kind, the Gratianas and Levidulcias of a corrupt society. Ford, his equal in penetration, chooses, but for Annabelle, one clearly defined group, the gracious, reticent, high aristocracy of a Calanthe, a Penthea, a Cleophila, a Spinella ; Marston is happy with his Dutch courtesan and her like, Ben Jonson with his pretentious citizens and his Dolls, Dekker with Margery Eyre, with the meek, patient Grissills and the converted Bellafrontes. Middleton alone, outside Shakespeare, moves equally among all these and more.[2]

---

[1] V, iii, 157-60.

[2] We may consider only a few, and those the most individual of fifty-odd studies in the plays. In the comic types, more frequent in the early plays but running up also into the later ones, are the excellent studies of citizens' wives, some virtuous, some less so, some frank, some hypocritical, but all busy and active, often the domineering wives of henpecked husbands or the unfaithful ones of deserving cuckolds : Mistress Lucre, Mistresses Glister and Purge, the Jeweller's Wife (in *A Trick to Catch the Old One*, *The Family of Love*, *The Phoenix*), the unforgettable Maudlin of the *Chaste Maid* and the equally unforgettable Mistress Gallipot of *The Roaring Girl*, Mrs. Allwit, chiefly remarkable for the company at her christening feast, Mrs. Knavesby with her pretty turn of spirited intrigue, that excellently balanced pair Livia and the Mother of Leantio. Of the same kind of character, chiefly belonging to the early plays, are four studies of courtesans as vivid as

It is perhaps again to his early training in comedy, his training, that is, in unprejudiced and open-eyed observation, that we may attribute both the range and the penetration of these studies. Had he begun work in romance, in tragi-comedy or in tragedy, it is likely that he might have made from the start assumptions which would have ruinously limited his range. But his freedom from the romantic, the sentimental or the heroic mood left him, undazzled, to the use of his own good sense. And an active use he made of it. He is one of the few writers of Jacobean comedy who is not so obsessed by the differences between the sexes as to be unable to see the likenesses. He is well aware of the exist-ence of whores and bawds—no one better—and his understand-ing of the peculiar turns that that life is liable to give to the temperament and the nerves is as precise as Dekker's or Mar-ston's. But he can see simultaneously the fierce, active vir-ginity in a character like Moll, the Roaring Girl, and can draw it clearly, in all its individuality and its significance, with-out scoffing at it as a pretence or a fantasy. He can draw in

Marston's, as sympathetically handled as Dekker's, but drawn with a detachment free alike of Dekker's poignancy and of Dekker's senti-ment, the Novice of the *Five Gallants*, the Country Wench of *The Michaelmas Term*, the good-hearted and spirited Imperia of *Blurt* and the delicious comedy figure of Gullman in *A Mad World*. Broad and strong as is the natural humanity of all these comic figures, there is as much of strength and perhaps more of originality in the figures which, though they are set in comedy or tragi-comedy, lie a little off the beaten track of Jacobean material, Lady Ager of *A Fair Quarrel*, who like so many more of the figures in that play, almost anticipates Steele, Valeria of *The Widow*, Thomasine who so determinedly rescues her future from her present husband in *The Michaelmas Term*, and Moll of *The Roaring Girl* with the masculine spirit of Webster's Vittoria, the vocabulary of a courtesan and the virginity and chivalry of Belphoebe. More sensitively drawn, but amply suggested, are the White Queen's Pawn in *A Game at Chess* and the subsidiary figures of *A Fair Quarrel*, Jane and the still more slightly touched-in sketches of Anne and the Colonel's sister. Finally, and nearly all in the later plays, come the great tragic or potentially tragic figures where Middleton's power is at its height : Francisca of *The Witch*, Clara of *The Spanish Gipsey*, Isabella and Bianca of *Women Beware Women* and Beatrice of *The Changeling*. This is a list of little more than two dozen characters but it ranges from the Dickensenian breadth of the gossips of Cheapside and courtesans of Pickthatch to the gracious dignity of the figures in *A Fair Quarrel* or the still reticence of Clara in *The Spanish Gipsey*, covering in doing so women of all ages and a wide range of class.

Clara [1] what is perhaps the most difficult of all studies.   Her nature, one of quiet and gracious dignity, is shocked into sudden development by Roderigo's rape.   There is first an overwhelmed stillness, then gravity that slowly steadies to an open-eyed sense of the practical situation, then the nature grows rapidly deeper and more compact as the effect of the catastrophe takes hold of it. We are upon the verge of one of those implacable pursuits of vengeance so frequent in this drama, when Middleton, taking us utterly by surprise and yet as utterly convincing us, by a modulation at once daring and yet just in every line, draws the gradual awakening of her love for Roderigo.   But beside this character he can draw with equal understanding the frank, free bonhomie of Livia, her easy morals, her coarse, merry tongue and her good-fellowship.   It is the simultaneousness of range and penetration that constitutes the virtue of Middleton's understanding of women's minds.   For each inevitably contributes to the other. In just the same way the interplay of tragedy and comedy makes the chief excellence of his work as a whole.   In comedy he early developed the ironic detachment which only a potential tragic sense can give, and into tragedy he carried the habit of clear, single-minded observation learnt during almost a lifetime's practice in naturalistic comedy.   No mist of sentiment confuses the delicate outlines in which he sparingly defines the processes by which a mind gropes, discovers, recoils from and is engulfed in the events with which it has entangled itself.   No rush of passionate identification of himself with its fate drives athwart his judgement or opens up vistas of perception into worlds beyond normal experience.   All his concern is with its experience in contact with a present actuality, and however deep or however rare be that experience he finds in it nothing which passes comprehension, never resigns into the hands of a circumambient mystery that soul upon which he has focussed so steady and so dry a light.   His sight is clear, his draughtsmanship of a fineness and rapidity that can cover in a single scene the growth that would seem to ask a whole play for its delineation. In these superlative scenes he, like his successor and pupil Ford, writes without faltering and without flaw ; each speech

[1] In spite of a growing conviction that Ford learnt much from Middleton, I am not yet prepared to see in this study more than Ford's hand alongside Middleton's.   I find it hard as yet to resign this character entire to Ford.   (But see H. Dugdale Sykes, *Sidelights*. . . .   1924.)

and often each sentence is the imperishable record of a stage in that progress which he is following step by step. What results is as clear of pathos as it is of colour or incidental poetry. It terrifies by the scientific clarity with which it reveals the operation of natural laws about the inevitable destruction of those who unawares have broken them. It stirs what is perhaps pity (lying, if so, too deep for instant or immediate expression), but what is left at the end is above all else the sense of passionless and ineluctable law, smooth, unhurried, lucid in its processes, dwarfing the men it overwhelms to something below the status of tragedy as they are dwarfed by those other great operations of nature, flood and earthquake and pestilence. We attend, as we rarely do in Jacobean drama, the destruction of a soul, not the gigantic triumph of the human spirit in uttermost physical catastrophe. No one in these plays cries ' I am Duchess of Malfi still '. No one speaks over the dead or dying those tributes which Shakespeare, Webster, Ford put in the mouths of the bystanders, often even of the very foes who have destroyed them. Their lives are indeed ' a black charnel ' but they do not redeem themselves in death ; their deaths are of a piece with their lives and become them no better. It is in this pitiless abstemiousness that Middleton stands alone in Jacobean tragedy, suggesting again and again to the reader of a later age that here was in germ the Ibsen of the seventeenth century. Faithful to his observation and to the record of underlying psychological laws which it revealed to him, he is untouched by the heroic, the romantic and the pathetic mood, to the very belittling of those human figures which his contemporaries, even to Ben Jonson himself in tragedy, exalt.

CHAPTER VIII

CYRIL TOURNEUR

I

THE work of Cyril Tourneur presents one extreme of early Jacobean tragic thought and presents it with a completeness and single-mindedness else only to be found in the deliberate self-absorption of much of the comedy in the evidence of the world about it. Like the middle comedy of Middleton and much of Ben Jonson, Tourneur excludes in his first play specific or implicit reference to that universe of the spirit to which Chapman and Webster in their different ways give positive or negative testimony, and in his later play the references are perfunctory and unconvincing. He, alone among the dramatists who seem to have brought to this problem clear and coherently conscious thought, appears to accept a world-order inherently evil. He alone among the tragic writers of the first decades seems untroubled by the sense of the conflict of two worlds, of the confounding knowledge with knowledge ; he accepts, if not the evidence of the world immediately around him, a consistent body of evidence from within his own imagination which gives to his plays a unity of mood absent from those of his contemporaries. He offers thus what is in fact a universe and since his interpretation is tragic, it is a universe of evil that he reveals. This is his peculiar contribution to the various but related conceptions of the major dramatists. His detachment from his characters is nearly as complete as Middleton's in tragedy, but they are produced upon a background of horror and evil fraught with emotional implications from which Middleton's are free. Beside the tragic uncertainty of Webster, on the other hand, who resembles him often in theme and choice of material, his definite affirmation of evil stands inflexible and positive.

Tourneur anatomizes minds. They are specimens that come into his laboratory. On the whole he analyses well and the resulting dissections and articulated skeletons tell us much of what is inside the man. There is far more scientific exposition, far clearer description of the parts and their relations than in the pictures of living people that Webster draws. But the difference is that Tourneur's do not live. He does not enter them and speak from within them. He draws them all (except Sebastian) by inspection from outside. They are laboratory specimens. He does not love them or sympathize with them. Nor do we.

How is it then that we have the effect of tragedy at all in these plays—or have we indeed that effect and not, instead, something approximating to it, imitating it and imposing itself on us for tragedy? Webster has a sense of tragic issues. Some at least of his characters—all the chief ones—he enters. He speaks from within them. Only the less significant remain unanimated, a record merely of observed characteristics. Many of them he loves, admires ; certain of their qualities—their resolution and dauntless bearing—move him and us through him to wonder, upon which the ineluctable fate imposes the mood of pity. Man, at war with a fate less noble than he, rouses, in Webster's plays, pity and admiration which become at moments pity and fear. There is a tragic system, if only by means of the implicit commentary on man and his fate. But with Tourneur there is no pity and, I think, no sympathy for his strange anatomies, either from us or from the author. A kind of comment there may be, but it is shrouded. What there is, especially in the *Revenger's Tragedy*, where he conducts himself more nearly in conformity with ordinary dramatic usage, is horror. This, strictly speaking, is the only emotion roused. Much interest we may experience, much speculation, much keen following up of thought, but the only emotion we are subjected to is horror and that comes to us, not from our entry into the characters' experiences but from extraneous aids, not from identifying ourselves with apparently living people, but from two things, one of them the very opposite of this ; from the aroma of evil with which Tourneur by the aid of diction and verbal music surrounds these walking anatomies, these galvanized laboratory subjects, and from the very fact that, being dead, they do so adequately mimic life. There is a hideousness (and its effect grows upon us as the play progresses) in the very separation of our observation from the emotions that should accompany it, in watching this simulacrum of experience where there is no experience. That absence of sympathy in

Ben Jonson which hinders sometimes the full experience of comic emotion in his reader and gives us a sense of detachment and so eventually of unreality is met and combated in Tourneur's work by the deep sense of horror implicit in the very circumstance of being.   And, paradoxically, when once that has got to work, it is only enhanced by the unnatural absence of normal human feelings.   It is not in fact tragedy which Tourneur offers us, but something which, by presenting a deeply inhering fear and by the lifelike movements of these figures so devoid of life, blinds us momentarily to the absence of the equally essential tragic pity which the approach to character by way of inspection can never give to us.   Tourneur, thus excluding from his mind and ours pity and that part of normal tragic fear which is sympathy, leaves us face to face with a form of horror that is in tragedy the logical inference from a universe denuded of spiritual significance.   It is Tourneur's peculiar function to accept single-mindedly this denuding and its implications where the other dramatists hesitate, confounding knowledge with knowledge.

II

To find a world vibrant with imaginative horror as was Tourneur's we must fetch a wide compass and shall not even so find it easily.   It swings between the tingling dread of Edgar Allan Poe or Ambrose Bierce and the 'implacable dejection' of James Thomson.   We have entered indeed a 'City of Dreadful Night', and if we pass beyond its bounds it is into that world where Hamlet dwelt for a time, 'a sterile and barren promontory', 'a pestilent congregation of vapours', where the 'intellectual tapers' are 'fed with Hell's flame' and the poet himself knows that the agony of his mind 'Doth make his gesture seem a troubled story':

> Ev'n from the artique to the antartique pole,
> All in a rowe in ranke proportionate;
> Subject unto th' unstedfast moones controle
> Do stand the lights that should truth animate;[1] . . .

It is indeed a universe upon which Mutabilitie has seized and in his earliest poems we find Tourneur still struggling in vain to compose it again with the 'Stedfast rest of all things firmely

[1] *The Transformed Metamorphosis*, stanzas 16, 42 and 44.

stayd upon the pillours of Eternity '.   For the ultimate guardian
of this universe is not for him, as for Spenser, ' Great goddesse,
great Dame *Nature* ', but a strange anticipation of a Nature more
like De Sade's, a ravening and dominating force, destroying and
urging on the destroyer.   Indeed, it is with De Sade and his
successors, particularly his later successors, the followers of
Baudelaire, that we next breathe the atmosphere of the *Revenger's
Tragedy* (an atmosphere which is hardly dissipated when it is
rationalized in the *Atheist's Tragedy*).   There is a metallic
quality, the acrid taste of brass, in this atmosphere ; the very
thoughts and words of the people have about them the clang of
a brazen gong and the light by which we see them comes from
a sky that is itself a brazen disk.   Like Satan in *La Révolte des
Anges* the author seems to wake into a world of shades.   ' Et
quand j'eus accoutumé mes yeux a l'ombre épaisse, j'aperçus
autour de moi mes compagnons d'armes gisant par milliers sur
le sol solfureux, où passaient des lueurs livides.   Mes yeux ne
découvraient que solfatures, cratères fumants, palus empoisonnés
. . . un ciel d'airain pesait sur nos fronts.' . . .   ' Un ciel
d'airain ', ' les compagnons d'armes gisant . . . sur le sol
solfureux ' ;   there we have the setting of Tourneur's drama.

It is by the great scenes of this kind in his two plays that we
at first remember him ;   Vindice waiting with the skull of his
mistress in the dark hunting lodge for the Duke her murderer ;
Lussurioso after his attempt on Vindice's sister unwittingly
swearing him to the performance of the very vengeance he seeks ;
D'Amville, his brain staggering under the sudden realization of
his crimes, repeating in an agony of fear and repentance the
very imagery in which he had earlier proclaimed his criminal
exultation ;   D'Amville again, in the last moment of his life,
searching feveredly for the Cause that can supersede the law of
that Nature he has hitherto worshipped.[1]

Vindice with his mistress's skull hardly recalls at all those
prototypes of his, Hamlet in the grave-yard, Hippolito of the
Honest Whore with his easily forgotten ritual,[2] for the scene
is no longer, as in these plays, a relief between two periods of

---

[1] *Revengers Tragedie*, III, v, and IV, ii.   *Atheists Tragedie*, IV, iii,
and V, ii.

[2] *Honest Whore*, Part I, IV, i.   Still less is it aesthetically related
to the opening of Chettle's *Hoffman's Tragedy*, which else it resembles
closely.

stress, but is itself the climax of the action, the skull the veritable reminder of deaths past and to come, and both deed and setting have a terrible economy and relevance. It is no longer an expression of the irrelevant arabesques of Hamlet's melancholy, but the concentrated and ironic malice of a mind which, if it were once melancholy, is now compact of action, formed all of an insane and fiendish purpose :

(*Enter* VINDICE, *with the skull of his love dresst up in Tires*.) [Vindice and his brother are waiting in the Lodge in the park for the Duke, the murderer of his betrothed, who has appointed that place for an assignation with a lady Vindice has promised him.]

Vin.   Madame, [speaking to the decorated skull] his grace will not be absent long.
      Secret ? nere doubt us, Madame ; twill be worth
      Three velvet gownes to your Ladyship—knowne !
      Few Ladies respect that—disgrace ?
      Ile save your hand that laboure Ile unmaske you.
Hip. Why, brother, brother
Vin.   Art thou beguild now ? . . . Here's an eye,
      Able to tempt a great man—to serve God,
      A prety hanging lip, that has forgot now to dissemble ;
      Heres a cheeke keepes her colour ; let the winde go whistle . . .
      Spout, Raine, we feare thee not, be hot or cold
      Alls one with us . . .
      Who now bids twenty pound a night, prepares
      Musick, perfumes, and sweete-meates ? All are husht.
      Thou maist lie chast now . . . See Ladies, with false formes
      You deceive men, but cannot deceive wormes.[1]

This has the right Thyestean ring, perhaps the only scene in Jacobean drama that is true kin to Seneca's own supreme imaginative achievement. Yet it is at the same time more than this, for the economy, the irony, raise it beyond Seneca's range into momentary comparison with those same qualities in *Oedipus Tyrannus*.

Vindice poisons the lips of the skull and draws on the mask again. ' Hide thy face now for shame ; thou hads't need have a mask now '—one of those jests which hold the essential flavour of Tourneur's mind, jests which, if we gather into recollection all that has preceded this in the play and before the opening scene of the action, are seen to be instinct with an insane horror, ushering the play in triumph to its fit climax. The Duke enters and all is ready.

[1] *R.T.* (ed. Nicoll), III, v, 46 seq., *passim*.

Vin.   Brother, fall you back a little
         With the bony Lady.

             .   .   .   .   .

Duke.   *Piato*, well done ; hast brought her, what Lady ist ?
Vin.   Faith, my Lord, a Country Lady, a little bashfull at first, as
          most of them are, but after the first kisse my Lord the worst is
          past with them, your grace knowes now what you have to doe ;
          sha's somewhat a grave looke with her—but——

Sophocles need not have been ashamed of this, one of the
moments when the pun, in its apotheosis, becomes no longer
the misplaced frivolity that Jonson so misliked in Shakespeare,
but, rather, the charged receptacle of bitter and terrifying irony.
The same quality runs through the scene where Lussurioso
unknowingly swears his own murderer to the performance of
vengeance, Machiavellian outwitted by Machiavellian :

Lus.   . . . The ingreatfull villayne,

   [The ' villain ' had been VINDICE spying upon him in disguise and
    the episode quite other than his description. But LUSSURIOSO
    had not realized this.]

          To quit that kindnes, strongly wrought with me . . .
          With jewels to corrupt your virgin sister.
Hip.   O villaine.
Vin.   *He shall surely die that did it.*
Lus.   I far from thinking any Virgin harme,
              . . . would not endure him.
Vin.   *Would you not my Lord?*
          Twas wondrous honorably donne.

             .   .   .   .   .

Lus.   Thy name, I have forgot it ?
Vin.   VINDICE, *my Lord.*
Lus.   Tis a good name that.
Vin.   *I, a Revenger.*
Lus.   It dos betoken courage, thou shouldst be valiant,
          And kill thine enemies.
Vin.   *That's my hope, my Lord.*[1]

Where the irony of Sophocles derives in part at least from the
motionless indifference of fate, Tourneur's has a restless,
mordant quality deriving from the infusion of implacable and
purposed malice.

   The *Atheist's Tragedy* is a later comment upon the imagined
world which is revealed in the *Revenger's Tragedy* without com-

   [1] *Revengers Tragedie*, IV, ii, 143 seq. The italics are mine, but, in
effect, every line of Vindice's italicizes itself.

ment, even with complete subjection and identification of the poet's mood with the unbroken mood of the world he watches. In the later play he detaches himself, portrays again this world of lust and intrigue but leads the virtuous characters to triumph and not merely to escape and sets the chief characters to work to analyse their motives and rationalize their moods. The world upon which they (and Tourneur through them) are working is less terrifying than that of the *Revenger's Tragedy* because it is less all-embracing, it is a world not darker but meaner, more sordid and more immediate. With the figures of Languebeau Snuffe and Levidulcia, it seems less detached from the world of Jacobean London than the *Revenger's Tragedy* with its deep imaginative coherence. But the last act and at least one speech in the fourth act have that strange fineness peculiar to Tourneur at the height of his power. They have the half-apocalyptic, half-hysterical quality—like the leap of lightning and the crash of thunder on a mountain—which alone can reflect the convulsions of D'Amville's mind :

D'Am.   Why doest thou stare upon me ? Thou art not
       The soul [1] of him I murderd. What hast thou
       To doe to vexe my conscience ? . . . And that Bawde,
       The skie, there ; she could shut the windowes and
       The dores of this great chamber of the world ;
       And draw the curtaines of the clouds betweene
       Those lights and me about this bed of earth,
       When that same Strumpet Murder and my selfe
       Committed sin together. Then she could
       Leave us i' the darke, till the close deed
       Was done : But now, that I begin to feele
       The loathsome horrour of my sinne ; and (like
       A Leacher emptied of his lust) desire
       To burie my face under my eye-browes, and
       Would steale from my shame unseene ; she meetes me
       I' the face with all her light corrupted eyes,
       To challenge payment o' mee.[2]

This imagery, magnificent as is its sustained and cumulative power, gains impressiveness in its setting by its close integration both with the preceding scenes and with the earlier scene of the murder of Montferrers, that scene where D'Amville hails in exultation the black night sky, the ' Beauteous mistress of a murderer '. This gathering up in one climactic speech of the

[1] scull, Q. 1611.   [2] *A.T.*, IV, iii, 239–58.

images whose tones have been running through the play, gathering them to such different purpose and with such reversal of
their earlier effect, is the work of a precise artist, just such, in
fact, as we recognize in Tourneur as soon as we attempt any
closer examination of his work.

For it is this very quality of control, this steady, cool handling
(even in the tempest of passion) of the forces he has set going that
distinguishes most notably Tourneur's conduct of a play, extending from his handling of imagery and metre (which most clearly
of all reflect the essential quality of his mind) to the revelation
and manipulation of the characters and even to the narrative
itself.

Isolated images in both plays have this sudden and surprising
virtue, this moving power which is yet precise in its minute
articulation : Spurio, in the *Revenger's Tragedy*, yielding at last
to the Duchess's persuasions :

> Oh one incestuous kisse picks open hell.

Vindice with his denunciation of the lust of the court, where
the changing rhythm and the imagery bear equal parts in the
apocalyptic, lightning-stroke of the words :

> O howre of Incest !
> Any kin now, next to the Rim ath sister,
> Is mens meate in these dayes, and in the morning,
> When they are up and drest, and their maske on,
> Who can perceive this ? save that eternall eye,
> That see's through flesh and all.

Or, yet again, D'Amville in the later play, after he has struck the
blow by which he kills himself :

D'Am.	What murderer was hee that lifted up My hand against my head ?
1st *Judge.*	None but yourselfe, my Lord.
D'Am.	I thought he was a murderer that did it.
1st *Judge.*	God forbid.
D'Am.	Forbid ? You lie Judge. He commanded it.[1] To tell thee that mans wisedome is a foole.

But there is more in Tourneur's precise art than mere isolated
flashes of power.   There is, in his use of imagery, a sensitiveness

---

[1] A reminiscence of *Faustus* that, like a later one in this same play,
is not unworthily applied.

to the underlying harmony of image and character, image and setting, or image and situation which deserves no less a term than the
much-loved Elizabethan ' decorum '. This appears already in the
earlier play, but it is almost invariable in the later one. To
D'Amville and to Vindice, the focuses of passion, fall most of the
images of strong imaginative or poetic power ; those of Sebastian
are homely in source, pithy and effective in application ; Charlemont's imagery, whatever his circumstances, is obvious and
simple ; Gratiana's is slipshod like her mind, superficially effective but uncertain in its clinch as often are the metaphors of
rapid, fluent talkers ; the Duchess's metaphors, like Levidulcia's,
have more force than Gratiana's, and, like Castabella's, though
they have little poetry, have a practical effectiveness and some
penetration. Nor is this all. Sometimes the most important
undertones of a scene are referred entirely to the imagery ; the
glib, profuse, conventional imagery that ornaments D'Amville's
speeches at the funeral of Montferrers and Charlemont,[1] the
elaborate but shallow artistry of Charlemont's parting speech
to Castabella,[2] even the conventional images of the unconvincing
mourning of Castabella at her lover's supposed tomb,[3] all these
give us warning, obviously or subtly, that something lying
beneath the actual statements is quite other (and far more
important) than the logical content of the words.[4]

The same subtle but precise impression is left, by the mood
of any given character, scene or situation, upon the metre, and
here again, with a meticulousness which shows Tourneur to
have been one of the most careful of all Jacobean workmen.
In the passages already quoted this has been apparent enough.
The lines are crisp and hard and clear more often than mellifluous, but they have a capacity for modifications of tempo
that makes them flexible to any mood and at all times a
ringing quality that reveals a mind alert and clear in command.
The rhythms are never sensational, though they sometimes,

---

[1] *A.T.*, III, i.   [2] Ibid., I, ii.   [3] Ibid., III, i.
[4] In one case (II, iv, 38–55) the lapse into lurid, Marstonian imagery
by a character (D'Amville) whose images at other times, though often
passionate and sometimes of the highest order, are never sensational,
is seen, upon closer view, to be exactly similar to Macbeth's words about
Duncan's ' silver skin laced with his golden blood ' and in an exactly
similar situation. Each man is overacting, in a crisis, the part of
the horror-stricken discoverer of a murder he has in fact himself
committed.

11

like Ford's, demand a training in the subtleties of their cadences :

D'Am.   Now to myselfe I am ridiculous.
Nature thou art a Traytur to my soule.
Thou hast abus'd my trust. I will complaine
To a superior Court, to right my wrong.
I'le prove thee a forger of false assurances.
In yond' Starre Chamber thou shalt answere it.
Withdraw the bodies.[1]

But they vary, within their own range, from character to character and from mood to mood :

Grat.   Dishonorable Act ?—good honorable foole,
That wouldst be honest cause thou wouldst be so,
Producing no one reason but thy will.
And t'as a good report, pretely commended,
But pray by whome ? Meane people ; ignorant people ;
The better sort Ime sure cannot abide it.
And by what rule should we square out our lives,
But by our betters actions ? [2]

The impression of a clear, presiding mind which we receive from a study of the details of Tourneur's work and particularly his correlation of detail in imagery and metre, is confirmed when we come to consider his control of his characters.   Hardly ever do we feel, as we do with the characters of Shakespeare, Marston, Webster and others of his contemporaries, that they are organic growths developing in the mind of the author, taking charge of the play and almost it might seem of the poet.   Rather are they, like the pair in Mr. Shaw's *Methuselah*, ' thought-out and handmade '.   Only Sebastian shows signs of breaking away and possessing the author ; the rest are all too obviously possessed by him.

In the *Revenger's Tragedy* they are for the most part embodied passions, the men clearly and definitely portrayed, but except for Vindice a little remote, the women slighter still, except for the figure of Gratiana where the workmanship is uneven.   This effect is emphasized by the perfunctory labelling with the descriptive names of the morality and humour comedy tradition : The Duke, Lussurioso, Spurio, Ambitioso, Supervacuo, Youngest Son, The Duchess, Castiza.   These all obey their names more or less faithfully and it is probably the absence of individualizing

---

[1] *A.T.*, V, ii.   [2] *R.T.*, II, i.

inconsistencies in this automatically moving body of evil spirits
that gives to the play its unique atmosphere of compact and irre-
fragable evil. Like corpses animated by Voodoo magic they
move about their tasks, horrible simply because, but for this one
trait of inhuman consistency, they are so nearly human. Castiza,
who has a slightly drawn but definite personality, is a preliminary
study for the far more fully thought-out Castabella of the later
play ; the Youngest Son, whose elimination was essential to the
survival of the atmosphere, anticipates Sebastian. Gratiana
alone seems to have puzzled the author, but the inconsistencies
or unexplained passages in her character are the result of gaps
in his observation, not of individuality in what he observed.
The first scene of the second act, for instance, is a mixture of
close and penetrating observation (' Ay, that's the comfort on't
. . .' or the hurrying anger of the speech ' Dishonourable act ! ')[1]
and lapses into undramatic self-analysis of which such a character in such a moment is generally incapable.[2]   In the main,
however, she is the most nearly human figure in the play, one
that Tourneur modified and developed in Leviduicia of the later
play.   He seems to know these women when they reveal themselves in emotion, though he cannot readily enter their minds in
everyday moods.   In the second act of *Revenger's Tragedy* he
portrays without faltering the hurrying, half-hysterical, breathless movement of the mind, where thought pours in upon thought
till persuasion rises to indignation, indignation to anger, in a
throbbing crescendo of emotion that feeds upon itself and at last
overbears pretence, laying bare the coarse, vulgar, scheming
mind of a shallow virago.   He knows their fluent, sentimental
repentances too, just as he knows their coarse, domineering
anger and the scene (IV, iv) so highly praised of Lamb, has its
chief merit in this unflinching revelation of facile tears.   The
same theme is worked out more fully in the death scene of
Levidulcia.

[1] See *supra*, p. 162.
[2] As when she receives money from Vindice to corrupt her own
daughter Castiza :

Gra.   These are
The means that governe our affections—that woman
Will not be troubled with the mother long,
That sees the comfortable shine of you,
I blush to thinke what for your sakes Ile do.
                                    (*R.T.*, II, i.)

In the later play a similar attitude to the characters produces a rather different group. Levidulcia and Sebastian seem integral and almost organically growing things, while an immense amount of thought has gone to the construction of most of the others, particularly Castabella, Charlemont, D'Amville. But these others, and the minor characters too, have ceased now to be embodied passions and are becoming embodied principles or ideas. The danger that threatened Tourneur from the beginning, of over-control amounting sometimes to manipulation of his personages, has grown more marked. He appears to think that the opinions a man holds (atheism, nature worship, conventional piety) can be regarded as the sources from which his actions spring ; in fact, that conduct rests directly upon principles and ideas. Thus his characters now tend to become aggregations of interesting problems or of qualities with no necessary relation each to each. Some show more unity of principle than others and some more connexion between principle and conduct, but all tend to the same unreality of effect because we are not aware, as we are with Shakespeare's people, of an underlying relation between the different qualities in the character and so of a relation between action and motive or sentiment and motive. The more carefully he works upon a character, the more fully he elaborates its ideas. This does not mean that he succeeds in making it move as a whole : the parts are excellent, but they do not integrate. Almost he would seem to tell us that what is not thought-out is not real, an unconscious misconception that seems to have been shared by Ben Jonson in his early comedy and Bacon as a psychologist and is peculiarly fatal to dramatic art. This is revealed very clearly in the figure of Levidulcia, the innate whore of Jacobean drama who must yet, in the middle of her instinctive, animal existence, first realize that ' the god [she] serves is [her] own appetite ' and then evolve a philosophy of appetite like any modern hedonist. It is a queer tribute to Tourneur's power and to the deepness of his conviction that she is never more convincing than when she is expounding this philosophy.[1] The *Atheist's Tragedy* is a play written primarily to satisfy this desire to think out positions, a play whose chief characters are nearly all self-conscious exponents of the springs of their own motives, simple or complex, related or unrelated.

[1] *A.T.*, I, iv.

D'Amville is the clearest and at the same time the extremest of these. He is a conscious theorist and as such might pass muster, were it not for the logical finality with which his every action, up to the time of his defeat and disintegration, is referred to his theory. A deliberate atheist (which seems to mean for Tourneur a nature-worshipper,[1] what we might call a materialist), he makes his every action a demonstration and delivers brief explanatory lectures on the application of his theory even in the heat of action, plotting or crime. We cannot say categorically ' This cannot be ', but we derive more pleasure from taking him to pieces and examining his philosophy in isolation than from contemplating him as a human being or as the agent of the plot. Castabella is clearly presented but is a rigid figure. She seems at first sight obsessed with a rather priggish sense of the importance of her virginity and on nearer view to be a study of what was probably becoming a common type on the fringe of the Jacobean court, a young girl suffering from a violent revulsion from the lasciviousness about her. This links her at once with Isabella of *Measure for Measure* (among other later studies) and indeed she seems to owe much to her ; even the inhumanity of her chastity, which has not escaped Tourneur's notice, is akin to Isabella's. But she has vigour and scorn and, in the scaffold scene, a touch of Belphoebe's or Brunhilda's quality, which redeems her. Charlemont is less of a piece than either of the others ; at one moment the mouthpiece of chivalric sentiment, he at another repudiates Castabella as basely as Claudio does

---

[1] The atheism of D'Amville is extremely interesting. It owes something to Jacobean Machiavellianism in its refusal of religious sentiment, in its cult of aggression and in its frank pragmatism. But his use of the term ' Nature ' (more frequent than his use of 'atheist ' or ' atheism ') goes back to the middle ages. Its connotation varies from passage to passage, but always, I think, within the scope of the three main medieval usages or an obvious modification of them. It is at one time the law that governs the physical universe, the creative power in the universe (controllable by man) (*Natura Naturans*), at another time the particular manifestation of the governing law in man or animal (*Natura Naturata*) and at others ' the loving Mother of us all ', who does not ' purpose anything for nothing ' (*Natura Dea*). The conflict between the idea of supreme Nature, *Natura Dea*, and the idea of a power above Nature relegating her, as with Bacon, to the position of Second Cause, or limiting her solely to her double aspect of *Natura Naturans* and *Natura Naturata* forms, of course, the climax of the spiritual career of D'Amville. (See *A.T.*, V, i, and V, ii *passim*.)

Hero ; the self-constituted redeemer of the revenge motive, he
is at one moment falsely romantic, at another falsely cynical.
A prig and a cad he yet conducts the action to a successful end
—supplying us by the way with some excellent annotations on
the psychology of dreams.   Did Tourneur mean to make this
of him or has the character, as it were, come apart in his hands
through his trying to make it represent simultaneously too many
groups of insufficiently related ideas ?   (Possibly the same
weakness is to be traced here as in Chapman's somewhat similar
figure of Clermont.)   We turn with relief to Sebastian.   Here is
the man after Tourneur's heart and, like Shakespeare in a similar
predicament with his blood-brother Mercutio, he was obliged
to kill him or he would have wrecked the play.   Sebastian and
his predecessor the Youngest Son in the *Revenger's Tragedy* are
(with the possible addition of Levidulcia) the only characters of
the two dozen odd in the two plays in whom Tourneur shows
any sign of joy in the creating or of affection to the creation.
They like the Bastard Falconbridge are staunch advocates of the
kind of truth that shames not so much the devil as the unco'
guid—there is better fun to be had out of the unco' guid than
out of the devil.   Sebastian is in fact a Jacobean Devil's Disciple,
from his first appearance, where he scandalously interrupts the
course of justice with a far too apt monosyllable, through his
whimsical redemption of Charlemont from prison, to the moment
when, uttering a jest worthy of Cyrano, he dies in a strumpet's
quarrel.   Like Blanco Posnet again, he never disappoints us
and is never quite predictable.   But he is alone—except perhaps
for Levidulcia, that frank and refreshing blend of Thierry and
the Insatiable Countess with a dash of Mistress Page ; in contact with her vital, salacious garrulity we forget (perhaps pardon-
ably) that this is all part of the service paid to the abstraction
Nature and remember only that we have here a blood-relation
of Doll Tearsheet, Mistress Quickly, Francischina and Frank
Gullman translated to a slightly higher social sphere.

The measure of the difference in the treatment of character
in the two plays can be seen in their titles : the revenger is the
incarnation of a passion and he acts ; the atheist is the receptable
of certain opinions and theories, and, though he also acts, his
prime function from Tourneur's point of view is to test the
operation of these theories in the theatre of the world.   And so
we are haunted throughout the play by a pair of protagonists

who do not appear on the character list, abstractions who threaten to push the human automata from the stage or at least to direct the action by pulling the cords that control them. If, as in Hardy's *Dynasts*, we could have a momentary transparency that showed us the cords at work upon the figures, we should see that the real causes and controls were these abstractions, Nature (or materialist philosophy) and her less clearly defined antagonist Heaven (or the religious sense). From them emanate the host of opinions and loyalties—the atheism of D'Amville, the piety of Montferrers, the animalism of Levidulcia, the chastity of Castabella, the stoicism of Charlemont. And these in their turn are not, as in Beaumont and Fletcher, the topics of debate bandied to and fro between the characters (who, when they come to their senses, act on instinct and disregard them); they are embedded deep in the action, acting as the springs of personality, so that D'Amville pursues his quest of Nature to the verge of life itself and Levidulcia, compact of lust, is yet never so powerful or so convincing a figure as when she rationalizes it as natural law.

The drama of Tourneur, then, is at bottom that of a poet-philosopher who approaches his theme with a thesis in mind and groups his abstractions, embodying them in dramatic persons whose first task is to expound them. His lucid and admirably thought-out psychological theories break through, again and again, in explicit analyses, especially in the later play ; D'Amville on atheism and natural causes, Charlemont on dreams, are lucid and logical theorists like their creator ; Levidulcia in self-analysis, Castabella disputing upon incest with D'Amville, have a surprising fluency and coherence of thought. But this does not mean that Tourneur is defective in his dramatic effect, still less in his sense of his theatre. His understanding of startling effects and settings, the vigour with which his people live in and plead for their theories would alone give power to the two plays, conceived as they are so entirely in terms of Jacobean tradition. Apparent weaknesses are often found to be short cuts to an effect desired by the audience with the help of a convention accepted by them. The acting quality is invariably excellent ; indeed, so obviously is this in the poet's mind that a passage, a line, is sometimes no more than a hint to be developed by the tones and gestures of the actors. The opening scene of the *Revenger's Tragedy* has already been discussed ; [1] here a fine dramatic and

[1] See above, Chap. I.

a keen theatrical sense are combined.   Other scenes, only second
in effect to this, stand out in the reader's memory : the murder
of the Duke in the hunting-lodge, the indictment of Gratiana
by her sons, the masquerade and murder of Lussurioso, all in the
earlier play ; and from the later, the murder of Montferrers in
the chalk-pit, the scene in the charnel-house, the judgement
scene and the death of D'Amville at the end.   There are parts
even of these which do not bear careful examination as drama,
but always they are effective theatrically and here, as in certain
cases where the work seems to be scamped with an almost perilous
indifference to illusion, the theatrical effectiveness will generally
be found to justify the dramatic weakness.   It is, of course, never
accompanied by metrical weakness (so far as we can judge from
such texts) and certainly never by slovenly imagery ; the final
effect therefore is not of careless workmanship but of indifference
to something not germane to his purpose as are metre, imagery,
philosophic reflection and theatrical effect.[1]

Even the weakness of the supernatural passages can be justified
by theatre convention.   Montferrers, a courteous old gentleman
in life, makes but a bald and mannerless ghost ; he has somewhat
elementary sentiments which he utter (once in four, once in
five lines) without expansion or circumlocution and forthwith
vanishes again.   But we are in, or about, the year 1610.   The
ghost of King Hamlet, with his full explanations and minute
instructions, is fresh in the audience's mind ; the revenge theme

---

[1] There is, in fact, only one passage in the two plays for which
there seems to be no sufficient justification, the criminal foolishness of
Charlemont and Castabella in being overtaken by slumber in a critical
moment in the charnel-house so that ' They lie downe with either of
them a Death's head for a pillow.'   True, this gives rise to a satisfactory
crop of catastrophes and confusions that save the play from a threatened
fourth-act decline and set it going robustly for another act and a half.
But probability has been too ruthlessly sacrificed.   The other cases
that come to mind, the unnaturally elaborate recital of Borachio in
II, i, D'Amville's similar over-acting his part in II, iv, the abrupt
arrival of the dead body of Sebastian at the moment of D'Amville's
exultation in V, i, would all fall into their place on the stage, the first
two in accordance with the law that a speech must be ludicrously
theatrical if it is to outgo the dramatic heightening of the rest of the
play and appear theatrical in the theatre, the second because, however
abrupt the stage direction (' Enter servant with the body of Sebastian ')
or the modern entry, the deep Jacobean stage would give an entry slow
and solemn enough for a pause of horrified realization most potent
in effect.

is familiar to them in this and other forms from ' a ' to ' z '.
They are not interested in ' supernatural soliciting ' and are
willing to accept the briefest of short-hand formulae for all that.
What they do want and what Tourneur proceeds to give them—
hastily and before their attention flags—is a new interpretation
of the position and duty of the avenging son, indicated and
summed up by Montferrers himself : ' But leave revenge unto
the King of Kings.' [1]

Tourneur's later critics have from time to time spoken well of
him, so well indeed that we must judge him one of those artists
who induce in those who make them their special study a fineness and precision of phrase not unlike their own.   J. Churton
Collins, in 1873, J. A. Symonds, in 1885, have summed up
Tourneur's genius (though Symonds took only two paragraphs)
with unforgettable insight.   Swinburne, in 1908, gives him the
highest and in some passages the most penetrating praise he has
ever received, commenting especially on his style, ' the hard
Roman style of impeachment by photography '.   Marcelle
Schwob and his French descendants have the same inspiration
and it continues among our immediate contemporaries : ' Mieux
que tout autre, il garde le farouche élan, l'éclair métallique ; et
les machinations de Vendice sont réglées comme une machine
infernale.' [2]   ' Its [the *Revenger's Tragedy*] motive is truly the
death motive, for it is the loathing and horror of life itself.   To
have realized this motive so well is a triumph : for the hatred of
life is an important phase—even, if you like, a mystical experience
—in life itself.' [3]

---

[1] Even the most unfortunate line in either play, that of the Execu-
tioner (*Atheists Tragedie*, V, ii, 263–4) as D'Amville strikes his own
death-blow :

> In lifting up the axe
> I think he's knocked his brains out,

is necessary for an audience that could not otherwise realize what it
was required to imagine, and presents, after all, no more difficulty to
an intelligent producer than Malcolm's notorious ' Oh !   By whom ? '
the bugbear of Shakespearian actors.

[2] *La Tragédie de la Vengeance*, traduit de l'anglais par Camille Cé
et Henri Sarvajean.   Paris, 1925.

[3] Cyril Tourneur.   T. S. Eliot, *Elizabethan Essays*.

CHAPTER IX

JOHN WEBSTER

I

JOHN WEBSTER, whose greatest surviving plays date from
the early part of the second decade, reveals the transition
from early to late Jacobean drama as clearly as Chapman represents the conflict between the Elizabethan and the Jacobean at
the turn of the century. For Webster, though more intimately
preoccupied with death than any predecessor except Shakespeare,
was touched for a moment with the illumination that spread over
the latest phase of that drama, replacing the darkness of the
earlier years by the assurance of a serener or the light-heartedness
of an indifferent generation. Light-heartedness was impossible
to Webster and he had become too deeply subdued to what he
worked in for serenity to be more than a passing mood, but he
remains the playwright who most clearly perceived the chaos and
conflict in which the tragic thought of his generation was caught
and, while unable to climb out of the ' deep pit of darkness ',
discerned for a moment through the eyes of one of his characters
the ' stars ' that ' shine still '.

Moreover, he perceives to some extent the nature of the two
protagonists in this fight, working now upon the figures of
' politicians ', the pseudo-Machiavellian materialists, Flamineo,
Monticelso, Bosola. the Cardinal, and now upon the figures,
Isabella, the Duchess, Antonio, Delio, who escape from this
imprisonment of reasoned limitation into a wider, unproved
universe of the spirit. Only, with him, there is no security in
the evidence of this second group. The Duchess dies before the
end of the play, Antonio is cut off, cynically, by an accident, and
Delio remains a mere chorus to reduce into terms of moral
sententiae the aspiration of the two clearer figures.

It is because of this perception, because he is never entirely
free from the presence of both these worlds, because, moreover,
he feels their presence in him as an unresolved, internecine fight,

that he brings to his questioning of man's profoundest knowledge such passionate curiosity. It is because of this that he concentrates upon the moments of high crisis and suffering, most of all upon the moment of death. He brings his characters to the verge of death and holds them there, suspended, subject to his questioning. He hovers, brooding, over the dying Flamineo, that high-spirited, dynamic figure, whose life, if it has been ' a black charnel ', has also been full-blooded, passionate and active, whose illumination at the last should therefore be of strange significance. ' What dost think on ? ' Lodovico cries as he is about to stab him. But it is Webster's own uncertainty that answers :

> Nothing ; of nothing : leave thy idle questions,
> I am ith' way to study a long silence,
> To prate were idle, I remember nothing.
> Thers nothing of so infinit vexation
> As mans owne thoughts.[1]

No answer can come from these figures because their looks are cast back over life, not forward into the ' long silence ' or the ' mist '. All that Flamineo can tell him is thus negative. ' We . . . cease to dye by dying ', ' At my selfe I will begin and end ', ' O, I am in a mist.' And Webster, knowing this, seems to relinquish the question ; in his last speech, Flamineo jests brilliantly with the multicoloured memories of the life he is leaving and there are no more ' idle questions ' :

> 'Tis well yet there's some goodnesse in my death ;
> My life was a blacke charnell : I have caught
> An everlasting could : I have lost my voice
> Most irrecoverably . . .
> Let no harsh flattering Bels resound my knell
> Strike thunder, and strike lowde to my farewell [2]

—but not before he has delivered himself of the only conclusion Webster can draw. Faced by this strange inconsistency of assessable experience troubled and disvalued by the intrusion of an undefinable uncertainty, invisible, impalpable and yet pervasive, that reveals itself among other guises, in the ' strange thing . . . compassion ', Flamineo makes, paradoxically, his most definite admission of the reality of the unseen world he resolves to exclude :

---

[1] *The White Devil*, V, vi, 203–7. [2] *W.D.*, V, vi, 269–76 *passim*.

> Noe, at my selfe I will begin and end.
> While we looke up to Heaven wee confound
> Knowledge with knowledge. O, I am in a mist.[1]

The Duchess of Malfi is the only character who sees, or thinks that she sees, beyond this mist that receives Flamineo, Vittoria and Bosola as the moment of highest significance approaches. She does indeed know that her pain is ' heaven's scourge stick ', sees ' the eternal Church ' in which ' We shall not part thus '. And in the moment of death itself the assurance heightens :

> Who would be afraid on't ?
> Knowing to meete such excellent company
> In th' other world. . . .
> . . . Pull, and pull strongly, for your able strength
> Must pull downe Heaven upon me : [2]

And so she, and with her what assurance there is that ' Heaven hath a hand in 't ', passes out of the play and the final commentary, after all, is given to Bosola the Machiavellian.

With significant implication it is the criminal madman Ferdinand who in the final moments of the play will ' affect high pleasures Beyond death '. Those who speak more steadily, the Cardinal, Antonio and Bosola, who are the repositories of Webster's more habitual thought, take leave far otherwise. Antonio, for all his earlier belief that ' Heaven hath a hand in 't ', knows now that

> We are meerely the Stars tennys-balls, (strooke and banded
> Which way please them),[3]

and that ' pleasure of life ' is only ' the good hours of an ague '. The Cardinal would be ' laid by and never thought of ' and Bosola, speaking last of all, can testify only to that ' mist ' which so fatally cuts off the answer to all Webster's questioning.

Indeed it is the only answer he ever gives to his own insistent questions ʃhe brings his people, by the most careful preparation, to the position in which, if ever, a man should see absolute reality—and before them is only ' a mist '.   It is for him as for a later dramatist, this negation, this quality of nothingness, this empty, boundless, indefinable grey mist that is the final horror, the symbol of ignorance, of the infinite empty space in which man

---

[1] *W.D.*, V, vi, 258–60.
[2] *The Dutchesse of Malfy*, IV, ii, 216–18, 237–8.
[3] *D.M.*, V. iv, 63–4.

hovers, the material and the spiritual world both in different terms unreal :

> Er der ingen, ingen i hele vrimlen—
> ingen i afgrunden, ingen i himlen—
> Saa usigelig fattig kan en sjael da gaa
> tilbage til intet i det taagede graa.[1]

His later plays have little to add to this. Webster may have outgrown the urgency of his own questions ; he does not appear to have answered them.

II

Webster has always been known best by his two great surviving tragedies, *The White Devil* and *The Duchess of Malfi*, and, judging by what else remains of his, it would seem that the popular judgement has here been a just one. It may be that the lost *Guise* play, which he himself classed with these two,[2] was of a like quality and theme, but, even were this so, it would still appear that in this small group was concentrated his most characteristic dramatic work, his sombre characters, his penetrating thought and his imagery at once powerful, swift and exquisite. In comparison with the two surviving tragedies the rest, with the exception of three or four remarkable scenes, seems to have lost the essential quality of his poetry. When we have remembered the great trial scenes of *The Devil's Law Case* and *Appius and Virginius* and the corresponding scenes in prison before the death of Appius and the duel of Romelio,[3] we have recalled all the later passages that can fitly compare with his earlier work. A scene or two from *A Cure for a Cuckold*, perhaps the duelling scene on Calais sands if indeed he wrote it,[4] might be added. Of the slightly earlier conjectural plays which have more recently

---

[1] Ibsen, *Peer Gynt*, V, x. ' Is there no one, no one in the whole swirling chaos, no one in earth and no one in heaven ? A soul can go, then, so unspeakably poor, back into nothing, in the grey mist.'

[2] In the Dedication to *The Devil's Law Case*. (See biographical note on Webster.)

[3] *The Devil's Law Case*, IV, ii, and V, iv, respectively, and *Appius and Virginius*, IV, i, and V, ii. The only scenes in *A.V.* with which Brooke credits Webster are I, i, and IV, i (see *John Webster and The Elizabethan Drama*, App. A, esp. pp. 203–4).

[4] III, i. For a discussion of Webster's share in this play and a summary of the views of previous editors, see F. L. Lucas' introduction to the play in Vol. III of his edition.

been associated with him, there is little that recalls the two great plays ; indeed the virtues of these comedies seem far more like those of the other associates,[1] while in the plays of his apprenticeship (*Sir Thomas Wyat, Westward Ho, Northward Ho*) his work is so far indistinguishable from Dekker's that Brooke specifically warns us against attempting a too definite assignment of shares.[2] And so it is to *The White Devil* and *The Duchess of Malfi* that we turn for the fullest expression of Webster's thought and poetry.

As we study the three chief plays, the two tragedies and *The Devil's Law Case* (but especially the first two), we become slowly aware, as with all his major contemporaries, of the profound originality of the mind at work beneath the drama. (Indeed, though the demeanour of the two writers is as different as could well be imagined in the same form, there is an underlying correspondence even between Webster's thought and ' the laboured and understanding works of Master Jonson ':) His judgements are his own, even when they most clearly derive in their immediate form from Sidney, Montaigne, Donne or a contemporary dramatist,[3] mature, grave judgements on the human mind and its creation, society. He offers us, of course, pictures of some of the same processes of those minds as do his contemporaries, but how deep his insight goes, how compact and pithy is his summary, we can only realize when we weigh the effect of his great scenes against any more slender work or of a less imaginative depth : how easily a quicker, lighter handling can appear a little florid, a little specious beside this brevity of Webster. The very way he sets about inducting us into the world of his play, again, is referable to no canons of dramatic structure but his own,[4] and the regardlessness with which in his early work he leaves the

---

[1] For reference to the evidence of authorship and date of *Anything for a Quiet Life* and *The Fair Maid of the Inn*, see biographical note on Webster.

[2] See Rupert Brooke : *John Webster and the Elizabethan Drama* (1916), Apps. C and D.

[3] Webster's habit of working from a commonplace book and the process by which he transmuted phrases and images from his sources has been described in three studies, all of the highest interest : C. Crawford, *Collectanea*, I, 20–46, II, 1–63 (1906, 1907) ; R. Brooke, *John Webster*, Chap. 5, pp. 141–56 ; F. L. Lucas, *Works*, Vol. I ; *Webster's Imitation*.

[4] For a fuller discussion of the structure of *The Duchess of Malfi*, see Chap. II, Sec. III, above

details of his plots unsecured and, in his later, crowds the intrigue with involutions that obscure the outline, shows his preoccupation with something other than the outward form. Even in a Jacobean, writing for a Jacobean audience, his disregard is noticeable. All that he seems to ask is that we should understand the bearings and relations of the events enough to realize the quality of the characters that begot them.

His purpose seems to be to create, as rapidly as is consistent with fullness and depth, a picture of the world in which his characters move ; a world created of their thoughts and of the deeds which are the outcome of their thoughts. Any process which will quickly make us free of this country is fitting for his purpose, whether dramatic revelation or repeated analysis of one character by the others ; any process that will bring us quickly to knowledge of and intimacy with these people, so that we may understand, as with a lifetime's familiarity, the field of the mind in which each moves. From this point of view, the first act is often given over to this induction ; by the end of it we see the characters his people present to the world and something also of the underlying character guessed at sometimes by the others, known with a greater or less degree of consciousness by themselves, and by the dramatist profoundly and subtly understood : ' Superficial flashes do indeed hang upon him for form ; but observe his inward character.'

Indeed he is preoccupied in these plays primarily with one particular phase of human experience, with life lived so that action and reflection go on simultaneously under conditions of high concentration illuminating and stimulating each other. And ultimately it is the reflections that are his main interest ; those that his people, in moments of illumination, make upon their own discoveries, and those that he, under the thinnest of choric disguises, makes upon them. This accounts in part for his habit of grouping his characters almost in series, returning to rehandle a certain study in fuller or modified form in the next play ; it accounts also for the deep attention he gives to certain reflective types, for his tendency to examine some characters so exclusively from one aspect that he sometimes ends by making them appear inconsistent. At the same time, his deep power of poetic utterance, in its own kind supreme even among Jacobeans, joined with his fine sense of the theatre and his often sure sense of drama, renders the findings of his two great tragedies unforgettable and gives to them that suggestion of inexhaustible significance which we associate with great tragedy.

Here then we enter Webster's kingdom ; the interplay of thought, the meeting of mind and mind in the double and simultaneous expression of action and reflection.   The true plot of his play is not the events which proceed upon the surface and are flung off, as it were, as a casual expression, but the progress of the minds of the central figures towards deeper and deeper self-knowledge, the approach to the impenetrable mystery of fate perceived in the moments of intensest suffering and action, which are also the moments of clearest insight.   Our interest in the figure of Bosola, for example, is not mainly because, in the service of Ferdinand's mania, he murders the Duchess and brings about unwittingly the death of Antonio, but because of the strange discrepancy between the man he appears, the man he would be and the man that, unknown to himself, he really is. Our interest is intense, first because we are watching the slow permeation of his outer consciousness by this inner self, the slow summation of all his findings in the knowledge of himself :

> An Actor in the maine of all,
> Much 'gainst mine owne good nature . . .[1]

and then because, when this self-knowledge has cleared away all illusion, he stands for a moment as near to truth as a man can stand.   His eyes are fixed on reality and he reports it, like Vittoria, ' a mist '.   In comparison with this, the ruin brought upon him by his belated resolve to ' be mine own example ' is only incidental, one of those events that, in Webster's drama, serve primarily the deeper purpose of showing where the thought is tending.

When we think of Webster's characters we find that, even in the limited group of the three main plays, there is a marked tendency for them to fall into series.   This may be partly due to limitation in sympathy, but it is also, I think, due to a desire to explore a certain territory of the mind more fully than the compass of a single play will allow ; in nearly every case the later study is an extension or modification of the earlier and not a contraction.   The group of ' politicians ', half stoic half Machiavellian, begins with Flamineo in the *White Devil* (an imperfect Machiavellian who bungles in practice though he is clear enough in intention), and goes on, in *The Duchess of Malfi,*

[1] *D.M.*, V, v, 106–7.

to study separately the fitful, complex and inconsistent plotter in Bosola and the pure, intellectual politician, the incarnation of Machiavellian doctrine, in the Cardinal, adding a highly interesting extension of the type in Romelio of *The Devil's Law Case*, the spontaneous, unanalytical but practical Machiavellian. The strong, clear-minded, masculine quality, again, which is a marked characteristic of Vittoria reappears, more briefly but with the same resoluteness, in Julia ; the more passive feminine quality, absorbed rather in being than in doing, which he sketches, not very clearly, in Isabella of the earlier play, becomes, in the *Duchess of Malfi*, a full and profound study of the

> . . . Simple vertue, which was never made
> To seeme the thing it is not ; [1]

even those two admirable choruses Delio and Pescara, whose rectitude and austerity runs like a tonic infusion through the nightmare of the world created by Ferdinand and the Cardinal, find a natural extension both of their mood and of their function in the shrewd and upright judge Crispiano.   These are only a few of the persons of Webster's world, but in so limited a character list there is some significance in the readiness with which they group themselves.

To see how Webster extended his knowledge by his imaginative exploration of certain territories of the mind, we have only to watch the growth of one of these.   And because of the significance which Webster attached to the Machiavellian interpretation of the universe (or to that attitude to man and society which he assumed to represent Machiavelli's interpretation) the group of ' politicians ' is perhaps the most interesting.   It contains four figures of great power, Flamineo, Bosola, the Cardinal and Romelio, alike in certain fundamental principles but differing in the degree of tenacity with which they retain them and the degree of clarity with which Webster develops in later characters the implications in the earliest.   Because for him, as for Marlowe before him, this particular approach to life held or seemed to hold the answer to his curiosity, to offer at least one consistent and coherent explanation of man's experience and destiny, he examined minutely a related series of figures that represented it.[2]

[1] *D.M.*, I, i, 513–14.
[2] As did Marlowe before him in the related series Barabbas (*Jew of Malta*), Guise (*Massacre at Paris*) and Mortimer (*Edward II*).

Flamineo is the least certainly drawn. He is a mean, treacherous, flattering pander, incapable of achieving that advancement for which he sinks his honour and his humanity and yet, in the clash and conflict of high event, manifesting side by side with this a grim humour and that dauntless resolution that was to Webster a cardinal virtue. It is as though with the admission of that

" . . . strange thing in mee to th' which I cannot give a name, without it bee Compassion."[1]

there was released also an underlying clarity of thought and nobility in endurance of which the poet himself had been unaware until he perceived it part of the character he had created.

Lod. Dost laugh ?
Flam. Woulds't have me dye, as I was borne, in whining ?
Gas. Recommend your selfe to heaven.
Flam. Noe, I will carry mine owne commendations thither.
. . . .
       I ever thought a Cutler should distinguish
       The cause of my death, rather than a Doctor.
       Search my wound deeper : tent it with the steele
       That made it.[2]

In the next play, accordingly, he makes a double study of the ' politician ', rearranging some of Flamineo's attributes so as to bring out more clearly the complexity of inconsistency in Bosola and the unflawed, perfect Machiavellian in the Cardinal. Bosola, richest of all his characters in mental disguisings, is fitly set over against the singleness of the Duchess, as the Cardinal, upon her other hand, opposes his vigilant guile to her innate frankness. Bosola sees himself as a Machiavellian, as clearly as ever did Flamineo, but it is a reflective Machiavellian, a man philosophizing upon ' policy ' itself. To the court, however, he presents not quite this character, but that of the conventional melancholy villain, despising a world that has despised him ; a disguise that is penetrated by the astute Antonio, who at the same time makes us aware of a third Bosola, the one who, underlying both of these, gradually emerges, to the point of self-recognition, as the play goes on :

Ant. You would looke up to Heaven, but I thinke
      The Divell, that rules i' th' aire, stands in your light.[3]

---

[1] *W.D.*, V, iv, 107–9.   [2] *W.D.*, V, vi, 195 seq.
[3] *D.M.*, II, i, 97–8.

Finally, the quality of compassion, that touched Flamineo in a
moment's bewilderment, is allowed to develop in Bosola, first
to the wrecking of his policy, then to the freeing of his understanding :

> Fare you well—
> It may be paine : but no harme to me to die,
> In so good a quarrell.[1]

But if this incompatible element in the politician and its
effects upon character and career are expanded in the study of
Bosola, the true Machiavellian which Flamineo nearly was finds
consummation in the figure of the Cardinal. Tò Bosola, the
Arragonian brethren are alike in perversion, ' Plum-trees that
grow crooked over standing-pooles ', but Antonio, who has
some of the shrewdness of a self-made man, distinguishes them
clearly. While Delio, looking at the Cardinal, only remembers
that he has been a brave soldier and is still gallant and brilliant,
' will . . . Daunce, court Ladies . . one that hath fought
single Combats ', Antonio takes him up at once : ' Some such
flashes superficially hang on him, for forme. But observe his
inward character : he is a mellancholly Churchman : . . .
He should have beene Pope.' And Antonio is right. The
flashes hang superficially on him throughout in the scenes with
his mistress Julia or his investiture as a soldier (in the third act),
but the ease with which he sets these things aside shows their
shallowness ; Julia he poisons within a few moments of perceiving her treachery (nor do we ever know precisely at which
moment he perceives it). A strong possession rises from the
depths of his nature, showing these things to be indeed superficial, of no account beside the cold dominance of the politician
who schemes his way to his end unshaken, undismayed and
never surprised into revelation of thought or emotion. When
the two brothers meet after the marriage of their sister, Ferdinand,
whose passions are already hurrying him to that madness he
founders in, exhausts his ingenuity in sinister, fantastic cursing.
The Cardinal, to whom it is even newer intelligence, takes the
shock without emotion ; while Ferdinand raves he reflects aloud
and then, coming out of his reverie, perceives his frantic brother :
' You flie beyond your reason.' ' How idlely shewes this rage.'
' Come, put your selfe in tune,' and then, in one of the few
lines in which he reveals his own nature (reveals, even, that

[1] *D.M.*, V. v, 122–4.

there is a personality still, with tastes and distastes, behind the
schooled and disciplined Machiavellian) :

> . . . there is not in nature
> A thing, that makes man so deform'd, so beastly,
> As doth intemperate anger.[1]

Nothing shakes him and nothing confuses him : his handling of
Bosola, who has discovered his complicity in the Duchess's
murder and has him in his power, is so rapid, clear and ruthless
that the lead comes again into his own hands against all expectation.   Though he lose ground a little in the last act by the net
which he weaves for himself (the consummate Machiavellian
should fall a victim to no man's machinations, only to chance),
he redeems himself at the last.   He too, in respect of fortune,
is but one of

> The Starres' tennys-balls (strooke and banded
> Which way please them),

but in respect of his own mind he is as secure a stoic as the upright
Delio and Antonio, having the courage of his own ill-doing, as
Appius after him, and redeeming himself by it much as Appius
does.[2]   His spirit, burdened with the very deed that has driven
Ferdinand mad, gives no sign.   ' How tedious is a guilty conscience,' he says ; he is ' puzzell'd in a question about hell '
and sees, in the clear water of the fish-pool, ' A thing, arm'd with
a Rake '.   That is all.   Never does Webster tell us more of this
character than when, leaving him alone upon the stage in soliloquy, he tell us only this.   Such, as Webster discovers it to us,
is the Machiavellian reticence ; at the end his brevity stands
compact against the loquacity of the dying Ferdinand and Bosola
and his last words, a suggestive variant of Hamlet's, close a
volume that we have never been able to read except obliquely.
He keeps his counsel to the end ; we are never suffered a sight
of the workings of that impenetrable mind ; death does not
move him from a life-time's reticence.   When he can no longer
scheme, direct and control, he asks not for pity, forgiveness or
understanding, but to be ' layd by, and never thought of '.
He alone, of the Jacobean stage Machiavellians, is worthy to
stand beside the prototype of all politicians.[3]

[1] *D.M.*, II, v, 74–6.
[2] See *Appius and Virginius*, V, ii, and *post*.
[3] From the point of view of Elizabethan dramatists, Cesare Borgia,
the central figure of Machiavelli's *Prince*.

But Webster was not done with the subject yet. From the pure, ideal Machiavellian, conscious of his method though never discussing it, he passes on to complete the group by a study of a more instinctive type. Strictly, Romelio, in *The Devil's Law Case*, is not a Machiavellian, but a character whose instincts for plotting have the same unscrupulousness as Flamineo's, the same power of rapid decision as the Cardinal's and the same resolution as both of them. There the resemblance stops and Webster has modified the rest of the character to such an extent that it deviates as far from the central type as does Bosola, though sharing hardly a quality in common with him. At the beginning of the play he is a realist, but not a cynic ; a practical business man, he has no delicate sensibilities but equally no time for the cynical melancholy of Bosola. He has the habit of carrying responsibility and of making quick decisions (not always sound ones) and a merchant's honour which at first stands comparison well with the more delicate personal honour of the aristocrats he is contrasted with. His speech has a kind of ripe brevity, full of observation and racy humour. We know that he will miscalculate the springs of honour in a chivalrous character and the strength of passion in a woman, but in other matters his shrewd vigilance will see him through. His personal morals are utterly unscrupulous, but he has a clear sense of himself as a public figure and, as the play develops and catastrophe comes upon him, the alertness of mind, the manliness and self-sufficiency, the unshaken firmness of his behaviour, link him, except for the exuberance of his energy, with the Arragonian Cardinal as one of the best losers even Webster ever drew. As circumstances darken round him his philosophy touches ever more serious themes, even to death itself. But unlike almost all the other characters of Webster who make discovery of themselves in such a progress, his mood and his philosophy, like the Cardinal's, remain the same. In the great trial scene his brain is working at top pressure, every faculty vigilant and awake, like Vittoria's in her trial ; there emerges an unexpected capacity for reticence while he measures his danger, and unexpected dignity as he finally refutes the charge. Most significant of all is Act V, Sc. iv, where, the night before the ordeal by battle, the supposed Capuchin tries to direct him into the proper Jacobean road to death. His steady, reasonable and completely unhysterical rejection of the proffered consolations, penetrated through and through with some of the sternest of Machiavelli's thought, is one of the finest studies of that perhaps most highly prized of all Jacobean virtues, resolution. Webster has examined again and more fully that quality which he indicated in greater or less explicitness in Vittoria, Flamineo, Lodovico, Julia and the Cardinal :

Cap. O you have a dangerous voyage to take.
Rom. No matter, I will be mine owne Pilot :
        Doe not you trouble your head with the businesse.
Cap. Pray tell me, do you not meditate of death ?
Rom. Phew, I tooke out that Lesson,
        When I once lay sicke of an Ague : I doe now
        Labour for life, for life ! Sir, can you tell me,
        Whether your Tolledo, or your Millain Blade
        Be best temper'd ?
                .   .   .   .   .   .
        Who has hired you to make me Coward ?
Cap. I would make you
        A good Christian.
Rom. Withal, let me continue
        An honest man, which I am very certaine,
        A coward can never be . . .
        I am to fight, to fight sir, and Ile doo't
        As I would feed, with a good stomacke.[1]

This man is not, like Bosola, to meet himself for the first time on the eve of death ; it is hard to resist the impression that this, though perhaps not the noblest, is the fullest and, in some ways, the most interesting character Webster ever drew.

This figure does not occur again, though certain modifications of it are to be found in the intrigues of *Appius and Virginius* and in the resolute criminal Appius. If we accept as Webster's the trial scene (IV, i) and the prison scene (V, ii),[2] we are struck at once by solidity of treatment in the first, the direct speeches, logical and compact, and by the explicitness of the commentary made in the second upon the foregoing action of the play. This commentary is almost a travesty of Webster's manner in the great tragedies, there is little poetry, but a clear definition of Webster's ideas on courage, crime and the breeding of an aristo-

[1] *Devil's Law Case*, V, iv, 57 seq.
[2] For a discussion of these scenes and the authorship of the play generally, see F. L. Lucas's introduction to the play in Vol. III of his edition, and for the argument which would give most of the play (including V, ii) to Heywood, see Brooke, App. A (esp. p. 186 for Heywood's use of ' strage ').

crat, to speak which, Appius at least, almost lays down his
character and comes forward to speak his own epilogue. But
as an epilogue it serves not only this play but the two early
tragedies and *The Devil's Law Case* ; it is a frank admission of
the redeeming virtue of resolution, no matter with what crime
it cohabit, and, as such, is an index to one of the most significant
of Webster's preferences :

App.   Think not Lords
      But he that had the spirit to oppose the Gods,
      Dares likewise suffer what their powers inflict.
      I have not dreaded famine, fire nor strage,
      Their common vengeance, poison in my cup,
      Nor dagger in my bosom, the revenge
      Of private men for private injuries ;
      Nay more than these, not fear'd to commit evil,
      And shall I tremble at the punishment ?
      Now with as much resolved constancy,
      As I offended will I pay the mulctt,
                   . . . Learn of me *Clodius*,
      I'l teach thee what thou never studie[d]st yet,
      That's bravely how to dy.

Virg. He dyed as boldly as he basely err'd
      And so should every true-bred Roman do.

Icil. And note the difference 'twixt a noble strain,
      And one bred from the rabble : both alike
      Dar'd to transgresse, but see their odds in death :
      Appius dy'd like a Roman Gentleman,
      And a man both wayes knowing.[1]

There is little more of great significance in either of the two
later plays in which Webster can reasonably claim a share.
Two scenes stand out in *A Cure for a Cuckold*, that of the meeting
of Lessingham and Bonvile on Calais sands (III, i) and that
between Clare and Bonvile at the end of IV, ii, but, if these are
Webster's, it must be acknowledged that they have neither the
passion and pith of the early tragedies nor the penetration and
sardonic shrewdness of the trial scenes in *Appius and Virginius*
or *The Devil's Law Case* or of the figure of Romelio throughout
this play. Though the play on the whole is good (until frivolous
complications of the plot and contradictions of character destroy
the fifth act) it is with a virtue which suggests, as Mr. Lucas
points out, rather his collaborator than Webster himself.[2]

[1] *Appius and Virginius*, V, 2, 125–75 *passim*.
[2] In the scene on Calais sands Lessingham is improbable, a fault
which can seldom be charged to Webster's characters. However

Thus it is finally to the great trial scenes that we return in the later tragedy and the tragi-comedy of Webster, scenes which demand and exercise some of his strongest faculties, blending passion and intellectual argument, so that the passion itself lends a finer clarity to the thought, and the nobler of them is that in *The Devil's Law Case*, where Crispiano's clarity of thought and firm conduct of the evidence (together with other more human and wholly delightful characteristics) make it one of the most interesting pieces of writing in this kind to be found in this drama.

III

It is perhaps not until these primary characteristics have become familiar that the reader of Webster's plays realizes to what extent they are interrupted or glossed by terse comments and gnomic couplets summing up the conclusions or the deductions drawn. For Webster's preoccupation with the reflections of his characters has a two-fold expression, the outcome, at some removes, of his endeavour to reconcile two aspects of the universe in his own imagination or to repress one and live at peace with the other. From the sententiae [1] of the play we perceive that

violent or strange their action or their setting, the words they speak in moments of crisis invariably convince us at sight. But Lessingham brings with him a curious aroma of unreality, as though his speeches did not spring from common human motive or experience, that we associate with the joint work in tragi-comedy of Beaumont and Fletcher and with a certain amount of Fletcher's individual tragi-comedy (Lessingham's discussions of his motives, conduct and emotions while intending to kill Bonvile are not unlike those of Maximus arguing with himself about the killing of Aecius in *Valentinian*). The scene points forward, of course, to Steele's *Conscious Lovers* (IV, i), a scene with which it is, moreover, not unakin. For a discussion of the relation of Webster's share (i.e. the main plot) of the play with Marston's *Dutch Courtesan* and Massinger's *The Parliament of Love*, to which he judges it to be clearly indebted, see Brooke, App. J. The whole question of motivation, especially of Clare's motivation, is also discussed at length there.

[1] It is perhaps not without significance that these apothegms, even the very short, epigrammatic comments, diminish in the later plays and are more frequent in *The White Devil*, where the conflict in Webster's mind is perhaps most violent and the effort to build a solid system with the aid of explicit statement is most marked. In *The Duchess of Malfi* they are not only fewer but are, I think, better assimilated to the character speaking them and to the situation (or to both). In *The Devil's Law Case* they are almost gone and are in general replaced by self-analysis which, like Leonora's, is consistent with the

he has built up for himself a moral system which does not
correspond wholly with his instinctive affections (which have
also by now become fairly clear) nor with the profounder and
hardly less instinctive doubts that troubled his spirit. Delio,
Pescara and Crispiano serve as choruses to expound the moral
system and we admire them, indeed, with increasing readiness.
But we do not necessarily notice them when we first read the
Duchess of Malfi or *The Devil's Law Case*.   In spite of their
comments on life, death and fate (germane enough to the matter
though they are), it is the characters Webster loves, not the
moralists through whom he preaches, that possess our minds ;
Romelio, the Arragonian Cardinal, Flamineo, Vittoria, characters with no moral scruples, who have indeed few virtues save
that kingly one of resolution.   And so the accompanying moral
commentary though pithy, clear and often deeply impressive is
seen to be not so much a different medium of Webster's thought,
but actually the vehicle for a group of ideas quite different from
his instinctive love of nobility and of courage, even if it be Satanic.
His comments in fact upon kingliness and the fate of princes,
upon statecraft and the nature of nobility, upon adversity and
virtue, policy, stoicism, reason, all these are made not indeed by
the lover of Flamineo, Arragon, Vittoria and Romelio, but by
a man endeavouring to bridge by explicit statement a gulf
between two worlds of knowledge to neither of which he can
give himself entire.   The divided mind is pulled between two
interpretations and the use of apothegm and abstraction are,
as so often, only the index of the endeavour to reconcile them.
The finest of these choric utterances is perhaps that which, on
Delio's lips, serves as epilogue to the *Duchess of Malfi* :

> These wretched eminent things
> Leave no more fame behind 'em, then should one
> Fall in a frost, and leave his print in snow—
> As soone as the sun shines, it ever melts,
> Both forme, and matter : I have ever thought
> Nature doth nothing so great, for great men,
> As when she's pleas'd to make them Lords of truth :
> *Integrity of life, is fame's best friend,*
> *Which noblely (beyond Death) shall crowne the end.*

---

character. Side by side with the loss of this explicit commentary
we may notice the decrease of Webster's characteristic poetry, itself
at least to some degree the outcome of the strife within his mind.

But even this, with its note of assurance and stability, comes too late when we have followed Bosola into that ' mist ' into which all the great figures of the play have gone, that mist which is our final memory of it and our deepest. Illumination cannot be shed into that ' deep pit of darkness ' by explicit commentary drawn from a moral system however noble : Delio's words ring true when he cries ' These wretched eminent things ', but the significance evaporates when he talks of ' Integrity of life ' as ' Fame's best friend '. Neither integrity nor fame will follow us into that mist.

Webster, as has already been said, makes one attempt to penetrate it dramatically and is far nearer reaching his solution that way than he ever comes by the most determined reiteration of *sententiae*. Only the Duchess enters it with any better clue than stoic resolution. In her Webster's struggle for illumination finds a momentary solution, but he cannot maintain it and recoils upon the idea of the confusion of knowledge with knowledge. For the truth is that Webster's instinctive affections carried him further than his conscience cared to follow. By nature he was endowed with a great love of resolution, courage, manliness and originality and a clear perception that good and evil are irrelev- ances beside the reality of these things. This comes out clearly in the figure of Vittoria, who has been praised with equal fervour as a study of innocence and of crime. Innocence and crime are irrelevant ; Vittoria is a study of the glory of resolution so burn- ing that it destroys, while it is operating, the superficial distinc- tions in the mind alike of author and of reader. Such, less completely, is Flamineo, such the Cardinal and such Romelio. But Webster consciously rejects his own instinctive kinship with this form of good and so inherits a divided universe. From this follows the need to unify a dislocated series of experiences, the attempt now to exclude the deeper, intuitive perceptions and to limit the world to the evidence of the senses and the deductions drawn from that, now to admit the disturbing suggestion that there is a realm of interpretation, a means of perception beyond that which he has admitted. Between the two, he oscillates and attempts now to unify the two groups of evidence by a system of calculated moral laws, now to urge the abandonment of one so that he may no longer confound knowledge with know- ledge. For paradoxically it was in his love of resolute evil that his deepest wisdom lay and to have followed that out might have

led him, as it later seems to have led Ford, to the realization that
between these figures and those of the nobler creatures in *The
Duchess of Malfi* was no ultimate divergence. The sense, with
which he invests the Duchess, of the continuity of life into an
eternity beyond definition, perhaps, but not beyond perception,
so suddenly lengthens the focus of the play that we feel him
upon the verge of perceiving, in the place of evil, only an inverted
nobility and in its very agents a purpose other than their own :

Ant.   Heaven hath a hand in 't : but no otherwise,
        Than as some curious Artist takes in sunder
        A Clocke or Watche, when it is out of frame
        To bring't in better order.
Duch.   . . . all our wit
        And reading, brings us to a truer sence
        Of sorrow : In the eternall church, Sir,
        I doe hope we shall not part thus.
           .   .   .   .
             naught made me ere
        Go right, but Heavens scourge-stick.[1]
Bos.   Doth not death fright you ?
Duch. Who would be afraid on't ?
        Knowing to meete such excellent company
        In th' other world ? [2]

What he perceives here is that at bottom there is but the union
of two forms of nobility : to have carried this realization into
his interpretation of the dual universe presented to him by his
imagination would have been to make that synthesis which
Shakespeare had made before him and to return again to the
Elizabethan and Shakespearian perception of the oneness of all
knowledge, that perception which neither Chapman had been
able to preserve nor he himself was able to regain.

IV

The stress of Webster's two great tragedies is almost unre-
lieved. And his instinct in this was sound. For so deep is his
absorption in the pattern of thought and emotion and in the
light he believes this ordered sequence may throw upon the
mystery of man's fate, that relief would generally be mere
interruption or hindrance. Being a good theatre-man, he leaves
his producer free to unbrace the tension of the audience's mood
here and there in both plays, but he prefers to do it with a mask

---

[1] *Duchess of Malfi*, III, v, 75 seq.   [2] Ibid., IV, ii, 215–18.

or a passage of grim dialogue capable of comic production, things which, though they can be used to vary the mood, do not necessarily interfere with the movement of the thought. So that the two great tragedies are without essentially comic elements.

The variations in mood constitute a kind of relief, akin to that of the Greek choric odes, but quite distinct from the mingling, whether close or loose, of the elements of tragic and comic in much Elizabethan and Jacobean comedy, tragi-comedy and tragedy. In Webster's plays, the elasticity of the emotions is preserved by variations of mood, tempo and force. Again and again, after a tempest of rage, the rushing together of two whirlwinds, there is a sudden pause ; the speech that follows seems barely audible by contrast with the thundering passions that have passed, but it falls into the silence with incalculable pathos, solemnity or awe. Sometimes this is no more than a line, a half-line even, as where Ferdinand, looking on his dead sister, perceives her truly for the first time since his rage possessed him, or where later, in the madness that the realization brings, he moves unnoticing through the crowd of courtiers, his mind turned inward upon the thought ' Strangling's a very quiet death ', or when Flamineo, wishing he ' were from hence ', makes discovery of that ' strange thing ', compassion. Sometimes it is the length of a brief scene, as in that (one of the most moving and sincere studies of a child in the whole of this drama) where Giovanni enters to his uncle Francisco with the news of his mother's death, hard upon the exit of Vittoria, when the violent tumult of the trial scene has hardly died away.[1]

Giov.   My sweete mother
          Is——
Fran.   How ? Where ?
Giov.   Is there—no yonder—indeed, sir, Ile not tell you,
          For I shall make you weepe.

---

[1] Giovanni is perhaps one of the best child studies in a drama not noticeably successful in its children ; in Shakespeare, only young Marcus of *Coriolanus* and Mamillius of *A Winter's Tale* seem as natural as he. He says little that a prematurely old, Elizabethan child might not easily have said. He is not (as so many children of Jacobean drama) the mouthpiece merely of pathetic or shrewdly significant sayings beyond his intention, nor yet (as so many more) a mere portrait of that precocity which was all too common a result of sixteenth-century educational ideals.

Fran. Is dead ?
Giov. Do not blame me now,
         I did not tell you so.
Lod.   She's dead, my lord.
Fran. Dead !
   . . . .
Giov. What do the dead do, uncle ? do they eate,
         Hear musicke, goe a-hunting, and bee merrie,
         As wee that live ?
Fran. No, cose ; they sleepe.
Giov. Lord, Lord, that I were dead
         I have not slept these six nights.
   . . . .
Fran. O, all of my poore sister that remaines !—
         Take him away for Gods sake.[1]

The only contemporary who makes so subtle a use of such
contrasts is Shakespeare. He also in tragedy gives these intervals of gentle, low-toned speech in the midst of tempest, he
alone can at once suspend and emphasize the tragic tension by
the half-heard murmurs of a mind moving absorbed upon the
path of self-discovery that may lead to madness. ' I did her
wrong,' says Lear in the midst of the Fool's babble when the
gates of the castle have been closed against him.[2] Ferdinand
echoes it ; ' She died young '.

Side by side with this varying of emotional mood and tempo,
intimately akin to it, in fact, is the imaginative relief of the
poetic imagery,[3] the momentary escape into the world called
up by the images, a world like that in which the events and characters move, but, by its very wealth of imaginative concentration,
less actual—a hidden country which, though full of macabre
and hideous, sometimes obscene, forms, is yet a land of escape,
into which we wander, are absorbed for a moment, immersed
in its fantasy, and from which we return, as from a dream, to
the hurry and clash of events. This world of imagery, which is
as different from the world of thought and reflection as that is
in its turn from the world of event and action, holds the third

[1] *White Devil*, III, ii, 323 seq.
[2] See *Lear*, I, v, ll. 8–45, a scene which, in the use of this particular
process, surpasses Webster himself.
[3] Webster's imagery has been finely described and analysed by
F. L. Lucas. See the Introduction to his edition, Vol. I, especially
pp. 30–42. For Brooke's comments upon the distinctive quality of
Webster's imagery and some of its characteristic processes, see *John
Webster*, Chaps. IV and V *passim*, esp. pp. 141–56.

place in Webster's dramas, a reality shadowed behind the other realities. Here Webster calls up by a few phrases and their juxtaposition trains of thought which, for a man of an easier habit of mind, would have made a whole dialogue. His is a style that, when the emotion grows intense and the tragic issues approach their climax, passes into that lucidity, those inevitable phrases that distinguish the great poetry of the Greek drama, or, in English, the closing scenes of *Hamlet* and *Macbeth*. It is characteristic, too, of the bitter force of Webster that some of the finest of these are found in his jests, concentrated flashes that illuminate the gloom with devastating revelation ; the laughter in these plays is like Duke Ferdinand's, ' A deadly cannon that lightens ere it smokes.'

So deeply is this imagery inwoven with the concept of the play, so essentially is its function part of the function of the whole drama, that in the great closing scenes of *The White Devil* and *The Duchess of Malfi* it is impossible to isolate passages without losing that essential part of their effect which they draw from their dependence upon the whole preceding drama. It is thus the range and interplay of mood, thought and imagery which gives them their richness and their variety, arriving at last at that impression of width and universality of implication which is an essential of great tragedy. For in these scenes Webster gathers together the streams of thought and purpose, bringing up to the surface undercurrents of action and relation hitherto unknown to the characters themselves. On the threshold of death they pause, like Shakespeare's people, to throw a last look back over the course of their lives, and delusion falls from them. In the strange illumination of those moments they see life also as something strange and new. Their last thoughts are cast back upon it, elucidating suddenly what had before been dark.

CHAPTER X
FULKE GREVILLE

I

THERE would, in the ordinary way, be no reason for the presence in a study of major Jacobean dramatists of so recluse and unprofessional a writer as Fulke Greville, Lord Brooke. His life was primarily that of a statesman, his private interests those of a scholar, he wrote two dramas only and those for the study, and he made it painfully clear that he despised the theatre.[1] It is by little less than a paradox therefore that his two plays, the direct result of the late Senecan revival under Daniel and Alexander,[2] should sum up so often and so clearly the passionate uncertainty that is reflected in the professional drama with which he disavowed association. Having no audience to refer himself to, he was troubled by no need to make his plays theatrical or even dramatic, and the long analyses of statecraft, the debates on religion, fate, war, learning and the variety of human knowledge extend themselves freely through speeches and inter-act choruses as they never could with Chapman, Tourneur, Webster or Shakespeare. He is as full of obstinate questionings as any of his contemporaries but, unlike them, he need neither check this habit nor convert it to dramatic purposes. In his dramas there is revealed not only a mind typical of its generation, bitterly at war with itself and deeply divided, but a group of ideas intimately connected with theirs, freely and explicitly set out. Like Webster, he mistrusts man's groping endeavours to understand the universe beyond his immediate experience, and like Webster he is haunted by the

---

[1] ' And if in thus ordaining, and ordering matter, and forme together for the use of life, I have made those tragedies, no Plaies for the Stage, be it known, it was no part of my purpose to write for them, against whom so many good and great spirits have already written.' (*The Life of the Renowned Sir Philip Sidney*, Cap. XVIII, 1652).
[2] Geoffrey Bullough, in his edition of the works of Greville (1939) weighs with great care and precision a large body of indirect evidence on the dates of Greville's two plays and arrives at the conclusion (vol. 2, p. 58) that *Mustapha* may be assigned to the years 1594–6 and *Alaham* to 1598–1600.

indefinable presence of what he cannot see and cannot turn away from. The reason in each case is different ; Flamineo will not ' look up to Heaven ' because it darkens counsel to mix the two forms of knowledge ; Greville will not approach it by way of man's understanding because all knowledge is to him corrupt and graceless, the means by which man has come to loss and disorientation :

> Now in this *twilight* of Deliberation,
> Where man is darke, because he will not see :
> Must he not trust to his selfe-constellation ?
> Or else grow confident, he cannot be ?
>   Assuming this, hee makes himselfe his end
>   And what he understands, that takes to friend.[1]

>   .   .   .   .

> Memorie doth worlds of wretchednesse assemble,
> Passion to ruine passion is intended,
> My reason is but power to dissemble ; [2]

> II

> And but one only way unto the right.
> A thorny way : where Paine must be the guide ;
> Danger the light.[3]

Our first impression of Greville, drawn from his plays, poems and prose, is of a man whose mind houses more conflicting

---

[1] *Fame and Honour*, stanza XI.

[2] *Caelica*, X, 2–4.

Upon this characteristic Jacobean division of mind in Greville, his latest biographer, Mr. G. Bullough, has written so clear and to my mind so just a summary that I would rather quote it than attempt to re-word it.

' He wrote only for those on whom " the Black Oxe " had trod, since only those who had given themselves to the sick hurry, the divided aims of the world and yet remained sadly aware of a higher reality could appreciate the truth of his " double " view of life, and the subtlety with which he tempered relativism in politics and morality with an apprehension of something nobler, that he was, however, too unheroic to pursue. Man cannot serve two masters—and be happy ; though the dilemma was magnificently ignored by many in the earlier Renaissance, it was increasingly recognized as ineluctable in the age of Donne. Donne himself, after temporizing for years, finally ' clutched at God's skirts ' and was swept up into the cloud from which he preached like an angel. Not for Fulke Greville this valiant self-surrender. Always he tried to serve both God and Mammon.' (*M.L.R.*, XXVIII (1933), p. 19.)

[3] *Mustapha*, II, iii. (Ed. 1633, p. 106. Page references throughout are to this edition unless otherwise stated.)

ideas than was usual even in his age of intellectual doubts.   He
abhors war (which destroys all but the military virtues of courage
and force), yet he despises alike the processes and the achievements of human art and reason ; he holds this world's fame and
honour a gilded dream, yet despatches contemptuously the
retreat of the stoic.[1]   He arrives indeed by that ' thorny way :
where Paine must be the guide ', to a position where ultimately
he is convinced of the unreality of the seen, the reality of the
unseen :

> That sensual unsatiable vaste wombe,
> Of thy seene Church, thy unseene Church disgraceth ;
> There lives no truth with them that seem thine own.
> Which makes thee living Lord, a God unknowne.[2]

A mixture of bitter asceticism which, when it touches learning
and art (and especially art), is sadistically vindictive and of
astute and penetrating analysis of the motives, feelings and
experiences of man in his political and religious life, Brooke's
qualities as a dramatist could almost be prejudged from his other
writings.   Almost, but not quite.   We might, indeed we almost
certainly should, anticipate from the poems and the sonnets the
severe and disillusioned survey of the ' wearisome condition of
humanity ', the soundness of his thought on broad issues of
statecraft and the nature of civilization, the acuteness of his
penetration into men's motives and processes of thought, especially into the motives of public men and the thought processes
of religious or semi-religious men ; we might even have anticipated the obscure concentration of style in which all this is
expressed.   What surprises us in the plays, in *Alaham* to some
degree but notably in *Mustapha*, is the passion which there gives

---

[1] See especially *A Treatise of Warres* (*passim*) ; *A Treatise of Humane
Learning*, especially the first 56 stanzas on the imperfection of the
' faculties of apprehension ', the uncertainty of man's ideas and consequently of the arts and sciences developed by him ; *An Inquisition upon
Fame and Honour* (*passim*) and, especially on the stoic attitude, stanzas
21–3 and 30–42.   This reaction against stoicism may be compared
with the debates in the drama of Marston, Chapman, Shakespeare,
Tourneur.
[2] *Caelica*, CIX, stanza 3.   But see the last twenty-five ' Sonnets '
passim for this idea, which underlies the whole of that group.   (See
especially 89, 96 and 99.)

13

depth and volume to the expression of these thoughts, bringing, as in the similar case of Donne, an unwonted clarity and inevitableness of utterance at the moments of supreme fusion of feeling and thought.[1] Granted that these plays were not, of course, written for performance, that they were, in fact, nothing more than contributions to the late Senecan revival begun by Daniel and passing through Alexander to Greville, yet they have certain dramatic qualities, more I think than those of either of the other two exponents. The relatively simple Senecan scheme limits his character list and the convolutions of his story ; for this perhaps we may be thankful. His passion, which was a little like Marlowe's in that it could fasten itself upon an abstraction and was relatively independent of the stimulus of character or personality, gave intensity to themes some of which in other hands might have been arid as the desert sand—the conflict between the rival parties at an oriental court, the struggle to overthrow one tyrant and set up another, the accompanying reflections on monarchy, democracy, the relations of the state and the individual, loyalty, honour, religion and, most promising of all, the relations of the governing power and the state religion, the part played by state religion in the control and even the oppression of the people. Thus without Dryden's verse, without Dryden's fluency and clarity of exposition, without his flexible effectiveness, Greville is already anticipating not only his themes and settings but something of his way of relating ' sentiment ' to action. He strikes out fine heroic sentiments as does Dryden and from similar themes, but in the end it is the more crabbed of Seneca's condensations that he recalls, while Dryden covers the same task with the unforgettable grace of a Terence.

Dramatic power is, then, I think, not lacking in these plays but the quality which cuts them off effectively from the theatre is Greville's peculiar, characteristic style. Had he intended (as how should one who so despised the arts [2] intend it ?) to produce

---

[1] See particularly, besides numerous single lines of startling quality (a mark of Greville's writing as of so many of his contemporaries) the fine sustained passages : *Alaham, Prologue* (p. 2), III, iv, last speech ; *Mustapha*, chorus 1, p. 97 ; II, iii, p. 110 (Camena's first speech) ; V, iv, p. 155 (Rossa's long speech) and the two choruses at the end of the play.

[2] See, especially, *Of Human Learning*, stanzas, 21–40.

practical theatre plays, his habit of writing would probably have
hindered him against his will. As he did not so intend, there is
no curb upon it and it shows all the marks of closet-writing at
any time and in any form. It separates immediately from that
of his fellow-dramatists, the working theatre-men, as the style
of Browne's *Hydriotaphia* separates from that of Jeremy Taylor's
sermons, not only because of the different musical and imagistic
qualities of the writers, but because of that major distinction
between writing which does not have to refer itself to a public
and writing, whether drama, sermon, polemic or narrative, which
does. The style of *Alaham* and *Mustapha* is, like that of the
Hydriotaphia, that of a man who is primarily concerned with
catching and setting down his thought for himself and a specialized public of a similar mental process ; the emphasis tends to
fall upon the subtleties rather than upon the plain and obvious ;
it develops characteristic and personal modifications of the
normal syntax and the customary connotations : [1]

> His Fame untimely borne : Strength strangely gather'd,
> Honnor wonne with honoring, Greatnesse with humblenesse,
> (A Monarchs heire in courses popular.)
> Make me divine some strange aspiring minde ;
> Yet doubtfull ; for it might be Art, or Kinde. [2]

In these passages the style could clog not only the theatrical but
the dramatic effect.

Greville moreover adds to this habit of thought that is in
itself difficult to communicate a natural preference for knotty
or contorted expression, as though he were born not only for
' whatever was arduous ' but with an almost perverse determination to make the process arduous if it were not already so ; a
method of expression best appreciated by contrasting it with the
Greek tendency to render all thought as limpidly as possible.
And where the Greek habit often results in a deceptive appearance of obviousness or shallowness, this stiff and inflexible

---

[1] Just as Sir Thomas Browne can write a clause such as ' a prerogative above that principle which makes no regression from privations '
(*Pseud.*, X) where nearly every word bears the stamp of an individual
usage, differing slightly or noticeably from the customary mid-seven-
teenth-century usage.

[2] *Mustapha*, I, i, p. 82 ; ll. 10–14. He has not outgrown the Elizabethan vice of incessant emphasis, nor realized that staccato apothegms
sooner become monotonous than almost any other habit of style.

speech of Greville's as often gives a fictitious appearance of depth like that of the sometimes incoherent vehemence of Chapman. Greville, however, is not vehement ; at his most characteristic he is slow, stiff, archaic and stately and it is the bitter gravity of his meditative and annihilistic commentary that, reflected in such a style, accounts for the depth of impression made, often long after reading, by his finest passages upon the minds of his somewhat limited public.

But this very habit of mind, this secretive engendering of thought, though at times it clogs the utterance, guarantees that the thought itself, if not necessarily profound, will be penetrating, original and sometimes arresting. Though this cannot by itself sustain a drama in which the characters are relatively undefined or only crudely outlined, it assures us of a running commentary upon their actions and their natures, more weighty than the text. Sometimes, like his master Seneca, he seizes upon a chorus as an excuse for a brief philosophic poem, and then there is very little to suggest that we are attending a play ; sometimes a similar poem is distributed through several speeches, and then the comparative heightening of the tension suggests that he had more innate dramatic force than he perhaps guessed himself possessed of. Consider, for instance, the subversive views on religion and the State scattered throughout *Mustapha*, falling chiefly to the Priest in IV, iv, and Achmat in V, ii. They occur, in a modified form, in the fourth chorus of *Alaham* also, but in *Mustapha* they are part of the substance of the play, their entry into the dialogue is as proper to the situation as Aureng Zebe's reflections upon the futility of life. Their passion gives a ring to them that is rare in the previous Senecans or the subsequent heroic playwrights, but that is akin to the originality of thought, the product of that marriage of thought and passion that characterizes the contemporary drama. Such topics as these could not be debated openly upon the stage, and much that Greville wrote may well have been in the minds of his contemporaries in whom the publicity of their utterance checked the full expression of their thought. Even Chapman, though he comes near it once,[1] could not have written the

[1] See Strozza's lines (*Gentleman Usher*, V, iv, 56–66) :

' And what's a prince ? Had all been virtuous men,
There never had been prince upon the earth . . .
A virtuous man is subject to no prince,' etc.

following lines in a play to be produced or published in the first
two decades of the seventeenth century :

Priest.   We are untrue,
      And spirituall forges under Tyrants might :
      . . . Where we doe preach your bodies to the Warre ;
      Your goods to Taxe ; your Freedome unto bands ;
      Duties, by which you own'd of others are ;
      And Feare, which to your harmes doth lend your hands.
      . . . Shall sorrow write this storie of oppression
      Onely in idle teares, and not in blood ?
Achmat. No People, No. Question these Thrones of Tyrants ;
      Revive your old equalities of Nature ;
      Authority is more than that she maketh.
      Lend not your strengths to keepe your owne strengths under.
      Proceed in Furie : Furie hath Law and Reason.[1]

Not only might Greville claim that ' Paine must be the guide ',
but, no less, ' Danger the light '.   The curious crossing of this
hard vein of Machiavellian pragmatism with the almost mystical
rejection of the seen in favour of the unseen is one of the abiding
puzzles in a mind as complex and as full of strange crannies as
was the style in which it was expressed ; it is, in its different form,
the counterpart of Webster's endeavour to bridge the gulf between the two worlds of his mind.   The uncompromising statement of Greville's conclusions on this theme on which he was

---

[1] *Mustapha*, IV, iv, and V, ii (pp. 136–9 *passim*, p. 153).   Altogether,
as neat a summary of the main positions of the ' Communist Manifesto '
as, presumably, Lenin himself would have demanded.   The originality
of this train of thought in the year 1609 is of course hard to realize at
first, but there are plenty of indications that the thought is not peculiar
to Greville among the dramatists, though, for reasons already suggested,
the frank expression of it was.   Derived, as its original positions
obviously are, from the famous passages on religion and kingship in
the *Discorsi* (the first three chapters of Book I and the second of Book
II) he yet arrives at conclusions that distinguish him clearly from the
purely pragmatical position of Machiavelli and in fact bring him a good
deal nearer, in this isolated deduction, to the thought of Lenin (' The
roots of modern religion are deeply embedded in the social oppression
of the working masses, and in their apparently complete helplessness
before the blind forces of capitalism. . . .   " Fear created the Gods."
Fear of the blind force of capital . . . this is the tap-root of modern
religion.' V. I. Lenin : *Proletarii*, No. 45, 26 May, 1909.) With
the passage from *Mustapha*, IV, quoted above, there should, of course,
be compared the *Chorus Quintus* of the same play.
      (The passage here quoted is from F. 1633, but the variations of
Q. 1609 are, at this point, such as to emphasize, if anything, the ideas
under discussion.)

best qualified to speak, the relation between his two most continuous and deepest interests, religion and statecraft, is as surprising as is Herbert's licensing for publication of a play containing these sentiments in the year 1632.

Moreover, penetration and originality of individual comments are not his only strength. Although these plays had probably little or no effect upon the main current of contemporary drama, they have an intrinsic value greater, after the lapse of three hundred years, than that of much of the material that made the common theatrical food of the contemporary public. They have dignity which is sometimes majesty, and if they have not much in them that we can call poetry, they have a severity of demeanour which is doubly welcome by contrast with the ready despatching of all things twixt earth and heaven which makes so unsatisfying the work, for instance, of the composite group represented in the second folio of Beaumont and Fletcher. Where in contemporary drama, outside the sternness of Ben Jonson in tragic mood, the momentary harshness for dramatic purpose of Chapman, Shakespeare, Webster or Tourneur, have we an effect that we can name beside the concluding scenes and choruses of *Mustapha*? The noble indictment of superstition in the fifth chorus gives us again his favourite Machiavellian conclusion, invested this time with the ironic bitterness of Marlowe's pseudo-Machiavellianism :

> Courage, and Worth abjure thy painted heavens.
> Sicknesse, thy blessings are ; Miserie, thy trial ;
> Nothing thy way unto eternal being ;
> Death, to salvation ; and the Grave to Heaven.
> So Blest be they, so Angel'd, so Eterniz'd
> That tie their senses to thy senselesse glories,
> And die, to clog the after-age with stories ;[1]

and, following it, comes the surprisingly clear summary of what had in effect been the prevailing Elizabethan and Jacobean practice, though of the dramatists only Cyril Tourneur had so far seen clearly enough to proclaim it, and he only under cover of dramatic form, refuting it by implication in the conduct of his play and explicitly in D'Amville's dying speeches.[2]

---

[1] *Mustapha. Chorus Quintus, Tartarorum*, ll. 17–23 ; cf. Machiavelli : *Discorsi*, II, ii (see Chap. I, above, pp. 14–15).

[2] The references to a force somewhat like the Nature of Lucretius are, in fact, fairly frequent in the later Jacobean drama ; they are, in

Man should make much of *Life*, as *Natures table*,
Wherein she writes the Cypher of her glorie.
Forsake not Nature, nor misunderstand her :
Her mysteries are read without Faiths eye-sight :
She speaketh in our flesh ; and from our Senses,
Delivers down her wisdomes to our Reason.[1]

We must go outside the professional drama to parallel this,
either in its uncompromising content or in the emphasis of its
plain and weighty style, but the implications behind it are there,
so far as they dare be uttered, in the speeches of the active
dramatists of his day ; in different modifications they appear, now
in Chapman's or Shakespeare's political thought, now in Chapman's or Webster's religious speculation, now in Tourneur's,
Shakespeare's or Middleton's reference back to Nature, the
' provident kind mother of increase '.   Nor is the inconsistency
and bewildering contrast of the sudden Lucretian declarations
with the argument on the fallibility of the senses,[2] other than
a type of the very conflict which lay at the roots of their thought,
manifesting itself in the explicit speech of Greville as it could
not, either for artistic or for political reasons, in the practical
theatre drama of his contemporaries.   This, then, is Greville's
function in the history of contemporary drama, that he makes
explicit statement both of the ideas themselves and of the conflict between them, which were characteristic of the thought of
his contemporaries.   Never is this, perhaps, clearer than in the
saturnine, Senecan bitterness of the final ' Chorus Sacerdotum '
of *Mustapha*.

Oh wearisome Condition of Humanity !
Borne under one Law, to another bound :
Vainely begot, and yet forbidden vanity,
Created sicke, commanded to be sound :
What meaneth Nature by these diverse Lawes ?
Passion and Reason, selfe-division cause :

---

any case, a probable sequel to the Machiavellian pragmatism of the
slightly earlier period.   Tourneur dwells upon it at greater length
than do most of the others (see *Atheists Tragedie*, D'Amville's speeches
passim, especially in V, i and ii), but Chapman, Shakespeare, Middleton
all touch it.   Montaigne's habit of liberal quotation from Lucretius
made him easily accessible after 1603, the date of Florio's translation.
    [1] *Mustapha*.   *Chorus Quintus, Tartarorum*, ll. 24–9 ; cf. of course
for both passages Lucretius, *De Rerum Natura*, I, *passim*, which must
share with the *Discorsi* the indirect parentage of these lines.
    [2] *Human Learning*, stanzas 6–9.

Is it the marke, or Maiesty of Power
To make offences that it may forgive ?
Nature herselfe, doth her owne selfe defloure,
To hate those errors she her selfe doth give.
For how should man thinke that he may not doe
If Nature did not faile, and punish too ?

Tyrant to others, to her selfe unjust,
Onely commands things difficult and hard.
Forbids us all things, which it knows is lust,
Makes easie paines, unpossible reward.
If Nature did not take delight in blood,
She would have made more easy waies to good.

We that are bound by vowes, and by Promotion,
With pompe of holy Sacrifice and rites,
To teach beleefe in good and still devotion,
To preach of Heavens wonders, and delights :
Yet when each of us, in his owne heart lookes,
He findes the God there, farre unlike his Bookes.

Relatively early though the first version of this play stands in the list of Greville's writings one is tempted to wonder whether the conclusion of that ' thorny way ' was not, in fact, the conclusion of this chorus, and whether the conflict of passionate thought which raises the play above all his other writings except the *Caelica* sonnets was not, after all, the true index of a mind which, like those of his great contemporaries in tragedy, continually found his innermost intuitions at variance with the evidence drawn from observation of the universe in terms of Machiavellian pragmatism.

CHAPTER XI

BEAUMONT AND FLETCHER

I

THE work of Beaumont and Fletcher escapes from the tyranny of Jacobean incertitude into a world of its own creating. It is bound neither by the weight and horror which oppresses the tragedy nor by the compensatory pragmatism which binds the comedy to realistic portraiture. It evades the great questions (except as debating topics) and it endows with remoteness all emotions, so that the strongest passions fail to engulf us, however fiercely the characters seem to be shaken by them. Through the tragi-comedies and the early joint tragedies in particular, there is transfused a colour of such singular beauty that we accept enchantment as we do a dream or a fairy-tale, not seeking in these plays, as in the great Jacobean tragedies, implicit answers to our urgent doubts, but escaping into them as into the moonlit stage of an exquisite opera-set, become suddenly real and co-extensive with life itself. Upon this stage and in this clear, remote radiance all the events of life take part and types of character of nearly as wide a range as can be found in all the rest of the Jacobean drama ; the air is full of reverberant rhetoric, melting cadences of word and music, clear, sweet pathos and sentiment more noble than can be readily found in the world outside. So bright is it, so self-contained, this sanctuary from the agonies of spiritual tragedy and the cynicism of observant comedy, that it dims the real world, bewilders our faculties and comes near to laying asleep in us the uneasy sense of sleep-walking illusion.

The names of Beaumont and Fletcher are often associated so closely with tragi-comedy that their work and that form of play are loosely spoken of as if they were co-extensive. This, which is obviously not the case, since there are at most only five surviving tragi-comedies of their joint workmanship, is yet one of those absurdities more literally than fundamentally untrue.   For Beaumont and Fletcher's collaboration covers most of the short career of Beaumont and of the early and formative period in Fletcher's professional life, and, coming at the moment when the tragic mood of the early part of the century was at its climax and very near its end, it gave, by its originality (not only of form but of temper) and by its immense popularity, an impression so deep that most of the subsequent drama bears testimony to it.   The large body of plays published in the second folio of 1679 under the name of Beaumont and Fletcher is directly of their fathering [1] and much of the work of Fletcher's later contemporaries only less so.   If we agree to regard the element of romance, the withdrawal from the pursuit of reality, as the distinctive quality of this tragi-comedy and the essential difference which separates them from their predecessors in tragedy or comedy, then perhaps we are not far wrong in deriving from them a large proportion of the extensive late Jacobean drama (whether tragi-comedy, tragedy or, in some cases, comedy) which is similarly characterized by this element.   In this respect, then, the body of tragi-comedy and the work of Beaumont and Fletcher and of Fletcher in collaboration with others can be connected, so that the old association of terms continues to hold significance.

When Beaumont and Fletcher escaped at once from the tragic oppression and the analytic comedy of their predecessors they did, in fact, create something not only in a new mood but in a new kind.   For their intimate blending, not only of the elements of tragedy and comedy but also of the emotions belonging to each kind, led, in their case, to an emotional type totally different not only from either of these others, but even from the earlier, Elizabethan combinations.   The artistic contrast between the world of comedy and of tragedy or potential tragedy had been perceived some twenty years back, as early as Greene's *Friar Bacon and Friar Bungay*, and indicated by the simple juxtaposition of the two in plots almost entirely separate.   Shakespeare's use of potential tragedy to enhance and ripen the mood of his late comedies, even in *Much Ado* and *The Merchant of Venice*, still leaves them distinct and separable.   At the same time, the

[1] On the division between the plays of Beaumont + Fletcher, Fletcher only, Fletcher + Massinger and Fletcher + other collaborators, see the note on the plays of F. 1679 in Appendix II, Book Lists.

serious plot remains to some degree realistic and reasonably probable and the springs of the motives are those of everyday men, even if their fortunes lead them to the Forest of Arden or cast them upon the sea-coast of Illyria. The fortunes are different and there is a corresponding modification of bearing in the characters, but at no point are we aware, as so often with Beaumont and Fletcher, of a difference of mental process resulting from their romantic or tragic surroundings. In the mixed plays of Middleton, from *The Phoenix* to *The Old Law*, and still more in Chapman's *Gentleman Usher* and *Monsieur d'Olive*, there has been some development away from the Elizabethan kind. The blending of the two kinds of action is closer ; in *The Gentleman Usher*, the romantic story of Vincentio and Margaret and the devices by which Vincentio manipulates the gullable Bassiolo are not two plots, but separate aspects of one. But the characters are rooted in normality ; even Strozza, who changes so rapidly from a vigorous, practical man of action to an almost prophetic mystic, does so on just such terms as did many of Chapman's contemporaries, most notably Ralegh himself, and each phase is understandable and reconcilable alike to the events which have prompted it and to the personalities by which he is surrounded. This phase of Chapman's romantic comedy links indeed the middle comedy of Shakespeare with the tragi-comedy of Beaumont and Fletcher,[1] but the likeness to its successors is a matter of structural technique rather than of thought or word.

Fletcher's definition of tragi-comedy (in the *Address to the Reader* prefixed to the first edition of *The Faithful Shepherdess* in 1609), though it was hardly an adequate description of the new form that he had already set going, shows that he had in mind something more than Chapman had reached in *The Gentleman Usher* ; he carried the definition straight over from his Italian predecessors in this form,[2] perhaps without realizing

[1] On this point, see T. M. Parrott's notes on *The Gentleman Usher* in his edition of Chapman's *Comedies*.

[2] See especially Guarini's account of the tragi-comedy, in the controversy which followed the publication of *Pastor Fido*, especially ' Il Verrato ovvero difesa di quanto ha scritto Messer Jason Denores contra le tragicommedie e le pastorali in un suo discorso di poesia ' (Ferrara, 1588). Guarini appears to lay, on the whole, more stress upon the mixture of tragedy and comedy in the third type, while Fletcher specifically points out that it is, in fact, neither. But see

that his own creation was, or was about to be a further development of theirs :

A tragie-comedie is not so called in respect of mirth and killing, but in respect it wants deaths, which is inough to make it no tragedie, yet brings some neere it, which is inough to make it no comedie : which must be a representation of familiar people, with such kinde of trouble as no life be question'd, so that a God is as lawfull in this as in a tragedie, and meane people as in a comedie.

That Fletcher has not specified all the characteristics of his new dramatic type here may be shown by a random application of the formula to some play which conforms to what is set down and yet is quite other than the specialized Jacobean tragi-comedy. Middleton's *Chaste Maid in Cheapside*, to take perhaps the most incongruous that could be chosen,[1] ' wants deaths ' and yet ' brings some near it ' ; it is ' representative of familiar people, with such kind of trouble as no life be questioned ' ; it does indeed hover on the borderline between tragedy and comedy, but no reader would hesitate for an instant to reject it from the category of plays which Fletcher had in mind. It has a grim sense of moral law, an unsparing realism of portraiture, an immediacy which Fletcher's have not ; it lacks the romantic vicissitudes, the romantic love plots and the exotic or at least foreign setting, the cunning succession of events, surprises and quick turns of plot which all or nearly all of his possess. It is clear then that the distinctive characteristic of Fletcher's new tragi-comedy was not the mixture of ingredients or the relatively greater closeness of the mixture, not even the refusal to go to the extreme in either direction, though these are necessary corollaries if we once accept the main characteristic, that of the non-realistic and romantic approach to the material. It is the mood of the play which is of so great importance, a mood which lies, as Fletcher suggests, somewhere between the light-heartedness of unshadowed comedy and the apprehension of

also F. H. Ristine, *English Tragicomedy* (Columbia University, 1910). While I accept the cogent argument put forward here, I incline not to equate Fletcher's ultimate theory and practice quite so closely with Guarini's, but to adopt a view rather nearer to that of Parrott.

[1] Though *Troilus and Cressida*, *Measure for Measure*, *All's Well*, *The Malcontent* and a good many more might equally be instanced, and are, indeed, covered by the broader definitions such as that adopted by Ristine.

shock and mystery which attend a tragic catastrophe. If this indeed be the fundamental distinction between tragi-comedy and the other two kinds (and Fletcher is careful to tell us that it is no mere mixture of the elements that he has in mind), then it is the creation of this middle mood which is the contribution of Beaumont and Fletcher to the subsequent drama.

Directly we think in terms of this distinction of mood, this creation of an imagined world neither tragic nor comic which yet, taking something from each, resulted in something different again from either, we are prepared to admit that a well-marked technique was likely to result from it and that the mood, once clearly created, could be introduced into any play, irrespective of formal distinctions between tragedy, tragi-comedy and comedy. This assumption is, indeed, confirmed early in the joint careers of the two authors. The plays which conform to Fletcher's definition, such as *Philaster* and *A King and No King*, are not essentially different in respect of mood, characterization or style from those, like *The Maid's Tragedy* and *Cupid's Revenge*, which, by reason that they do not ' want deaths ', are classed as tragedies. It is, I think, impossible, up to the moment at which Evadne murders the king, to gather from the tone of the play that catastrophe will, in this case, touch the characters instead of, as in *Philaster*, just missing them. There is no stronger sense of horror than might be felt at the situation offered in *A King and No King*. There are no stronger apprehensions of immanent evil than there. And in *Cupid's Revenge* the opening is deceptively light-hearted ; even when Urania and Leucippus are stabbed we expect that it will turn out to be but a wound (as with Bellario and Philaster before them) and that they will rise and walk away unharmed to the happy inheritance of the kingdom. It takes the stage directions to convince us they are dead. Something, then, in the mood which is the peculiar creation of Beaumont and Fletcher has disabled us from distinguishing, in the world we are now moving in, the characters, emotions and events that will lead to tragedy from those that will lead through romantic stress to escape. What, then, are those further implications in this mood ?

II

Whatever be suggested in the phrase ' It wants deaths, which is enough to make it no tragedy ', we cannot therefrom assume that Fletcher supposed the converse, that deaths necessarily constituted tragedy. Dramatists had not yet touched the type of tragedy which dispenses with the catastrophe of death, and the practice of the whole body of contemporary work is witness that ' deaths ', whether or not the individual writer supposed them to constitute tragedy, were at least regarded as an inseparable part of it. What is, rather, borne out by the immediate practice of these two tragi-comedy writers (and is equally in harmony with Fletcher's theory) is the desire to escape from the weight and profundity of tragic thought no less than from the accuracy and exactness of comic portraiture. They were minded equally to let the great questions rest and to refuse the painstaking research into human nature to which the work of Ben Jonson pointed them. Irresponsibility then is an essential part of their attitude, the irresponsibility which creates fairy-tales either as an escape from what is threatening to overwhelm the mind, or as a welcome and reasonable reaction against an overlong period of strain, or as an extension of the domain of imaginative experience. And the mood in which Beaumont and Fletcher approached their early plays seems to have something in it of all three and to be that of the pure romance or fairy-tale, not referable to any criteria but of artistic satisfaction and effectiveness, not concealing under its narrative a hidden or secondary series of moral implications, not at all concerned to preach, however far debating of the issues of their conduct may preoccupy some of the characters.

It is moreover characteristic of a certain type of fairy-tale (not necessarily of all) that the characters themselves are affected by the atmosphere in which they move, so that they do not necessarily act like those of everyday life, and the rare and strange events that befall them beget emotions and motives that are themselves a little strange, a little unaccountable. They do not do what ordinary people in such circumstances, illuminated by the light of common day, would do, but, more happily for the author (and for the reader if he be of like mind), what he would, in a kind of dream-world, have them do, in order that such and such further situations might arise. They do not, when once he has begotten them, take charge of him and his tale and dictate to him what he shall write ; rather, he foresees situations which he will enjoy exploring, plans for them emotions and experiences in which he will enjoy watching them and then sets them therein.

There is, of course, enough consistency of character to make it superficially convincing ; even a fairy-tale fails of its consummation if there is no sufficient evidence that these things are happening to people reasonably like those we know. The emotions must be strange enough to give us the sense of escape, but the people who experience them must be like enough to persuade us that it is we in them who achieve that escape. And so the fairy-world of Beaumont and Fletcher is, even at its most fanciful, peopled by beings who act plausibly most of the time and only rarely strain our credulity. But the distinction between them and those other people of the earlier Jacobean drama is that, with Beaumont and Fletcher, we have an impression that the motives have been supplied after the situations and emotional crises have been determined upon ; they have been thought-out carefully and articulated delicately but, nevertheless, they are only part of the apparatus of illusion, made to conceal the real springs of the machine, which are situation and action. When there is a difficulty in making them co-operate, it is the situation or emotional crisis that is preserved, while the motivation shows unmistakable signs of patching.[1] When Leucippus (in the fourth act of *Cupid's Revenge*) deliberately insists in a moment of danger on trusting his life to the word of Timantus (a man of whom he has hitherto known nothing but evil and who has always been associated with his enemies), can there be any reason but that it is necessary for the conduct of the narrative that he should be lured back into the power of those enemies ? Can any amount of noble sentiment conceal the innate absurdity of his action and the sudden disappearance of normal motivation ? Ismenus, his friend, has protested, very reasonably, at this sudden and hazardous credulity :

Leu. Peace, peace for shame, thy love is too suspitious, 'tis a way offer'd to preserve my life, and I will take it : be my Guide *Timantus* and do not mind this angry man, thou know'st him : I may live to requite thee.

---

[1] This might appear at first glance to be closely akin to Webster's habit of concentrating on certain key situations and neglecting to elucidate both plot and motive. But with Webster the situations, however much he neglect all else for them, are the outcome of the personality he has first conceived. There is no suggestion that the situation or the emotional crisis itself was what he sought, but, rather, that he sought it as a means to illuminate that particular character.

Ism. . . . Sir, for wisdoms sake court not your death, I am your friend and subject, and I shall lose in both. . . .
Leu. So much of man, and so much fearful ; fie, prethee have peace within thee : I shall live yet many a golden day to hold thee here dearest and nearest to me : Go on *Timantus.* . . .

Not even the attempt of the author to forestall criticism by putting that very criticism into the mouth of the outraged friend, Ismenus, can cover up the joinery here. Either Leucippus is too fantastically wrong-headed to hold our sympathy, or, a far likelier alternative, he is not a homogeneous and continuous human being, but a series of imperfectly associated groups of responses to the stimulus of carefully prepared situations. He is in this only one of a number of heroes similarly constituted and similarly circumstanced, and the same inconsistency is likely to creep into them all ; even Philaster defers and plays into the hands of his opponent in a way which reveals that the guiding principle of the play is not the revelation of his character in event, but the celebration of event itself.[1]

Less obvious, but no less significant, I think, is the sacrifice of consistency of behaviour not immediately, for the sake of plot, but, less directly, for the development of the action through some improbable but persistent attribute in the character. The fantastic loyalty, nobility and scrupulousness of the heroes in the early plays again and again fills us with impatience if we come to them fresh from the fundamental veracity of Shakespeare, Middleton, Jonson, Tourneur or Webster. Philaster procrastin-

---

[1] This government of character by situations occurs, if only momentarily, in many of the plays, especially of the early group. Philaster's conduct at the end of IV, iii, is hardly consistent with the quixotic nobility he has so far professed, but it is eminently useful in bringing on the next turn of stage affairs, while the character of Maximus in *Valentinian* suffers repeatedly and more deeply from this kind of violation, from the third scene of the third act onwards. (In this case, the latter part of the play is not really consequent upon the first and what should have been an impressive situation, from V, iii, onwards, is flawed by the insufficiency of motive upon which it rests.) Rather similar is the light-hearted lie by which Dion (an otherwise dependable character) separates Philaster and Arethusa (III, i) ; it has a casual irresponsibleness, which the character has not hitherto suggested, and a flourishing progeny of events, misconstructions and emotional crises. The text of the Cambridge edition is followed in the quotations in this chapter, but scene references are added, from the Mermaid edition, in the footnotes for purposes of readier reference.

ates and so does Hamlet, but in Hamlet the putting off of a doubtfully noble task is a part of his being, springing from certain well attested and openly recognized qualities of his mind, admitted and commented on by himself and others, while in Philaster it is part of a vague, incoherent fastidiousness, inexplicable alike to his friends and to the audience.[1] Hamlet has scruples about accusing his mother, genuine, fundamental and natural scruples which deflect the action of the play as they would in common life ; Leucippus has scruples too, but of so fantastic, ungrounded and strained a loyalty that he submits with patience and reverence to the insults, hostility and plotting of his own cast mistress Bacha simply because, by hoodwinking the old king Leontius, she has married him and become Leucippus's queen and mother. Here is a character rooted in unreality, with motives that seem to rest upon words only, with no perception of the nature of fact (' la verità effetuale della cosa '), paying a ridiculous respect to a woman who, for seducing his own father, should be doubly hideous to him, and for her plans to undo the kingdom should be stamped out like any other contagious disease. The salt of common sense that meets us on every page of Ben Jonson, and that stayed by the major Jacobean dramatists at all but their wildest moments, has vanished from the fairy-land of Beaumont and Fletcher.

Leu. All you have nam'd but making of me sin
With you, you may command, but never that ;
Say what you will, I'll hear you as becomes me,
If you speak, I will not follow your counsell,
Neither will I tell the world to your disgrace,
But give you the just honor
That is due from me to my Father's wife.
      I see 'tis in your power
To work your will on him : And I desire you
To lay what trains you will for my wish'd death,
But suffer him to find his quiet grave
In peace. . . . I beseech you pardon me,

---

[1] See especially Philaster's dialogue with Dion (III, i), where all the answer he gives to the entreaty that he will come forward and deliver the kingdom, is the vague and unexplained ' my designs Are not yet ripe ', ' the time Is short of what I would '. There is no attempt on his own part or on that of the others to give reasons for this melancholy inertia ; rather it is accepted as the indication of a sensitiveness and nobility beyond criticism.

14

> For the ill word I gave you, for how ever
> You may deserve it, it became me not
> To call you so, but passion urges me
> I know not whither.[1]

This unmanly acquiescence, this enchanted passivity, sinking back upon endurance and eschewing action cannot with any justice be laid to Hamlet's charge ; [2] it is not even a bastard of his begetting, but is the child of that same mood of fairy-tale unreality in which motive is strained beyond credulity in order that accumulated stresses may fall into a preconceived place in a crucial scene.

Less extreme cases, because better concealed and set in greater beauty of sentiment, situation and speech, are the better known figures of Evadne and Philaster. The speeches of Evadne immediately after her interview with Melantius (IV, i) and in the scene (V, i) in which she murders the king are, though not difficult for an actress to portray effectively, hard to believe when they are read. Something there is, perhaps, of Bonduca in her tigerish resolve, something of Webster's masculine women, Julia and Vittoria, something it might be of Lady Macbeth and again of Goneril.[3]   But with all of these it is possible to identify ourselves, provided the play has been followed to that point with an alert imagination. With Evadne, no amount of imaginative submission to the earlier part of the play seems to avail us any-thing. She seems to move suddenly on to another plane of being. The springs of motive do not seem to be like our own, nor the processes of the mind. This does not suggest a momen-tary failure, confusion or weakness of imagination, but rather a break in the continuity. Approaching it with the memory of

---

[1] *Cupid's Revenge*, III, i.   (The reader may indeed long for the entry of a figure like Romelio of *The Devil's Law Case*.

> ' Death
> Phew !   I tooke out that Lesson,
> When I once lay sicke of an Ague.   I doe now
> Labour for life, for life ! '

A grain of the old Elizabethan ' resolution ' is worth a world of en-chanted figures, waiting thus, in love with their own deaths.)

[2] To be ' pigeon-livered and lack gall ' no longer makes ' oppression bitter '.   On the contrary, in this looking-glass world of motive and action, it is gradually becoming a cardinal virtue.

[3] Edith, in *The Bloody Brother* (V, ii), comes nearest of all, but there it is blood that calls for blood and the whole bearing of the woman is more believable.

such a play as *Cupid's Revenge* clear in the mind (a play inferior in beauty and technical skill to this), we are inclined to attribute the difficulty here to the same cause that was so patent there. The situation required the murder, and some violation of the character, albeit subtly concealed and delicately overlaid, was the inevitable outcome of the clash of interests between character and plot. Philaster fills us with the same uneasiness (and we may be forgiven if we trace it to the same cause) when he suspects Arethusa and Bellario (III, ii), accepting the words of court gossips rather than their own straightforward statements.[1]

From this weakness of motivation, then, this wanton interference with character in the interests of plot and situation, comes the pervading atmosphere of falseness and unreality which spreads through the early plays, a fundamental unsoundness which from time to time builds beauty of sentiment and conduct on insecure foundations [2] or lends the exquisite descriptive poetry of *The Faithful Shepherdess* to a story in which chastity, like the player-queen, doth protest too much.

[1] Posthumus, in *Cymbeline*, who never lays claim to such nobility of sentiment and scruple as does Philaster, is the victim of deliberate and determined machinations, he does not yield up his faith without severe pressure and the revulsion of his mind against his own action is complete long before Iachimo's confession confirms it. This, though the situations are similar, gives the measure of the difference between the naturalness of Posthumus's behaviour and the disjointedness of Philaster's.

[2] For this faulty relation of sentiment and conduct with the main mood of the play, we may consider the speech of Dorialus in IV, i, of *Cupid's Revenge* (' Thou angry power, whether of Heaven or Hell '). There is a fundamental impropriety—not only moral, but, I think, also aesthetic—in raising the tragic, religious emotion here on a substructure of light-opera mood and motive. The same characteristic is discernible even in comedy, as when in *The Wild-Goose-Chase* (IV, iii), the supposed madness of Oriana draws on such apparent beauty of sentiment and just such pathos as have moved us in the serious or tragic plays. Mirabel's lines as he looks at the wreckage his heartlessness has supposedly caused are exquisite—but not as the sequel to a joke which the audience shares against him. For a moment we wonder whether Fletcher had confused his commonplace books and set in the wrong speech. Then we realize that he is, as Ward suggests, parodying his own pathos. This is indeed neither right tragedy nor right comedy ; this is a greater aesthetic crime than to ' match Hornpipes and Funeralls ', this employing the very note of Jacobean tragedy in the mood of burlesque. Something similar is again at work even in the finest scene (IV, i) of *Thierry and Theodoret*.

But these are avowedly the weak points in this fairy-tale tragi-comedy and its descendants, the inevitable indications of the unreal world into which the drama, with Beaumont and Fletcher, has escaped. A measure of unreality is perhaps inseparable from such an escape. It is generally easier to trace first in the weaker plays (like *Cupid's Revenge*) because it is only when the workmanship falls a little below the excellence they usually maintain that we can see the strain imposed by a structure that subordinates character to situation in a serious play.

But in general we abandon quite early the demand for homogeneousness of mood, thought and character, abandon the unsuitable effort to think of the plays as organic growths or to see in each its individual spatial form and look instead at the bewildering variety of beauty in situation, episode, sentiment and language. We are bewildered, dazzled, intoxicated by cadence, variation, unexpected change of action, of sentiment, of tempo until we lose the power of integrating this magic world into which we have strayed and surrender ourselves to a beauty which, however it be rooted in falsity, bears again and again a singular and lovely flower. Whether it be the excellence of the structure, the rapidity and variety of the movement in comedy and the sudden breathless turns of fate in the serious plays ; whether it be the vigour and effectiveness of the characters in the later tragedies, the brilliance and variety of those in the comedies, the perfumed beauty of certain isolated, pathetic figures in the tragi-comedies and tragedies ; whether it be the solid vigour of individual speeches, the long passages of sustained dialogue or the poignant snatches of verse and image ; whether it be the spellbound atmosphere that holds the romances or the gaiety and geniality of the comic plots and comic interludes, enough is here to satisfy us—once we have admitted the dispersal of the elements, the disintegration of mood, character and thought, which sets these writers and those who entered their territory apart from the strict Jacobean tragedy and comedy.

Since much has been sacrificed to structure in the art of Beaumont and of Fletcher, it is fitting that that structure should be good. It is indeed superlatively good. It surpasses that of any other Jacobean dramatist in its own kind, combining the complexity of Jonson with the ease with which Middleton manipulated his somewhat simpler machinery. And this is true whether the play be tragedy, tragi-comedy or comedy, whether we examine the conduct of the whole intrigue, the relations of tempo and mood of adjoining scenes, the original use of old devices and the development of fresh ones, or the minutiae of stage conduct, the very exits and entries of the characters. All that can be regarded as strictly structural (not as belonging to the domain of the relations of character and structure) is beyond cavil, and would, I believe, prove itself so in action. What, for neatness of comedy plotting, for variety without confusion and proportioning of the phases of intrigue and its resolution, could be better theatre-work than, say, *The Coxcomb* upon the one side or *The Wild-Goose-Chase* [1] upon the other ? Or than the clear, easily followed and yet unexpected developments of the tragic action of *The Maid's Tragedy, Bonduca* or *Valentinian* ? [2] Or, if we choose a tragi-comedy, how excellently do the authors control, not only the action but the relations of tempo and mood in, say, *A King and No King, Philaster, Two Noble Kinsmen.* This is not merely a matter of intrigue only, but is clearly seen in the conduct of individual scenes. To the crucial scene between Mardonius and Arbaces [3] they have given some of the best of their skill in this kind. First comes the natural dialogue between the two friends, Arbaces again and again approaching his confession and as often flinging away from it, while Mardonius grows more and more aware of his agony. Then, after the slow, hesitant and stumbling approach, follows the rush of words, the outburst of passion, with which the fact comes out, and the withdrawal of Mardonius into a matter-of-fact plainness (indicated by the subtle passage from verse to prose) designed to sober the passionate Arbaces. This is interrupted abruptly by the entry of the comic figure Bessus. In the quick dialogue that follows, the callous lightness of this trivial creature serves, as no serious admonitions of Mardonius could, to reveal the depth of moral misery in which Arbaces' mind is struggling. The same skill is to be found in the disclosure at the end of the

[1] A range that includes such variety of theme and comic technique as there is in *The Scornful Lady, The Woman Hater, The Little French Lawyer, The Humourous Lieutenant, The Spanish Curate, Wit Without Money* and *The Chances.*

[2] The unsoundness of the character of Maximus notwithstanding. We do not rebel against the course of the action, but against the idea that a man of that character should take it.

[3] *A King and No King*, III, iii.

play, where the unravelling, though just slow enough for us to
follow readily and delivered piecemeal so that suspense is maintained, is yet rapid enough for apprehension to wait upon event
and not outrun it.   How skilful again (to consider a detail of
theatrecraft) is Fletcher's handling of the battle scenes in *Bonduca*
where he ranges over the whole of his wide and flexible Elizabethan stage, using its magnificent possibilities to the full, so
that, by his manipulation of its different resources, we may follow
both the conduct of the fight as a whole and the fortunes of the
individual fighters in whom we are most nearly interested.[1]
In all this, it is the theatre that is the authors' main concern ; not
the content of the play, the underlying thought or implicit commentary, but the effectiveness of the successive and related
episodes.   And just as this skilful handling of the course of the
plot evidences at every turn their keen sense of the theatre, of its
demands at once and its facilities, so do the individual situations,
and they also remain sharp in our memory.   In the comedies
they are reached, like Middleton's comic climaxes, on the crest
of a swiftly moving wave of action and are rich in implications
drawn from the preceding action.   Nor are they essentially
different in the serious plots : ever and again the characters fall
into a striking, often an unexpected grouping ; the group dissolves and, as suddenly, another takes its place, pauses for the
length of a scene or half-scene and melts away again.   A series
of brilliant tableaux or episodes remains ; the interim, confusion
and it may even be inconsequence.   There is no attempt at the
presentation of a continuous growth of circumstance or event
like the inevitable growth of one of Shakespeare's tragedies to
its inevitable end, nor at the solid, articulated architecture of

---

[1] See *Bonduca*, III, iii–v.   Caratach, as leader of the British forces,
first stations himself in a position from which he can see the plan of
the field and he and Nennius discuss the movements of the Roman and
British armies as they engage.   He then withdraws to enter the fight
himself.   There is a short scene in which we gather up the fortunes of
Junius, Curius and Decius and then Drusus and Penyus appear above
and discuss the next stage of the general battle.   This information
is provided quite naturally (although everybody else is now engaged in
fighting) by Penyus, who has refused to join the Roman army and is
standing aside from the engagement.   The third phase of the battle
can then be easily indicated in the usual Jacobean manner by a series
of running fights upon the stage and the entry of one side or other with
captives.   All the individual plots in the play are thus carried forward
under our eyes and yet the general progress of the action remains clear.

Ben Jonson's plots. At its best it is more like the sequence of groupings in a ballet ; even when the workmanship falters a little the splendid episodes emerge and impress themselves on the memory. What we recall is the dialogue at the central moment or the finely moulded and detachable set speeches that form the climax of the scene ; the words in which Philaster at last speaks out his long-repressed indignation and denounces the king at the same time as, with a magnificent gesture, he offers to make sacrifice of his own life ; [1] the long soliloquies of Maximus torn between honour and vengeance ; [2] the convulsive conflicts of Arbaces and the dialogues between him and Panthea ; [3] the passionate pleading of Edith with Rollo for her father's life and the later scene in which she avenges herself for that father's murder ; [4] the battle speeches of Suetonius and Caratach ; [5] the grave deportment of the dialogue between Ordella and Thierry ; [6] speech after speech of vigorous emotion, solid and well defined, sometimes in crisp quick dialogue or soliloquy, sometimes touched with beauty and gravity of sentiment.

Cel. . . . Can these, Sir,
These precious things, the price of youth and beauty ;
This shop here of sin-offerings set me off again ?
Can it restore me chaste, young innocent ?
. . . The Kings device ! [7]
The sin's as universal as the Sun is,
And lights an everlasting Torch to shame me.
. . . .
Thou seemest to me a Souldier.
Ant. Yes, I am one.
Cel. And hast fought for thy Country ?
Ant. Many a time.
Cel. Maybe, commanded too ?
Ant. I have done, Lady.
Cel. O wretched man, below the state of pity !
Canst thou forget thou wert begot in honour ?
A free companion for a King ? a Souldier ?
Whose Nobleness dare feel no want, but Enemies ?
Canst thou forget this, and decline so wretchedly,

---

[1] *Phil.*, V, iii.   [2] *Val.*, III, iii ; V, iii.
[3] *K.N.K.*, I, i ; III, i ; IV, iv.   [4] *B.B.*, III, i ; V, ii.
[5] *Bond.*, I, i ; I, ii ; III, i ; III, ii.   [6] *T.T.*, IV, i.
[7] The Cambridge editors here read ' device ' ; I have ventured to modernize the punctuation in the interests of clearness.

> To eat the Bread of Bawdry, of base Bawdry ?
> Feed on the scum of Sin ? fling thy sword from thee ?
> .   .   .   .
> *Ant.* I command ye stay.
> *Cel.* Be just, I am commanded.
> *Ant.* I will not wrong ye.
> *Cel.* Then thus low falls my duty.
> *Ant.* Can you love me ?
>   Say I, and all I have—
> *Cel.*   I cannot love ye ;
> Without the breach of faith I cannot hear ye ;
> Ye hang upon my love, like frosts on Lilies :
> I can dye, but I cannot love : you are answer'd.[1]

For the handling of a single dramatic moment, the sudden check of the action, as it were, in full career and the turn which carries it, sometimes in a single sentence, from unsuspecting geniality into tragic intention, nearly every play written at the height of their powers gives evidence. To Melantius, fresh from the scene with Amintor, when he has at last been persuaded of his sister's adultery with the king, comes in his younger brother Diphilus full of the merry mood of the wedding celebrations and utterly unsuspicious alike of Melantius's knowledge and of the tragic motive which has enveloped him and Amintor and is waiting to overspread the laughter of the court.

> *Mel.*   Sword, hold thine edge,
>   My heart will never fail me :   [*Enter Diphilus*]
>   Diphilus !
>   Thou com'st as sent.
> *Diph.* Yonder has been such laughing.
> *Mel.* Betwixt whom ?
> *Diph.* Why, our Sister and the King.
>   I thought their spleens would break,
>   They laught us all out of the room.
> *Mel.* They must weep, *Diphilus*.[2]

In the ease and economy of this there is consummate skill ; with this check Melantius swings round the career not only of his brother but of the whole action of the play.

Single characters, in the same way, detach themselves from the background ; some, especially in those plays which Fletcher is generally considered to have written alone, are refreshingly free from the inexplicable motives that interfere with our full acceptance of the tragi-comedy and early tragedy heroes. Aecius in *Valentinian* (and, up to a point, Maximus), Aubrey

---

[1] *The Humourous Lieutenant*, IV, i.   [2] *M.T.*, III, ii.

in the *Bloody Brother*, Petillius, Caratach, Penyus and Suetonius
in *Bonduca*, and many more, are all coherent, clearly drawn
figures. There is no pretence at undue nobility of sentiment
or super-normal sensitiveness, but there is plenty of good sense
and workmanlike treatment side by side with passages of no
mean degree of percipience. Being mainly involved in action,
they need not be drawn minutely, but the proportions are true
and the drawing by no means always rough. Caratach is in
fact a kind of touchstone of good sense, practical capacity and
manly steadiness of conduct, balanced by the same qualities in
the Roman general Suetonius and contrasted with the hysteria
of Bonduca. His longer speeches, even on the eve of battle,
are temperate and sane ; his affection for the child Hengo
never threatens to become mawkish ; his respect for his foe is
as genuine as his determination to beat him if he can, and both
stop short of hyperbole. Indeed, in this and other plays of the
kind, Fletcher develops a plain manliness of style and treatment
which seems to be carried over from Mardonius, Melantius and
Ismenus, the straightforward soldiers whose presence in the
earlier group threw into relief the gusty passions or melancholy
inertia of the other characters. Just such another is Aecius,
a man with the gift of moderate, sane speech (upon all but the
dangerous, debatable topic of kingship) and with a certain innate
decency of demeanour whatever vicissitudes he passes through :

Max.   If I should dye, would it not grieve you much ?
Aeci.   Without all doubt.
Max.   And could you live without me ?
Aeci.   It would much trouble me to live without ye.
       Our loves, and loving souls have been so us'd
       But to one household in us : but to dye
       Because I could not make you live, were woman,
       Far much too weak.[1] Were it to save your worth,
       Or to redeem your name from rooting out,
       To quit you bravely fighting from the foe,
       Or fetch ye off, where honour had ingag'd ye.
       I ought, and would dye for ye.[2]

While Fletcher can create and maintain characters like this,
and they are relatively numerous in the middle and later plays,

---

[1] The Ff. read ' weak, were ' and are followed by the Cambridge
editors. I have ventured to alter the punctuation in accordance with
modern usage in order to make the meaning more immediately clear.
[2] *Val.*, III, iii.

even when there is inconsistency in the mood of the rest of the play, it is idle to suggest that theatre romance pervaded the whole of his work. There are in fact plays in which it only occurs sporadically, when his sense of the theatre is revealed in a very different way, in the effectiveness with which he groups, in striking situations and in rapid action, characters which are natural, unpretentiously drawn and yet strongly coloured and distinct.

There is, finally, one group of characters in the serious plays in whom the romantic conception appears with almost unflawed beauty, the characters whose fates, temperaments, sentiments, even the very cadences of their speech, are instinct with a clear pathos upon which no other responsibility is laid than to run like a minor melody, through the action of the play.[1] Even the memory of the great tragic figures of the earlier drama cannot destroy the haunting beauty of the slight figures of Aspatia, Arethusa, Bellario, Spaconia, Panthea and their kindred, though they demand a double share of the willing suspension of disbelief, and even as we accept their control over our authors we know that we are entering a cloud-cuckoo land of sentiment. These characters are generally clear in their main lines, not subtle or complicated, but simple and limpid. Indeed, Aspatia is perhaps too transparent ; she seems, after a time, to lack colour and definition. But the clear note of simple pathos persists, brings with it its own cadences, its own lucid and gentle imagery and often a quiet plainness of utterance, empty of any imagery at all, that re-appears later as one of the characteristic marks of the work of Middleton. In Lysippus' description of Aspatia's melancholy, in Arethusa's speeches when Philaster disowns her, in some of Philaster's own at the nadir of his fortunes, in Spaconia's and Panthea's scenes together, and most movingly of all, in Bellario's words with Philaster, the same mood runs.[2] Often these scenes, like that in which, at the beginning of *Philaster*, Arethusa finds her way out of the tangled events besetting her, ring true for the duration of a whole dialogue and have a note, like the pathetic cadences of Ford, to which

[1] In the tragedies and the tragi-comedies this is often the quintessence of the play. Fletcher is capable, however (as has been suggested), of introducing the same pathos in settings so incongruous that his use of it seems almost mechanical and suggests, rather disquietingly, that he could write as movingly for a burlesque as for a tragedy.

[2] *M.T.*, I, i ; *Phil.*, III, ii, and IV, iv ; *K.N.K.*, II, i, and *Phil.*, III, i.

the habitual readers of the tragi-comedy respond unconsciously, it may be unintentionally, no matter in what setting it occurs :

[*Enter* ARETHUSA *and a* LADY.]

Are. Comes he not ?
La. Madam ?
Are. Will *Philaster* come ?
La. Dear madam, you were wont
    To credit me at first.
Are. But didst thou tell me so ?
    I am forgetful, and my woman's strength
    Is so o'recharged with danger like to grow
    About my Marriage that these under-things
    Dare not abide in such a troubled sea :
    How look't he, when he told thee he would come ?
La. Why, well.
Are. And not a little fearful ?
La. Fear Madam ? sure he knows not what it is.
Are. You are all of his Faction ; the whole Court
    Is bold in praise of him, whilst I
    May live neglected : and do noble things,
    As fools in strife throw gold into the Sea,
    Drown'd in the doing : but I know he fears.
La. Fear ? Madam (me thought) his looks hid more
    Of love than fear.
Are. Of love ? To whom ? to you ?
    Did you deliver those plain words I sent,
    With such a winning gesture, and quick look
    That you have caught him ?
La. Madam, I mean to you.
Are. Of love to me ? Alas ! thy ignorance
    Lets thee not see the crosses of our births :
    Nature, that loves not to be questioned
    Why she did this, or that, but has her ends,
    And knows she does well ; never gave the world
    Two things so opposite, so contrary,
    As he and I am : If a bowl of blood
    Drawn from this arm of mine, would poyson thee,
    A draught of his would cure thee. Of love to me ?
La. Madam, I think I hear him.
Are. Bring him in :
    You gods that would not have your dooms withstood,
    Whose holy wisdoms at this time it is,
    To make the passion of a feeble maid
    The way unto your justice, I obey.[1]

---

[1] *Phil.*, I, ii. If the plays had always maintained this clear honesty of simple emotion, natural and morally unpretentious, ' it had been vain to blame and useless to praise them '.

Not a line could be cut out of this without loss ; it is an emotional study, though only episodic, that is simple, definite and self-absorbed.   Such passages are in nearly every serious play and where they are not sustained as here, they break through in sudden, poignant snatches of verse or in potent or pithy summaries :

> Those have most power to hurt us, that we love ;
> We lay our sleeping lives within their arms,[1]

' some man Weary of life that would be glad to die ',[2] ' I did hear you talk Far above singing ',[3] ' the Night Crowned with a thousand stars and our cold light '.[4]   The spellbound pathos that holds the earlier plays like an enchantment and appears again and again in snatches in the later is summed up in that scene in which Philaster, not recognizing Euphrasia under the disguise of Bellario, threatens to kill her as the betrayer of Arethusa.   The scene is heavily fraught already ; the burden of unrequited love, of hearing continually Philaster's longing for Arethusa and of acting as messenger between the lovers while hiding her own breaking heart, have laid upon Euphrasia such accumulated sorrow that death at Philaster's hands is, as for so many of Beaumont and Fletcher's love-crossed maidens, more joy than sorrow :

Phil.   Fearest thou not death ?
　　　 . . . thou dost not know what 'tis to die.
Be.   Yes, I do know, my Lord ;
　　　'Tis less than to be born ; a lasting sleep,
　　　A quiet resting from all jealousie,　　·
　　　A thing we all pursue ; I know besides,
　　　It is but giving over of a game that must be lost.[5]

It is in scenes like these that the finest flowering of the tragi-comedy romantic mood is to be found, working in its own proper medium and uncontaminated by incongruous association, moral or aesthetic, uncontaminated, too, by reference to that world of tragic doubt and horror or satiric exposure that was the Jacobean tragedy and comedy.   Beaumont and Fletcher have escaped alike from Vindice and from Volpone before them and from Sir Walter Whorehound and from de Flores who are yet to come. A new world has been discovered, and though Middleton and

---

[1] *M.T.*, V, iv.　　　　[2] *Phil.*, IV, iv.　　　　[3] Ibid., V, v.
　　　　[4] *M.T.*, I, ii.　　　　[5] *Phil.*, III, i.

Webster (and such of their contemporaries as survive) never enter it, even when, like Middleton,[1] they seem most nearly to do so, it is a world irresistibly desirable to a generation that no longer needs to live at the edge of eternity or in whom that habit has not been too deeply grained to be laid aside.

The comic plots and the comic episodes in the serious plays, whether long or brief, seem to belong to another world ; they are rooted in reality, resting on commonplace motives and emotions. When the comic mood takes possession, with Beaumont and Fletcher, alone or jointly, the fairy-land of romantic feeling or inflated sentiment vanishes. Brief snatches of dialogue between the courtiers in *Philaster* [2] or *Valentinian*,[3] glimpses of life behind the scenes at a court festival in *The Maid's Tragedy* [4] or *The Bloody Brother* [5] drop at once to the same matter-of-fact, merry or cynical level of everyday feeling as the more broadly comic elements of the comedies from *The Woman Hater* to *The Noble Gentleman.* The soldier scenes of *Bonduca* and *The Loyal Subject*, the sailors in *The Sea Voyage*, the talk of the citizens in *The Knight of the Burning Pestle*, the excellently comic, detachable character of Bessus in *A King and No King*, the absurdities of Lazarello in *The Woman Hater*, above all the crowds in *Philaster*, *A King and No King*, *Cupid's Revenge* and *The Knight of the Burning Pestle* again, have a vulgar, hearty, Rabelaisian geniality which witnesses to the love and keen observation of London life with its variety of types and matter.[6]

In all this, the lighter and gayer side of their work, there is the same excellent familiarity with the types they draw from and the treatment they give them. They range from the satirical-farce of Beaumont's earliest play, through delicate

---

[1] The plays, formally tragi-comedies, of the Middleton-Rowley group (*A Fair Quarrel*, *The Witch*, *The Spanish Gipsey*), are, upon inspection, just such plays as fulfil the letter of Fletcher's definition without sharing his distinctive mood.

[2] *Phil.*, II, ii, and II, iv.   [3] *Val.*, II, i.

[4] *M.T.*, I, ii, the brief dialogues during the preparation for the mask.

[5] *B.B.*, II, iii. One would like to add the scenes in the royal kitchen, but it is at least doubtful whether these are Fletcher's.

[6] The same intimate familiarity is there as we find simultaneously in Middleton, but with Beaumont and Fletcher there is almost a note of conscious affection for the town that we do not meet else till the Restoration. ' There's music in the worst cry in London ! ' Etherege's words are almost anticipated in the descriptions of specific London scenes, as in *K.B.P.*, IV, v, *Mons. Thomas*, IV, ii, or *W.H.*, I, iii.

mixture of romance and broad comedy in *The Coxcomb* and the delicate, fanciful mockery of *The Wild Goose Chase* to the vigorous breadth of low life in *The Beggar's Bush* or the mixture of romance and Aristophanic laughter in *The Humourous Lieutenant*. The variety of range in characters is enormous. Few, if any, are profoundly drawn. All are effective either by their natural vitality and frankness, by a kind of straightforward originality of conduct (like that of Mercury in *The Coxcomb*), by sharp, satiric observation (like that of *The Little French Lawyer*) or by a kind of spirited honesty found in many of the women, Honora, Celia, Oriana, Rosalura and many more.

The mood of the tragi-comedy very seldom (and then only slightly) invades these characters or the plays to which they belong, and it might seem at first that they differed in no essential (except in the finer finish, the easier grace and lightness of movement) from the main body of Jacobean comedy. Indeed, in some of the plays which, like *The Woman Hater* at the beginning or *The Little French Lawyer* towards the end, border in part on Jonsonian humour studies, it is hard to distinguish them from the comedy now of Marston, now of Jonson, and especially of Middleton. But upon nearer view it appears that the total result of the comedies of Beaumont and Fletcher is different ; we miss the painstaking research of Jonson and the detached photographic record of Middleton, and we find, as a rule, a total effect of geniality and gaiety too unchequered to belong to the older Jacobean world where ugly and discordant jars forced themselves in and must be reckoned with in the orchestration. This would not be noticeable in one play, I think. It is only when it is perceived in several, or in similar sections in several plays, that it becomes of account. In the crowd scenes, for instance, whether in the early studies of city crowds in *The Knight of the Burning Pestle*, *Philaster*, *A King and No King*, *Cupid's Revenge* or in the rather later studies of soldiery in *Bonduca* and *The Loyal Subject*, it may occur to us after a time that there is a persistent assumption of good-will and right-headedness in these groups which is not there with certain other mobs such as Shakespeare's, that the intervention of these genial, hearty, Rabelaisian citizens and soldiery is too uniformly felicitous, that all tends to work together too consistently for the best for it to be the same stuff of which the background of Jacobean comedy is made. With Shakespeare's mobs increasingly, from that led by Jack Cade to that led by the tribunes Sicinius and Brutus, there is a sinister implication behind the voluble excitement ; it may be touched in so lightly that the atmosphere is hardly disturbed, but it still gives a veracity and soundness to Shakespeare's pictures which meets the test of repeated reading in widely varying moods. Here is, perhaps, another manifestation, indirect and hardly at once perceptible, of the deep inhering tendency of Beaumont and Fletcher to use as their base a transparent wash of romance in the composition even of those scenes whose colouring seems least associated with it.

III

It has been suggested that Beaumont and Fletcher, with their excellent sense of the theatre upon the one hand and of the appetite for romance in their audience upon the other, were content to avoid the great questions which, in their profundity, trouble the form and sometimes confuse the substance itself of the earlier Jacobean tragedy. This, with some qualification, is often true ; they do not raise, by the implications of the material they choose and the passions they stir, those issues touching the meaning of life and the destiny of man which run through those tragedies. But alongside this there is a marked increase in explicit statement and in discussion, if not of the main tragic issues, of topics of still living and immediate concern ; the nature of kingship, of friendship, of honour (particularly of woman's honour), of the conduct proper to a gentleman. They bring the claims of these deliberately into conflict in the serious plays, so that, in the central scenes, they may be debated between the characters in all the heat of immediate experience. They make of a situation, of an episode, a test case upon which the cause of both claimants may be tried ; Amintor's honour over against his loyalty, Melantius's friendship against his duty to his sister's good name ; Maximus is divided in just such a way as Amintor, and Aecius between his friendship for Maximus and his loyalty to Valentinian. Like motifs in a pattern, they are grouped and regrouped, always with the practical case as the foundation of the debate. It reads as though it would be well within the reach of an intelligent audience, [1] even though

---

[1] Those, at least, of these plays which have been produced in the last twenty years have generally proved easy to follow—but not easy enough to allow of any slackening of attention.

hearing it for the first time ; it is not profound and it is never confused ; it is original only so far as a definite, explicit state-ment of what has long been in many men's minds bears claim to originality ; it is a little like wit as Pope understood it and has most of the stimulating effects we associate with that wit ; it must have given its audience a pleasant sense of being abreast of the newest thing that was being thought and discussed. What it does not do, on the other hand is to fill the mind with images from which the hearer could deduce his own reflections ; to provide, as Shakespeare does, an imaginative experience from which conclusions could be drawn, without specifically drawing them. Beaumont and Fletcher do not, partly for the very reason that Shakespeare has already done it, build up a group of closely connected history plays, which, with the help of some later tragedies, lay before us almost every relevant experience connected with statecraft and government, approached in turn from the point of view of almost every relevant group or in-dividual in the state and interspersed with the brief comments inevitable to men whose lives are mainly engaged upon these things. Instead, they give us the crucial situations (those test cases that Shakespeare for some reason so seldom seems to meet) which introduce clearly the conflict between two views on king-ship, and let it be debated to and fro, sometimes in a running series of scenes, between Amintor and Melantius, Maximus and Aecius, Rollo and Aubrey, the problem resolving itself into a series of points set over against each other : private honour against public loyalty, reverence for the monarch against hatred of the man, the rights of the individual against the demands of the State.[1]

Akin to this, and in some degree perhaps arising out of it, is the tendency to group characters in series, repeating, often with only slight modifications, the same type in one play after another : the blunt but faithful friend (Mardonius, Ismenus, Melantius, Dion) ; the virtuous hero, wronged and long-suffer-ing (Leucippus, Amintor, Philaster) ; the wronged maid or wife (Euphrasia, Urania, Aspatia, Arethusa, Spaconia), who often takes to a page's disguise to serve her lover : the wicked,

---

[1] See, among several passages that might be cited, *M.T.*, II, i ; *Phil.*, IV, ii ; *Val.*, I, iii ; III, i, IV, iii ; *B.B.*, I, i, and Aubrey's speeches throughout the play. Of the same nature are the debates on friendship in *M.T.*, III, ii, and *K.N.K.*, I, i, upon honour in *M.T.*, II, i ; IV, ii.

scheming woman (Bacha or Brunhalt); the tyrannous (often usurping) king and the plotting villain.

Yet in all this body of plays, though written for the most part by three men (but, in the later years of Fletcher's more various collaboration, undoubtedly by several more), there is a kind of consistency, whether we are considering the joint work of Beaumont and Fletcher, the single-handed work of Fletcher or that body in which he, in collaboration with Massinger, still manages to preserve much that was characteristic of his early tragi-comedy.   All three of the main contributors must have been consummate dramatic journalists; there is balance and ease and a sense of contact with the audience throughout. Other Jacobeans may protest that their work was for the theatre only, but none were so completely its children, or knew so well how simultaneously to obey and lead the public taste.   ' Shakespeare, to thee, was dull.'   We can well believe it.

For this seems as nearly perfect theatre-work as is possible to imagine.   The characters are distinct, varied, unencumbered with the subtle modulations that are wasted on the stage, shallow enough to be grasped quickly by a few salient qualities, well-enough proportioned to sustain their parts and hold the attention fast through five acts of playing; all inconsistency or rough workmanship is lost in the heat of rhetoric and the brilliance of sentiment.   The plots are delicately articulated; no confused undercurrent of philosophic thought breaks up the action or disturbs the balance of interest; they are full of suspense, surprises, recoveries, disguisings, sudden turns of fate and fortunate disclosures.   The sentiment, which plays an important part here, as in all English plays with a strong sense of the theatre, has just enough reflection behind it to give at first hearing an impression of profundity without effort.   It adds colour to event and character, suggesting, like the shadows on a back-cloth, that the play has the three-dimensional quality of life itself; the topics that are debated are popular and they are boldly and freshly handled, like a good leading article in a paper catering for a good, average public.   The very language is easy to follow, but not so empty as to seem trivial.   Imagery, metre and diction are always of the kind which could be fully appreciated when heard; they do not, like Shakespeare's, demand familiarity and re-reading before anything like full appreciation can be approached.   The diction of Beaumont and Fletcher seems to reach the height of exquisite

15

stage speech and there is nothing there to which the theatre cannot do full justice.   Above all, the balance of all the elements, whether for comedy, tragi-comedy or tragedy, shows the finest theatrical tact, the discrimination that can control or release at need passions, events, descriptions, sentiment, poetry and verbal music, keeping the proportions of the whole truly balanced, providing the necessary variety in what is yet a happy synthesis ;   storm of mind and calm, vicissitudes of fortune, exotic and familiar scenes ;   the foaming torrent of accident and passion or the slow, enchanted embassy of death.

CHAPTER XII

JOHN FORD

I

FORD stands at some distance from his Jacobean predecessors and the work of his maturity seems separated by more than the actual space of a decade from that of the latest of these. Yet it is to the latest that his affiliations reach, to Webster in the phase of *The Duchess of Malfi*, to the ease of cadence and mood in Beaumont and Fletcher and to the limpid quietness of the later Middleton. Most of all, to the latest phase of Shakespeare's work, who, anticipating all of these in date, surpassed them in completeness of solution. Ford is the inheritor of the security of the later Jacobean mood, after the great questions had died down, deriving his serenity and stability alike from Beaumont and Fletcher who had not worked through the period of disintegration and from Shakespeare who alone, having done so, was able to re-integrate his universe.

This admittedly is not apparent at first glance because, superficially, Ford's plays show all the signs of a late and decadent art in their use of sensational episode and setting. But as one approaches him more closely it becomes clearer that these groupings and situations are, like the utterly incongruous comic subplots of his plays, concessions to the needs of the theatre rather than a spontaneous expression of his thought. They have, in fact, no valid part in the main business of his plays which is, as with the greatest of his predecessors, the illumination of character and thought by the aid of event.

Ford, then, comes, if not chronologically yet in effect, at the end of a period of dramatic evolution, gathering up its conclusions and leaving in his work the final expression of certain moods, ideas and technical habits which there find their natural close. The great storm of Jacobean tragedy had blown itself out : its range, confined though in one direction it had been by its spiritual doubt, had in another direction opened into immensity by the very hypothesis there implied. The spirit of man, brought suddenly into the foreground, had assumed dimensions so vast as to blot out for a time the absence of much else. But this very enlarging of the figure had concentrated attention upon it, and the progress of the major tragedy, after Webster's and after Shakespeare's later plays, is towards closer and closer concentration upon the mind of man and its secret processes. Fletcher's vigorous plays of action, the *Valentinian*s and *Bloody Brother*s, gave valuable service here by satisfying the audience's desire for healthy melodrama, while Middleton proceeded in the quite different direction of close analysis of hitherto disregarded or less fully examined movements of the mind. When tragedy came into Ford's hands, either alternative was, technically, possible for him, but his mind was attuned to that of Middleton to whom he was a true successor. In his plays, then, the focus is closed down to the narrow limits of this field only. In scope, his work is microscopic ; it excludes everything beyond the area of a few minds and those of like processes. Its greatness lies in the profundity of the study thus made in so narrow limits, and its universality lies in the knowledge of the ultimate oneness of the roots of human feeling and experience to which his concentration upon a few processes of the mind has led him. It may, however, be reasonably claimed that Ford, while specializing the tragic drama of Webster, Shakespeare and Middleton, so limited its scope as to bring it to an inevitable conclusion.

He again appears as the agent of its concluding phase, in his choice of theme, a choice intimately linked with that of his predecessors but leading almost inevitably to the extinction of the form. Side by side with the violence and sensationalism of the theatrical element in his plays, Ford pursues what was indeed the theme to him of major interest, the study of characters whose strongest quality was a reticent dignity in endurance. Like Shakespeare and Webster before him he recognizes the potency of the silent griefs, but, unlike Webster, he pursues that theme to the gradual exclusion of all others. Like Middleton, he prefers to work in a clear, cold light, but, unlike Middleton, he turns it not upon crudely or richly coloured minds but upon those of ever-increasing delicacy and neutrality of tint. After the loudness of the early Jacobean colour-scheme this is

most welcome, but, in essence, it is undramatic and can only
lead to the extinction of the dramatic form in the hands of any
artist who persists in it.

Ford is, then, in every sense a conclusion. He gathers into
his own tragedy, with sensitive response, the best of the discoveries of Beaumont, Fletcher and Middleton ; he brings
tragedy to a point at which it would have been well-nigh impossible for any successor to have received it at his hands, for in
concluding it he practically extinguishes it ; nevertheless it is
a true conclusion, perhaps the worthiest that could be given to
the great imaginative drama of the Elizabethans and the Jacobeans. It is written in major harmonies which may sound
commonplace after the tumult of tragic protest that has gone
before it. Actually there is, in its quiet stability, nothing
commonplace, nothing too easy. It brings us back, serenely,
economically, untheatrically, to the dominant which last sounded
clearly in Greene and Peele and in the early work of Marlowe.
' Look you. The stars shine still.'

II

Sibelius was once reported as saying that he offered his
audiences pure cold water instead of the cocktails of his immediate predecessors and contemporaries ; and, apart from some
melodramatic episodes and the ineffable silliness of his comic
sub-plots, this is equally true of Ford. There is coldness and
restraint in much of his work ; a grave and chill dignity in which
the emotions seem to be recollected rather than felt ; recollected
not merely in tranquillity, but in spellbound stillness. There
is also a quality, at once firm, solid and motionless, which affects
progressively his diction, his prosody, the demeanour of his
characters and finally their groupings and relations and even the
architecture itself of the inner form of the play. There are fore-
tastes of this in the earliest play of his sole authorship, *The
Lover's Melancholy*, and, in the latest play which bears the sure
mark of his hand, *The Lady's Trial*, the quietness of his utterance robs the play of theatrical, if not of dramatic, effect. At its
finest, in *The Broken Heart*, this distinctive quality deserves
comparison with that of Sophocles' drama, and there are continuous stretches of dialogue in which phrase after phrase
brings to the mind of the reader imaginative expansions and

reconstructions only to be checked again in the moment of utterance by the spell of Ford's own reticence.

The plays which give us anything significant are relatively few. *The Witch of Edmonton* [1] and *The Sun's Darling* show more of Dekker's work than of Ford's, *The Fancies Chaste and Noble* [2] and *The Queene* have at best a few scenes apiece that add to our knowledge of his mind. The essential part of his dramatic work is to be found in the six plays that fall between these two groups.

The Lover's Melancholy owes something, as Ford openly acknowledges, to Burton's *Anatomy of Melancholy* (1621), but it owes more to Ford himself, and, though more slender and lighter hearted than his later plays, it is also happier and gentler and its diction and metre have what is for Ford an almost decorative quality. Taken as it stands, without too severe a judgement, it is a lovely thing. We miss the later massive treatment of character and the solid interlocking of group with group, but we find instead a play of moods like the interplay of plain-song and prick-song melodies (carrying us back to the tragi-comedy of Beaumont and Fletcher at its sweetest), each one, Thamasta, Cleophila, Menaphon, Palador, Eroclea, complete in itself, yet all consorting together with that faultless tact in the blending of tragic or pathetic moods, not always within the reach of Beaumont and Fletcher, which was to grow clearer and firmer as Ford developed. We miss those dialogues which, in the later plays, run page after page in sustained beauty with never a failure of insight or judgement, but we find instead a melody of single lines such as we never meet again, for in the later plays these are severely subsidiarized to paragraph structure and to the continuous metrical effect of scenes taken as a whole. This ' lamentable tale of things Done long agoe, and ill done ' is no unfitting introduction to the work of that poet who stands alone for knowledge of ' the silent griefs that cut the heart-strings '. The words in this early play often give a very echo to the mood in which all Ford's tales unfold themselves and

---

[1] For *The Witch of Edmonton*, see Chap. VI.

[2] There are excellent passages in Ford's late subdued and temperate style (III, ii ; IV, ii ; the end of V, i ; V, iii *passim*), and the relation between the brother and sister, Romanello and Flavia, is good ; but Ford has carried so far his favourite theme of hidden love, that it is now hidden even from the audience and realization comes too late for dramatic effect (V, iii, 80–5).

they hold in them the quintessence of his verbal music at its sweetest :

> *Parthenophill* is lost, and I would see him ;
> For he is like to some thing I remember
> A great while since, a long, long time ago.[1]

That grave piety, too, which is part of the groundwork of the early plays written under the partial influence of Dekker, has an explicitness here that is gone in the later plays where judgement is given, like Sophocles' or Shakespeare's, by implication. *'Tis Pity She's a Whore* differs from his other work not in degree, but in kind. *The Lover's Melancholy* is an obvious younger brother of *The Broken Heart, Love's Sacrifice* and *The Lady's Trial*, but *'Tis Pity* seems to have suffered from its startling theme both at Ford's hands and at his critics'. The passions are more violent, there are fiercer emotions at work, and the play stands in consequence a little apart from the others in the greater emphasis of its lines and the higher colours of its characters and its emotions.[2] Except for the great scenes with Giovanni and Annabella,[3] we are liable to think less highly of this play every time we read it, while the others grow upon the mind—slowly, according to their slow nature—and ultimately possess it utterly. But to say this is only to put it second to the *Broken Heart*.[4] Already we find in it Ford's maturer characteristics ; there is less music in the individual lines, but there is a firmer and clearer expression throughout ; we notice, as in the late work of Middleton, less the style (though that is masterly) than the wisdom lucidly and unobtrusively expressed. The same advance can be traced in the revelation of the characters and in their grouping.

[1] *L.M.*, IV, iii.

[2] Leaving aside the maniacal exultation of Giovanni which makes his last speeches like those of D'Amville, there are moments of passion quite unlike the usual mood of Ford. (As, for example, the explosive indignation of Donado and Florio at the legalized hypocrisy of the Cardinal in III, ix, a scene which wants little to pass into the mood of Webster or of Tourneur, or Annabella's speeches to Soranzo in IV, iii.)

[3] *'Tis Pity*, V, i, iii, v, vi.

[4] Where, indeed, Lamb placed it. Havelock Ellis (Introd., p. x., Mermaid Ed.) says of *'Tis Pity*, ' in it he touched the highest point that he ever reached. He never afterwards succeeded in presenting an image so simple, passionate and complete.' This is, of course, the case, but in my view he never afterwards attempted it. In his later plays, he attempted (and reached) something far other.

The Broken Heart is, to most of Ford's readers, the supreme reach of his genius. If the comic plot were excised, and we have the evidence of Maeterlinck's translation [1] and of Marcel Schwob's comment upon the acting version thus obtained [2] to show us that nothing is lost and much is gained by excising it, a play is left which for simplicity and compactness of line, for dignity and for compression of emotion, thought and phrase is unsurpassed in Jacobean drama. Here there needs no apologist ; it is written without haste and without distraction, in the full maturity of Ford's power. Any attempt to describe or analyse the peculiar virtue of his poetry draws inevitably upon this play as the main source of its illustration.

Love's Sacrifice is an imperfect and inconsistent play, with flashes of Ford's power. He reproduces situations, relations and effects from his greater plays (*'Tis Pity* and *The Broken Heart*) and the result is a few fine fragments in a welter of inconsistent plot and character. [3] Gifford's strictures, though they take no account of the firm design of the fifth act partially executed, are on the whole justified. Its comic sub-plot puts even Ford's other attempts in the shade and has the more jarring effect in that it suddenly and unexpectedly takes a tragic direction ; never were his touch on comedy more unsure and his attempt at tragi-comedy more destructive. [4] The very morality of the main action is asquint, a rare fault with Ford. The

[1] *Annabella*, translation by M. Maeterlinck (1895).
[2] *Annabella et Giovanni. Conférence faite par Marcel Schwob au Théâtre de l'Oeuvre, le VI Novembre MDCCCXCIV.* (*Mercure de France*, 1894.)
Schwob here refers to the performance which he had seen of Maeterlinck's subsequently published version. He likens the effect of the play, denuded of its comic scenes, to that of the *Choephori* ; it had, he says, a 'fatalité grecque '. ' Le drame n'est plus autour des personnages : il se joue au plus profond de leurs coeurs.' . . . Schwob's criticism of the play is, here and there, penetrating and just : ' leur destin s'élève entre leurs âmes et se termine entre leurs âmes ; ils l'ont créé ; ils le détruisent ; ils sont leurs maîtres.'
[3] The main plot is tangled and hastily constructed ; Roseilli's disguise is without proportionate motive or results. Indeed, as Gifford pithily remarks : ' Ford seems to have lost his way through a great part of this drama.' (Gifford ed., Vol. I, p. 382, fn.)
[4] The climax of this action (III, iv), hovering as it does between the tragic and the farcical, is, for a modern audience, unfortunately precipitated in the latter direction, by the far more justifiable use of precisely the same effect in *The Beggar's Opera*. . . .

attempt to build in some fine solid speeches in the part of Bianca, especially in the scene in which she saves her lover from the vengeance of her husband, are worthy of a better structure and do but tear their flimsy setting. No attempt to repeat in the Duke and Ferdinand the relations of Orgilus and Ithocles or to touch again the marble dignity of Calantha, not even the grave conduct of the ending, will redeem the play. However nearly we may guess at the intentions thus imperfectly executed, we tend to borrow our verdict from Thersites : ' All the argument is a whore and a cuckold.'

Perkin Warbeck is in nearly every way a contrast to its predecessors ; it lacks certain characteristic marks of Ford's genius but it shows a certain capacity, notably for structure and objective and varied character drawing, which we do not otherwise meet. Like *Edward II* in the series of Marlowe's plays, it is likely to please best those who least appreciate the author's individual flavour. His grasp of political ideas is unexpected, much though it obviously owes to Shakespeare ; unexpected too is the clear drawing of all the characters including the minors, the elimination of incongruous farce and the wide range of sympathy. Even the love of Warbeck and Katherine never gathers impetus enough for Ford's peculiar treatment of constancy and silence ; that theme is, very properly, subordinated to the wider ideas of kingship and government with which the play is primarily concerned.

The Lady's Trial, which Gifford rightly coupled with *Perkin Warbeck* as a play up to then insufficiently appreciated, has remained neglected, as the history play has not. It is interesting rather as showing the final development of Ford's tendency to work more and more in reticent undertones in action, in character and in sentiment, than as adding much to his positive poetry. Some of it at least seems hastily written and shows Ford's usual weakness in such cases, inadequate motivation and imperfect interlocking of the parts of the plot, but we gratefully acknowledge with Gifford that ' Either by accident or design, the humbler characters of the *Lady's Trial* are inoffensive ; they are occasionally even amusing '. And we remember scenes between Spinella and Auria or Auria and Aurelio without which our knowledge not only of Ford's development but of his values themselves would be the poorer.

III

Even the melodramatic terrors with which Ford, for the reasons suggested above, invests the action of many of his plays,[1] do not seriously disturb his treatment of emotion and thought, which remain quiet and penetrating by virtue of his preoccupation with the processes of the mind rather than with event. In his earliest work, and to a less degree in some of the later, a pathos akin to that of Beaumont and Fletcher's romance is his initial response to a theme. Meleander's ' tale of things Done long agoe, and ill done ' is a fit summary of the mood of the early *Lover's Melancholy* ; the note is echoed again and again through the play. It can still be found in the later plays, lingering on even in *Perkin Warbeck*,

> A subject of the rarest kind of pity
> That hath in any age touched noble hearts,

and in the half-enchanted, romantic preoccupation of Warbeck and Katherine with the thought (so near to Philaster's love of death) that ' If they fail, Yet the report will live ', that habit of perceiving themselves and their lives as (in the words of a later poet) ' A story that shall be told for ever '. But in the later plays this is no longer the main theme. Ford has moved out of the mood of romantic unreality which envelops Beaumont and Fletcher's tragi-comedy lovers and those of his own early play, into a world of reality in which pathos is only incidental, a world whose preoccupation is nearer to that of Middleton with the inner experience of the mind, concentrating the major scenes more and more upon the hidden or half-hidden emotions and thoughts.[2]

[1] Such, to instance the most notorious, as are Giovanni's entry, at the end of *'Tis Pity*, with Annabella's bleeding heart upon his dagger, the ' cunning engine ' with which Orgilus traps Ithocles in *The Broken Heart*, or, worst of all, but in a play of less power than these two, Fernando's unexpected appearance in his winding sheet at the gate of Bianca's tomb in *Love's Sacrifice*. Where, as in the first two, these are closely wrought into the action of the play, they are still seen to hinder hardly at all the revelation of thought and emotion with which Ford and his readers are mainly concerned.

[2] A habit clearly perceived by Lamb, Havelock Ellis and Schwob. ' He is a master of the brief, mysterious words, so calm in seeming, which well up from the depths of despair. He concentrates the revelation of a soul's agony into a sob or a sigh. The surface seems calm ; we scarcely suspect that there is anything beneath ; one gasp bubbles up from the drowning heart below, and all is silence.' Havelock Ellis : Introduction to Ford's plays (*Mermaid Series*, pp. xiv–xv.)

At a slightly later stage it would seem that Ford was distracted from this main purpose by the fever and heat of a kind of psychological melodrama, by the fascination of a theme of incest or some other relatively abnormal experience of the mind. But this again is no more Ford's essential theme than is the physical melodrama of setting and episode, and no more interferes with his final statement than does the momentary response to pathos. The friar, speaking to Giovanni near the beginning of 'Tis Pity, seems for the moment to reveal in the author that mingling of horror and fascination into which some minds are thrown at their first meeting with this theme :

> Peace, thou hast told a tale, whose every word
> Threatens eternall slaughter to the soule :
> I'me sorry I have heard it,[1]

but, far more surely than in this somewhat sensational outburst, come the notes of certain later speeches, even from the friar himself, and more notably from Giovanni. Giovanni's cry ' Mercy ? why I have found it in this Justice ! ' indicates an interpretation that reconstructs the accepted relations of good and evil, and in the friar's words, ' The throne of mercy is above your trespass ', we recognize a response very like our own to the individual quality of Ford, to that serenity of judgement and clarity of perception whose possession led him to explore territory that his predecessors and contemporaries had not often cared to enter.[2]

When we have penetrated these superficial moods we recognize the essential quality of the plays ; the deep experience of certain emotions and the clear, distinctive analysis of the experience ; the constant worship of high, aristocratic virtues and the subdued sobriety of expression which reminds us that, for Ford, the greatest of these virtues was continence.

There are in fact three cardinal virtues in his world, continence, courage and chivalry, and the best of the plays is devoted

[1] T.P., II, v.
[2] Actually, the number of Ford's predecessors who treated or skirted the theme of incest is greater than might at first be supposed. Beaumont and Fletcher juggled with it in King and No King, Middleton approached it in The Phoenix as Tourneur did in The Atheist's Tragedy only to shy away from it again. Middleton later boldly incorporated it in the subsidiary plot of Women Beware Women, though it is characteristic of his detached and critical spirit that he accepts it without any sign of shock or recoil, such as we find in the early scenes of 'Tis Pity.

to the progressive revelation of these under differing aspects. The essential continence which is so marked a quality of Ford's own temperament is reflected primarily in his characters, though its effect is clear also in his style, in the conduct of his plot and in the tempo of his major scenes.   The reticence which endures in equal silence, love or sorrow, the sense of the sanctity of deep, inward grief,

> a secret that hath been
> The only jewel of my speechless thoughts,

these meet us in the first play and develop continuously until the last. Thamasta, Parthenophil, Flavia, Dalyell, Auria, Spinella, all reveal it, and his finest play is but a succession of such studies from the unbroken stillness of Penthea's opening scenes to the tenacity of Calantha at the end, balanced against the fortitude of Orgilus and Ithocles.   Never perhaps is it better revealed than in the madness of Penthea,[1] whose speech never rises above the low, broken, faltering music of a mind that is ' sworn brother . . . to dire necessity ' and with it ' will keep a league till death '.[2]

> Make me the patterne of digesting evils,
> Who can out-live my mighty ones, not shrinking
> At such a pressure as woulde sinke a soule
> Into what's most of death, the worst of horrors.[3]

In the great fifth act so deep a stillness possesses passion and speech that, though the action continues to unroll itself in event, the characters seem locked, by this pressure within and without, in an endless immobility of tension.

---

[1] *Broken Heart*, IV, ii.

[2] Penthea in this scene owes much and obviously to Ophelia, nearly as much (though less obviously) to Imogen, with whom she is clearly related in some of the earlier scenes in which her mind is still normally balanced.   There is present, too, in the mad scene, an echo, though at greater distance, of Beaumont and Fletcher's Euphrasia, Aspatia and Spaconia.   Yet Ford's character and its relations to the other figures are drawn in colours as different from Shakespeare's as from Beaumont and Fletcher's.   She has, indeed,

> ' . . . seal'd a covenant with sadnesse,
> And enter'd into bonds without condition
> To stand these tempests calmely.'
>
> (*B.H.*, V, ii.)

[3] *Broken Heart*, V, ii.   The dramatic impropriety of giving these lines to Bassaneo in no way alters their significance as a comment upon the action.

But it is not only in this region of silence and stillness that we find the innate continence of Ford's mind revealed. It is there no less in the dignity, the exquisite grace with which he invests at one time or another all his serious figures. ' Here lives majesty At league with love ', and the gravity which we first perceive in the figure of Cleophila in *The Lover's Melancholy* becomes in the later plays an austerity that almost forbids emotion. What quality but this could have guided Ford (and his characters) through Parthenophil's confession to Thamasta,[1] leaving both with their dignity unflawed, ending all without violence of passion ? ' My extasie of ioyes would speake in passion,' says Palador in another scene,

> But that I would not lose that part of man,
> Which is reserv'd to intertaine content,[2]

and Palador is a man after Ford's heart, of high breeding and unremitting courtesy, one of those men who give to each other in the drama that reverence which the author in his portraiture gives to them. Katherine in *Perkin Warbeck*, Spinella in *The Lady's Trial*, do but carry this a stage further. Shakespeare himself has hardly a fuller understanding than Ford of the immensity of feeling that finds few words or none, but those words, when they come, a revelation of a whole country of the mind. Outwardly unexpected, often even to the other characters, they are yet a revelation of some experience whose profoundity alone hides its connexion with the situation that gave rise to it.[3]

[1] *Lover's Melancholy*, III, ii. The resemblence between this scene and the corresponding one (II, ii) of *A King and No King* is superficially obvious. The distinction, in sensitiveness and dignity, is the measure of the difference between Beaumont and Fletcher and Ford.

[2] *L.M.*, IV, iii.

[3] Take, for instance, Spinella's lines in IV, i, when she hears, after many vicissitudes, that her husband's causeless suspicion is laid to rest :

Castanna.	But as for jealousie of your dishonor
	Hee both laughes at and scornes it.
Spinella.	Does a'.
Malfato.	Therein
	He shewes himselfe desertfule of his happinesse.
Castanna	Methinks the newes should cause some motione sister.
	You are not well.
Malfato.	Not well.
Spinella.	I am unworthy.
Malfato.	Of whom ? what ? why ?

Or take again the clear revelation of the characters and relations of

Truly, for Ford, the virtue which covers the multitude of sins is continence. The courage and chivalry, which are, indeed, derived from this in Ford's code, are no less clearly defined and no less constant. There is little daring or aspiration among his figures with the single exception of Giovanni ; Tamburlaine and Hotspur find no kinsmen here. But there is constant fortitude and often something more, the swift and sudden courage that, though it will not court catastrophe, knows that ' the meeting it is all '. Orgilus dies calling upon his friends to

> looke upon my stedinesse, and scorne not
> The sicknesse of my fortune,

and Calantha, who will ' die smiling ', ' has a masculine spirit '. Her speech, when the dance ends and ' the custom of this ceremony ' has at last made room for the successive messengers of death, is princely :

> Peace crown his ashes : we are queen then.
> . . . We begin our reigne
> With a first. act of Justice : thy confession,
> Unhappy *Orgilus*, doomes thee a sentence ;
> But yet thy fathers, or thy sisters presence
> Shall be excus'd : give, *Crotolon*, a blessing
> To thy lost sonne : *Euphranea*, take a farewell,
> And both be gone.[1]

It is indeed ' well done, and fitting for a princess ' ; Orgilus being the murderer of her lover and betrothed husband.[2]

There is something added yet to his ideal figures ; above their continence and their courage is a chivalry that is the flowering of late Jacobean civilization. The innate nobility which is part generosity and part humility and almost inseparable from

---

Auria and Aurelio in III, iii, of the same play. In both these scenes the previous work of Middleton is clearly suggested. But the discipline of his delicate, accurate draughtsmanship was all that Middleton could pass on to Ford. The uses to which the two men put this technique were entirely different ; Middleton drew his characters with the detachment of a scientific analyst, Ford with the passionate worship of a lover.

[1] *B.H.*, V, ii.

[2] Ithocles, again, suddenly betrayed by Orgilus, meets with instant courage the instant calamity ; Ferdinand, discovered by the duke, shows for the moment the same balance of faculties and composition of character, even Bianca calls down imminent death with the unshaken courage of a resolute liar.

generations of simultaneous responsibility and independence (the quality, whether in crofter or nobleman, whose freedom is perfect service), is for Ford the summit of human development ; that ' bon sang ne peut faillir ' no man was ever more sure than he.   The response to another man's beauty or nobility which Marlowe's robust sense seems to have missed, which Greene perceived at times and Peele continually, which Shakespeare understood and Beaumont and Fletcher manipulated, which was a cardinal point of Webster's creed ; that worship of the kingly mind, which had been defining itself as the drama developed, reaches, at the end of the Jacobean period, its full florescence in Ford. Amethus, Amyclas, Flavia, Malfato, Spinella, all echo his belief ; Calantha embodies it in nearly every line ; it is left to *Perkin Warbeck* to analyse it most clearly and to the scene of Orgilus' death to present it in its extremest form.   In the noblemen of *Perkin Warbeck*, Oxford, Surrey, Stanley, Dalyell, and sometimes Warbeck himself, he has drawn characters in whom dignity and magnanimity are assured and established by tradition ; and in Warbeck's fall, and still better in Stanley's, we have one of those stories (so dear to Jacobean dramatists and historians) fitly summed by Shakespeare's epitaph on Cawdor.   In an age in which it was indeed part of the necessary deportment of a gentleman to be ' studied in his death ', a gallant death and a chivalric acknowledgement of an enemy's virtue—or might we say virtuosity ?—in so dying went hand in hand.   Better even, in Ford's plays, than the deaths of Warbeck and Stanley, are those linked deaths of Ithocles and Orgilus. Everything is there, the prompt unfaltering courage, the acceptance of a turn of fate, however sudden, that cannot be avoided, the ceremonial killing (each man bearing with dignity his fit part in the ritual), the unfaltering death and the eulogy spoken by the avenger-executioner :

Orgilus.   Farewell, faire spring of manhood . . .
          . . . Sweet Twins shine stars for ever.
                    . . . bravery
          Of an undaunted spirit, conquering terror,
          Proclaim'd his last Act triumphant over ruine.[1]

---

[1] *B.H.*, IV, iv, V, ii. In the scene of Orgilus' own death Ford attempts something more dangerous, an idealization of noble death which becomes a long drawn out ritual of official suicide, while the other nobles deputed to see the sentence carried out become the priests of a

From this it will be apparent that his treatment of character is largely subjective ; with the exception of the people of Perkin Warbeck [1] (Huntley, Frion, Henry VII and Warbeck himself, that excellent study of a romanticist in a realist world), they speak on the whole a similar language and share the same constant virtues, the same processes of mind. The revelations made are the result of penetrating thought ; whether in sustained dialogues of faultless tact and perception [2] or in those brief phrases charged with long reflection, the plays are full of delicate indications, too fragile for the relatively coarser art of the theatre. [3] He is concerned only to penetrate to and reveal the fundamental relations of human hearts ; his perception is as sure as Webster's but less sudden and more detailed. We feel that Webster's knowledge has come with the shock of a sudden revelation, poignant or immense ; but we feel that Ford has always possessed his knowledge, that he is letting slip, from time to time, a still and almost frigid comment. Perhaps his main contribution to the technique of character drawing is to be found in his repeated study of a character consolidated under the impact of the blows of fate. The process is examined in the earlier plays, slightly in Cleophila, fully in Giovanni ; in the later plays the result is assumed, he is working almost entirely in terms of character (Penthea, Calantha, Orgilus, Ithocles, Flavia, Spinella) that has been thus formed. When Giovanni exclaims

> Despaire or tortures of a thousand hells
> All's one to mee ; I have set up my rest . . .
> Be all a man my soule . . . [4]

the process is already at work and ushers in the catastrophe throughout which he conducts himself, under pressure of this

---

strange cult in which the victim is also the god, exhorting him to the height of his spirit. ' This pastime Appeares majesticall.' Admittedly this scene is tainted by deeply inhering sadism, but the attempt is at something beyond that, and Orgilus' own lines are noble.

[1] There are earlier instances of such observations in Corax, Soranzo, Vasques and Bassanes, but these are isolated and incompletely developed. Beside the Shakespearian figure of Huntley they are elementary work.

[2] See especially *L.M.*, III, ii ; *T.P.*, II, i (beginning), V, v ; *B.H.*, III, ii, v, IV, iv, V, ii, iii ; *P.W.*, II, ii, III, ii, IV, i ; *L.T.*, V. ii.

[3] This is especially true of the parts of Parthenophil, Thamasta and Eroclea in *L.M.* and Calantha and Ithocles in *B.H.*

[4] *T.P.*, V, iii.

resolve, no longer as an hysterical boy, but as a man responsible
to himself, determined. There is a growing quietness in his
speech and singleness in his deeds :

> . . . the Powers
> That guide the motions of Immortall Soulles
> Could not prevent mee . . .

He makes for himself a bridge through untrodden experience
which carries him above and beyond the conditions of his world
of incest, murder and death.

Indeed this impression of an elastic solidity, whether in the
characters of the chief persons, in the language or in the shape
of the scenes themselves, is probably our last impression of
Ford's art. In his best scenes there is the same massive compactness, in which the single lines or speeches are rather units
than individuals ; so, almost, in the great final acts of *'Tis Pity*
and *The Broken Heart* are the characters themselves in relation
to the shaping thought. The true effect of Ford's art is to be
found in this firm elasticity, this enduring simplicity of proportion which gives form to the idea, somewhat as, in his imagery,
the illumination is not that of a lightning flash or a solitary ray,
but of a wide, clear luminosity without heat and without any
but the clearest colour. If one of the main scenes of, say, the
Broken Heart be analysed, it will be seen that his treatment of
tempo is a simple adjustment of movement which again gives a
statuesque, almost an archaic, effect, rapidity of inner realization
and stillness of outward demeanour simultaneously indicated.
Rapidity of dispatch, too, marks his initial revelation of plot and
character, a swiftness only possible to his packed phrasing ;
there is often speed too in the early parts of a scene, curtailing the
necessary but preliminary adjustments of the mind before the
phase to be examined in detail is reached.[1] But when this is
touched, there is a cessation of action, sometimes, as at the end of
'Tis Pity, like the sudden stillness of Webster's storms, and the
scene changes to the slow tempo essential to the revelation of the
processes and experiences most significant to him.[2] It is in
these scenes that we find most markedly those qualities of style
which are, indeed, a main factor in these effects of stillness and
silence, that plain style so solid in its gravity, so unforgettable in

---

[1] Especially is this noticeable in *B.H.*, II, iii, and the first part of
IV, iv.

[2] See *L.M.*, IV, iii, V, i ; *B.H.*, III, ii, and *T.P.*, V, vi (end).

16

its brevity and commonplace simplicity [1] and those echoes and musical cadences [2] which afford to the other the simplest and yet the most satisfying counterpoint.   In these moments of high tragedy it is, with Ford, a pellucid word, a hard, irreducible phrase or two that escapes ; nothing more.   Rhetoric is crushed by the pressure of inexpressible grief, the silent griefs that stifle and extinguish.   Lady Macbeth, after the banquet, speaks so, with just such dulled, slow and unfeeling accents.

Ith. Death waits to waft me to the Stygian bankes,
And free me from this Chaos of my bondage,
And till thou wilt forgive, I must indure.
Pen. Who is the Saint you serve ?
Ith.   Friendship, or nearness
Of birth to any but my sister, durst not
Have mov'd that question, as a secret, Sister :
I dare not murmure to myselfe.
Pen   Let me,
By your new protestacions I conjure 'ee,
Partake her name.
Ith.   Her name,—'tis,—'tis,—I dare not.
Pen. All your respects are forg'd.
Ith.   They are not.—Peace
Calantha is the Princesse, the Kings daughter,
Sole heire of *Sparta*—Me most miserable,
Doe I now love thee ? for my injuries
Revenge thy selfe with bravery, and gossip
My treasons to the Kings eares.   Doe ; *Calantha*
Knowes it not yet, nor *Prophilus* my nearest.
Pen. Suppose you were contracted to her, would it not
Split even your very soule to see her father
Snatch her out of your armes against her will,
And force her on the Prince of *Argos* ?

---

[1] This is especially noticeable in the scenes already indicated.   Its supreme achievement is perhaps that of *B.H.*, IV, ii, but there is fine work in this kind in *L.T.*, especially IV, i.

[2] These echoes form one of the gentler musical effects that run through Ford's work.   They tend to increase in his later work, replacing to some extent the peculiar verbal music which is a marked feature of the early plays.   They are hard to quote because, like a recurring note in a theme, they lose their significance when they are taken from their setting, but some dozen or more will be noticed in the most casual first reading of the plays :

' 'Tis buried in an everlasting silence,
And shall be, shall be ever.'

(*B.H.*, II, iii.)

Ith.   Trouble not
        The fountaines of mine eyes with thine owne story,
        I sweat in blood for't.
Pen.   We are reconcil'd,
        Alas, Sir, being children, but two branches
        Of one stocke, 'tis not fit we should divide :
        Have comfort, you may find it.
Ith.   Yes in thee :
        Onely in thee, *Penthea* mine.[1]

                        .   .   .   .

Pen.   I lov'd you once. [*To* ORGILUS.]
Org. Thou did'st, wrong'd creature, in despite of malice ;
        For it I love thee ever.
Pen.   Spare your hand,
        Beleeve me, I'le not hurt it.
Org.   My heart to.
Pen. Complaine not though I wring it hard : I'le kisse it ;
        O 'tis a fine soft palme : harke in thine eare,
        Like whom doe I looke, prethe ? nay, no whispering.
        Goodness ! we had beene happy : too much happinesse
        Will make folke proud they say—but that is he ;
                                        [*Points at* ITHOCLES.]
        And yet he paid for't home ; alas, his heart
        Is crept into the cabinet of the Princesse ;
        We shall have points and bride laces.   Remember
        When we last gather'd Roses in the garden,
        I found my wits, but truly you lost yours :
        That's He, and still 'tis He.
Ith.   Poore soule, how idely
        Her fancies guide her tongue.
Bass. Keepe in vexation,
        And breake not into clamour.
Org. She has tutor'd me.[2]

One more thing remains to be examined before we can attempt
to define the nature of that ideal that Ford so steadily keeps
before us.   It will have been noticed that the growing clarity
of thought, stillness and subjugation of passion, the growing
purity of form, cadence and phrasing, seem to be won in spite
of an obsession with abnormal areas of experience.   The incest
of Annabella and Giovanni is a theme which few predecessors
had dared to touch and the sadism underlying the deaths of
Annabella, Ithocles, Orgilus, and Bianca is in evident contrast
with other Jacobean death scenes.[3]   And the relations of

[1] *B.H.*, III, ii.   [2] Ibid., IV, ii.
[3] Webster's death scenes are as long drawn out as Ford's but the
death-blow is given by an enemy in the heat of a quarrel ; Ford's are

Amethus and Menaphon, Henry and Stanley, James and Warbeck, the Duke and Fernando, Ithocles and Orgilus vary between
a sharp and chivalric sense of the nobility of an enemy (common
enough to the drama) and love only slightly more restrained
than that of other lovers in Ford's plays.   In the sudden illumination, the blazing light that falls upon the dead man, the
slayer is seen not as the avenger he claimed to be but as the
victim himself of the remorseless law, ' On finit toujours par
tuer la chose qu'on aime '.   In an age in which homosexual
relations, at least between men of equal age, were apparently so
unregarded as to be passed without comment, there is a heightened brilliance in the light Ford turns upon Orgilus' sacrificial
murder of Ithocles and his subsequent suicide.   Whether the
peculiar purity of his art is distilled from these emotions or
survives in spite of them, the unavoidable fact is that they
proceed side by side and that both reach their finest, though not
their ultimate, development in the same play, *The Broken Heart*.

There are of course instances not only of abnormal taste but
of actual moral obliquity in Ford.   The friar in *'Tis Pity* suffers
from it at intervals all through the play and Richardetto in the
opening speech of IV, ii.   In *Love's Sacrifice* it is still more
marked, the conduct of the tragi-farcical sub-plot is utterly
insensitive, and in the fifth act most of the characters of the
main plot are touched by it one after another.   It may be that
both admit of the same solution.   Ford, whether in his exploration of the abnormal or of the less well understood roots of
normal experience, prefers generally to walk where few or none
have walked before him ; if his judgement staggers for a moment
or his inspiration flags, the result is confusion and contradiction ; he cannot fall back upon a tried convention or upon
deductions from recorded experience.   Small wonder if in
these little known territories an explorer, in the absence of
previous records, is now and again for a time bewildered.
When, on the other hand, his mind is working at high pressure
and all his faculties are alert, he cuts his way through his material
with a sureness that irradiates and dissolves the evil he has
chosen for his theme.[1]   Again and again he draws a distinction

generally given by a friend or a lover moved in some degree by a sadistic
impulse disguising itself as avenging anger.

[1] In *'Tis Pity*, for instance, the central figures are sure and clear in·
mood ; the confusion and obliquity lies in the vacillations of other

between a man's fate and his character, even more, between his
very deeds and an inner quality that shines in spite of them :

> Looke upon my steddinesse, and scorne not
> The sicknesse of my fortune.

It is very like the distinction the reader inevitably draws between
Ford's own themes and the mood in which he handles them,
the purity of form, music and language.

For among Jacobean dramatists Ford, the latest of high merit,
alone perhaps at his best shows that quality of thought which
Matthew Arnold selects as the distinguishing mark of Wordsworth's :

> The cloud of mortal destiny,
> Others will front it fearlessly—
> But who, like him, will put it by ?

He destroys evil, not by showing us in triumph the partial survival of the good, as does Webster, but by an illumination,
shared in a very different way by Shakespeare, that convinces
us that evil never was.[1]   It is inevitable, as for Sophocles in
Oedipus or for Dostoeievsky in his novels, that the evil chosen
should be the deadliest, the very Archtype, if it may be, of evil
itself.   But we assist, in Ford's plays, at the conversion of the
seven deadly sins, not at their overthrow.

He is a psychologist of clear, steady and slowly progressing
insight whose field is by preference abnormal conditions of mind

---

characters such as the Friar and Richardetto.   In *Love's Sacrifice*
the relations of Bianca, Fernando and the Duke are themselves touched
with this uncertainty, but even there we can reconstruct, from the
wreckage of the hastily written fifth act, the design from which Ford
meant to build.

[1] We may contrast in this connexion the effect of *'Tis Pity* and
The Broken Heart on one hand and that of the work of a modern
psychologist of exquisite perception, H. L. Lenormand, upon the other.
Simoun and *L'Homme et ses Fantômes*, to take the plays which touch
the themes of incest and homosexual relations, are plays of horror and
dismay.   Lenormand believes in his evils ; the whole conduct of his
play might, indeed, be said to proceed ' *A l'ombre du Mal* '.   The
mood of nightmare bewilderment is utterly foreign to Ford.   For
Lenormand ' Les disques rouges et vertes d'évènements mystérieuses
s'allument et s'éteignent sans cesse dans ma nuit '.   For Ford there is
neither crime nor expiation, the artificial divisions of good and evil
are down ; even his Giovanni exhorted to pray for mercy sees clearly
enough that ' I have found it in this justice '.

or unusual experiences and relations. These he approaches
with a grave and unfaltering faith in the ultimate prevalence of
underlying virtue in the universe of mind, robbing them of
their terrors and showing them for what they are, the follies
of children on a background of the immutable virtues ; courage,
continence and chivalry.

CHAPTER XIII

THE SHAKESPEARIAN TRANSMUTATION

I

ERGO vivida vis animi pervicit, et extra
  processit longe flammantia moenia mundi
atque omne immensum peragravit mente animoque,
unde refert nobis victor quid possit oriri.

It is no mere eccentricity of criticism that has insisted, for
upwards of two hundred years, on setting Shakespeare apart
from his fellow-dramatists, either on the ground that he stands
outside the Jacobean drama or (on the alternative and actually
similar ground) that he comprehends it. For though it is
admittedly easy to trace resemblances between him and his
fellows (nearly every line he certainly wrote has been tested and
discussed in relation to the ' borrowings ' or ' influences ' or, at
least the likenesses to which it seems to point), and though the
content of his plays is so clearly related to the content of theirs
that we cannot point to themes, groups of characters, situations,
devices, or even, easily, to vocabulary that is peculiar to him
(sometimes, as in *I Henry VI, Henry VIII, Two Noble Kinsmen*,
it is difficult to agree as to whether or no he had a share in a play
and, if so, what share), yet the total impression that we take
from the works refuses to fit into any scheme made primarily to
describe the other Jacobeans, however liberal that design appears
to be. None of us quite dares to treat him as one of these,
assigning him a like place among them, however dearly we may
estimate those others.

This attitude rests on a just, universal, if often only instinctive,
perception of difference ; a difference the unlettered man is as
capable of realizing as the scholar, for it depends upon the
presence in Shakespeare of something that dispenses with
scholarship's interpretation. Indeed, the unlettered man, being
unprejudiced either for or against, often gives his evidence more

cogently, testifying to a reality he finds in Shakespeare [1] and so, unconsciously, to Shakespeare's own recognition, beneath the many manifestations of Jacobean life, of the reality which, being universal, can be understood again by a man familiar only with the many manifestations of some other age. This testimony never fails, for all his faith, to come with a shock of joy to the scholar, for it is the index of something beyond all other achievement. The corruptible has put on incorruption. Lettered and unlettered alike, we testify in our different ways to this transmutation of the common thought and the common experience of Shakespeare's contemporaries. Whether we prefer to seek it in Aeschylus or in Job, in Sophocles, in Shakespeare or in Wordsworth, we know it for the mark peculiar to those who have ' understood the causes of things '.

For Shakespeare, if we think of him for a moment as a Jacobean, this has a peculiar significance. For the causes of things bulked hugely, if only as an undecipherable black shadow, in the minds of the most serious of his fellow dramatists. But since, in the nature of things, this experience is wordless, incommunicable except by something implicit in the orientation of matter and theme, we are left, as we began, with that indefinable yet equally undeniable sense of Shakespeare's simultaneous detachment from his contemporaries and comprehension of them.

II

Yet the signs of some such magnitude of conclusion, some deep-lying but as yet inarticulate perception of the one in the many, some instinctive moving towards synthesis, are there in Shakespeare's work from the beginning, making, out of the fragments of contemporary comment and reflection, a coherent body or world of thought, feeling towards the final resolution by which, of many such worlds, there grew a universe. Always, from the shaping of the whole play, down to details of imagery, there is, in Shakespeare's treatment, what seems an instinctive

---

[1] The response of an audience like that of the justly famous gallery of the Old Vic Theatre is an admirable test of this. Not having enough education, in many cases, even to have a prejudice against Shakespeare and having, as a rule, no criterion of art except that rough, but sound, one, its effect on their own emotions and its relation to their own experience, their testimony has a value peculiarly its own.

knowledge of the roots of being from which phenomena spring. Where his contemporaries at one time draw with photographic accuracy the thing as they see it, at another dispute and conjecture on its nature and hidden relations, Shakespeare, without conjecture and without dispute, seems to work with a deep, unconscious awareness of its true being. The shaping of his material, the handling of the source from which he drew it, the treatment of characteristic figures or dominant ideas with which his contemporaries were preoccupied (often before he touched them), theatre habits, devices, even language itself, all reveal variously this awareness, and simultaneously with it, the shaping power at work.

Shakespeare's transmutation of his sources, the various kinds of modification that he makes in the material offered him, according as it is the biographical narrative of Plutarch, the chronicle narrative of Holinshed, contemporary prose romance, Italian novella or the narrative poetry of Chaucer, is too well known to his readers to call for comment. Where character is outlined clearly and to his purpose, he makes little modification, where episode or dialogue or phrasing is already dramatic in content or tension, he takes it sometimes almost as it stands ; but where the narrative is diffuse or the orientation of theme implies a mood quite other than that in which he is then working, he alters drastically and economically. All these are the expected and natural procedure of a great dramatic artist. What is perhaps more peculiarly his own is the intimate and fundamental coherence which emerges, that inexplicable substratum of reality whose presence so modifies the total effect of the play that generations of readers have in all sincerity hailed *Macbeth* as a perfect piece of unified conscious art although it has (as we now suspect) been, all along, an altered and abbreviated stage version of Shakespeare's play.[1] It is the impression of the inward nature of the characters and the events that has dominated the effect of the play, not that of the corrupt or interpolated passages that stray momentarily from the essential quality. The same power is at work here that took, a few years before, the situation and relation of some of the chief characters in Marston's *Antonio's Revenge* and reproduced them in *Hamlet* so modified in their

[1] See, for a brief indication of the possibilities involved in the transmission of this text, Professor J. D. Wilson's Introduction to the Facsimile of the First Folio.

bearings, in the responses drawn from the characters by the events, that not until we set them down, stripped of the Shake-spearian implications, do we admit the closeness of their likeness.[1]

The same transformation overtakes, at his hands, the characteristic figures and the dominant ideas of his contemporaries. Kings, courtiers, clowns ; melancholy men and Senecal men ; the *miles gloriosus*, the Senecan tyrant, the Machiavellian politician ; these and a hundred more that we can still recognize as types among his predecessors are, with Shakespeare, unrecog-nizably transmuted into individuals.   So with the theatre habits and devices, the disguisings, the battle scenes, the discoveries, the traditional theme of vengeance, of ambition, of madness : the traditional conventions of soliloquy, entry and exit, of exposition and of conclusion.   Even his imagery, that most intimate and characteristic aspect of his expression, is an index of this same quality.   A phrase, a picture of Holinshed, a word or two in the play of another dramatist, is transmuted from the commonplace of its earlier form into something instinct with significance, penetrating, revealing ' the before unapprehended relations of things '.

Out of all these, we may perhaps look more closely at two instances of Shakespeare's peculiar power of transmutation, one indicative rather of that supreme penetration that, taking what his contemporaries had already discovered, discerns, not alone its practical theatre effect, not the details of its appearance and the technique of its displaying, but the fundamental significance of the thing itself that those predecessors merely recorded ; the other, indicative rather of that organizing and synthesizing power that gathers the scattered comments and the isolated explorations of his contemporaries into a continent of imaginative knowledge.

The dramatic possibilities of the theme of madness were recognized before Shakespeare and were even brought to a high pitch of technical excellence before he attempted any serious treatment of a mind distraught or unhinged.   Kyd, Marlowe

---

[1] This likeness is gradually becoming accepted as an instance of Shakespeare's power to transmute material that has been handled before by another playwright.   Those critics who believe in the existence of an ' Ur-Hamlet ', preceding the version extant in the first Q. (1603), of course reverse the verdict and assign the borrowing to Marston.   For the view indicated above, see F. Radebrecht : *Shake-speares Abhängigkeit von John Marston* (1918).   See also Chap. IV above (*Marston*).

and Marston at least had all made their contributions before his [1] and in all of them, in Hieronimo, in Zabina and in Piero, we recognize a close enough observation and recording of the manner of distraction momentarily to stir the audience with pathos or to shock them with horror. But, excellent as is the theatre sense in all three pictures, there is little or no identification of the dramatist with the object of his study ; in no case has the experience so passed into his life by virtue of his imaginative sympathy that he can perceive at once the relation of the sick mind to its former self and the relation between the imminent dissolution and the unknown values of the enveloping universe. Nor is this wholly a matter of imaginative failure in these (and other) dramatists ; Marlowe, who drew with terrifying nearness the disintegration of the mind of Faustus in the hour of death, could assuredly, had he perceived its value, have drawn also this other. But, for the moment, all three are working rather for stage effects, using to its full capacity a splendid piece of theatrical material, rather than subjecting themselves imaginatively to the experience they are recording. It was a habit of Shakespeare's critics at one time, when speaking of his touch upon the theme of madness, to quote in that connexion Dryden's words, ' Within this circle none dare walk but he ', but it might be claimed with equal truth that many, both before and after him, were willing enough to walk there ; few or none knew their act for a daring one or the circle they exploited for a demon-haunted place of terror. Only Ford, long after him, seems to perceive this clearly and a little examination of his mad scenes will show how watchfully he is following Shakespeare's steps.

For with Shakespeare all is changed. He does not merely take over a useful dramatic effect, does not merely carry it further and develop the technique of its treatment ; the very nature of the material and of the effect is changed, as the molecular structure of an element may be changed.

When Zabina [2] runs mad after discovering the dead body of Bajazet, Marlowe picks up with some skill the echoes of the

---

[1] The study of Constance (*King John*, III, iv), of course antedates *Antonio and Mellida*, though not *The Spanish Tragedy* or *Tamburlaine*. But this is not Shakespeare's mature treatment of the theme. Ophelia, Hamlet, Lady Macbeth and Lear all succeed a fairly thorough stage exploitation by his contemporaries.

[2] I *Tamburlaine*, V, ii.

tragic events and speeches of the immediate past or of her
memories of that further past when she was the empress of the
east ; the slaughter of war, the insults of Zenocrate, the changing colours of Tamburlaine's flags, her ceremonial coach and
throne crowd upon each other in a sequence whose apparently
illogical confusion is logically deduced :

> Ah, save that Infant, save him, . . . I, even I, speake to her, the
> Sun was doune. Streamers White, Red, Blacke, here, here, here.
> Fling the meat in his face. *Tamburlaine, Tamburlaine*, Let the souldiers
> be buried. Hel, death, *Tamburlain* . . . make ready my Coch, my
> chaire, my jewels, I come, I come, I come.

This is by no means careless work, but it is, I think, imperfectly felt. Marlowe knows what she might say, he knows the
value of the whirling, kaleidoscopic succession of images, but
it is not his voice that speaks through hers, he is not concerned
to feel as she might feel. The fury and the confusion are there,
but he has not penetrated to where, in the broken and half-
meaningless echo of what once were living words, there looms
the horror of the shade :

> One : Two : Why then 'tis time to doo 't : Hell is murky. Fye,
> my Lord, fie, A Souldier, and affear'd ? what need we feare who knowes
> it, when none can call our powre to accompt : yet who would have
> thought the olde man to have had so much blood in him ? . . . Wash
> your hands, put on your Night-Gowne, looke not so pale : I tell you
> yet againe *Banquo's* buried ; he cannot come out on's grave. . . .
> To bed, to bed : there's knocking at the gate : Come, come, come,
> come, give me your hand. What's done, cannot be undone. To bed,
> to bed, to bed.

> I hope all will be well. We must be patient ; but I cannot choose
> but weep, to think they should lay him i' the cold ground. My brother
> shall know of it ; and so I thank you for your good counsel.—Come,
> my coach !—Good-night, ladies ; good-night, sweet ladies ; good-night,
> good-night.

Here are passages that use the very method of Marlowe's
earlier one ; the broken fragments of a former world of experience toss to and fro in the disabled mind, with the same confusion
of chronology and the same incongruity of sequence. But
Marlowe's logical statement of fact has become the revelation
of an unsuspected world, each phrase like a sudden illumination
dropped into the else hidden depths, showing for an instant the

sunken memories of event, the submerged agonies and the strange relations set up between them, only to go out again, resigning that lawless chaos back into its own obscurity. In one line of Ophelia's speech Shakespeare has taken over Marlowe's very words, but what was, again, a logical (we might almost say a reasonable) echo for the Turkish Empress bred in pomp and state, becomes upon the lips of the girl Ophelia a fantastic and exaggerated hyperbole, as significant an index of the obsessions of her dislocated mind as are her faint echoes of Hamlet's obscenity, both utterly unlike the sane Ophelia, yet turned to a purpose of double significance in their very unlikeness. Shakespeare's lines have penetrated beyond the manifestation to a perception of the nature itself of the experience, such that those who have themselves approached it find in his lines not indeed the echo only of their own thoughts, but intimations of the nature of their experience beyond, sometimes, what the experience itself had given.

Another phase of this distinctive Shakespearian process may be studied in the history plays. Here we are concerned not so much with his penetration of the essential nature and relations of an experience as with the synthetic process (in the final result inseparable from the first, both being but single aspects of the whole perception) which brings together into a coherent unity the great body of thought on the nature of kingship and government which was scattered throughout contemporary drama and political literature and practice. Three of Shakespeare's contemporaries claim serious consideration here, Marlowe for his exploration of the Machiavellian system, Chapman for his study of the conflict between individualism and the beginnings of democratic liberalism, and Beaumont and Fletcher for their enunciation of the almost mystical doctrine of the divine right of kings. One of these, Marlowe, works side by side with Shakespeare, while the two later groups of plays draw liberally upon his findings as the bases of their special doctrines. The contrast, moreover, between the solid body of Shakespeare's political thought (touching, at one time or another, nearly every important aspect of sixteenth-century politics possible to drama) and the more or less isolated and specialized contributions of each of the others is only less notable than the differences in method and purpose. Marlowe makes the most acute examination of the Machiavellian system that Elizabethan literature can show, but his interest in it derives from its value as a working hypothesis and his imaginative reconstructions of Machiavellian characters and their impact on society are at least partially designed as tests. His curiosity is concerned with the question whether or no this is a valid interpretation of the else disjointed phenomena of human society. Shakespeare's question, during the period (a short one) in which he studies the system, is quite other. He is concerned to know what constitutes a Machiavellian and whether it is a credible figure at all or only a fantasy. And since the answer can best be found by seeing how it came into being, his Machiavellian studies are at least half concerned with the genesis of the Machiavellian. Already in his first study of Richard of Gloucester he knows that Richard is ' determined to prove a villain ' because life has queered his pitch from the beginning. And when Shakespeare (rather more rapidly than Marlowe) satisfied himself that the Machiavellian system as it was transmitted contained no valid solution of social or political problems, he carried forward from his exploration certain fundamental conclusions about the nature of individualism and that perversion of individualism which is villainy. He has answered his own question on the genesis of the Machiavellian ; Richard of Gloucester, Don John (a casual sketch, but in the tradition) and the far more significant Edmund are all malicious plotters for the same reason, because of an injury (deformity or bastardy) done them by life before they had the power to control it. Marlowe has examined the theory as a working hypothesis, Shakespeare has tested its premises against what he instinctively knows of the half-hidden processes of the human mind.

So with Chapman and with Beaumont and Fletcher, who, though their conclusions are independent, sometimes differing from his, had yet the material of his history plays to work upon and, in the case of Fletcher, of the late Roman plays also. With both of these, though Chapman's is the more soundly based, the more thoroughly thought-out, it is again a theory of state which is put forward. In passage after passage, especially in the two Biron plays, Chapman states his theory of government and kingship, of the relation of state and individual as explicitly as ever Shakespeare did in Odysseus's speech on degree or in the opening scenes of *Measure for Measure*. It is compact, condensed political theory, almost, as it stands, in debating form, and Chapman's exposition of his view, though his system is often more liberal and comprehensive than Fletcher's, has the same explicit form.[1]

Shakespeare, in the history plays, has gone to the root of the experience involved, reading it simultaneously with the eyes of all the people concerned. In the early histories his findings are mainly negative, studies of individualists such as Henry VI and Richard of Gloucester who are, for opposite reasons, unfit for kingship, the one through preoccupation with his own sanctity, the other by reason of his aggressive material self-seeking. Following these come the preliminary sketches of men endowed with kingly qualities, the bastard Falconbridge, Theseus and the figure of Henry IV, imperfect rather through the great flaw in his position as a usurper than by defect of character, and simultaneously the contrasting figure of the self-centred individualist Richard II, interpreting kingship solely in terms of privilege. All these lead on to the conclusive figure of Henry V, the servant of the state, possessed at once of the kingly quality of service and an unflawed title, assessing privilege at its true value as the compensation for responsibility. Throughout these studies, Shakespeare is clearing his idea of kingship, defining it rather in a series of portraits than in abstract discussions, laying aside one by one the men who, for one reason or another, were unfit, and arriving at last at a character whose private self is sunk in his public life, such a man as the service of the state requires.

This by itself would form a body of material more positive, coherent and comprehensive than any that was attempted before or after him, but Shakespeare does not leave it there. Throughout the Jacobean period of his work he extends it, now qualifying, now developing what had before been indicated, pausing now and again to sum up his deductions in a passage on the hierarchical nature of the true state or the technique of popular government.[2] The studies of the individualists and of the qualities which incapacitate them for rule appear again in Hamlet's ' thinking too precisely on the event ', in Brutus's inability to estimate the baser element in his fellows, in Macbeth's

[1] See especially the relations of individualist subject and democratic monarch in *Biron's Tragedy* and the opposite grouping in *Chabot*, and contrast them with Aecius's speech on the divine right of kings (*Val.*, I, iii).

[2] As in *Troil. Cress.* (I, iii, 75–156) and *Meas. for Meas.* (I, i).

delirious vision, ' For mine own good All causes shall give way ', in Coriolanus's medieval ideal of soldiership, in Lear's slender self-knowledge. In all these the question is no longer that of his Elizabethan period : ' What does the state require of the man who rules it ? ' for that has been answered. A new question takes its place, a question impossible to answer fully, because for each individual it takes a different form : ' What does the state make of the man who rules it ? ' What, in fact, has his relation to the state (as ruler or potential ruler) made of Brutus, Hamlet, Claudius, Macbeth, Coriolanus, Lear ? That is the focus of Shakespeare's later interest in this theme. The conclusions and implications, and they are manifold, may be illuminated if we make certain suggestive groupings, Claudius with Henry IV, Falconbridge with Edmund, Macbeth with Richard III, Coriolanus with Henry V. The last two may perhaps serve as an instance of the kind of corollary that Shakespeare is, I think, drawing in this later period.

In Henry V he had studied the voluntary submission of the private character and life to the public character and office, a submission so voluntary as to become a conversion, taking with it the character entire, leaving no unresolved confusion, no indication of a divided mind. The private qualities, even it may be, certain of the private virtues, disappear in creating this figure of a public man, this servant of the state, a great Tudor [1] monarch. But, as though some aspects of the subject had been insufficiently developed, Shakespeare defines the figure further in another and far later study. For Coriolanus is also a man in whom the public figure has submerged the private character, but in his case the process has been different. The standards of public conduct have been imposed on him from without, the ideals of Volumnia and certain of the patricians making a ready impression upon the haughty imperiousness of his fighting nature. But there is no conversion of the whole character. The acceptance has hardly been spontaneous and so is not complete. It has left him with a divided mind, the underlying character so undeveloped and so rigidly disciplined by a convention of conduct that it is inarticulate, blind and dangerous—like the Roman mob which is its outward prototype in the play. When in the last scene Volumnia speaks with a single mind from the foundations of her belief and

---

[1] Shakespeare, of course, endows his Henry V with the characteristic Tudor virtues, many of them those of Elizabeth herself.

practice, Coriolanus speaks like an actor who has learnt a part,[1] who knows the code by which he should direct his actions but cannot connect it with his passions, so that his speeches increase in hollow staginess until his final collapse before her coherent purpose. The contrast between these two figures is, I think, a vital part of the commentary that Shakespeare added, towards the end of his career, both on the nature of the public and private virtues [2] and on the danger to a man in an eminent position of having ' ever but slenderly known himself '.

When, therefore, by the study of all the plays which bear in any way upon political or social thought, we realize the significance of Shakespeare's repeated pictures of leaders, rulers and their relations with the ruled, we are ready to understand the nature of that social and political hierarchy in whose constitution he so firmly (but not as a result of abstract deduction) believed :

> The Heavens themselves, the Planets, and this Center,
> Observe degree, priority, and place,
> Insisture, course, proportion, season, forme,
> Office, and custome, in all line of Order :
> . . . How could Communities,
> Degrees in Schooles and Brother-hoods in Cities,
> Peacefull Commerce from dividable shores,
> The primogeniture, and due of Byrth,
> Prerogative of Age, Crownes, Scepters, Lawrels,
> (But by Degree) stand in Authentique place ?
> Take but Degree away, un-tune that string,
> And, hearke, what Discord followes.[3]

---

[1] The very imagery of Coriolanus, in the latter part of his career, turns instinctively to the stage for its sources, culminating in the sound psychological truth of the commonplace image,

> ' Like a dull Actor now, I have forgot my part,
> And I am out, even to a full Disgrace.'
> (V, iii, 45–6.)

This is in fact, though he hardly means it when he speaks, precisely, what has happened to him.

[2] Shakespeare never explicitly points the contrast between these, but enough is, I think, implicit in the studies of kingship to suggest that he, like Spenser, would have accepted, at least in part, the Aristotelian distinction upon which the divisions of the twenty-four books of the *Faerie Queene* were to have been made : ' the twelve private morall vertues, as Aristotle hath divised . . . the other part of polliticke vertues ' (*Faerie Queene, A Letter* . . . to . . . *Sir Walter Raleigh*.)

[3] *Troilus and Cressida*, I, iii, 85 seq.

17

We understand, moreover, out of many conclusions implicit in these studies why he so often emphasizes certain axioms of state, the almost mystic virtue of an unflawed, hereditary title, the sanctity of law, the difference between the private and the public virtues which allows Henry to reject Falstaff, which would have made of Hamlet an extremely poor ruler and makes of Claudius, the murderer and usurper, an efficient and, on the whole, a beneficent one.

The scattered fragments of thought in the earlier and contemporary drama, in *Gorbuduc* and Bale's *King John*, in Greene's *Friar Bacon* and *James IV*, in Peele's history plays and in Marston's and Ben Jonson's tragedies, and the solid if limited territories mapped by Marlowe before him and Chapman after him, thus cohere in Shakespeare's wide political scheme, into a body or world of thought.[1]

But even this phase of his work, reflecting as it does the double process of penetration and synthesis, is but preliminary to the great Shakespearian resolution of the deeper-lying Jacobean problems of man's nature and his relation to that circumambient reality that shapes his ends.

III

Because such resolution can only be complete when it has included all things in its experience, and belief in world order only impregnable when all evil has been gathered into its embrace, Shakespeare is supreme (like Sophocles, choosing and

---

[1] What Shakespeare has done is, of course, much what Sidney adumbrated or Bacon deduced when speaking of the relations of history and poetry :

' The Historian, wanting the precept, is so tyed, as not to what shoulde bee, but to what is ; to the particular truth of things, and not to the general reason of things, that hys example draweth no necessary consequence. . . . Hee [poetry] excelleth Historie, not only in furnishing the mind with knowledge, but in setting it forward to that which deserveth to be called and accounted good.' (Sidney : *Defence of Poetry*.)

' The use of this feigned history hath been to give some shadow of satisfaction to the mind of man in these points wherein the nature of things doth deny it, the world being in proportion inferior to the soul ; by reason whereof there is agreeable to the spirit of man a more ample greatness, a more exact goodness, and a more absolute variety, than can be found in the nature of things.' (Bacon : *Advancement of Learning*.)

transmuting the theme of *Oedipus*) because into him there pours, as perhaps into no other single dramatist, the full flood of the early Jacobean dread of death and horror of life. The significant period opens with *Hamlet, Troilus and Cressida* and *All's Well*, reaches a pausing place in *Measure for Measure* and then leads on to *Macbeth, Lear* and *Timon*. Never was the characteristic doubt of that age more searching, more nearly comprehensive of everything within its reach than in the first of these sequences that leads down to *Measure for Measure* ; never did the sense of chaos, of disjunction and flying apart of the very bonds of earth, of mutiny in the spheres themselves, find so nearly apocalyptic expression as in the sequence in which *Macbeth* and *Lear* lead up to *Timon*. Even Tourneur himself whose youth saw in a vision ' the frame of things disjoint ', and who in *The Revenger's Tragedy* made his sternest attempt to portray a world thus driven down through destruction to chaos, cannot quite reach the mood, much less the implications, of either phase in Shakespeare's experience. For, with Shakespeare, the continual extension of scope and deepening of penetration, joined to an ever-growing tendency to unification, leads, when this incipient universe of half-co-ordinated worlds suffers disruption, to doubt and destruction on a colossal scale, beyond the spiritual anarchy of his contemporaries. The elements then desecrated or destroyed are those most precious and the laws impugned those that reach out beyond the universe of common experience till Mutability lays hands upon the stars themselves. The all-comprehending doubt, the dead disgust of *Measure for Measure* sounds a lower note than does the burning satanism of *The Revenger's Tragedy*. It is the laws that integrate civilization itself, no less than those that wall in the human mind, that break apart in *Lear* and *Timon*. In these plays ' Natures germens tumble all together, Even till destruction sicken ', and this is possible to perhaps no other English dramatist, because, it would seem, there was no other with the power (the growth of a long habit of simultaneous synthesis and penetration) to lay hold on laws so fundamental.

Whatever be the order in which the first group of these plays was written, the descent to *Measure for Measure* is clear enough. In *Hamlet*, however deep be the weariness of spirit, the keen air of tragedy still moves through the play and the conclusion is in terms of tragedy, in the direction, that is, of faith, of poetry and of order. The next three plays are not tragedies ; the glory that is an inseparable part of tragic vision has gone from them and they no longer make a positive, a coherent comment.   Faith gives place gradually to cynicism, poetry to loathing and order to contradiction and discontinuity.   *Troilus and Cressida* shows the onset (though not the full development) of this mood.   The central theme is indeed no more than ' a whore and a cuckold ', its fit commentary in Thersites' imagery of disease ; the chivalrous Hector is killed by a hole-and-corner plot and Pandarus' epilogue suffuses what is past with the associations of the brothel. But there are still continuous passages in which the poet's thought escapes into a positive, constructive world of ideas. The ideas are chiefly concerned with statecraft, with the nature of law, with the nature of values, with the objective and subjective aspects of worship, with the experience of the mind in apprehending these, with themes, that is, as remote from the central theme as they are different from it in the dignity of the imagery and music in which they are treated.   With *All's Well*, the mood has become more homogeneous, the ' twylight of deliberation ' has deepened.   The conclusion is as cynical as that of *Troilus* ; more so, perhaps, in its implications.   It is huddled up hastily, the reactions of the main characters perfunctorily indicated.   Helena, who for courage, tenacity, sweetness and good sense is one of the most lovable of Shakespeare's women, accepts gratefully a man who has repudiated her, slandered Diana in the open court, behaved throughout like a graceless, spoilt schoolboy and at the end only promises to love her if she can give substantial proof of the trick she has played him.   There is weary acceptance of this central situation, but many of the subsidiary figures still belong to that brighter world from which Helena also comes.   At worst we have merely made ' modern and familiar things supernatural and causeless '.

In *Measure for Measure* the lowest depths of Jacobean negation are touched.   Cynicism has taken on a kind of diabolic vigilance ; with the exception of the kindly, timid Provost, there is no character who is not suspect, and those whose claims to goodness or decency seem most vigorous are precisely those in whom meanness, self-regard and hypocrisy root deepest. The theme of the main plot is Isabella's triumphant preservation of physical chastity against Angelo's cunning and at the risk of

Claudio's life ; that of the underplot, the shifts of a company
of brothel-keepers to maintain their trade.   Before the end of
the play we prefer the company of the second group to that
of the first.   Vile, dull and lacking even in the redeeming
virtue of humour, they are at least plain in their intents and
practices.

Claudio, selfish and self-indulgent, is another Bertram, with
something in him, too, of that other Claudio of *Much Ado*, but
fortune does not conspire to save him from the consequences of
his deeds.   To Isabella he is a craven weakling, but Shakespeare, to whom man is now no more than 'an angry Ape ', one
who

> Plaies such phantastique tricks before high heaven
> As makes the Angels weepe,

sees to it that, in his most contemptible abasement, he speaks the
language of generic humanity, so that, in his words on death, all
men may hear the echo of their own terrors, see him no other
than the mirror of their own nothing.   In Angelo the elements
are more thoroughly mixed and the picture drawn with cynicism,
not pity.   The man who traps Isabella with a perfidy at which
even the intellect staggers, who admits, between his administra-
tion of the law and his own observances, a breach so wide that
its impudence leaves the beholder breathless, who, finally,
refuses the reward for which he has exacted in advance a nefarious
payment, this man is no stage Machiavellian, but only an upright, decent citizen who has forced upon his nature a standard
beyond its capacity and warped it with the strain.   Here is the
soul of evil in things good, thus does ' corruption boil and
bubble ', spreading and searching till it tinges the innermost
sanctuary of the mind :

> When I would pray, and think, I thinke and pray
> To severall subjects : heaven hath my empty words ;
> Whilst my Invention, hearing not my Tongue,
> Anchors on *Isabell* : heaven in my mouth
> As if I did but onely chew his name ;
> And in my heart the strong and swelling evill
> Of my conception.[1]

This is indeed the very type of that division of mind that beset
the Jacobeans ; the inseparable mingling of evil with good here

---

[1] *M. for M.*, II, iv, 1–7.

is such as Middleton later did indeed perceive, though with him it is mainly a record of scientific observation, while with Shakespeare at the stage of *Measure for Measure* it constitutes the denial, not only of the nobility of man, but of the very laws which pretend to guide him. What seals our impression of a world-order ineradicably corrupted and given over to evil is the character of Isabella, where the same method is followed as in that of Angelo, but with a mingling of the elements so much deeper as to call in question the sanctity of religion, sex, marriage and even ' the holiness of the heart's affections '. Isabella, the novice already entered upon the religious life, pleads, despite her own severe chastity, for the life that Claudio's incontinence has forfeited. When nothing will move Angelo else, she applies the ultimate test of earthly judgement :

> Why, all the soules that were, were forfeit once,
> And he that might the vantage best have tooke,
> Found out the remedie : how would you be,
> If he, which is the top of Judgment, should
> But judge you, as you are ?

With the words hardly cold on her lips she meets Angelo again and hears his nefarious offer to release Claudio only if she will commit with him the very deed for which Claudio is condemned. For a moment she feels only normal horror at this duplicity. Then the obsession of ' abhorred pollution ' takes hold of her, the virtue of her chastity fills her universe. Hard as an icicle she visits Claudio in prison and lays before him the terms and her decision. She does right to ' fear ' him, for primitive humanity is at all times stronger in him than in her. But because of her very inhumanity she can watch unmoved while he faces the awful realization of immediate death, her pitilessness only growing with his pleading. Weak as he is, his self-indulgence cannot stand comparison with hers, with the pitiless, unimaginative, self-absorbed virtue which sustains her.

> Die, perish : Might but my bending doune
> Repreeve thee from thy fate, it should proceede.
> Ile pray a thousand prayers for thy death,
> No word to save thee.[1]

This is another divided mind, but more deeply so than Angelo's because unaware of its own division. We know from this

---

[1] *M. for M.*, III, i, 142–5.

moment that a nunnery contains no cure for Isabella's malady and we have a shrewd suspicion that she will not end there. But we are not quite done with her, nor with Shakespeare's final comment. In the next scene or two she agrees contentedly to Mariana taking her place with Angelo, arranges the deception, gets the keys of admission from him, breaks the plan to Mariana and gives her a few last words of business-like admonishment. Finally, when the Duke proposes to make her his Duchess, she gives silent consent, all thought of the religious life abandoned without comment and all backward reflections, apparently, full of self-content.

Before the comprehensiveness of this exposure, the imagination staggers, all the cynicism in individual speeches is as nothing beside the cynicism implicit in this orientation of the material ; it is a world in whose fetid air no wholesome thing can grow. It is, in Shakespeare's thought, the very nadir of disgust and cynicism, a world where ' nothing is but what is not ', where such order as there is is evil, where all passion and all enterprise is only ' the expense of spirit in a waste of shame '.

It is indeed the lowest point. From it we move up into the world of tragedy again, to the great plays that have for their common theme the disintegration of all order, even of a world order that is evil. Poetry returns to these plays, if for no other reason because Shakespeare's fundamental belief in ultimate co-ordination and in an ordered universe, is marshalling its forces against the uttermost of denial and loathing, against final immersion in the rising tide of Jacobean negation. The imagery of *Macbeth* is thick with this ; ' the frame of things disjoint ', ' the yesty waves Confound and swallow navigation up ' and ' natures germens tumble all together '. But it is not until *Lear* and *Timon* that the full force of the conflict breaks and then it is fought out in these terms, disintegration spreading ever wider and penetrating deeper and deeper towards the ' deep base of the world '. In *Lear* the laws of nature itself are caught into this whirling, chaotic conflict and subverted ; Lear's curse upon Goneril, the storm on the heath, symbolizing the storm in man's brain and in its macrocosm society, show a world whose warring elements are on the verge of disjunction. As the play proceeds there comes again and again an invocation to chaos, the rising *hysterica passio* that finds relief from the growing disjunc-

tion of this sick society in the image of a cataclysm mighty
enough to blot out its memory :

> And thou, all-shaking thunder,
> Strike flat the thick rotundity o' th' world !
> Crack nature's moulds, all germens spill at once
> That make ingrateful man ! [1]

But deep beneath this passion for destruction, this backward
seeking of primeval, whirling chaos, is the half-hidden sense of
pity and the breathless wonder as at some ritual of purification,
too colossal for man's thought to enclose, comprehending him,
in default of his comprehension :

> Let the great gods,
> That keep this dreadful pudder o'er our heads,
> Find out their enemies now. . . . Close pent-up guilts,
> Rive your concealing continents and cry
> These dreadful summoners grace. [2]

Timon defines the theme that *Lear* had touched, and loses little
of its magnitude in definition.   Lear's cry ' Off, off you lendings ' is also Timon's first impulse ;   to strip away the horror of
corruption that is civilization and fight back to the bare, essential,
natural condition of man.   It is the subversion of society only
that he seeks at first, but he moves step by step through the
gradually unfolding experience of destruction until the boundaries of thought themselves dissolve and the mind itself, the
very instrument of consciousness, is drawn out into chaos.

Timon's denunciation is directed specifically against society
and civilization, aimed directly at the relations of the parts that
hold the hierarchy together.   It is the very inversion of that
speech of Ulysses on degree that redeems for a moment the
oncoming gloom of *Troilus*, reading its clauses, as it were, backward, like a cosmic Black Mass.   The two speeches [3] give the
measure of the distance travelled in this experience of destruction ;   the positive belief of Ulysses is gone and what he holds
up as a threat, Timon calls down in instant doom.   Nature,
the destroyer (no longer nature the understanding, or nature
the ultimate and impartial law-giver), is called in to the subversion both of the civilization man has built and of the

---

[1] *Lear*, III, ii, 6–9.   [2] Ibid., 49 seq.
[3] *Timon*, IV, i, 1–40 ;   *Troilus*, I, iii, 75–134.

'lendings' that his soul in its pretensions has borrowed therefrom.

> That Nature, being sicke of man's unkindnesse
> Should yet be hungry : Common Mother, thou
> Whose wombe unmeasureable, and infinite brest
> Teemes and feeds all . . .
> Dry up thy Marrowes, Vines and Plough-torne Leas,
> Whereof ingratefull man, with Licourish draughts
> And Morsels Unctuous, greases his pure minde,
> That from it all Consideration slippes.[1]
>
>   Call the Creatures,
> Whose naked Natures live in all the spight
> Of wrekefull Heaven, whose bare unhoused Trunkes
> To the conflicting Elements expos'd
> Answer meere Nature,[2]

until nature, herself attainted, becomes no longer the agent of this centrifugal destruction, but a disintegrating chaos of force and matter at the mercy of that self-generating destruction which alone remains, working alike through the material universe and the moral universe of thought and society :

> The Sunnes a Theefe, and with his great attraction
> Robbes the vaste Sea. The Moones an arrant Theefe,
> And her pale fire, she snatches from the Sunne.
> The Seas a Theefe, whose liquid Surge, resolves
> The Moone into Salt teares. The Earth's a Theefe,
> That feeds and breeds by a composture stolne
> From gen'rall excrement : each thing's a Theefe.
> The Lawes, your curbe and whip, in their rough power
> Ha's uncheck'd Theft.[3]

Good and evil change their places ; the blessed light of the sun becomes the accursed engenderer of plague and rotten mist. Finally, Timon, stripped bare of the 'lendings' of society, down to the limit of primeval, individual man, finds, not an absolute foundation on which he can rest secure against betrayal, but only further and further depths of dissolution.   Beyond the dissolution of society, beyond that of nature's laws themselves, there remain deeper reaches of this experience in which the mind itself becomes a negation, emptied alike of properties and of cohesion.   The world-order is no longer evil.   There is no

---

[1] *Timon*, IV, iii, 177 seq.   [2] Ibid., 220–92.
[3] Ibid., 442–50.

longer any discernible world-order. All is resolved into disparate, warring elements. He has attempted to penetrate and analyse something beyond expression, beyond what can be contained in the mind of man. Chaos is come again :

> My long sicknesse
> Of Health, and Living, now begins to mend,
> And nothing brings me all things . . .
> *Timon* hath made his everlasting Mansion
> Upon the Beached Verge of the salt Flood,
> Who once a day with his embossed Froth
> The turbulent Surge shall cover ; thither come,
> And let my grave-stone be your Oracle :
> Lippes, let soure words go by, and Language end :
> What is amisse, Plague and Infection mend.
> Graves onely be men's workes, and Death their gaine ;
> Sunne, hide thy Beames. . . .[1]

IV

What indeed lies beyond such expression or analysis as Timon can attempt, Shakespeare does not set out in explicit terms. He indicates its presence as he had indicated the wild resolution into elemental factors of the laws of the material and the spiritual universe in Lear's or Timon's brain. Nor does he ever define it except by implication. But the implications are unmistakable, their solemn and pervasive presence is there in various forms through the great plays of his last period, clear in the tragic exaltation of *Anthony and Cleopatra*, in the orientation of material and of emotion in *Pericles*, *Cymbeline* and *The Winter's Tale*, in the symbolic imagery of *The Tempest*. Through these plays there runs a steady crescendo of assurance, of a comprehension that, whether or not we can follow its progress (and it becomes increasingly difficult to follow as Shakespeare's interpretation develops in profundity and universality), is undeniable in its effect. There grows steadily in these plays a solemn radiance that is wholly positive, the manifestation of that comprehension which, in its very nature, is beyond communication.

The deep base of the world has remained untouched and upon that base, whatever be its nature, the chaos of disrupted elements has re-formed into a universe. Timon, in the midst of his wildest denunciations, checked for an instant by the sight of the one good man yet left in a universe of evil, was visited by

[1] *Timon*, V, i, 191–3, 220–8.

a momentary vision of this unmoving base which else his agony denied :

> Let me behold thy face : Surely, this man
> Was borne of woman.
> Forgive my generall, and exceptlesse rashnesse,
> You perpetuall sober Gods ! . . .
> How faine would I have hated all mankinde,
> And thou redeem'st thy selfe.[1]

The ' perpetuall sober Gods ' are at their tasks, the still and sure subjection of negation and chaos to harmony.

This is first clear in *Anthony and Cleopatra* where the central theme of the tortured debates of *Troilus* and *Measure for Measure* is answered, not by debate or argument, but by the deep assurance, reflected from line after line throughout the play, ' The nobleness of life Is to do thus '. In the final act there is so much less of pain than in *Timon*, *Lear* or *Hamlet* that we hardly think of it as tragedy. Yet it is tragedy of the highest quality. So little are the glances of the actors cast back upon the lives they are leaving, so instinct is every movement with their ' immortal longings ', that the world of actuality dims and dislimbs in the clear illumination of their faith. It is Dolabella, Proculeius, Caesar and the Roman guards whose voices come to us faintly and unreal, who seem to move like puppets seen from a great distance, carrying out, perforce, what is of importance to them, but of none to us. From the moment of Cleopatra's words, ' There is nothing left remarkable Beneath the visiting moon ', we never again look backward ; it is not an end, but a beginning. There is no suffocating sense of unfulfilment, of that frustration in which ' the rest is silence '. There is not even the sense of escape from suffering into the peace of non-being, the best gift that Webster can give his characters or Kent's lifelong service offer Lear. All, instead, reaches forward, as surely as in Manoah's concluding speech in *Samson Agonistes*, which, despite its defined and specific dogma, yet draws its assurance, by however different a road, from the same source.

> I am againe for *Cidnus*,
> To meete *Marke Anthony* . . .
> Give me my Robe, put on my Crowne, I have
> Immortall longings in me.

---

[1] *Timon*, IV, iii, 502 seq.

So strong is the vitality of their exultation that even Caesar, the most unlikely instrument to catch this harmony, can only echo it.

> she lookes like sleepe,
> As she would catch another *Anthony*
> In her strong toyle of Grace.

Beyond *Anthony and Cleopatra* there is, it may be, no step further for tragedy to go.   What yet remains must be spoken, perhaps, in a form that is wholly positive, or in which the positive so far subdues the negative as to remove the tragic conflict and the exultation of tragic triumph.   So, it would seem, it was with Shakespeare.   When we have perceived with Cleopatra the ineradicable nobility of man, seen not alone the ' cinders of my spirits through the ashes of my chance ', but known also that positive assurance,

> It is well done, and fitting for a Princesse
> Descended of so many Royall Kings,

when we have focused the mind not upon the life that ends in death but upon the transmutation that can befall the spirit, the function of tragedy is ended, and what follows, being throughout instinct with assurance, must make to itself a new form.

In the three last plays, *Cymbeline, The Winter's Tale* and *The Tempest,* this process sets in.   The outward form lay ready to Shakespeare's hand ;   the tragi-comedy of Beaumont and Fletcher which ' hath no deaths ' but ' brings many near it '. The moment of death being no longer part of Shakespeare's purpose, the form fitted his content as would probably no other form then known have done.   He, like Romelio, had ' taken out ' that lesson of death and was now concerned with the basis, not of death, but of life.   And so, by one of those paradoxes which this drama continually offers us, Shakespeare used for the culminating expression of his faith in reality that form which its inventors had devised as a means of escape.   The fairy-tale with him becomes charged with those implications which the more immediate types of story could not present, becomes the vehicle of imaginative experience and interprets the real world more truly than do the records of actuality.

In the first two plays of this group, in *Cymbeline* and *The Winter's Tale*, this is deeply implicit, not obscure but never defined either with exaltation like that of Cleopatra's death or with the symbolic imagery of *The Tempest*.   Throughout these two it is by the orientation of the material, the emotions and the experiences of the characters, that this is implied, no less than in the emotions themselves, pity, forgiveness and comprehension, which fill the play. There is from the first an almost supernatural sense of sureness, of the soul of goodness now never to be subdued even in things evil, of the knowledge of some inherent, ineluctable glory stabilizing the changing forms of fate and event.

> A Touch more rare
> Subdues all pangs, all feares.

In *The Tempest* this knowledge has passed beyond either of these forms of expression into a symbolism co-extensive at once with the whole frame of the play and with the details of symbolic imagery. In so far as one can follow this (and I would not claim to follow it as yet more than a little way), the same powerful and assured comprehension of some positive fact about the nature of the spiritual universe is at work, revealed no longer simply by the evidence of its presence in stability and serenity of mood, but by suggestions, often terrifying in their half-perceived significance, of an understanding so clear that it could, were men able to receive it, give positive and defined assurance. Shakespeare's utterance in this play is, I believe, like that of the mystics, definite but comprehensible only to the initiate. It brings to the uninitiate that awe felt in the presence of mysticism, derived in part from our failure to comprehend but hardly less from the sight of a familiar figure passing, like Cleopatra herself, beyond our terms of life and thought. Into the region in which he no longer doubts as we do we cannot follow ; now that he can testify to it, we can no longer understand his testimony as when he doubted with us.

His comment upon the unresolvable evil of the universe, though little more than a passing phrase or two, contains the gist of the answer to *Measure for Measure* and *Timon*. Prospero, listening to Ariel's account of Caliban's conspiracy, dismisses this element of evil as beyond cure but also beyond concern :

> A Devill, a borne-Devill, on whose nature
> Nurture can never sticke : on whom my paines
> Humanely taken, all, all lost, quite lost.[1]

---

[1] *Tempest*, IV, i, 213–15.

Different, but resting upon the same deep base of serenity and assurance, is his comment upon that other, older conspiracy that robbed him of his dukedom :

> Though with their high wrongs I am strook to th' quick,
> Yet, with my nobler reason, gainst my furie
> Doe I take part : the rarer Action is
> In vertue, than in vengeance.[1]

And the lines that follow are instinct with that mysterious implication of positive knowledge that yet cannot be transmitted, of that understanding that sees order, a just design, where had been chaos :

> I have bedymm'd
> The Noone-tide Sun, call'd forth the mutenous windes,
> And 'twixt the greene Sea, and the azur'd vault
> Set roaring warre : to the dread ratling Thunder
> Have I given fire, and rifted *Joves* stowt Oke
> With his owne bolt : the strong bass'd promontorie
> Have I made shake, and by the spurs pluckt up
> The Pyne, and Cedar. Graves at my command
> Have wak'd their sleepers, op'd, and let 'em forth
> By my so potent Art. But this rough Magicke
> I heere abjure. . . . I'le breake my staffe,
> Bury it certaine fadomes in the earth,
> And deeper than did ever Plummet sound,
> I'le drowne my booke.[2]

In the concluding scene this is resolved into the utmost simplicity, into the breathless comments of Miranda's wonder, and the simple piety of the good old man Gonzalo. It is as though, any expression being but a symbol of the incommunicable truth it expresses, the final commentary may be as well made in their symbolism as in any other :

Miranda.   O wonder !
> How many goodly creatures are there heere !
> How beauteous mankinde is !   O brave new world
> That has such people in't.

Prospero.   Tis new to thee . . .[3]

---

[1] *Tempest*, V, i, 31–4.   [2] Ibid., V, i, 48–64.
[3] Ibid., 213–7. The editors of the New Cambridge *Tempest* insert at this line of Prospero's the words ' smiling sadly '. I am inclined to doubt whether there is anything sad in it. Prospero's comment is Shakespeare's, and the world *is* ' new ' to him, as to Miranda.

Gonzalo.   Look doune you gods
        And on this couple drop a blessed crowne ;
        For it is you, that have chalk'd forth the way
        Which brought us hither.[1]

Much in these latest plays must necessarily be spoken of
inconclusively, with uncertainty as to Shakespeare's actual
declaration (though never, I think, as to the direction of his
thought). To attempt more, without some share of the experience upon which these plays obviously rest, would defeat its
end. Concerning one thing, however, there is no question.
Shakespeare, in the final stage of his thought, transmutes the
doubt of his contemporaries into something positive, draws
together their conflicting worlds into a universe and disperses the
twilight of deliberation to reveal the stars that ' shine still '.
He, like an earlier contemporary, but with an even deeper
assurance, perceives the

            stedfast rest of all things firmely stayd
        Upon the pillours of Eternity.

Like Spenser, he knows this for the ultimate testimony of
Nature, and harmony for the soul of the universe.

Pericles.   But harke what Musicke ?
        Tell *Helicanus*, my *Marina*, tell him
        Ore, point by point, for yet he seems to dout :
        How, sure you are my daughter ; But what musicke ?
Helicanus. My Lord I heare none.
Pericles.   None,
        The Musicke of the *Spheres*.

---

[1] *Tempest*, ibid., 238–41.

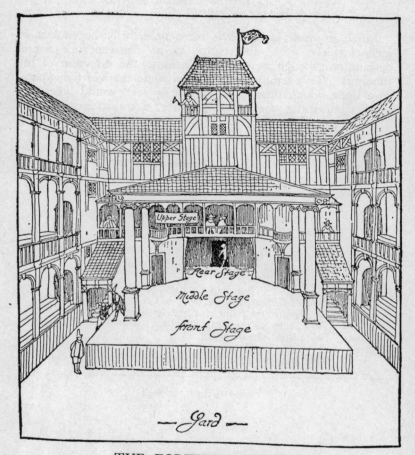

Upper Stage

Rear Stage

Middle Stage

front Stage

— Gard —

THE FORTUNE THEATRE
Mr. W. H. Godfrey's reconstruction from the builder's contract

CHAPTER XIV

THE JACOBEAN STAGE

[FOR the convenience of those readers who wish, while reading, to refer to an illustration of the Jacobean stage, I include the reproduction of Mr. W. H. Godfrey's reconstruction from the builder's contract of the Fortune Theatre, to represent the Elizabethan public theatre. The mental image of any modern village, parish, school or college hall which has a raised platform at one end will serve as the basis from which the private theatre may be pictured. I have added a few notes to draw attention to those aspects of the Elizabethan stage which seem to me most significant for the plays referred to in this book. They are not intended to offer a systematic survey of the characteristic features of either type of play-house in respect of architecture, scenery, costume, stage effects, lighting, properties, hand properties, production methods and standards, acting, constitution and relation of companies, music, constitution and distribution of the audience, repertoire, theatre economics or any of the many other aspects of the Elizabethan theatre treated by the relevant authorities. For this (and much more) information, including extensive bibliographies, the reader should of course consult E. K. Chambers : *The Elizabethan Stage* (4 vols.) (especially Vol. II), supplemented by the same author's *Medieval Stage* (2 vols.) and by two works of later date and consequently not included in his bibliographies : E. Welsford : *The Court Masque* (1927), W. W. Greg : *Dramatic Documents from the Elizabethan Playhouse* (1931). Very clear and easily accessible brief summaries of the main facts are to be found in E. A. G. Lamborn and G. B. Harrison : *Shakespeare The Man and His Stage* (O.U.P., 1924), pp. 86–96, and C. J. Sisson : *The Theatres and Companies*, in *A Companion to Shakespeare Studies* (ed. H. Granville-Barker and G. B. Harrison, C.U.P., 1934). A valuable contribution to our knowledge of private theatre methods is made by J. Isaacs : *Production and Stage-management at the Blackfriars Theatre*. (*Shakespeare Association* 1933.) For still more recent discussions and deductions, the reader should consult the later additions to the book-lists in App. II.

IN the development of the English stage from the platform-stage of the Middle Ages to the picture-stage of to-day, the Elizabethan and Jacobean types occupy an intermediate position. The platform was large (43 feet × 27 feet 6 inches at the Fortune to an overall measurement of roughly 80 feet square for the whole theatre) but it could bring the actor at any minute close to the audience and had not lost the immediacy proper to the area and platform types. The space behind the traverse, however, was already an embryo picture stage and could be used for inset effects and for sudden disclosures, focusing the attention of the audience on a particular grouping as does the modern stage. From the inn-yard of its most recent setting, it had retained the gallery overhanging at the back which formed the upper stage (accessible from back-stage) and thus gave two practicable acting levels. The three entrances on the ground level were two doors and the traverse itself, all at or towards the rear of the acting area. There was of course little artificial lighting beyond, where necessary and practicable, that of torches, tapers or lamps ; the theatre, with its open-pit and partly open acting area, is in this respect a type intermediate between the wholly open-air and naturally lighted Greek theatre (or the medieval market-place) and the indoor European type which, dating from the early Renascence in Italy,[1] appears in England in the private theatres of noblemen's houses, palaces and college halls in the sixteenth century and remains in essence to the present day. It was the fashion at one time to apologize for this theatre as though it were intermediate not only in historical development but in artistic merit between the medieval and the modern. Few stage historians, of course, hold this view now.

The theatre of the Elizabethans had, in fact, one of the finest types of stage known to history ;[2] a stage to whose limitations our greatest drama adapted itself without apparent detriment and upon whose liberal facilities it drew to such an extent that it invariably suffers from their absence in modern productions. The advantages of the Elizabethan stage are, of course, known to every student, but they are not always remembered by the readers of the drama, or, perhaps, not sufficiently remembered while reading.[3] Roughly they are of two kinds. First those

[1] Indirectly, of course, from the late Roman Theatre as described by Vitruvius. (See E. K. Chambers : *Elizabethan Stage*, Vol. III, Chap. XIX.)

[2] I suggest as the finest types of stage (having reference to the dramas they at once served and modified) the Greek, the classical Japanese and Chinese, the Elizabethan English and the modern intimate theatres.

[3] I should like to induce all readers of Jacobean drama to visualize the plays (while reading) as productions on the Jacobean stage. This habit, though it requires a little practice, is not intrinsically more

of intimacy and immediate association with the audience, the result of the physical proximity of the audience on three sides of the platform in ordinary daylight, twilight or torch-light.[1] This implies the forfeiture of the effects derived from distancing, whether by physical distance and absence of enclosure helped by artificial enlarging of the figures and the voices, as in the Greek stage,[2] or by an elaborate concentration of light on an inset acting-area to-day.[3] In short, if the finest type of distanced stage is that of the Greek (where the members of the audience are visible as normal men, but the actors appear something at several removes from man, and moving on the setting of a great natural panorama), the Elizabethan is perhaps the most effective type of undistanced or immediate stage, where the main endeavour is to bring the actor into touch with his audience and natural daylight and the physical structure of the stage combine to do this. It is hardly necessary to remark that playing under such conditions is a severe task for poor acting or weak drama but offers perhaps finer possibilities than any other set of conditions to a great actor and a great dramatist. Somebody once pityingly remarked, ' When Burbage played the stage was bare . . . '; but Burbage's language, if asked to play on the modern stage, supported (or out-acted) by the modern switchboard, would probably be unprintable. This is illustrated by the difficulty

difficult than that of visualizing Mr. Shaw's or Mr. Galsworthy's plays as productions of a modern stage—a feat which most habitual play-readers can achieve in a year or two. (The first is made slightly more difficult by our ignorance of certain particulars.)

[1] These conditions, however much some of the playwrights complain of them (as does Webster in the preface to *The White Devil* (1612)), were not necessarily altogether adverse. A wild late autumn or early spring sunset, reflected in the open sky above the theatre during the end of a Jacobean tragedy, was probably of far stronger psychological value than any modern lighting, a value corresponding with that of the distant hills, sky and sunshine giving a wide and limitless background to an Aeschylean trilogy.

[2] The medieval outdoor production, though obviously the acoustics of a village square or green limited the effective audience to a few hundreds as against the Greek 17,000 odd (see A. E. Haigh : *Attic Theatre* (ed. 1907), pp. 99–101), probably had some effect of distance though nothing like so great as the Greek.

[3] This, while effectually concentrating the attention on the stage, loses something of the sense of immediacy by concealing the audience from each other and so interrupting the current from stage through audience and back to stage again.

a modern producer or actor often finds in the Jacobean soliloquy. Modern methods try to make this wholly dramatic and so vastly increase its difficulties. The Jacobean stage allowed of its being an intimate communication, almost extra-dramatic, between audience and actor, the actor's function becoming for the moment that of reciter of a poem.

The second advantage possessed by the Elizabethan stage is its freedom from undue definition. This, it is true, depends partly on the audience ; a modern audience, trained in the convention that a change of scene must be indicated by a black-out or a lowering or raising of the curtain (or both), would not be able to exercise the privilege offered by the Elizabethan stage of moving rapidly from one place to another in imagination. This is the positive side of what is negatively expressed as an absence of scenery and major properties. Actually the absence of scenery, in a stage with the architectural subtlety of the Elizabethan, represents an immense and more than compensating access of freedom. A very brief indication in the dialogue, often the grouping of the characters themselves, indicates a change of place convincing enough to an audience that has not made so sharp a distinction between drama and narrative as we have done, an audience that can shift the imaginary background of spoken drama as readily as it can that of read or heard narrative.[1] But, granted an audience that has not been imaginatively sterilized, this theatre, with its double level, its well-defined sections of the ground-floor acting area (front or lower stage to the edge of the platform, middle stage roughly between the two doors, upper or inner stage behind the traverse) has a flexibility that we are only now painfully recovering. (Meyerhold with his various levels, his removal of the proscenium arch and wings and his opening up of the whole cavity of the stage area secured several years ago for the Russian stage many of the virtues of the Elizabethan.) But even the immense variety of effect thus offered is of less significance than the great increase of tempo, the rapidity of action which is seen to be presupposed in many Elizabethan plays. Several of these are in fact so written —with such an assumption of technical facilities now for the

[1] Even an audience used mainly to the Elizabethan private theatres would have been accustomed to the multiple stage setting, descended from the Roman ' Houses ', which is only slightly less elastic than that of the regular public theatre.

most part lost—that they are unproduceable on the modern stage. The battle scenes at the end of *Macbeth* (at once the most familiar example and one of the most notorious) are literally impossible on a stage which has only one permanent level and is tied to realistic scenery. To the Elizabethan producer, juggling with the four areas of his stage, it must have presented no difficulty and the kaleidoscopic effect, the impression of an almost epic width of view, the sense of flying to and fro between two armies, must have made a magnificent crescendo to the audience's emotional experience.[1]

The private or indoor theatres of the Jacobean age were a different type, further developed towards the modern stage, but not yet, so far as we can judge, forfeiting the main advantages of the public type. There is far less direct evidence about these theatres (of which, for our purposes, the second Blackfriars theatre is the most important), but it is clear first that the indoor productions used far more artificial effects (especially of lighting and scenery) than the public theatres, but that at the same time many plays were performed on both stages and that the line of demarcation between the two types should not be drawn too sharply.[2] Admittedly, the development of the masque setting affected directly plays written primarily for the private theatre and only less directly those written for the public.[3]

The indoor productions, since they admitted of the use of candles, could develop the concentration of light upon the stage, and presumably, though there is little evidence for it, the use of lighting effects on the setting,[4] while the position of the stage,

[1] With this we might compare the admirable use made of the different areas by Fletcher in the battle scenes of *Bonduca* where, by means of them, he can intersperse a survey of the whole battle with brief presentations of the fates of the individual fighters.

[2] An excellent survey of the evidence is given in J. Isaacs : *Production and Stage-Management at the Blackfriars Theatre* (*The Shakespeare Association* : 1933). See also App. II, Section B. i.

[3] On this question see L. Campbell : *Scenes and Machines on the English Stage during the Renaissance* (1923) ; E. Welsford : *The Court Masque* (1927) ; E. Boswell : *The Restoration Court Stage* (1932). Some of the evidence collected even in the last of these can be applied to the Jacobean period as well as to the Caroline with which the author is primarily concerned.

[4] This, of course, was well known in Italy as early as the middle of the sixteenth century (see Sebastiano Serlio : *Architettura* (1551), f. 31, *Di Lumi arteficiali delle Scene*, a delightful piece of theatre history).

with the audience all facing the front and having approximately the same angle of vision, allowed of a freer use of scenery (side wings as well as back-cloth) and the development of picture effects and the art of grouping. All this, combined with the greater ease with which quiet speech would carry in the enclosed halls, with their more orderly audiences, and the greater distinctness with which facial expression could be seen, points to a development of intimate playing, and allows of the growth of interests mainly psychological (as in Ford's plays), mainly philosophic (as often in Chapman's) or the intimate comedy of manners with its quick by-play (as often in Beaumont and Fletcher's).

In describing some of the possible uses and effects of the Jacobean theatre and the facilities which it offered the dramatists I have admitted once or twice that its effectiveness depended upon the ability of the audience to appreciate its possibilities as much as upon the corresponding ability in the dramatists. This might be carried further, for, admittedly, the audience for whom Jacobean dramatists and actors catered was, by the seventeenth century, theatrically trained to a fairly high pitch along certain lines. I do not mean to imply that they were docile, easily controlled or homogeneous in taste or demands, but simply that they had certain habits of mind which resulted partly from the conditions of their daily life and education, partly from their habituation to the material, dramatic conventions and stage technique of the theatre of Elizabeth's reign. All audiences who are the product of a sound and sufficiently established theatre tradition acquire such a technique and are thereby one of the surest means by which a theatre tradition is preserved. In ages where the drama is anywhere near the centre of the national life, not only the subject-matter of the drama, but the thought and language of the dramatists moulds to some degree the habit of mind of the audience, who thus return to it, by their demands, their selection and their sympathy, part of what they have received from it. The Greek audience of the best period was clearly in such a relation to its drama, so were the medieval European audiences, so (in its limited way and in regard to its

Whether or not any of Serlio's ingenious devices were used in England for plays (not masques) and as early as the Jacobean period is difficult to say; there seems to be no evidence of its occurring. Of course it would only be possible in a ' private ' house.

limited theatre) that of the Restoration ; so that of the French
and the Russian theatre to-day, and so, certainly, was that of the
Elizabethan age.

First and most important is sympathy, that almost undiagnos-
able factor which, running between stage and auditorium,
stimulates the effectiveness of the acting and the tempo of the
play to a degree that cannot be realized until it has been experienced. It has long been realized that, in the case of the Elizabethan audience, that looked to its theatre to fulfil the functions
of our daily newspaper, B.B.C., circulating library, extension
lectures and films, that found in it comments on news, current
politics, philosophy and science, there must have been some
peculiarly close relationship between stage and audience, an
eagerness not easily paralleled to-day. Something like it can,
it is true, be experienced to-day when the audience is a specialized
one, brought together on a basis of a common and vital interest
to see a play concerned with topics of the utmost significance to
it. Something of the kind happened at a performance of the
former Left Theatre where, though the basis of sympathy was
a social philosophy, the artistic merit of the plays produced was
by no means low. The flow of sympathy from the auditorium
to the stage and back again raises the standard of the acting and
overcomes the raggedness (a difficulty that must have beset the
Elizabethans) to which repertory playing is liable. Any ordinary member of the audience is swept into a current of feeling,
which is not hysteria but a steady, compulsive virility of emotion,
and recognizes that here is a first-rate example of true theatrical
heightening.

But in addition to this, the Elizabethan audience had specific
qualifications peculiar to itself.[1] The work proper to its imagination, of calling up at will pictorial images, had not atrophied as
a result of watching films and theatre settings ; it was accustomed to visualize in response to words and, as a great part of
it could not read, especially in response to spoken words.
Those that could read had not had their imaginations choked
by sensational news and easily read novels. What they did
read they probably read more slowly and assimilated more

[1] Upon this question of the nature of the audience and its constitution, the reader should consult the admirable article, *Shakespeare's
Audience*, by M. S. Byrne, in *A Series of Papers on Shakespeare and
the Theatre by members of the Shakespeare Association*. O.U.P., 1927.

thoroughly than we do, and for the most part it was not so written as to minimize imaginative effort. This, indeed, is true of all their experience : they probably responded more sharply, assimilated it more completely and, as their leisure and the ordinary goings and comings of life left them free of wireless programmes, advertisements and, in general, traffic problems and street noises, as they were less distracted and superficially stimulated than we, they were free to extract its significance by unconscious rumination if not by conscious reflection. In short, the inhabitants of Jacobean London were, as regards mental alertness, an ideal audience. A great part at least of the lives of most of them had been spent in a small country-town which yet offered its inhabitants the experience, or the spectacle, of all the important events in the life of a state or an individual, a town at once its country's chief port, the residence of the court and reigning sovereign, the seat of Parliament and law-courts, the chief market and trade centre of the country, the headquarters of foreign ambassadors and merchants, and of the country nobility when in town, all this on so small a scale that any one man was almost bound to be aware of it all. He was thus accustomed to meet directly experience which a large part of a modern population only hears of or sees in reproduction. Crime, robbery, street-fights, death ; the obvious evidences of plague and disease, the immediate effects of rumour or panic, official executions and official celebrations ; tavern meetings, sailors' yarns, coney-catching, gambling ; all these were not only transacted to a larger extent in public, but were concentrated into a relatively small area. So that the average citizen of the early seventeenth century had a fair chance of meeting most of them at first hand, where his unfortunate descendant to-day meets at first hand few, or even none, of those natural occurrences. The average member of the Elizabethan audience was a man with a pretty varied and well-balanced experience of the cruder and more representative events of human and national life ; what conclusion he drew from it depended upon his intelligence, but he possessed a touch-stone of reality, whether he used it consciously or not. If he were of average intelligence he had a vivid sense of the importance of the affairs among which he moved, whether prosperous and expansive as in Elizabeth's reign or sinister and threatening as in the early years of the reign of James. In either case, he made up an ideal audience, with the quick wits of the city-bred but the equally ready emotions of men who have never lived in terms of second-hand experience, sometimes crude in his taste and often brutal, but equally quickly moved by an appeal to his sentiment and capable of responding to, if not imitating, a certain fineness of feeling.

It is indeed necessary not to underestimate the brutality of the Elizabethan or Jacobean audiences, but the flexibility of their emotions must also be allowed for. It is true that some of the jokes that they enjoyed most heartily turned upon disasters for which our generation feels nothing but horror ; venereal disease and lunacy being, perhaps, the most notable. They took their country cousins for an afternoon's jollification to Bedlam as we take ours to the Zoo (a practice which will probably also appear brutal in the eyes of our descendants). A hanging, or better still a treason execution, was as good an entertainment as a Jubilee is to us—they bespoke their places well in advance. But, without accepting at its face value everything that Beaumont implies, we can judge, from the citizens in *The Knight of the Burning Pestle*, of the quick successions of gusty sentiment (and by no means unvocal) which could be guided or provoked by a word, a tone or a gesture from the stage. The great advantage of the element of frank brutality in Jacobean life is shown by the fact that the major drama is practically free from genuine sadism —a mood which does not appear until we reach the repressed and involuted emotions of Ford's drama.

Finally, the Elizabethan audience had, of course, that training in the peculiar habits of its own drama to which reference has already been made. This would be of less interest to us, were it not that, occasionally, a modern reader leaves it out of account in assessing the theatrical effectiveness of a given play, scene, character or situation. I think it possible that the Jacobean audiences found fewer difficulties than we find for them. They could accept what may be called the shorthand references of theatre convention which, until we are familiar with them our-selves, appear to be defects in the dramatist's explication. The Jacobeans knew certain types of stage characters from long association, could, at a hint, presuppose a certain body of char-acteristics common to all members of the class and be prepared to find in the play before them modifications and elaborations of a familiar theme. The same holds good of intrigue and plot-structure. So that modern readers, approaching for the first time some of the Jacobean drama, may feel a little as though they were entering the concert-hall at the beginning of the second movement of a symphony ; it is intelligible enough to those who already know the first movement but may be a little bewildering to those who do not. Contrast, for example, Kyd's careful explication of the revenge theme and the characters of the vengeful ' politician ' about the year 1586. How childish his obviousness sometimes seems, but, upon reflection, how necessary for an audience untrained in the twists and turns of a plotter's mind :

> Thus have I with an envious forged tale
> Deceived the king, betraid mine enemy,
> And hope for guerdon of my villainy.[1]

Kyd's technique was not as crude as this—but that of part of his audience may have been. And it was essential that no innocent mind in the pit should have been misled into taking Villuppo's earlier speeches literally. So we find the equivalent of the equally necessary nineteenth-century melodrama ' aside '. Now if we turn to the Jacobean revenge plays, we come upon material written for an audience sophisticated and highly trained in this type of work ; it has a firm grasp of the essentials of the character of the revenger-politician and of the usual intrigues. It is ready for modifications—in fact, it will be impatient if it does not get them. So that Marston in *The Malcontent* can show them the tortuous processes of two plotters double-crossing each other. and this plot, which would, I believe, baffle a modern audience, was apparently assimilated with ease within twenty years of the *Spanish Tragedy's* cautious pioneering. In the same way, the quick procedure of *The Revenger's Tragedy*, Webster's concentration on characters and indifference to preliminaries, Chapman's modification of the revenger in Clermont D'Ambois, Tourneur's sudden traversing of the tradition in *The Atheist's Tragedy*, all of these presuppose a familiarity with types of character and intrigue, which can be nicely paralleled by the really considerable pitch of technical familiarity demanded of a modern audience at a good detective play.[2]

[1] *Spanish Tregedy*, I, ii, 93–5.
[2] This was most happily illustrated at a recent production of the *White Devil* by the New Phoenix Society, when a large part of the audience was puzzled by the relation of Lodovico to the rest of the play. A Jacobean audience, familiar with the figure of the vengeful

This, of course, could be illustrated by innumerable cases, throughout the Jacobean drama, where what looks to us at first glance like a piece of scamped work is probably a piece of dramatic shorthand, a technical convention, tacitly agreed upon by dramatist and audience.

and embittered man (Roderigo, Laertes, the murderers in *Macbeth*, Piato, Borachio), as the instrument of the main intriguers, would have known what he was there for, set him aside for the cipher or short-hand sign that he was, and attended to the main business of the play. They would have known, in fact, that he was 'a wondrous necessary man', but only to the action, not to the emotion or thought of the play.

BIOGRAPHICAL NOTES

1. CHAPMAN

GEORGE CHAPMAN was born in 1559 or 1560 [1] in Hitchin, Hertfordshire. According to his father's will,[2] discovered by one of his latest biographers, Mr. R. L. Hine,[3] he was the son of Thomas and Joan Chapman, the former being a freeholder in the Hundred of Hitchin, and one of a family consisting of an elder son and three married daughters. Anthony a Wood tells us that he went to Oxford. He may have left the university without a degree and then entered the service of Sir Ralph Sadler; he was certainly in his service in 1583, was abroad for a time (possibly in the Low Countries in 1591–2) and was imprisoned in 1599.[4] In 1594 he published his first poem, *The Shadow of Night*, which connects him with the philosophical coterie of which Ralegh and Hariot were members. In 1595 he published a volume of poems containing *Ovid's Banquet of Sense*, *Coronet for his Mistress Philosophy*, *The Amorous Zodiac* and a translation of an earlier Latin poem. This was followed the next year by the *de Guiana, Carmen Epicum*. By 1596 or earlier, as Henslowe's *Diary* shows, he was writing comedies for the Admiral's company. *The Blind Beggar of Alexandria*, referred to by Henslowe as ' ne ', was produced in February 1596. (It was entered and published in 1598, the year of the publication of Chapman's translation of the first seven books of the *Iliad and Achilles' Shield* and also of his continuation of the *Hero and Leander* left unfinished by Marlowe.) The following year, 1597, the Admiral's produced *An Humorous Day's Mirth* [5] (published in 1599). Before

---

[1] The Parish Register does not begin until 1562 but the portrait prefixed to *The Whole World of Homer* is inscribed ' Georgius Chapmannus Homeri Metaphrastes. Aeta : LVII. MDCXVI.'

[2] Dated Jan. 1581 and proved London 5 June 1589. (Somerset House : P.C.C. Wills, 52 Leicester.)

[3] R. L. Hine ; *Hitchin Worthies* (1932) contains a biographical chapter on Chapman. For other recent biographies see E. K. Chambers, *Elizabethan Stage*, III, 249, and Havelock Ellis, *George Chapman : Prefatory Essay and Selections*. 1934. And see note 4 below.

[4] For these facts and suggestions, see Jean Robertson : ' The Early Life of George Chapman,' *R.E.S.*, July, 1945.
Comedies of George Chapman, p. 685, agree that Fleay's identification of this play with the ' Comedy of Umers ' played on 11 May 1579 on the evidence of the inventories is justified.

breaking off his connexion with the Admiral's, Chapman wrote five other plays [1] which are either lost or not extant in their original form. The lost play, *The Old Joiner of Aldgate*, belongs to the year 1602.[2] *The Gentleman Usher*, registered in 1605 as ' A book called Vincentio and Margaret ' and published in 1606, was apparently written for the Children of the Chapel, between 1602 and 1604.[3]   *All Fools* [4] and *Monsieur D'Olive* [5] appear to have been written in or about 1604. (The first was performed on January 1, 1605, and published in the same year ; the second was published in 1606.)   To the same year, 1604, probably belongs *Bussy d'Ambois* (entered and published in 1607).   The next year he collaborated with Marston and Jonson in *Eastward Ho* [6] which landed him in prison in Jonson's company. Chapman was again in trouble in 1608 when the *Conspiracy and Tragedy of Biron* was acted and by its injudicious references to the French court gave offence to the French ambassador.[7]   Chapman, who appears to have escaped imprisonment, wrote forcibly to the

---

[1] E. K. Chambers, ibid., p. 249.   *The Isle of a Woman*, afterwards called *The Fount of New Fashions*, *The World Runs on Wheels*, afterwards called *All Fools but the Fool* (Jan.–July 1599), *Four Kings* (Oct. 1598– Jan. 1599), a Tragedy of Bengemens plotte (Oct. 1598–Jan. 1599) and a pastoral tragedy (July 1599). W. W. Greg notes the entry of a playbook of Chapman's on 23 Oct. 1598. (See Henslowe's *Diary*, ed. W. W. Greg, ii, 51–2), but does not identify it with the *Four Kings*, an anonymous play (see E. K. Chambers, ii, 167, 169).

[2] See Charles Sisson, *Keep the Widow Waking*. (*Library*, June 1927, p. 41.), and *Lost Plays of Shakespeare's Age*, 1936.

[3] Parrott, ibid., 753, fixes the date of writing at 1602, though E. K Chambers, ibid., III, 251, finds 1604 equally possible.

[4] Parrott, ibid.,p. 701, identifies this with the Admiral's play, 'The world rones a whelles and now all foolles but the foolle ', and accordingly dates it 1598–9, assuming it was performed again at the Blackfriars in 1605. E. K. Chambers, ibid., p. 252, suggests a possible 1604 as date of composition.

[5] Stoll, *M.L.N.*, XX ; Parrott, op. cit., p. 773, and E. K. Chambers, op. cit., p. 252, agree as to 1604 for the date of composition, mainly on the evidence of internal allusions.

[6] According to Jonson, *Conversations* (Herford and Simpson, Vol. I, p. 140), he was ' delated by Sir James Murray to the King for writting something against the Scots in a play, Eastward hoe '.   The Hatfield MS. contains a letter from Jonson on his and Chapman's imprisonment dated 1605.   In the *Athenaeum*, 1901, i, 403, Dobell prints this and 3 more of Jonson's letters together with 3 of Chapman's from MS. petitioning for release. E. K. Chambers, ibid., p. 254, thinks imprisonment was due to publication, not to the presentation of the play. See also biographical notes 2 and 3, Marston and Jonson.

[7] For a summary of the evidence on this matter, see Parrott, *Tragedies*, pp. 591–2.

licenser of the press protesting against the resulting dismemberment of the play for publication. His comedy, *May Day*,[1] published in 1611, was probably written in 1609 and possibly in the same year his last comedy, *The Widow's Tears*, entered and published in 1612. *The Revenge of Bussy d'Ambois* is generally considered to have followed in 1610. Apart from his career as a dramatist very little is known concerning the facts of Chapman's life during these years. In 1609 he published a poem, *The Tears of Peace*, and must have continued the translations of Homer, probably at the command of his patron, Prince Henry (to whom he had been appointed sewer in ordinary at the beginning of James' reign). In 1609–10 the first twelve books of the *Iliad* were published, followed in 1611 by the complete *Iliad*. But in the same year the Prince died and Chapman did not receive at the king's hands the life pension promised by him nor did he retain his post, being 'now put from his place under Prince Charles '. Letters of this or a later period speak of a crisis in his fortunes in their references to poverty and debts. In 1612 he published his translation of Petrarch's Seven Penitential Psalms, together with the Hymn to Christ upon the Cross. On 13 February 1613 a masque by Chapman was performed by the Middle Temple and Lincoln's Inn for the Princess Elizabeth's wedding celebrations. It is to this year that Parrott and E. K. Chambers tentatively assign the tragedies *Chabot Admiral of France*, not published till 1639, and *Caesar and Pompey*, published in 1631. These complete the list of Chapman's dramatic work unless the plays [2] assigned to him by various authorities are his. After this, with the exception of the *Andromeda Liberata* written for the marriage in 1614 of his new patron Somerset, Chapman seems to have devoted himself to his work of translating. In 1614 the first twelve books of the *Odyssey* were published, followed immediately by the whole *Odyssey* and two years later by the whole *Works* of Homer and his translation of Musaeus. In 1618 he dedicated his translation of Hesiod's *Georgics* to Bacon and finished his work on Homer in 1625 with the publication of the *Batrachomyomachia*. *The Justification of a Strange Action of Nero's*, published in 1629, was his last known work. Save for the record of a quarrel [3] with his friend of long standing, Ben Jonson, we know

[1] E. K. Chambers finds Parrott's arguments for 1602 ' on the grounds of reminiscences of 1599–1601 plays ' inconclusive, a later date being more probable from a reference to *The Gull's Horn Book*, published 1609. Boas agrees substantially with Parrott.

[2] See E. K. Chambers, ibid., 260, and Vol. IV, Chap. 24, where the arguments of the various authorities are summarized.

[3] *Invective written by Mr. George Chapman against Mr. Ben Jonson.* See also article by P. Simpson, *T.L.S.*, 3 March 1932, suggesting a reason for the quarrel in Jonson's criticism of Chapman's scholarship written in the margin of a copy of *Whole Works of Homer* in the FitzWilliam Museum.

nothing of his life during his later years until we hear of his death on 12 May 1634 and of his burial in a tomb designed by his friend Inigo Jones, in the churchyard of St. Giles in the Fields.

2. JOHN MARSTON [1]

Marston's biographer, Dr. R. E. Brettle, has recently put forward some convincing arguments in favour of finally identifying the two John Marstons of the late sixteenth and early seventeenth century, connected, the one with Oxford University and the Middle Temple, the other with the stage. Beginning with the references in the preface to the *Parasitaster* (1606) and Sheares' epistle dedicatory to the 1633 collection of Marston's plays, both of which serve to show that the two were of similar age, he couples with them the evidence of Ben Jonson's remark to Drummond (1619), ' Marston wrote his father-in-law's preachings ' and the records of a lawsuit in 1610 which reveal John Marston, a ' preacher of the word ' at Barford St. Martin in Wiltshire, as a shareholder in the very company for which the dramatist John Marston had written his plays. From this leading, he suggests that we may incorporate in the life of the poet the facts known about ' John Marston gent.' (b. 1576, d. 1634), who married Mary, only daughter of William Wilkes, D.D., chaplain to James I, one of his favourite preachers and rector of Barford St. Martin in Wiltshire. He further identifies in part the husband of this Mary Wilkes with the John Marston who matriculated at Oxford as a member of Brasenose College in 1592 and thereupon incorporates his record. If, Dr. Brettle suggests, we accept these last two sets of facts, we can give a fairly detailed life of the poet—very full in comparison with what is similarly known of, say, Webster.

John Marston, son of John Marston a Shropshire lawyer and of his wife Maria Guarsi, was christened on October 7, 1576, at Wardington, Oxford, having been born possibly in Coventry. On February 4, 1591/2, he matriculated at Brasenose College, Oxford (' Joh : marston War[r] gen : fil. aet s—16.'), having possibly been in residence since the Trinity Term of 1591. On August 2, 1592, he was admitted ' specially ' to the Middle Temple ' by Mr. Marston his father,

---

[1] The following note is derived directly from the results of the researches of Dr. R. E. Brettle. For a far fuller account than is possible here of the newly discovered facts of Marston's life and of Dr. Brettle's deductions therefrom, the reader is referred to the following articles (where, also, any discrepancies between his view and my note will be apparent) : *John Marston, Dramatist, some new facts about his life*, *M.L.R.*, XXII (1927) ; *John Marston, Dramatist, at Oxford, R.E.S.*, III (1927) ; *Marston born in Oxfordshire, M.L.R.*, XXII (1927) (317–19); *John Marston* (University of Oxford. Abstracts of Dissertations for the degree of D.Phil., Vol. I, 1928).

Reader '. On February 4, 1593/4, he supplicated for his degree, describing himself as the eldest son of a squire, and was admitted on February 6, being entered on the Register of Congregation on February 9. The first indication of his residence in the Middle Temple does not occur until 1595 ; there is evidence that he resided also in 1596, 1597, 1599, 1600, 1601, finally forfeiting on November 21, 1606, for discontinuance. It is probable that he shared his father's chamber there until 1599. In this year his father died, leaving his law books to him, ' whom I hoped would have profited by them in the study of the law, but man proposeth and God disposeth ' (God, we cannot help feeling, disposing in this case better than Mr. Marston).

His first appearance as a writer was in 1598 with the *Metamorphosis of Pygmalion's Image and Certain Satires*. This was followed in the same year by *The Scourge of Villainy* by W. Kinsayder, some of which satires are variously interpreted as attacks on Ben Jonson or on Gabriel Harvey. In 1599 a second edition of the *Scourge* appeared with an additional satire (satyre x). On September 28 of the same year Henslowe paid £2 on behalf of the Admiral's Company for ' Mr. Maxton the new poete ', an entry sometimes supposed to refer to the share Marston took in the lost *King of Scots* with Chettle, Dekker and Ben Jonson.[1]

At or soon after the setting up of Paul's Boys a second phase of Marston's career as a writer began. Between 1599 and 1601 he revised for them *Histriomastix*, wrote or revised *Jack Drum's Entertainment* and wrote *Antonio and Mellida*, the first part of which was produced in 1600 and the second, *Antonio's Revenge*, in 1600–1. The first two involved Marston in the famous stage quarrel or theatre war [2]; it is generally supposed that Ben Jonson is satirized, or imitated, or both in Chrysoganus in *Histriomastix* and as Brabant Senior in *Jack Drum*. These precipitated Ben Jonson's reply, with Marston (probably) as Hedon in *Cynthia's Revels* (1600–1) and as Crispinus in the *Poetaster* (1601). Simultaneously his earlier satires brought down another attack upon him in the form of the *Whipping of the Satire* by W. I. (1601) and provoked Nicholas Breton and an anonymous author to his defence. In any case, he was for a few years near the centre of a satiric storm. He probably did not, as is generally thought, collaborate with Dekker in the *Satiromastix* (1601), but in the same year wrote for Paul's Boys *What You Will*, in which Ben Jonson again appears, probably as Lampatho Doria. It is presumably to this period that Ben Jonson referred in the *Conversations*, when he said that ' He beate Marston and took his pistoll from him '.[3]

[1] On the other hand, it is now often believed that the gloss ' Mr. Mastone ' above the line is a forgery. This still does not remove the possibility that ' the new poete ' was Marston.
[2] See Appendix I.   [3] Herford and Simpson, Vol. I, p. 136.

19

So preoccupied was he with these controversies, apparently, that he forfeited at the Middle Temple for non-payment on October 14, though he was restored on November 27.

About this time his connexion with Paul's Boys seems to have ended, for he wrote the *Dutch Courtesan* for the Queen's Revels children (1603–4) and in 1604 took a share of one-sixth in the syndicate formed to exploit that company. For it he wrote during the rest of his career and it is not fantastic to see in the vigorous but indiscreet career of the company a reflection of his satirical temper. His relations with Ben Jonson had in the meantime become friendly, as is shown by his verses on *Sejanus* (1603) and his dedication of his own *Malcontent* (1604) in which he defends himself against the charge of personal satire. Certainly he was collaborating with Ben Jonson and Chapman in *Eastward Ho!* in 1605 and probably, when the play was performed without licence and offence given to the king, he was involved with Chapman. His part here is a little obscure because, while Ben Jonson's and Chapman's letters [1] make it unlikely that Marston was imprisoned with them, Ben Jonson speaking in 1619 specifically said that he was.[2]

Between 1604 and 1606 he wrote the *Fawn*, in 1606 part of the City Pageant for King James and King Christian of Denmark and *Sophonisba*. In 1607, when he may have been living in Coventry, he wrote the *Entertainment* at Ashby-de-la-Zouche and probably at the same time began studying for the ministry. In unfortunate juxtaposition comes the next detail in his career—he was committed to Newgate on June 8, 1608. (But the Privy Council Register in this case leaves us free to suppose a relatively innocent occasion, such as an infringement in connexion with the breaking-up of the Queen's Revels Company.) At all events his career as a playwright was now ended and his interest sold now (or earlier) to Robert Keysar. He left unfinished the *Insatiate Countess*. This may have represented a part of his share and have been sold with it ; it was finished by Barksted in 1611 and played by the children of Whitefriars. A letter of his to Sir Gervase Clifton is extant from 1607 [3] and the record of his Deacon's ordination in the Parish Church of Stanton Harcourt on September 24, 1609.

From now onward the record is entirely ecclesiastical and academic. On December 7, 1609, he was at S. Mary's Hall, Oxford, on December 24 he was ordained priest, on June 18, 1610, he was referred to as a ' clerk ' of Barford in Cuthbert Burbage's affidavit. On August

[1] For a discussion of this problem, see Herford and Simpson, *Jonson*, I, 24–31.
[2] *Conversations*, ed. cit., p. 140.
[3] For the date, see R. E. Brettle, *The ' Poet Marston ' letter to Sir Gervase Clifton*, 1607, *R.E.S.*, IV, 1928.

10, 1616, he appears to have been the victim of a highway robbery in Knightsbridge, on October 10 in that year he was appointed to the living of Christchurch in Hampshire and was instituted on November 7. He compounded for the first-fruits on February 12. There is a record of the death of his only son in 1624 and then nothing until he resigns the living on September 13, 1631. His will was made (but not signed) on June 17, 1634 ; he died on June 25 and his funeral certificate was given the same day. He was buried on June 26, 1634, in the Temple Church by the body of his father and under a stone with the words ' Oblivioni sacrum '—an envoy curiously reminiscent of that he himself gave to his *Scourge of Villainy* thirty-six years before.[1]

3. BEN JONSON

The facts of Ben Jonson's life are relatively better known than those of any contemporary dramatist and there is less need for a note of this kind in his case. The reader will naturally turn directly to the ample and authoritative biography of Professor Herford and Mr. Simpson in the first volume of their edition of Jonson's works. But for convenience of reference and for the sake of uniformity the main events and dates are listed here in a very much abbreviated form.

He was born in or near London in 1572, the posthumous son of a ' grave minister of the gospel ', attended Westminster school where he was taught by Camden the antiquary, to whom he refers devotedly, who made him a sound scholar. He was removed by his stepfather about the year 1589 and put to the bricklaying trade instead of to the university. There is a gap at this point in our knowledge of his life in which two episodes only can be vouched for, that he was at the wars in Flanders as a volunteer and that in 1594 he married Anne Lewis. It is assumed, partly on the evidence of the material of his plays, and their relevant satire, that he was living in London during the early nineties. In 1597 he played in a strolling company of actors and it would appear from Dekker's references in *Satiromastix* that he played the part of Hieronimo. About this time he seems to have come into touch with Henslowe and to have been on his literary ' staff ' for a time, completing Nashe's *Isle of Dogs*, for the satirical references in which

---

[1] No attempt has been made here or in the chapter on Marston to discuss the textual and biographical problems of some of the plays. That is outside the scope of the present work. Much valuable information will be found in the articles of Dr. R. E. Brettle and in his review of *The Plays of John Marston*, Vol. I, ed. H. Harvey Wood, in *R.E.S.*, April 1935, and in the review of the same work by W. W. Greg in *M.L.R.*, Jan. 1935. This last contains some extremely valuable indications as to the nature of the problems of the *Malcontent* texts.

he was arrested (and subsequently released). During the year 1598 he was presumably writing comedies (alone and in collaboration) and one lost tragedy.

From about 1598 our knowledge is more definite. *Every Man In His Humour* was played by the Chamberlain's company at the Curtain in September, Shakespeare being a member of the cast. The play was entered in the Stationers' Register (twice) in 1600 and published, in its ' Italian ' form, in 1601. (The revised ' English ' form in which we generally read it belongs to the Folio of 1616).[1] In the same year, 1595, he fought a duel with a fellow actor, Gabriel Spencer, and killed him, for which he was again arrested and subsequently released. His long connexion with the Children of the Chapel Royal began about the same time, with their playing his Plautine comedy *The Case is Altered*. In the following year, 1599, he collaborated with Dekker and two others in two lost tragedies for the Admiral's ; the Chamberlain's produced his *Every Man Out of His Humour* at the Globe and the famous ' Stage Quarrel ', ' Theatre War ' or ' Poetomachia ' began.[2] The view of Herford and Simpson on this much-discussed episode may be briefly summarized here. Marston recognized or thought he recognized himself as Clove in *Every Man Out of His Humour* and replied with some allusions to Jonson in his next play, *Jack Drum's Entertainment* (1600). Jonson in *Cynthia's Revels* (1601) dealt with Marston and Dekker (whose offence is not now known) as Hedon and Anaides. Marston replied with the satirical parts of *What You Will* and brought down Jonson's devastating attack in Crispinus of the *Poetaster*. This roused up more enemies for Jonson, and Dekker's attack in *Satiromastix* was followed by a storm. The *Apologetical Dialogue* which Ben Jonson appended to *Poetaster* purported to close the episode, though, as might be expected, the element of apology is to seek.

For a few years after this Jonson was cut off from his usual work and in great poverty. He left his home and was supported for five years by Sir Robert Townshend. He abandoned comedy for a time and took to writing tragedy, possibly in collaboration with Chapman. To this time also belong his *Epigrams*, the ' additions to Jeronymo '[3] that he wrote for Henslowe and some critical writings many of which were subsequently lost in the burning of his library in 1623. In 1603 he returned to the stage with *Sejanus*, which was

[1] Both forms are readily accessible in the extremely useful collection of his plays, in two volumes, in Dent's Everyman's Library.

[2] See Appendix I.

[3] Whatever may be the force of Henslowe's allusions, it is now generally held that these are not the additional passages found in the 1602 edition of *The Spanish Tragedy*. Upon this question see Herford and Simpson, Vol. II, pp. 237–45.

unpopular with the public and was supposed by the authorities, nervous from the recent conspiracy of Essex, to contain some dangerous satire. He was called before the Council to answer it, but no results followed and the play was entered in the Stationers' Register in 1604 and published in 1605. In 1604 he collaborated with Chapman and Marston (now reconciled again) in *Eastward Ho* ; the satire on the Scots in this play led to the imprisonment of Chapman and Marston and to Jonson's voluntary surrender of himself. All were acquitted, but not without the use of both Jonson's and Chapman's influence. (He seems to have lost no ground by the episode, for in 1605 he was employed by the government in finding the conspirators of the Gunpowder Plot.) It was about this time, too, that he came into prominence as a writer of court masks. From the year 1604/5 until the end of the reign of James I, he wrote a mask every Christmas that he was in London. He was rising in reputation with the King, the court and the leading men of the state. The fact that he had been a Catholic since 1598 did not hinder this, although he and his wife were ' presented ' at the consistory Court of London in 1606 for habitual absences from Church services and communion.

From 1606 to about 1616 comes the period of his greatest success and prosperity. *Volpone*, produced in 1606, was an immediate success with all sections of the audience ; some of his most famous masks, *The Hue and Cry after Cupid*, *The Masque of Queens*, *The Masque of Beauty*, &c., belong to the years immediately after *Volpone* ; *Epicoene* (1609-10) and the *Alchemist* (1610) were notable triumphs and the failure of *Catiline* (1611) did nothing to hinder his ascendancy over younger poets, or his friendships with courtiers, scholars, poets and statesmen. In 1612 he was abroad as tutor to Ralegh's son and about the same time he began to prepare that definitive edition of his own works which ultimately became the Folio of 1616. In 1614 came *Bartholomew Fair*, a success alike with the public and the court. His best work in drama was now done, but his masks, in spite of quarrels with Inigo Jones, were as successful as ever and as good ; *The Golden Age Restored* (1615-16) and *Pleasure Reconciled to Virtue* (1617-18) both belong to this period. But his next comedy, *The Devil is an Ass*, in 1616, is generally acknowledged to show some decline in his genius and there is no new play for nine years. In 1618-19 he visited William Drummond at Hawthornden and was responsible for the conversations which Drummond records. In 1619 he was inducted into the degree of M.A. at Oxford and from then onwards, a scholar who was never at a University, he stood at the head of English letters until his death. Judging by the references in his *Execration upon Vulcan*, where he describes the writings destroyed by the fire in his library in 1623, it would appear that his work for the last five or six years had been mainly non-dramatic ; translation, criticism, history, an epic and an English grammar.

But in 1626 he returned to the stage with what is perhaps his last play of genius, *The Staple of News*. Shortly after this began a period of decline in his fortunes, dating from the death of James I. This was followed by the death of his old master Camden and by the loss of his own health and the loss of his income from the court masks. In 1628 paralysis set in and he turned back to the stage for a livelihood. *The New Inn* in 1629 was a failure, though the *Magnetic Lady* (1631) was slightly more successful. In 1634 his series of quarrels with Inigo Jones culminated in a satire on him and *The Tale of a Tub* is his last comedy. He wrote two more masks which were reasonably successful and left the *Sad Shepherd* unfinished at his death in 1637.

4. THOMAS DEKKER

Thomas Dekker is another of the dramatists whose life presents as yet many gaps to his biographers. He was born probably about 1572 [1] in London but has not as yet been definitely identified with any of the London families of the name. He was certainly writing for the Admiral's Company in 1598 and may, of course, have been working for them from 1594–8.[2] From 1598 he was almost continuously at work and the list of plays which can plausibly be associated with his name is considerable. He appears to have written for the Admiral's, Worcester's, the Chamberlain's, Paul's and Queen's, and it is generally agreed that he must have written or contributed to between forty and fifty plays. He involved himself in the Theatre War,[3] to which he contributed his *Satiromastix*, but continued his activities as playwright and pamphleteer with the possible exception of the period spent in King's Bench for debt (1613–19). In 1624 he was concerned with Webster, Ford and Rowley in writing *The Late Murther of the Sonne upon the Mother*, or *Keep the Widow Waking*, the play which, by the lawsuit which followed it, gave occasion for the evidence from which Dr. Sisson has deduced some highly valuable information on the collaboration method of this team of playwrights.[4]

The principal plays in which he is generally acknowledged to have a hand are seventeen. The earliest, *Old Fortunatus*, is assigned

---

[1] In the Epistle of his *English Villanies*, 1632, he refers to ' my three score years '. The inference is therefore reasonable that he was born about 1572, and it has been generally accepted by his biographers.

[2] See Henslowe's Diary, ad loc. In the years 1594–8 Henslowe does not give any names of authors.

[3] See Appendix I.

[4] See *The Library*, Vol. VIII, Sept. 1927, p. 245 *et seq.*, *pass.*

on strong evidence [1] to the year 1599 ; it was entered in the Stationers' Register on February 20, 1600, and published the same year. The next play, *The Shoemaker's Holiday*, is, on equally good evidence, assigned to the same year ; it was published by Valentine Simmes in 1600, but the first entry in the Stationers' Register is April 19, 1610, a transfer from Simmes to J. Wright. *Patient Grissill* appears to have been written (in collaboration with Chettle and Haughton) [2] in 1600 ; it was entered in March 28, 1600, 'stayed' and eventually published in 1603. *Satiromastix*, possibly in collaboration with Marston, belongs to 1601 ; its Stationers' Register entry is November 11, 1601, and it is published in 1602. *Sir Thomas Wyat* was written in collaboration with Webster [3] (possibly also Chettle, Heywood and Smith) and is generally identified with Henslowe's '*1 Lady Jane*' which puts it in 1602 ; it was published in 1607 and 1612 (Thomas Archer) but no Stationers' Register entry appears. *The Honest Whore* (*1*) (with Middleton) is generally assigned to 1604 ; it was entered on November 9 and published in the same year. *The Honest Whore* (*2*) is now generally agreed to belong to *c*. 1605 [4] ; it was entered in the Stationers' Register in April 29, 1608, for Thomas Man Junior, again on June 29, 1630, for Butler, and published in 1630. *Westward Ho !* (with Webster) [5] was probably written in 1604 ; it was entered in the Stationers' Register on March 2, 1605, and published in 1607. *Northward Ho !* (also with Webster [6]) belongs to the end of 1605 [7] ; it was entered in the Stationers' Register August 6, 1607, and published the same year. *The Whore of Babylon* falls between 1605 and 1607 (with the possibility of an earlier version

[1] See, for a summary of the evidence for the date of this and subsequent plays, E. K. Chambers, *The Elizabethan Stage*, Vol. III, pp. 291–300.

[2] For the most recent view of this collaboration, see Harold Jenkins, *Life and Work of Henry Chettle*, 1935, and W. L. Halstead in *P.Q.*, 1939.

[3] See, for recent comments on the authorship of this play, F. L. Lucas' edition of Webster's works, Vol. IV, pp. 239–41. (See, also, biographical note vii, John Webster.) It has recently been suggested that, in this same year, Dekker may have written the 1602 additions to *The Spanish Tragedy*.

[4] See Sir Edmund Chambers, Fleay, Hunt, &c. (It has, however, been suggested that the second part was not finished until just before 1630, the date of its first publication ; see for this view, E. Rhys, Thomas Dekker (*Mermaid Series*), Introduction, p. xxix.)

[5] See, in addition to the summary of opinions in Sir Edmund Chambers, *The Elizabethan Stage*, III, 295, F. L. Lucas, op. cit., IV, 241–2, and, on the three plays in collaboration with Webster, R. Brooke, *John Webster*, Apps. C. and D.

[6] See ibid. and Lucas, IV, 243–4.

[7] Stoll places it in 1606 (See *Elizabethan Stage*, Vol. III, p. 295.)

in 1600) ; it was entered on April 20, 1607, and published the same year. *The Roaring Girl* (with Middleton) is now assigned to 1607–8 ; it was published in 1611. *If It be not Good, the Devil is in It* falls between May 1610 and 1612, the year of its publication. *Match Me in London* is extremely difficult to date and conjectures range between 1594 and 1623 ; it was entered in the Stationers' Register on November 8, 1630, and published in 1631. *The Virgin Martyr* (with Massinger) also presents difficulties and 1620 seems the likeliest date ; it was entered in the Stationers' Register on December 7, 1621, and published in 1622. *The Witch of Edmonton* (with Ford and W. Rowley) is generally agreed to have been written soon after the publication of what may have been its source [1] in 1621 ; it was not entered in the Stationers' Register until May 21, 1658, and was published the same year. *The Wonder of a Kingdom* was either the product of collaboration between Day and Dekker in 1623 or was the result of revision by Day in 1623 of an old play by Dekker ; it was entered in the Stationers' Register on May 16, 1631, and on February 24, 1636, and published in that year. *The Sun's Darling* (with Ford) was licensed for March 3, 1624 ; it was published in 1656. *The Noble Soldier* (with Day and S. Rowley) is generally believed to have been written about 1600 and revised later, at any time up to 1631, when it was entered in the Stationers' Register on May 16 ; it was published in 1634. Dekker died in 1632, the record of his death being entered on August 25.[2]

5. THOMAS MIDDLETON

Thomas Middleton was born in 1580 and christened on April 18 at St. Lawrence in the Old Jewry.[3] We next meet him in 1597 with the publication of *The Wisdom of Solomon Paraphrased* which has been confirmed as his by Mr. Dugdale Sykes [4] and indirectly by Mr. Eccles' discovery of the date of his birth, which, by making him only seventeen at the time, frees him from the odium of having perpetrated this work at years of discretion. Shortly after this he went to the university, not Cambridge as has been generally supposed, but Oxford, where he matriculated from Queen's College in April 1598, signing at subscription on the seventh of that month.[5]

---

[1] Generally agreed to have been Henry Goodcole's (lost) pamphlet on the trial of Elizabeth Sawyer for witchcraft in 1621.

[2] See C. J. Sisson (op. cit.), *The Library*, Sept. 1927, p. 238, fn.

[3] A fact, which has vitally affected our estimate of Middleton's work and questions of the canon of his plays, only recently brought to light by Professor Mark Eccles. See *R.E.S.*, 1931, pp. 431–41.

[4] *Thomas Middleton's Early Non-Dramatic Work*, *N. and Q.*, June 20, 1925.

[5] See Mark Eccles, loc. cit., where he points out that the Cambridge University Registers give no Thomas Middletons of suitable date,

The next point in his career is the publication of *Micro-Cynicon or Six Snarling Satires* in 1599 [1] and of *The Ghost of Lucrece* in 1600. He is mentioned by Henslowe in the *Diary* in 1602 (he appears to have been, as Mr. Eccles puts it, ' a minor accomplice in *Caesar's Fall* '), but there is no real evidence that he was a playwright before this. In the same year was published *Blurt, Master Constable* which, though first attributed to Middleton only in 1661, was not seriously questioned until 1926.[2] Now Mr. Oliphant and Mr. Eccles have both doubted that he was the main author of this play, but it is probable that his career as a playwright began about this time ; as Mr. Eccles has shown,[3] he was never at any Inn of Court, though he might have had a brief experience of an Inn of Chancery. The only other event of this date is his marriage in 1603 to the niece of Dr. Roger Marbeck, Provost of Oriel, who was also a daughter of Edward Marbeck, one of the six clerks in Chancery and sister of Thomas Marbeck the actor. If we accept R. C. Bald's approximate dates for the composition of the early plays and combine it with his listing of the dates of his Entertainments [4], we can make out a rough scheme of his activities for the next few years.

The Phoenix (acted by Paul's boys and published in 1607) probably belongs to 1602, as does also *The Famelie of Love* (acted by His Majesty's Revels and published in 1608). Early in 1603/4 Middleton appears to have written one speech (at least) for the Entertainment given by the City of London to James I on March 15. This was arranged mainly by Dekker, who, however, acknowledges Zeal's speech as by Middleton. To this period belongs also his collaboration with Dekker in *The Honest Whore, I*. His *Michaelmas Term* (Paul's. Pub. 1607) and *A Mad World, My Masters* (Paul's. Pub. 1608) were probably both written before the middle of 1604. In the same year were published the pamphlets, *The Blacke Book* and *Father Hubbard's Tales*. *Your Five Gallants* (Paul's. Pub. n.d. S.R. 1607/8) and *A Trick to Catch the Old One* (Paul's. Pub. 1608) are less easy to

---

with the very doubtful exception of a Queens' B.A. in 1593–4. At Oxford, on the other hand, the Thomas Middleton who matriculated in April 1598, was of London, ' pleb. fil ' and eighteen years of age. Here age, place of residence and social rank all tally with what else we know of the dramatist.

[1] Again vouched for by Dugdale Sykes (op. cit.) and confirmed by Mark Eccles' evidence of date.

[2] E. H. Oliphant, *Studies in Philology*, XXIII.   [3] Op. cit.

[4] For the listing of Middleton's civic activities from the year 1603/4 onward, see R. C. Bald, *Middleton's Civic Employments*, *Mod. Phil.*, XXXI, Aug. 1933, pp. 65–78. For the most recent estimate of the dates of the plays, see the same author's ' The Chronology of Middleton's Plays' (*M.L.R.*, Jan. 1937).

determine, but were presumably written before 1606, when the Children of Paul's came to an end.

The plays written after this date are, until we reach the last three, very difficult to date. R. C. Bald, in the article already drawn upon, arrives at a conjectural order which will be provisionally adopted here. (The reader is referred to the article itself for further details and for the balancing of evidence in each case.) Bald would assign the following dates to the large and uncertain group of Middleton's plays that fall between 1606 and 1622: *The Roaring Girl* (1607–8); *A Chaste Maid in Cheapside* (1613); *More Dissemblers Besides Women* (c. 1615); *No Wit, No Help, like a Woman's* (c. 1615); *A Fair Quarrel* (1615–16); *The Witch* (1616); *The Widow* (1616); *The Old Law* (c. 1616); *The Mayor of Quinborough* (1615–20); *The World Tossed at Tennis* (1619); *Anything for a Quiet Life* (1621); *Women Beware Women* (c. 1621). Perhaps the most notable difference between this and the earlier groupings is the far later dating of *The Mayor of Queenborough*; the detailed evidence for this will be found in Bald's edition of that play (1938).

At the end of Middleton's career as a dramatist there is again greater certainty. The last three plays were licensed by Sir Henry Herbert, *The Changeling* on May 7, 1622, *The Spanish Gipsey* on July 9, 1623, and *A Game at Chess* on June 12, 1624. *Anything for a Quiet Life*, though not published till 1662, has been reasonably assigned to about 1621 by Mr. F. L. Lucas.[1]

Though the last thirteen or fourteen years of Middleton's career seems to have produced fewer plays than the period of corresponding length at its beginning, there is a considerable increase of activity in other directions which perhaps accounts for this.[2] From the year 1613 onwards R. C. Bald[3] has collected together a formid-

---

[1] F. L. Lucas, *The Works of John Webster*, vol. iv, p. 65.

Separate mention should perhaps be made of *The Puritan* (pub. 1607), which was attributed to Middleton by Fleay, Bullen and others, though it is now generally grouped with the anonymous plays of the period. Eccles has, however, proved that the knowledge of Oxford life shown in the play can now no longer be regarded as evidence against Middleton's authorship.

[2] Though here, again, allowance should probably be made for the fact that Middleton's share in the 'lost' and 'doubtful' plays of this period cannot easily be estimated.

[3] *Middleton's Civic Employments*, *Mod. Phil.*, Aug. 1933, pp. 65–78.

able list of civic entertainments of different kinds, chiefly Mayoral
pageants, which together with the office of City Chronologer (held
from 1620) might account for a fair proportion of the energy even
of so prolific a writer as Middleton.[1]   On September 29, 1613, was
produced his entertainment known as the *Running Stream Entertainment* for Sir Thomas Middleton.   This was printed with the second
issue of the *Triumphs of Truth* (1613).   In 1613 (October 29) he
was responsible for *The Triumphs of Truth* in honour of Sir Thomas
Middleton, mayor ; on January 4, 1613/14 for *The Mask of Cupid*
in The Merchant Taylors' Hall [2] ; on November 4, 1616, for *Civitatis
Amor*, a water-entertainment celebrating the creation of Charles Prince
of Wales ; in 1617 for the Mayoral Pageant *Triumphs of Honor and
Industry* of which some interesting accounts survive [3] ; on January 1,
1619/20, for the *Mask of Heroes* at the Inner Temple and later in
the year for the Mayoral Pageant *The Triumphs of Love and Antiquity*
and, with Rowley, for *The World Toss'd at Tennis*.   On September 6,
1620, he was appointed City Chronologer,[4] his salary being augmented
on June 23 following and special grants being made him by the
Court of Aldermen.   The year 1621 is represented by the *Honourable
Entertainments . . . for the service of this Noble City* and by the
Mayoral Pageant of *The Sunne in Aries*.   On April 17 of this year
appears his nomination ' to be made free of this Cittye by redemp-
cion '.[5]   In 1622 come the Mayoral Pageant, *The Triumphs of Honor
and Virtue*, and the *Invention . . . for Ed. Barkham, Lord Mayor*.
On September 17, 1622, February 5, 1623, and September 2, 1623,
there are entries of £15, £20 and £20 respectively given to Middleton
by the Court of Aldermen for services of the kind recorded in the
' Invention ' for the Lord Mayor's Feast in 1622.   In September 1623
comes another Mayoral Pageant, the *Triumphs of Integrity* and in
1626 the *Triumphs of Health and Prosperity*.   Bald notes that this
was, apparently, unsatisfactorily done as there was some difficulty
over the payment.   In 1624 the *Game at Chess*, with its indiscreet
political references and its great popular success, caused both author

[1] As R. C. Bald indicates, much more was involved than the mere
writing of the words for these entertainments, and the authors appear
to have supervised, in many cases, the production, designing and
planning as well.
[2] This mask has been lost, but an account of the documents referring
to it is given by Dyce in his *Works of Middleton*, Vol. I, pp. xix–xx.
The rest, unless otherwise stated, have survived.
[3] See R. C. Bald, op. cit., p. 72.
[4] R. C. Bald points out that the records of his work as Chronologer
have perished, though they were extant in MS. in 1735.   The salary
appears to have been £6 13s. 4d., raised to £10.
[5] Though unable to suggest the monetary value of this privilege,
R. C. Bald notes that it occurs again on May 7, 1622, and April 24, 1623.

and actors to be summoned, at the instance of Gondomar, the Spanish ambassador, before the Privy Council. Middleton seems to have disappeared, though his son, after a few days, appeared in his place. The players were for a time suspended. He died in 1627 in the parish of Newington Butts, where he had been living since at least 1623 [1] and was buried on July 4th.

THOMAS MIDDLETON : NOTE ON CANON

The canon of Middleton's plays is still under dispute and the subject is one of such intricacy, allowing for divergence of opinion even among experts, that no adequate survey of the problem can be attempted here. The reader is referred in the first instance to the recent work of Sykes, Oliphant, Dunkel, Eccles and Bald where the question is discussed in the light of modern discovery.[2] All that can be done here is to indicate the assumptions—and some of them, I admit, are frank assumptions—on which I have proceeded in discussing the plays used in the text. A nucleus of plays is undoubtedly his, those attributed to him by a title-page reference of contemporary or nearly contemporary date : *A Trick to Catch the Old-one*,[3] *A Mad World*,

[1] As shown by the entry in the pedigree of the College of Arms (C2, Vis. Surrey, 1623, p. 328, and Harl. MS. 1046, fol. 209) reproduced by Dyce and Bullen (I, xii) : ' Thomas Midleton de Newington in com. Surrey chronographus civitatis London 1623.'

[2] The subject was first treated by P. G. Wiggin, *An Inquiry into the Authorship of the Middleton-Rowley Plays. Radcliffe College Monographs*, IX, 1897, now to a certain extent superseded. See, for later views, H. Dugdale Sykes, *Sidelights*, 1924 (where Ford is proposed as the author of the *Spanish Gipsey* in place of Middleton) ; *Thomas Middleton's Early Dramatic Work* (*Notes and Queries*), June 20, 1925 ; E. H. Oliphant, books and articles on the Beaumont-Fletcher canon *passim* and especially the article in *Studies in Philology*, XXIII, 1926, where he suggests the rejection of *Blurt, Master Constable* from Middleton's work ; W. D. Dunkel, ' Anything for a Quiet Life ', *P.M.L.A.*, Sept. 1928, which dissents from Lucas and would give the play back to Middleton, *The Authorship of ' the Puritan '*, *P.M.L.A.*, Sept. 1930, and *The Authorship of ' the Revenger's Tragedy '*, *P.M.L.A.*, Sept. 1931, giving these to him also, and finally, *Did not Rowley merely revise Middleton ? P.M.L.A.*, Sept. 1933, where he rejects many of the findings of Miss Wiggin (see above) as to the collaboration of Rowley and Middleton and substitutes revision for collaboration in *A Fair Quarrel, The Changeling* and *The Spanish Gipsey*. The question of Middleton's relation with Rowley is again treated by C. W. Stork, *William Rowley*, and in his introduction to *Rowley's All's Lost by Lust and A Shoemaker a Gentleman*, *Univ. Penn. Pubs.*, xiii, 1910. See also E. C. Morris's edition of the *Spanish Gipsey* and his article on the *Date and Composition of ' The Old Law '*, *P.M.L.A.*, XVII.

[3] Attributed to T.M. in 1608 and to T. Middleton in 1616.

My Masters,[1] *The Roaring Girl,*[2] *A Chaste Maid in Cheapside,*[3] *A Fair Quarrel,*[4] *A Game at Chesse.*[5] Of practically equal value are late (but still seventeenth-century) t.p. ascriptions, especially as in nearly every one of the cases of that kind the play very closely resembles one piece or other of Middleton's known work : *The Old Law,*[6] *The Mayor of Quinborough,*[7] *The Widow,*[8] *No Wit . . . Like a Woman's,*[9] *The Spanish Gipsey,*[10] *The Changeling,*[11] *Anything for a Quiet Life,*[12] *Women beware Women,*[13] *More Dissemblers besides Women,*[14] *Blurt, Master Constable*[15] and *The Witch.*[16] Finally, there is the more difficult group of plays with no t.p. ascription ; naturally it is within this group that disputes mainly arise, though some even of them (*The Phoenix* (pub. 1607), *The Famelie of Love* (pub. 1608), *Michaelmas Term* (pub. 1607)) are never seriously doubted, either because of irresistible internal evidence of his hand or because of early association with his name or both. The main problem of authorship thus resolves itself into two branches. First, how much did Middleton write of the plays originally ascribed or subsequently attributed to him and Rowley or to him and others and what was the nature of the collaboration or revision ; second, did he write part, all or none of *Blurt, Master Constable, The Puritan, The Old Law,*[17] *The Mayor of Quinborough,*[17] and *Anything for a Quiet Life?* Blurt,

[1] T.M., 1608. [2] T. Middleton and T. Dekker (1611).
[3] Thomas Middleton Gent., 1630.
[4] Thomas Middleton and William Rowley (1617).
[5] Though without t.p. ascription this play was associated with Middleton immediately by contemporary reputation.
[6] Phil. Massinger, Tho. Middleton, William Rowley (1656).
[7] Tho. Middleton (1661).
[8] Ben Jonson, John Fletcher, Tho. Middleton (1652).
[9] Tho. Middleton (1657).
[10] Thomas Midleton and William Rowley (1653).
[11] Thomas Midleton and William Rowley (1653).
[12] Tho. Middleton (1662). [13] Tho. Middleton (1657).
[14] Tho. Middleton (1657).
[15] Published 1602 with no author's name. Generally attributed to Middleton since 1661.
[16] Recovered in MS. by Isaac Reed and first published in 1778. Identified as Middleton's work by the dedication to Thomas Holmes, signed Tho. Middleton.
[17] Doubt has from time to time been thrown on his sole authorship of both these plays. The presence of an older play or a collaborator's or reviser's hand has been suggested. The most recent comment on this question is to be found in Mark Eccles, *Middleton's Birth and Education, R.E.S.,* 1931, where he would date both plays about 1606 or 1606–7, traces Rowley's hand in *The Old Law* but does not wish to deny Middleton the main part, and in Bald's article referred to above (p. 297. n. 4) and in his edition of *The Mayor,* where he assigns both plays to the period 1616 or somewhat later.

Master Constable (1602, no author named, ascribed to Middleton only in 1661) has been rejected by Oliphant and latterly by Eccles [1]; *The Puritan* (1607) was rejected by Brooke [2] but retained in the Middleton canon by Fleay, Bullen, Dunkel, &c., and has latterly been restored by Eccles who shows that the discovery that Middleton was an Oxford man has removed the last objection to his authorship of *The Puritan* by explaining the source of the Oxford terminology; *The Roaring Girl* (1611) was ascribed to Dekker and Middleton jointly on the t.p. and the question with this play has been how far Middleton's hand can be traced in it and where. *Anything for a Quiet Life* was ascribed to him on the t.p. of the 1662 edition; Sykes first pointed out in 1921 [3] that Webster should be given at least a share and was followed by F. L. Lucas who included the play, in the appendix, in his edition of Webster in 1927; Dunkel has recently [4] preferred to restore it to Middleton. *The Witch* was associated with Middleton by the signature to the dedication and late though the discovery of the MS. was, there has been no serious attempt to consign it elsewhere. *The Honest Whore* (1604), on the other hand, though ascribed only to Dekker, is generally considered to contain also Middleton's work. One or two other plays have been from time to time associated with his name either as author or part-author (the *Birth of Merlin*, the *Second Maid's Tragedy* and *Wit at Several Weapons*, among others); the most recent accession to this list is, somewhat improbably, *The Revenger's Tragedy*.[5] I have included, in attempting to estimate Middleton's work, all of the first two categories and all of the third with the exception of *The Puritan* (which in any case offers little help to an understanding of the main body of his work), the doubtful *Birth of Merlin*, *Second Maid's Tragedy* and *Wit at Several Weapons* and the highly improbable *Revenger's Tragedie*.[6]

[1] Mark Eccles, *Middleton's Birth and Education*, R.E.S., 1931, pp. 431–41. The author finds the play unlike Middleton's other work in style, poetry and humour, would make Dekker responsible for Violetta and Imperia and, indeed, mainly responsible for the whole play. Bald brackets the play, as doubtful.

[2] *The Shakespeare Apocrypha*, p. xxx.

[3] See *N. and Q.*, 1921, and *Sidelights on Elizabethan Dramatists* (1924).

[4] See *P.M.L.A.*, Sept. 1928. W. D. Dunkel, *Anything for a Quiet Life*.

[5] See W. D. Dunkel, *The Authorship of 'The Revenger's Tragedie'* (1931).

[6] See Chap. VIII (*Cyril Tourneur*) and my article, *The Imagery of 'The Revenger's Tragedie' and 'The Atheist's Tragedie'* (*M.L.R.*, July 1935).

6. CYRIL TOURNEUR

His latest biographer, Professor Allardyce Nicoll,[1] has collected and added to the hitherto meagre facts known of the life of Cyril Tourneur. The dates of his main works, the date of his death, the fact that he was a soldier connected with the Cecils and the Veres and that he may (if identified with a certain William Tourneur) [2] have been also a secret service agent, these comprise, when all is said, the sum of knowledge and of justifiable conjecture.

His birth is not recorded, but it is probable that it fell within the decade 1570–80. He may have been the son of Edward Turnor of the Middle Temple, of a family connected with the Cecils and Sir Francis Vere, with whom Cyril Tourneur was certainly in his later life closely associated.[3] There are no records of a school or university education, though he shows himself to have had some education. The first date we can name with certainty is that of the publication of the *Transformed Metamorphosis* in 1600, a poem whose allusions have been so variously interpreted that they cannot at this point help us to much further knowledge of his career or associates.[4] The next date that we associate with him is 1605, when the pamphlet *Laugh and lie downe : or The Worldes Folly*, assigned to him by some scholars and rejected by others, was published.[5] In 1607 *The Revengers Tragedie* was entered in the Stationers' Register and published, though without indication of authorship in either case. The association with Tourneur derives from mid-seventeenth century attribution and there has been considerable controversy on the question for the past forty years.[6] The date of writing of this play cannot be exactly determined and no stage history of it has survived beyond the title-page statement that it was acted by the King's Men. I agree with

[1] *The Works of Cyril Tourneur*. London, Fanfrolico Press, 1930.

[2] See Nicoll, pp. 32–7, for a detailed consideration of this possibility.

[3] See Nicoll, *passim*. And J. R. Sutherland, *T.L.S.*, April 16, 1931, where a reference in the Trumbull papers is quoted to confirm previous conjectures. Under date Nimuegen, Aug. 14, 1614 (O.S.) James Bathurst writes of ' one Mr. Cirrill Turner, that belongs to General Cecil and was in former times Secretary to Sir Francis Vere . . . He is now gone to the army with his Colonel.'

[4] For a summary of these interpretations and an additional one see Nicoll, pp. 11–16.

[5] The dedication is signed C.T. and his biographers have differed as to the importance to be assigned to the initials. In the absence of conclusive evidence of any kind, Nicoll includes it in his edition but abstains from any positive verdict. (Nicoll, 16–18.)

[6] For a summary of the arguments and grounds of dispute up to 1930 see Nicoll (18–20). For references to the later articles on the subject see the book list to the present volume under ' Tourneur '.

Professor Nicoll that the year 1606 is the most likely date.[1] In 1609 comes the Stationers' Register entry and publication of *A Funerall Poeme Upon the Death of the Most Worthie And True Souldier, Sir Francis Vere*. In 1611 was entered and published *The Atheists Tragedie* which was attributed to Tourneur [2] in both cases. There is again no indication of the date at which the play was written and a large number of scholars accept the year 1610 or 1611—just before the date of publication.[3] His lost play, *The Nobleman*, was entered in the Stationers' Register on February 15, 1611/12, and a good deal of the stage history of this play survives and possibly a fragment of the incidental music.[4] In 1612 he wrote a *Character* of Robert Cecil, Earl of Salisbury,[5] who died on May 24th, a document whose tone, as Nicoll points out, suggests close association with the Cecil family. In the same year came another elegiac poem, *A Griefe On the Death of Prince Henrie*, printed early in 1613 in a volume containing similar laments by John Webster and Thomas Heywood. He is associated, through a reference of Robert Daborne (June 5, 1613) with another lost play, *The Arraignment of London*, but in this case there is not even a Stationers' Register entry. This is the last work of which we have any note and for the rest of his life Tourneur appears from time to time as a government emissary and in various other quasi-military connexions : as carrying letters from London to Brussels (Dec. 23, 1613), as in receipt of a pension from the United Provinces, as cited before the Privy Council (Sept. 1, 1617), as being arrested and subsequently released (Oct. 18, 1617). He was a member of Edward Cecil's expedition to Cadiz in 1625, was put ashore in Ireland on December 11 and died at Kinsale on February 28, 1625/6.

If in addition to this we accept the tempting suggestion—put forward only as a suggestion—by Professor Nicoll that he may be identified with a certain William Turnour [6] whose life agrees in some particulars with his and plays a convenient complementary part to it, we should be able to add that between 1598 and 1617 he was from time to time in Paris, Venice and other parts of the continent, seemingly as a member of Cecil's secret service department.[7] The correspondence between the two Tourneurs rests, as Professor Nicoll

---

[1] See Nicoll (20–21) and my article in *M.L.R.* (July 1935).

[2] The Atheists Tragedye : Or the honest Man's Revenge. As in divers places it hath often beene Acted, Written by Cyril Tourneur. [Device]. At London Printed for John Stepney etc. 1611.

[3] See Nicoll (22–3) and my article cited above.

[4] Reproduced by Nicoll in his edition.

[5] Established as Tourneur's and reprinted from the transcript (Harl. 36 ff., 495–7) by Nicoll. For references to later articles on the *Character* and variant MSS., see the book list to the present volume.

[6] Nicoll (32–7).   [7] Ibid.

points out, on the fact that both were soldiers and both in close association with the Cecils, on the substitution of the name William for that of Cyril in one transcript of the *Character* and on the possibility of a likeness in their spelling, all combined with the interesting fact that when one enters, approximately, the other disappears.

7. JOHN WEBSTER

There is less to be said of Webster's life than of many of the dramatists with whom we are concerned in these notes. The little, moreover, that is known with any certainty has been thoroughly investigated by his biographer and editor, Mr. F. L. Lucas, within recent years.[1] In this note I follow his conclusions in practically all particulars.

John Webster was born free of the Merchant Taylors' Company, this much the title page and epistle of his mayoral pageant, *Monuments of Honour*, tells us in 1624. The date of his birth is more difficult to determine and must for the present be assumed to lie between 1570 and 1580. He was perhaps admitted to the Middle Temple in 1598. He is first mentioned in connexion with the stage by Henslowe in 1602. Five payments are entered during that year, in which his name occurs variously associated with those of Chettle, Dekker, Drayton, Heywood, Middleton and Munday. In the same year were published his verses prefixed to the third part of Munday's *Palmerin of England*. We next hear of him in 1604 on the title page of the *Malcontent* and as the author of the *Ode* prefixed to S. Harrison's *Arches of Triumph*.[2] In this year and in 1605 he was again collaborating with Dekker, first in *Westward Ho* and then in *Northward Ho*. In 1607 these plays were both published and also the third play of their joint workmanship, *Sir Thomas Wyat*.[3] Thus what survives of Webster's prentice work is all written in collaboration with Dekker. (It is not now usual to assign to him *The Thracian Wonder*; the ascription of this play to him, as Dr. W. W. Greg points out, 'possibly rests on a mere blunder', and even Dyce turned it out of his second edition.)[4] Somewhere during the years 1611–12 *The White Devil* was probably written; this, the first surviving or recorded work of his sole author-

---

[1] *The Complete Works of John Webster.* Edited by F. L. Lucas. London : Chatto & Windus. 1927. 4 vols. The life of Webster, with references to various conjectures that have from time to time been put forward, is summarized in the first volume.

[2] See F. L. Lucas, Vol. III, pp. 259 and 264.

[3] On these three plays and their authorship see F. L. Lucas, Vol. IV, Appendix I, 'Webster's early collaboration with Dekker', and R. Brooke, *John Webster and the Elizabethan Drama*, Apps. C and D. On Webster's lost early plays, see Brooke, App. B.

[4] See *R.E.S.*, Oct. 1928, p. 450.

ship, was published in 1612.[1] To the same year belong his verses [2] prefixed to Heywood's *Apology for Actors*. In 1613 was written and published *The Monumental Column* on the death of Prince Henry. *The Duchess of Malfi*, though not published until 1623, probably belongs to the years 1613–14,[3] and the lost play *The Guise* may date back as far as 1614, though the upper limit for its date is 1623.[4] In 1615 comes his contribution to the sixth edition of Overbury's *Characters* in the thirty-two studies generally believed to be in part at least his.[5] In 1617 some satirical verses on Webster appear by H. Fitzjeffrey in *Certain Elegies done by Sundry Excellent Wits*. *The Devil's Law Case* probably belongs to the years 1619–20 (it is published in 1623) and *Anything for a Quiet Life* (in collaboration with Middleton) to about 1621. In 1623 come his verses prefixed to Cockeram's *Dictionary*, in 1624 his *Monuments of Honour* (for the Lord Mayor's Pageant of that October) and the lost play *A Late Murther of the Sonne upon the Mother* (in collaboration with Dekker, Rowley and Ford).[6] To 1625 perhaps belong the *Fair Maid of the Inn* (with Massinger and Ford) and *A Cure for a Cuckold* (with Rowley and perhaps Heywood). *Appius and Virginia* [7] (probably with Heywood) falls somewhere after this ; before 1634 if we accept that date for his death, before 1637/8 if we accept the later date.[8]

We are thus concerned here primarily with three plays, the two great tragedies of *The White Devil* and *The Duchess of Malfi* and the tragi-comedy *The Devil's Law Case* and with such portions of *A Cure*

---

[1] For a discussion of the date of this play, see F. L. Lucas, Vol. I, pp. 67–9.

[2] See F. L. Lucas, Vol. III, pp. 260 and 264–5.

[3] For a discussion of the date of this play, see F. L. Lucas, Vol. II, pp. 3–5.

[4] That is, the date at which Webster himself refers to it in the dedication of *The Devil's Law Case* to Sir Thomas Finch. It may, on the other hand, belong to the same period as the two plays mentioned with it there, *The White Devil* and *The Duchess of Malfi*. See F. L. Lucas, Vol. II, p. 321.

[5] See F. L. Lucas, Vol. IV, pp. 6–14, where the evidence for Webster's authorship of at least part and probably all of these additional thirty-two characters is set out.

[6] See C. J. Sisson, *Keep the Widow Waking* (*Library*, Sept. 1927, p. 243).

[7] Brooke considers Webster's share in this play to be ' very small compared with Heywood's,' to whom he gives the majority of the work. See *John Webster*, App. A (pp. 161–205).

[8] C. J. Sisson, op. cit., p. 238, fn. 1. ' I am tempted to suggest that a third of the four men engaged on this play for the Red Bull is referred to in another entry ' [Harl. Soc. Publ. Vol. IV] ' which records the burial of John Webster on 3 March 1637/8.'

for a Cuckold and *Appius and Virginia* as we believe to be his. *Anything for a Quiet Life* and the *Fair Maid of the Inn*, though not often hitherto ascribed to him, are now considered by some authorities [1] to contain portions of his work.

8. FULKE GREVILLE

Fulke Greville was born in 1554 at his father's seat, Beauchamp Court, in Warwickshire. He entered Shrewsbury School with Philip Sidney in 1564, and matriculated at Jesus College, Cambridge, in 1568. His lifelong interest in his University culminated in his foundation in 1627 of a history lectureship, which, however, lapsed on his death in the next year.[2] He obtained an office under the Court of the Marches of Wales in 1576, and in 1577 accompanied Sidney on the Casimir embassy. He became Secretary for Wales in 1583, and was M.P. for Warwickshire in 1592–3, 1597 and 1603 and from 1598 was Treasurer of the Navy. He was knighted in 1597. He had ' the longest lease, the smoothest time without rubs of any of her [Elizabeth's] favourites ' [3] but his influence he ' used honourably and did many men good '.[4] Among those he generously recommended to the Queen's Grace were Bacon, Bp. Andrewes, Bp. Overal, Sir John Coke and Samuel Daniel. His private benefactions were equally great ; they are acknowledged by Camden, Speed and D'Avenant among others. He was associated with Dyer and Sidney in literary and philosophical interests ; he entertained Bruno in 1583, and the early poems of *Caelica* must have been written during these first years at Elizabeth's Court, before he became more closely involved in affairs. On the accession of James he retired more and more, after loss and disappointment, to his estates, where he probably occupied himself with study, revising his earlier poems and writings. *Mustapha* may be assigned to the neighbourhood of 1595 and *Alaham* to a year or two later.[5]

[1] See F. L. Lucas, Vol. IV, pp. 66–9 and 148–52.
[2] For an account of this, see G. Bullough, *Fulke Greville, Lord Brooke*, M.L.R., XXVIII, Jan. 1933.
[3] Sir Robert Naunton, *Fragmenta Regalia* (1642).
[4] Bacon, *Apophthegms*, 1625.
[5] The most recent authority is G. Bullough. His edition, *The Poems and Dramas of Fulke Greville, first Lord Brooke*, (2 v. Edinburgh, 1939) reviews the problem of date in the light of earlier conjectures and later evidence, and places *Mustapha* between 1594 and 1596, and *Alaham* between 1598 and 1600.

Soon after Cecil's death in 1612 he returned to public life, becoming Chancellor of the Exchequer in 1614. He was active as a Privy Councillor, and in 1621 was created Baron Brooke of Beauchamps Court. He gave advice on the Spanish marriage, and continued to serve on councils of war and foreign affairs into the reign of Charles I. He died on 30 September 1628, as the result of a wound given by a servant who evidently believed himself unjustly left out of his will.

9. FRANCIS BEAUMONT [1]

Francis Beaumont was born in 1584 or 1585, was the son of Francis Beaumont and descended from a family of Leicestershire landowners. He entered Oxford (a member of Broadgates Hall) on February 4, 1597 ('aetat 12'), and the Inner Temple in 1600. He does not appear to have taken a degree. He seems to have taken part here in at least one set of Christmas revels (though it is not known which), to which he contributed a mock grammar lecture. He had written at least one poem before there is any record of his connexion with the stage, *Salmacis and Hermaphroditus*, published anonymously in 1602. His first play, *The Woman-Hater*, published in 1607, was probably written about 1606. It is a Jonsonian comedy and that fact, together with Jonson's epigram,[2] his own commendatory verses to *Volpone* in 1607 and the testimony of Drummond and his verse epistles to Ben Jonson,[3] points to a fairly close friendship between them.[4] His next verses are those for Fletcher's *Faithful Shepherdess* [n.d. probably 1608 or 1609], and it is generally assumed that his collaboration with Fletcher began at about this date. This presumably included the seven plays *Philaster* (1610), *The Maid's Tragedy* (1611), *A King and No King* (1611), *Four Plays in One* (?), *Cupid's Revenge* (1612), *The Coxcomb* (1608–10) and *The Scornful Lady* (1613–17), so that these, together with *The Knight of the Burning Pestle* (c. 1607), which is generally considered to be by his hand only, probably represent substantially his dramatic output. The period of collaboration, during which plays were written for the Queen's Revels, the Lady Elizabeth's and the King's, appears to have ended with Beaumont's marriage in about 1613. All that can be assigned to him with any sureness so late as that year is the mask for Princess Elizabeth's wedding (Feb. 20, 1613) and the still later traces of his work in *The*

---

[1] For a detailed biography of Beaumont see C. M. Gayley *Beaumont the Dramatist* (1914). The arrangement of the facts in the present note follows Chambers, *Elizabethan Stage*, III, 215–16.

[2] *Epigr. lv.*

[3] See on both of these, Herford and Simpson, *Jonson*, Vol. I, pp. 49–50.

[4] See Drummond, *Conversations*, I, 154, 183, 226. [Herford and Simpson, *Jonson*, Vol. I, App. I.]

Scornful Lady. So that the bulk of the work assigned jointly to him and Fletcher in the 1679 Folio cannot be his. In fact, it is probable that not more than nine plays (whole or in part) and a mask are to be attributed to him. He died on March 6, 1616.

10. JOHN FLETCHER

Fletcher was the son of a clergyman who became successively bishop of Bristol, Worcester and London (1594). He was born at Rye in Sussex in December 1579. It is not known whether he went to either university, the John Fletcher of London whose name is recorded at Corpus Christi, Cambridge in 1591 is now generally considered not to be the son of the bishop. The interval in his life until he appears as a dramatist is thus a blank. He appears first with *The Faithful Shepherdess* about 1608–9 and then in the plays already listed under Beaumont's name between 1508–9 and about 1613. A John Fletcher was married at St. Saviour's, Southwark, on November 3, 1612, and this is sometimes supposed to be the dramatist. If so, it would suggest that the collaboration with Beaumont ended before the marriage of the latter in about 1613 or that that marriage itself was slightly earlier. The condition under which the two poets are described as living hardly admits (if we accept it) of marriage in either case.[1] After the separation from Beaumont he continued to write a certain number of plays single-handed and is supposed to have collaborated, during the next twelve years or so, with Massinger, Jonson, Field, Tourneur, Daborne, Middleton, Rowley and Shirley but chiefly with Massinger.[2] He died in August 1625.

11. JOHN FORD

Ford was born in 1586 and baptized at Ilsington in Devon on the 17th of April of that year. He belonged to a family of well-established landowners who continued to reside there, though he himself apparently did not. On his mother's side he was related to Lord Chief Justice Popham. It is sometimes believed that he went to Oxford, as there is a matriculation entry for a John Ford at Exeter College in 1601. In November 1602 he became a Member of the Middle Temple. Our knowledge of his residence there has recently

[1] Aubrey reports that they ' lived together on the Banke side, not far from the Play-House, both batchelors ; lay together ; had one wench in the house between them . . . the same cloathes and cloake &c. betweene them.' (' *Brief Lives* ', *Chiefly of Contemporaries, set down by John Aubrey*. Ed. A. Clark, 2 vols, 1898. See Vol. I, p. 96.)

[2] For a list of the plays assigned to Beaumont and/or Fletcher in conjectural chronological order and suggestions as to authorship, see Appendix II, Book Lists.

been extended by Miss J. Sargeaunt[1] who has shown that he not only entered on November 16, but that he was later expelled for debt and readmitted on June 10, 1608, after payment of a 40s. fine and that he was probably involved, as late as May 1617 in a protest against the wearing of caps in Hall. This would make his residence, or at least his connexion with the Middle Temple long enough to warrant us in supposing him a practising member of some branch of the legal profession.

Soon after his entry into the Middle Temple he must have begun to write, for three early poems, *Fame's Memoriall, Honor Triumphant ; or the Peeres Challenge* and *The Monarches Meeting* were published in 1606. His writing cannot obviously have been profitable or the expulsion for debt would not have occurred in 1608. In May of 1609 his father died, bequeathing the manor to his wife and to John Ford ' my sonne tenn poundes of lawfull money of England ' only. His father was a rich man and the other sons received more.

We first hear of Ford in connexion with the stage in 1613 when his lost play *An Ill Beginning has a Good End* [2] is recorded as acted at the Cockpit. In 1615 he seems to have produced a now lost poem *Sir Thomas Overbury's Life and Untimely Death* which is known only by its Stationers' Register entry on November 25. On September 17, 1616, his brother Henry Ford made his will (dying two days later) with the interesting proviso ' To John Ford gent. my Brother, Twenty pounds a yeare for terme of his lief, . . . upon Condicion he surrenders the estate he hath in two Tenements upon Glandfields groundes Bilver parke and willow meade lyinge in Ipplepen and Torbryam to the use of my children.' This, though hardly afflu-ence, was in itself a slender livelihood, but whether or not he ceased to practise as a lawyer, Ford seems to have turned more vigorously than ever to theatre work. In 1620 he wrote his prose pamphlet *A Line of Life*, but after that his works are mainly plays. If, with Mr. Dugdale Sykes, we attribute to him a large share in *The Spanish Gipsey* and if we date that play just before or in the early 1620's, then, at this crucial point in Ford's dramatic career, he will have collaborated closely with Middleton, whose influence upon his later work appears most significant. He collaborated with Dekker in *The Witch of Edmonton*, which must, by reason of its close relation to the events it commemorated, have been produced soon after the trial of Elizabeth Sawyer in 1621. In 1624 *The Sun's Darling* (also in collaboration with Dekker) was acted at the Cockpit. To the same year belongs the lost play *Keep the Widow Waking, or A Late Murther*

---

[1] J. Sergeaunt, *John Ford*. Blackwell, 1935. The facts recorded in this work have, in general, been represented in the above note.

[2] His authorship of this play has recently been disputed by T. M. Parrott : ' A Note on John Ford ' (*M.L.N.*, April 1943).

of the Sonne upon the Mother, written in collaboration with Dekker, Webster and Rowley,[1] and probably the other two lost plays *The Fairy Knight* and *The Bristow Merchant*. In 1628 his *Lover's Melancholy* was acted at the Blackfriars and the Globe by the King's Men, having been licensed by Sir Henry Herbert ; it was published in 1629. To the years immediately after this belong (though there is no evidence as to their order) *Tis Pity She's a Whore*, acted by the Queen's Men at the Phoenix in Drury Lane, *The Broken Heart*, acted by the King's Men at Blackfriars, and *Love's Sacrifice*, acted by the Queen's at the Phoenix. All three were published in 1633. In 1634 *Perkin Warbeck*, also a Phoenix play, was published and in 1638 another Phoenix play, *The Fancies Chaste and Noble*. *The Lady's Triall*, his last recorded play, was acted at the Cockpit in Drury Lane in 1638. No record of his death has yet been discovered, nor is it possible to date either *The Queene* [2] or the three lost plays *The London Merchant*, *The Royal Combat* and *Beauty in a Trance*.

[1] See, for fresh light upon this play and its composition, C. J. Sisson, *Keep the Widow Waking* (*Library*, June and Sept. 1927).

[2] *The Queene Or the Excellency of her Sex*, published in 1653, attributed to Ford by W. Bang, who first reprinted it in his *Materialien*, Vol. XIII.

APPENDIX I

THE THEATRE WAR

[The Stage Quarrel of the years 1599–1601 affects the lives of Jonson, Marston and Dekker and can most conveniently be set out as a separate note. I follow here mainly the conclusions of the Oxford editors. (See *Ben Jonson*, ed. C. H. Herford and Percy Simpson. Oxford, 1925. Vol. I, pp. 24–31.) Certain differences in interpretation of individual passages, allusions, &c., may be found in the discussions of this episode in J. H. Penniman, *The War of the Theatre* (1897), and R. A. Small, *The Stage-Quarrell between Ben Jonson and the so-called Poetasters* (1899). Reference should also be made to the article by M. Castelain, *Shakespeare and Ben Jonson* (Jan. 1907. *Revue Germanique*), and to a somewhat different interpretation recently set upon the events by G. B. Harrison, *Shakespeare at Work* (Chaps. VIII and IX) 1933.]

The outline of the events can best be set down as follows. In 1599 (probably about August) Marston revised the old play of *Histrio-Mastix* and in rehandling the figure of Chrisoganus had introduced certain characteristics which he intended to represent Ben Jonson and, almost equally surely, intended as complimentary comments. Ben Jonson either did not so understand it or was irritated by the clumsiness of the intended flattery. Without giving the matter undue notice, he nevertheless introduced into the figure of Clove in *Every Man Out of His Humour* (III, iv) some half-dozen words from the strange and conspicuous vocabulary by which Marston had already made himself known. The quarrel may thus quite well have begun as Drummond reports, with Marston's ' representing him on the stage '[1] and with Jonson's rather casual reply. Perhaps Marston saw rather more in Clove than it occurred to Jonson that he would see, for in his next play, *Jack Drum's Entertainment* (1600, about August), he portrayed Jonson more recognizably and less respectfully in Brabant senior. Here again a good deal of the character seems to have nothing to do with Jonson, but parts of the satire are unmistakable.[2] In Jonson's next play, therefore, *Cynthia's Revels*, acted by the Children of the Chapel, probably in January

---

[1] Using the punctuation of the Oxford editors (which is also that of Penniman, Small and Castelain), this is now considered to be the whole of the reason which Drummond intended to assign.

[2] Yet the play exploits, as far as was possible to Marston's understanding of it, Jonson's discovery of the principle of Humours as a

1601, he introduced (perhaps when the play was already part written) a severer comment on Marston in the character of Hedon. He dealt at the same time with Dekker in the person of Anaides, the companion study to Hedon, though it is not yet clear what Dekker had done to incur this. The portraits seem to have been recognized easily and Dekker and Marston planned a vigorous reply. Jonson appears to have heard of this and set about a retort which should effectually dispose of his opponents. While Marston was preparing *What You Will* (where Jonson is presumably Lampatho Doria, though he might perhaps be sought in Quadratus) [1] Jonson was writing *Poetaster*, against time, in fifteen weeks. Marston won by a short length, apparently, but Jonson's was by far the more effective rejoinder and it came in hard on his heels ; as Crispinus in Jonson's play, Marston must have achieved even more notoriety than his own works had yet given him. Marston's hostility seems to have died down after this ; indeed, his original admiration for Jonson was resumed not much later. There is a clear suggestion that Shakespeare was also involved ; the well-known reference in *The Return from Parnassus*, Part II, IV, iii (' O that *Ben Jonson* is a pestilent fellow, he brought up *Horace* giving the Poets a pill, but our fellow *Shakespeare* hath given him a purge that made him bewray his credit '), has reasonably been taken [2] to refer to the character of

---

foundation of comedy. The admiration, then, is strong enough still, but Jonson's ' eye Only create to censure from above ' (*J.D.*, IV, 320–1) had apparently roused in Marston an irritable fury that drove him to denounce and parody even while imitating. He seems, in fact, to have passed through a succession of phases very like those we can trace in Greene's attitude to Marlowe ten years earlier : admiration and imitation in *Alphonsus*, soured, for some reason, into parody, satire (less open than Marston's) and still unwilling imitation in *Orlando*.

[1] That Quadratus is really Marston himself is, however, easier to believe ; he has the convulsive, volcanic and variable spleen of the author of the satires. Moreover, when we meet in one character a bitter and uncompromising satirist, terrifying in his ruthlessness, a court gallant, easy, gay and debonair, and a high-souled artist-philosopher, what are we to suppose but that we have Marston upon Marston ? Lampatho, though he is a mixture of spiteful satirist and sycophantic versifier, has some startling revolutions of mood obviously intended to be more like those of Jonson. He can be as fearless as Quadratus in satire (he too ' would not flatter though he saw death ') and can rise somewhat unexpectedly to the really remarkable, penetrating cynicism of the Senecan-Timonese speeches on scholars in II, i.

[2] By Fleay, Small and the Oxford editors. It has, on the other hand, by the editors of the New Shakespeare been taken to refer to Nym (*1 Henry IV*). See, for the more literal interpretation, G. B. Harrison, *Shakespeare at Work*, p. 316.

Ajax in *Troilus and Cressida* and is supported by Jonson's own reference in the Apologetical Dialogue of *Poetaster* to the ' better natures ' who were drawn by the players to join in the quarrel [1]—on the wrong side. But if Marston was quieted and Shakespeare's comment was a momentary mood of bitterness, Dekker was not yet suppressed. In fact, he had the last effective word in his *Satiromastix* (a few weeks after *Poetaster*), where he borrowed Jonson's own Captain Tucca. Since *Poetaster* had satirized and enraged several other professions besides the poets (soldiers, lawyers and actors) it is not astonishing that at this point Jonson left the writing of comedy and professed himself (at the end of the Apologetical Dialogue) dedicated to tragedy. The two original protagonists disposed of, the quarrel died away.

The main difficulty in outlining the order of events with any certainty lies in the lack of evidence as to the order of the plays after *Every Man Out of His Humour*. This allows for certain variations in the interpretation of the relations of *Jack Drum's Entertainment*, *Cynthia's Revels*, *What You Will* which can be traced in the works referred to at the beginning of this note and in the summaries in *The Elizabethan Stage*, Vol. III.[2]

[1] See Herford and Simpson, *Jonson*, Vol. I, p. 28, fn. i.
[2] See, especially, pp. 293, 362–3, 364, 365–6, 430. For the most recent discussions of various aspects, see App. II, sections B. i, and B: ii, under names of individual dramatists.

APPENDIX II

BOOK LISTS

[*Note.*—The publication of Sir Edmund Chambers's *Elizabethan Stage* (4 vols., 1923) with its exhaustive book lists has modified the function of such lists as the present. It is no longer necessary, even were there space, to name the most important pieces of work that have been done in this field. Sir Edmund Chambers's volumes are available in every library and duplication can therefore be avoided. The present list confines itself to the following ground:

  A. A list of books in which can be found general, or very important special bibliographies in the field of Jacobean Drama.

  B. A list of works, general or referring to individual dramatists, which have appeared since 1923 (and are therefore not listed in *The Elizabethan Stage*), or which have appeared since the publication of any later special book list already referred to under A. (In the case of Webster, for example, the present list would enter only the notices, &c., after 1927, the date of F. L. Lucas's edition.)

  C. A short list of the early editions of the plays of those dramatists who are not or who are only partly included in *The Elizabethan Stage* (Middleton, Beaumont and Fletcher, Ford) and a somewhat fuller list of recent works upon them.

A list of the abbreviations used in referring to standard works and periodicals will be found on p. xv.

SECTION A. BIBLIOGRAPHIES

(i) *The Elizabethan Stage.* E. K. Chambers. 1923. Oxford. 4 vols. [This contains comprehensive bibliographies (up to the year 1923) on general dramatic and stage history and cognate subjects : special lists prefixed to the individual chapters ; complete lists of editions of all plays written before 1616 and lists of important references to the authors, treated alphabetically, in vol. iii. This covers the field of the Jacobean drama except :

    (*a*) Plays written after 1616.

    (*b*) References and editions published since 1924.

(ii) *William Shakespeare : A Study of Facts and Problems.* E. K. Chambers. 1930. O.U.P. 2 vols. The bibliographical material is similarly arranged. The field covered is that of Shakespearian studies, widely interpreted. A valuable index to these two volumes and to the four of *The Elizabethan Stage* has been published by the Shakespeare Association. (O.U.P., 1934.)

(iii) *The Medieval Stage.* E. K. Chambers. 1903. Oxford. 4 vols. The bibliographical material is similarly arranged. Appendix X constitutes a full list of medieval dramatic texts, with later editions up to the year 1903.

(iv) *The Year's Work in English Studies.* Edited annually for the English Association since 1919. The relevant chapters here list, with full and very helpful summaries, the work done since 1919 and, after 1923, constitute an indispensable supplement to *The Elizabethan Stage.*

(v) The Annual *Bibliography of English Language and Literature* of the Modern Humanities Research Association, published since 1920. A somewhat fuller list than that of *The Year's Work in English Studies* but without summaries.

(vi) The revised bibliographies of *The Cambridge History of English Literature.* (*The Cambridge Bibliography of English Literature.*)

(vii) The bibliographical material prefixed to or incorporated in commentary and footnotes in certain recent editions of Jacobean dramatists is of great value.

Ben Jonson, edited C. H. Herford and P. Simpson, O.U.P. 1925—in progress (7 vols. issued).
The Works of John Webster. 4 vols., ed. F. J. Lucas. Chatto & Windus. 1927.
The Works of Cyril Tourneur. 1 vol., ed. Allardyce Nicoll. Nonesuch Press. 1930.

(viii) *Annals of English Drama.* A. Harbage. O.U.P. 1940.

(ix) *Chronological List of Extant Plays, 1581–1642.* H. W. Wells. O.U.P. 1940.

SECTION B. CLASSIFIED LIST OF WORKS SINCE 1923. SUPPLEMENTARY TO *THE ELIZABETHAN STAGE*, &c.

(i) GENERAL

Sidelights on Elizabethan Drama. H. Dugdale Sykes. O.U.P., 1924.
The Evidence of Theatrical Plots for the History of the Elizabethan Stage. W. W. Greg. (*R.E.S.*) July 1925.
English Actors in Paris during the Lifetime of Shakespeare. F. A. Yates. (*R.E.S.*) Oct. 1925.
Women on the Pre-Restoration Stage. T. S. Graves. (*S. in Ph.*) April 1925.
Prompt Copies, Private Transcripts, and the Playhouse Scrivener. W. W. Greg. (*Library.*) Sept. 1925.
English Literary Autographs, 1550–1650 : Part I—Dramatists. W. W. Greg. O.U.P. 1925.
Plays and Masques at Court. M. S. Steele. O.U.P. 1926.
The Child Actors : A Study in Elizabethan Stage History. H. N. Hillebrand. 1926.
The Court Masque. Enid Welsford. C.U.P. 1927.

Dramatic Publication in England (1580–1640). E. M. Albright. O.U.P. 1927.

The Physical Conditions of the Elizabethan Public Playhouse. W. J. Lawrence. O.U.P. 1927.

Pre-Restoration Stage Studies. W. J. Lawrence. O.U.P. 1927.

Posting Henslowe's Accounts. T. W. Baldwin. (*J.E.G.P.*) Jan. 1927.

An Elizabethan Journal . . . 1591–4, by G. B. Harrison. Constable. 1928.

Das Englische Drama im Zeitalter der Reformation und der Hoch Renaissance. Eduard Eckhardt. 1928.

Aspects of Elizabethan Imagery. Elizabeth Holmes. Blackwell. 1929.

Das Englische Drame der Spätrenaissance. E. Eckhardt. 1929.

Shakespeare and his Fellow Dramatists. E. H. C. Oliphant. Pitman. 1929.

The Elizabethan Jig and Related Song Drama. C. R. Baskervill. C.U.P. 1929.

The School Drama in England. V. Motter. Longmans. 1929.

The Dedication of Early English Plays. W. J. Lawrence. (*Life and Letters.*) July 1929.

Prayers after Plays. W. J. Lawrence. (*Fortnightly Review.*) Nov. 1929.

The Extra-Dramatic Moment in Elizabethan Plays before 1616. D. Fenton. Philadelphia. 1930.

The Bibliography of the Commedia dell'Arte. K. M. Lea. (*Library.*) June 1930.

The Elizabethan Private Playhouse. W. J. Lawrence. (*Criterion.*) April 1930.

Dramatic Documents from the Elizabethan Playhouses. W. W. Greg. O.U.P. 1931.

The Malone Society Collections, Vol. II. Part III, ed. W. W. Greg. 1931.

A Study of Patriotism in the Elizabethan Drama. R. V. Lindabury. O.U.P. 1931.

Elizabethan Stage Conditions. M. C. Bradbrook. C.U.P. 1932.

Selected Essays, 1917–32. T. S. Eliot. Faber. 1932.

The Length of Elizabethan and Jacobean Plays. A. Hart. (*R.E.S.*) April 1932.

The Time Allotted for Representation of Elizabethan and Jacobean Plays. A. Hart. (*R.E.S.*) Oct. 1932.

An Introduction to Tudor Drama. F. S. Boas. O.U.P. 1933.

The Lost Plays and Masques : 1500–1642. G. M. Sibley. O.U.P. 1933.

Shaksperian Scraps and other Elizabethan Fragments. S. A. Tannenbaum. O.U.P. 1933.

The Broken English of Foreign Characters of the Elizabethan Stage. W. O. Clough. (*P.Q.*) July 1933.

Tudor and Stuart Dramatizations of the Doctrines of Natural and Moral Philosophy. H. K. Russell. (*S. in Ph.*) Jan. 1934.

The Audience and the Revenger of Elizabethan Tragedy. F. T. Bowers. (*S. in Ph.*) April 1934.

Italian Popular Comedy. A Study in the Commedia dell'Arte, 1560–1620, with special reference to the English Stage. K. M. Lea. Oxford. 2 vols. 1934.

A Companion to Shakespeare Studies, ed. H. Granville-Barker and G. B. Harrison. C.U.P. 1934.

Elizabethan Essays. T. S. Eliot. Faber. 1934.

Themes and Conventions of Elizabethan Tragedy. M. C. Bradbrook. C.U.P. 1935.

Shakespeare's Imagery and What it tells us. Caroline F. E. Spurgeon. C.U.P. 1935.

Those Nut-Cracking Elizabethans : Studies of the Early Theatre and Drama. W. J. Lawrence. The Argonaut Press. 1935.

Dumb-Show in Elizabethan Drama. B. R. Pearson. (*R.E.S.*) Oct. 1935.

Logic in the Elizabethan Drama. Allan H. Gilbert. (*S. in Phil.*) Oct. 1935.

Lost Plays of Shakespeare's Age. C. J. Sisson. C.U.P. 1936.

The Theme of Revenge in Elizabethan Tragedy. Percy Simpson. British Academy Shakespeare Lecture. O.U.P. 1936.

Death and Elizabethan Tragedy. Theodore Spencer. Harvard Univ. Press and O.U.P. 1936.

Elizabethan and Seventeenth Century Play Manuscripts. Addenda. A. Harbage. (*P.M.L.A.*) Sept. 1937.

The English Renaissance. V. de Sola Pinto. Cresset Press. 1938.

Elizabethan and Jacobean Playwrights. H. W. Wells. New York, Columbia Univ. Press and O.U.P. 1939.

Hill's List of Early Plays in Manuscript. J. Q. Adams. (*Library.*) June, 1939.

Elizabethan Plays and Players. G. B. Harrison. Routledge. 1940.

Elizabethan Revenge Tragedy. F. T. Bowers. Princeton Univ. Press and C.U.P. 1940.

The Invisible World : A Study of Pneumatology in Elizabethan Drama. R. H. West. Univ. of Georgia Press. 1939.

The Staging of Elizabethan Plays at the Red Bull Theatre, 1605–1625. G. F. Reynolds. New York, M.L.A.A. and O.U.P. 1940.

The Jacobean and Caroline Stage : Dramatic Companies and Players. G. E. Bentley. O.U.P. 1941.

The Globe Playhouse : Its Design and Equipment. John Crawford Adams. Harvard Univ. Press and O.U.P. 1942.

Notes on early Stuart stage history. C. J. Sisson. (*M.L.R.*) Jan. 1942.

Charles Lamb and the Elizabethan Drama. F. S. Boas (*Essays and Studies*). O.U.P. 1943.

The Elizabethan World Picture. E. M. W. Tillyard. Chatto and Windus. 1943.

Shakespeare's Audience. H. S. Bennett. (British Academy Shakespeare Lecture, O.U.P.) 1944.

Shakespeare's History Plays. E. M. W. Tillyard. Chatto and Windus. 1944.

Elizabethan and Jacobean. F. P. Wilson. O.U.P. 1945.

An Introduction to Stuart Drama. F. S. Boas. O.U.P. 1946.

(ii) Individual Authors

[*Note.*—A list of early editions is not given, as these can be readily found in *The Elizabethan Stage*, Vol. III, under the dramatists' names, except in those cases which fall outside the categories covered by that work. The standard modern edition (or editions) is mentioned in each case.]

1. CHAPMAN
Editions : Single Works

Eastward Hoe. J. H. Harris. (Yale Studies in English, 73.) O.U.P. 1926.

The Blind Beggar of Alexandria. (Mal. Soc. Repr.) 1928.

Elizabethan Tragedy : Six Representative Plays. [Includes *Bussy D'Ambois.*] George Rylands. 1933.

Editions : Selections

Chapman : with Illustrative Passages. Havelock Ellis. Nonesuch Press. 1934.

Critical and Biographical

Hero and Leander. (*T.L.S.*) Nov. 6, 1924.

Chapman's Ethical Thought. Janet Spens. *Essays and Studies.* (Engl. Ass.) Vol. XI. 1925.

George Chapman. G. Thorn-Drury. (*R.E.S.*) July 1925.

Etudes sur l'humanisme continental en Angleterre à la fin de la Renaissance. F. L. Schoell. 1926.

Stuart Politics in Chapman's 'Tragedy of Chabot'. N. D. Solve. Univ. of Michigan Publ. Vol. IV. 1928.

Chapman, 'The Tragedy of Chabot', III. ii. 147–68. A. S. Ferguson. (*M.L.R.*) Jan. 1928.

Shakespeare and Chapman as Topical Dramatists. Percy Allen. 1929.

Shakespeare, Chapman, and Sir Thomas More. Arthur Acheson. Quaritch. 1931.

Hitchin Worthies. R. L. Hine. 1932.

Les Sources de 'Bussy D'Ambois'. C.-E. Engel. (*Rev. de Litt. Comp.*) XII. 1932.

The Plays of Shakespeare and Chapman in Relation to French History. Percy Allen. Archer. 1933.

Les Vers de Pibrac sur La Mort de Bussy D'Ambois. H. Vaganay. (*Rev. de Litt. Comp.*) XIII. 1933.

George Chapman. (*T.L.S.*) May 10, 1934.

George Chapman. James Smith. *Scrutiny.* March, June 1935.

Notes on Chapman's Plays. G. G. Loane. (*M.L.R.*) 1938 and 1943.

A Fragment from Henslowe's Diary. W. W. Greg. (*Library*). 1938.

Another Fragment from Henslowe's Diary. J. Q. Adams. (*Library*.) 1939.

Die Philosophisch-poetische Entwicklung George Chapmans. N. von Pogrell. Hamburg. 1939.

The Early Life of George Chapman. J. Robertson. (*M.L.R.*) 1945.

Chapman's Senecal Man. M. Higgins. (*R.E.S.*) 1945.

Textual and Bibliographical

Extant Autographs. (*Library.*) X. 310. 1929.
Keep the Widow Waking. C. J. Sisson. (*Library.*) VIII. 1927.
An Introduction to Bibliography. R. B. McKerrow. 1927. Pp. 192–3.

Standard Modern Edition

The Plays and Poems of George Chapman. T. M. Parrott. Routledge.
(*Tragedies*, 1910. *Comedies*, 1914.)

2. MARSTON
Editions : Single Works

The Scourge of Villainy, ed., with Introduction, by G. B. Harrison.
(*Bodley Head Quartos*, XIII.) 1925.
Eastwood Ho, ed. J. A. Harris. (*Yale Studies in English*, 73.) O.U.P.
1926.
The Metamorphosis of Pigmalion's Image. Golden Cockerel Press. 1926.

Editions : Collected

The Plays of John Marston. Vol. I, ed. H. Harvey Wood. Oliver
& Boyd. 1934.

Critical and Biographical

John Marston, Dramatist : Some New Facts. R. E. Brettle. (*M.L.R.*)
1927.
John Marston, Dramatist, at Oxford. R. E. Brettle. (*R.E.S.*) 1927.
John Marston. R. E. Brettle. 1928. (University of Oxford. Com-
mittee for Advanced Studies. *Abstracts of Dissertations for the
Degree of Ph.D.* Vol. 1.)
Allusions to James I. and his Court in Marston's 'Fawn'. A. W.
Upton. (*P.M.L.A.*) Dec. 1929.
Marston and Everard Guilpin. S. H. Atkins. (*T.L.S.*) June 9, 1932.
The Dates of 'Hamlet' and 'The Malcontent'. H. R. Walley.
(*R.E.S.*) Oct. 1933.
Shakespeare's Conception of Hamlet. H. R. Walley. (*P.M.L.A.*)
Oct. 1933.
The Date of 'The Malcontent' : A Rejoinder. E. E. Stoll. (*R.E.S.*)
Jan. 1935.
Senecan Elements in Marston's ' Antonio and Mellida '. J. O. Eidson.
(*M.L.N.*) 1937.
A New Date for ' Antonio's Revenge '. D. J. McGinn. (*P.M.L.A.*)
1938.
An Explanation of the two editions of Marston's ' Fawe '. W. L.
Halstead. (*S. in Ph.*) 1943.
The Convention of the Stoic Hero. M. Higgins. (*M.L.N.*) 1944.

Textual and Bibliographical

A John Marston Letter. W. H. Grattan Flood. (*R.E.S.*) Jan. 1928.
The 'Poet Marston' Letter to Sir Gervase Clifton, 1607. R. E. Brettle.
(*R.E.S.*) April 1928.

Marston Bibliography : A Correction. R. E. Brettle. (*Library*.) Sept. 1934.

The Plays of John Marston. [Review of H. Harvey Wood's edition above.] W. W. Greg. (*M.L.R.*) Jan. 1935.

The Plays of John Marston. [Review, ibid.] R. E. Brettle. (*R.E.S.*) April 1935.

Standard Modern Edition

A. H. Bullen. 3 Vols. 1887.

3. BEN JONSON
Editions : Single Works

The Spanish Tragedy, ed., with Introduction, W. W. Greg. (*Mal Soc. Repr.*)

Eastwood Hoe, ed. J. Harris. (*Yale Studies in English*, 73.) O.U.P. 1926.

Every Man in His Humour, ed. J. K. Peel. Knopf. 1928.

Ben Jonson's 'Volpone'. Freely adapted into German by Stefan Zweig. Trans. Langner. New York. 1928.

Every Man in His Humour, ed. J. Hampden. (*Nelson Playbooks*.) 1929.

The Sad Shepherd, ed. L. J. Potts. C.U.P.

The Masque of Queenes. Eyre & Spottiswoode. 1929.

Volpone. Italian trans. by Allisandro de Stefani. (*Nuova Antologia*.) 1929.

Editions : Collected

Ben Jonson, ed. C. H. Herford and Percy Simpson. In progress. (Vols. I–VII. O.U.P. 1925–41).

Ben Jonson : Best Plays, ed. B. Nicholson and C. H. Herford. 3 vols. Boston. 1930.

Critical and Biographical

B. J. [Review, Oxf. ed.] W. W. Greg. (*M.L.R.*) April 1926.

Some Notes on B. J.'s Works. W. W. Greg. (*R.E.S.*) April 1926.

Jonson and Drummond, their Conversations . . . C. L. Stainer. Oxford. 1925.

The Staple of News. F. A. Pottle. (*M.L.N.*) April 1925.

B. J.'s Ode to 'The Phoenix and the Turtle'. Sir I. Gollancz. (*T.L.S.*) Oct. 1925.

B. J.'s Art. E. C. Dunn. Smith College, Northampton, Mass. 1925.

The Riddle of Jonson's Chronology. W. W. Greg. (*Library*.) March 1926.

A Tale of a Tub. E. R. Brown. (*T.L.S.*) May 10, 1928.

B. J. and the Elizabethan Tacitus. Sir I. Gollancz. (*T.L.S.*) May 10, 1928.

    See also : Percy Simpson, June 14 ; Sir I. Gollancz, June 21 ; M. J. Ryan, July 19.

B. J., Stow and Drummond. O. F. W. Lodge. (*T.L.S.*) May 31, 1928.

A Jonson allusion . . . B. M. Wagner. (*P.Q.*) July 1928.

B. J. and Rabelais. H. Brown. (*M.L.N.*) Jan. 1929.

The Plots of B. J. E. C. Knowlton. (*M.L.N.*) Feb. 1929.

B. J. and Cecilia Bulstrode. P. Simpson. (*T.L.S.*) March 6, 1930.

B. J. and Hoskyns. L. R. Osborn. (*T.L.S.*) May 1, 1930.
See also : H.H.C. May 8, 1930.

B. J. on Chapman. P. Simpson. (*T.L.S.*) March 3, 1932.

A Note on 'The Gypsies Metamorphosed'. S. A. Tannenbaum. (*P.M.L.A.*) Sept. 1932.

The Memoirs of Sir Robert Sibbald (1641–1722), with . . . a Refutation of the Charge against Sir R. S. of forging B. J.'s 'Conversations'. F. P. Hett. O.U.P. 1932.

'The Alchemist' and 'Epicoene'. R. G. Howarth. (*T.L.S.*) April 26, 1934.

Ben Jonson on the English Stage. R. G. Noyes. Harvard Univ. Press and O.U.P. 1935.

Topographical Comedy in the Seventeenth Century. R. H. Perkinson. (*E.L.H.*) Dec. 1936.

Jonson's Marriage. Mark Eccles. (*R.E.S.*) July 1936.

The Dramatic Construction of 'Poetaster'. O. J. Campbell. (*H.L.B.*) April 1936.

Drama and Society in the Age of Jonson. L. C. Knights. Chatto and Windus. 1937.

Ben Jonson : Poet. The Social Background of the Plays. (*T.L.S.*) June 5, 1937.

Ben Jonson the Actor. F. T. Bowers. (*S. in Ph.*) July 1937.

Jonson and the Spies. Mark Eccles. (*R.E.S.*) Oct. 1937.

Classical Mythology in the Plays, Masques, and Poems of Ben Jonson. C. F. Wheeler. Princeton Univ. Press and O.U.P. 1938.

Seventeenth-Century Allusions to Ben Jonson. G. E. Bentley. (*P.M.L.A.*) Oct. 1941.

The Language of Satirized Characters in 'Poetaster'; a socio-stylistic analysis, 1597–1602. A. H. King. Williams and Norgate. 1942.

Unity of Time in 'Every Man in His Humour' and 'Cynthia's Revels'. Martin Kallick. (*M.L.N.*) 1942.

Jonson and Dickens. E. Simpson. (*Essays and Studies.*) O.U.P. 1943.

Ben Jonson and the Devil Tavern. K. Esdaile. (*Essays and Studies.*) O.U.P. 1943.

New Light on Ben Jonson's Workmanship. E. W. Talbert. (*S. in Ph.*) 1943.

The Classical Mythology and the Structure of 'Cynthia's Revels'. E. W. Talbert. (*P.Q.*) 1943.

The Function of the Masques in 'Cynthia's Revels'. A. H. Gilbert. (*P.Q.*) 1943.

The Imagery of Ben Jonson. D. J. Gordon. (*J.W.C.I.*) 1943.

Jonson's 'Cynthia's Revels' and the War of the Theatres. R. W. Berringer. (*P.Q.*) 1943.

Shakespeare and Jonson. G. E. Bentley. 2 vols. Chicago and Cambridge Univ. Presses. 1945.
Jonson and Juvenal. Kathryn A. McEuen. (*R.E.S.*) April 1945.

Textual and Bibliographical

The Genuineness of the Drummond Conversations. P. Simpson. (*R.E.S.*) Jan. 1926.
Was there a 1612 Quarto of 'Epicoene'? W. W. Greg. (*Library.*) Dec. 1934.

Standard Modern Edition

C. Herford and Percy Simpson (*above*). In progress.

4. DEKKER
Editions : Single Works

Shoemaker's Holiday. J. R. Sutherland. O.U.P. 1928

Critical and Biographical

'*The Shoemaker's Holiday*' *and* '*Romeo and Juliet*'. R. A. Law. (*S. in Ph.*) April 1924.
The Bloodie Banquet. E. H. C. Oliphant. (*T.L.S.*) Dec. 17, 1925.
'*Keep the Widow Waking*': *A lost play by Dekker.* C. J. Sisson. (*Library.*) June and Sept. 1927.
The Topography of Dekker's 'The Shoemaker's Holiday'. W. L. Chandler. (*S. in Ph.*) Oct. 1929.
The Sources of the Characters in 'The Shoemaker's Holiday'. W. L. Chandler. (*Mod. Phil.*) Nov. 1929.
The Life and Works of Henry Chettle. H. Jenkins. 1935.
A Fragment from Henslowe's Diary. W. W. Greg. (*The Library.*) 1938.
Another Fragment from Henslowe's Diary. J. Q. Adams. (*The Library.*) Sept. 1939.
Note on Dekker's 'Old Fortunatus'. W. L. Halstead. (*M.L.N.*) May 1939.
Dekker's Arrest by the Chamberlain's Men. W. L. Halstead (*N. and Q.*) Jan. 21, 1939
Thomas Dekker : Burial Place. Mark Eccles. (*N. and Q.*) Aug. 26, 1939.
New Source Influence on 'The Shoemaker's Holiday'. W. L. Halstead. (*M.L.N.*) Feb. 1941.
Surviving Materials in Dekker's 'Old Fortunatus'. W. L. Halstead. (*N. and Q.*) Jan. 17, 1942.

Textual and Bibliographical

The Early Editions of Thomas Dekker's . . . 'Honest Whore', I. M. Baird. (*Library.*) June 1929.
'*The Honest Whore*' *or* '*The Converted Courtesan*'. W. W. Greg. June 1934.

The undated Quarto of I 'Honest Whore'. H. Spenser. (*Library*.) 1935.
The *1602* Additions to 'The Spanish Tragedy'. H. W. Crundell. (*T.L.S.*) 1937.
Dekker's 'Phaeton'. W. L. Halstead. (*N. and Q.*) 1938.
Collaboration in 'The Patient Grissill'. W. L. Halstead. (*P.Q.*) 1939.
The Authorship of the 'Spanish Tragedy' additions. H. W. Crundell. (*N. and Q.*) 1941.
The Merry Devil of Edmonton, ed. W. A. Abrams. Duke U.P. 1942.
The Authorship of 'The Welsh Embassador'. B. Lloyd. (*R.E.S.*). 1945.

Standard Modern Edition

[R. H. Shepherd.] Pearson Reprints. 4 vols. 1873.

5. MIDDLETON

[As, in the case of Middleton, several plays were undoubtedly written after 1616 and are consequently omitted from *The Elizabethan Stage*, it has seemed advisable to give a complete list of his extant dramatic works, arranged in approximately chronological order. I have here followed Bald's dating.]

Early Editions

Blurt Master-Constable. 1601–2.
The Phoenix. 1602.
The Family of Love. 1602 (revised 1606 or 1607).
The Honest Whore, I. 1604.
A Mad World, My Masters. 1604 (revised 1606 or 1607).
Michaelmas Term. 1604.
Your Five Gallants. 1605 (revised 1607).
A Trick to catch the Old One. c. 1606.
The Roaring Girl. 1607–8.
A Chaste Maid in Cheapside. 1613.
More Dissemblers besides Women. c. 1615.
No Wit, No Help, like a Woman's. c. 1615.
A Fair Quarrel. 1615–16.
The Witch. 1616.
The Widow. 1616.
The Old Law. c. 1616.
The Mayor of Quinborough. 1615–20.
The World Tossed at Tennis. 1619.
Anything for a Quiet Life. 1621.
Women Beware Women. c. 1621.
The Changeling. 1622.
The Spanish Gipsey. 1623.
A Game at Chesse. 1624.

Editions : Single Works

A Game at Chesse by Thomas Middleton, ed. R. C. Bald. C.U.P. 1929.
Hengist, King of Kent: or the Mayor of Queenborough, by Thomas Middleton, ed. R. C. Bald. Scribner. 1938.

Critical and Bibliographical

Un Embajador de España en la Escena Inglesa (Del Homenaje a Menendez Pidal. Vol. III). Antonio Pastor. 1925.

Thomas Middleton's Early Non-Dramatic Work. H. Dugdale Sykes. (*N. and Q.*) June 20, 1925.

The Dramatic Technique of Thomas Middleton in his Comedies of London Life. W. D. Dunkel. Chicago. 1925.

Middleton and the Fashion in Playmaking. H. B. Bullock. (*P.M.L.A.*) Sept. 1926.

The Social Mode of Restoration Comedy. K. Lynch. 1927.

Thomas Middleton's 'The Viper's Brood'. H. N. Hillebrand. (*M.L.N.*) Jan. 1927.

Middleton's 'A Game at Chesse'. L. B. Wright. (*T.L.S.*) Feb. 16, 1928.

Middleton's 'A Game at Chesse'. R. C. Bald. (*T.L.S.*) May 17, 1928.

Campion's 'Art of English Poesie' and Middleton's 'Chaste Maid in Cheapside'. E. L. Buckingham. (*P.M.L.A.*) Sept. 1928.

'Anything for a Quiet Life'. W. D. Dunkel. (*P.M.L.A.*) Sept. 1928.

Shakespeare and his Fellow Dramatists. E. H. C. Oliphant. N.Y. 1929.

Middleton's 'A Game at Chess'. R. C. Bald. (*T.L.S.*) Feb. 6, 1930.

A New Manuscript of Middleton's 'A Game at Chesse'. R. C. Bald. (*M.L.R.*) July 1930.

The Authorship of 'The Puritan'. W. D. Dunkel. (*P.M.L.A.*) Sept. 1930.

The Authorship of 'The Revenger's Tragedy'. W. D. Dunkel. (*P.M.L.A.*) Sept. 1931.

Middleton's Birth and Education. Mark Eccles. (*R.E.S.*) Oct. 1931.

Middleton's Civic Employment. R. C. Bald. (*Mod. Phil.*) Aug. 1933.

Did not Rowley merely Revise Middleton? W. D. Dunkel. (*P.M.L.A.*) Sept. 1933.

A Middleton Forgery. S. A. Tannenbaum. (*P.Q.*) Jan. 1933.

A Note on Moll Cutpurse—'The Roaring Girl'. M. Dowling. (*R.E.S.*) Jan. 1934.

Thomas Middleton's Use of 'Imprese' in 'Your Five Gallants'. W. S. Hoole. (*S. in Ph.*) April 1934.

Middleton's Acquaintance with the 'Merrie Conceited Jests of George Peele'. M. G. Christian. (*P.M.L.A.*) Sept. 1935.

The Chronology of Middleton's Plays. R. C. Bald. (*M.L.R.*) Jan. 1937.

Swinburne on Middleton. T. Larson. (*T.L.S.*) June 17, 1939.

Middleton's 'No Wit, No Help, Like a Woman's' and Della Porta's 'La Sorella'. D. J. Gordon. (*R.E.S.*) Oct. 1941.

The Date of Middleton's 'Women Beware Women'. Baldwin Maxwell. (*P.Q.*) 1943.

An Early Version of Middleton's 'Game at Chesse'. R. C. Bald. (*M.L.R.*) 1943.

Middleton's 'Michaelmas Term'. Baldwin Maxwell. (*P.Q.*) 1943.

Textual and Bibliographical

A Lost and Found Volume of Manuscript Plays. F. S. Boas. (*T.L.S.*)
1935.

Standard Modern Edition

A. H. Bullen. 8 vols. 1885–6.

6. TOURNEUR

Edition : Collected

The Works of Cyril Tourneur, ed. Allardyce Nicoll. Fanfrolico Press.
1930.

Critical and Biographical

The Authorship of 'The Revenger's Tragedy'. E. H. C. Oliphant.
(*S. in Ph.*) April 1926.

Cyril Tourneur. *T.L.S.* (Leading Article.) Nov. 13, 1930.

Tourneur and 'The Revenger's Tragedy'. E. H. C. Oliphant. (*T.L.S.*)
Dec. 18, 1930.

Tourneur and the 'Revenger's Tragedy'. The Reviewer. (*T.L.S.*)
Jan. 1, 1931.

    See also : E. H. C. Oliphant, Feb. 5, 1931 ; B. M. Wagner,
        April 23, 1931 ; F. L. Jones, June 18, 1931.

Cyril Tourneur. J. R. Sutherland. (*T.L.S.*) April 16, 1931.

The Authorship of 'The Revenger's Tragedy'. W. D. Dunkel.
(*P.M.L.A.*) Sept. 1931.

A Tourneur Mystification. S. A. Tannenbaum. (M.L.N.) March
1932.

The Imagery of 'The Revenger's Tragedie' and 'The Atheists Tragedie'.
U. M. Ellis-Fermor. (*M.L.R.*) July 1935.

Tourneur and Mr. T. S. Eliot. E. H. Oliphant. (*S. in Ph.*) 1935.

'The Revenger's Tragedy' and the Morality Tradition. L. G. Salingar.
(*Scrutiny*.) 1938.

Cyril Tourneur. Harold Jenkins. (*R.E.S.*) 1941.

The Influence of Calvinistic Thought in Tourneur's ' Atheist's Tragedie '
Michael H. Higgins. (*R.E.S.*) 1943.

Textual and Bibliographical

Textual Errors in the Malone Society's 'The Second Maid's Tragedy'.
S. A. Tannenbaum. (*P.Q.*) July 1930.

Cyril Tourneur. W. W. Greg. (*T.L.S.*) Jan. 1931.

Standard Modern Edition

A. Nicoll (above).

7. WEBSTER [*after 1927*]

Critical and Biographical

'Appius and Virginia': by Webster and Heywood. H. D. Gray.
(*S. in Ph.*) April 1927.

English Hymns and Ballads and other Studies in Popular Literature.
Peter Haworth. Oxford. 1927.

John Webster : Playwright and Naturalist. E. W. Hendy. (*Nineteenth Century.*) Jan. 1928.
Webster's Debt to Guazzo. Marcia Anderson. (*S. in Ph.*)   1939.

Textual and Bibliographical

The Complete Works of John Webster. [Review, Lucas's ed.] W. W. Greg. (*R.E.S.*) Oct. 1928.

Standard Modern Edition

F. L. Lucas. Chatto & Windus. 4 vols. 1927.

8. GREVILLE
Edition : Collected

Poems and Dramas of Fulke Greville, first Lord Brooke, ed. Geoffrey Bullough. Edinburgh. 1939.

Critical and Biographical

The Influence of Robert Garnier on Elizabethan Drama. A. M. Witherspoon. Yale U.P. 1924.
Fulke Greville, Lord Brooke. (*T.L.S.*) (Leading Article.) Aug. 30, 1928.
Fulke, Greville, Lord Brooke. B. M. Ward. (*T.L.S.*) Sept. 6, 1928. And the following : W. W. Greg, Sept. 13 ; B. M. Ward, Sept. 20; W. W. Greg, Sept. 27; B. M. Ward, Oct. 4.
The Warwickshire Poets, ed. C. H. Poole and Russell Markland. Lytham. 1929.
Poems and a Defence of Rime, by Samuel Daniel. Ed. A. C. Sprague. O.U.P. 1930.
Samuel Daniel and Fulke Greville. (*T.L.S.*) [Rev.] June 5, 1930.
The Sources of Fulke Greville's 'Alaham'. W. G. Rice. (*J.E.G.P.*) April 1931.
Fulke Greville, First Lord Brooke. G. Bullough. (*M.L.R.* XXVIII.) Jan. 1933.

Textual and Bibliographical

'*Certaine Learned and Elegant Workes*'. W. W. Greg. (*Library,* VII, 217.) Sept. 1926–7.
Fulke Greville, Lord Brooke. W. W. Greg. (*T.L.S.*) Sept. 1928.
Fulke Greville's Works (1633). G. Bullough. (*T.L.S.*) Oct. 15, 1931.

Standard Edition

G. Bullough. 2 vols. 1939 (*above*).

9 BEAUMONT AND FLETCHER
[See introductory note to book-list for Middleton.]
Early Editions

[The following is a list of the plays included in F. 1679, with the addition of the non-Folio plays now generally attributed in part to

Fletcher. They are arranged approximately in chronological order
and the date most usually accepted for the writing of each (in cases of
great difficulty, the range of dates suggested) follows in round brackets.
The early editions are then indicated, up to the date of the second
folio. The letters B, F, M, following these indicate that the presence
of Beaumont's, Fletcher's, Massinger's hand is generally traced in the
given play ; the names of other playwrights known or supposed to
have taken a share follow these. This list makes no claim to bibliographical completeness or to offer any fresh information. It is merely
inserted for convenience of reference from Chapter XI and from the
biographical notes IX and X.]

1. *The Woman Hater.* (c. 1606.) Qq. 1607, 1607, 1648, 1049
   (reissue). F. 1679. B.
2. *The Knight of the Burning Pestle.* (1607.) Qq. 1613, 1635, 1635.
   F. 1679. B.
3. *The Faithful Shepherdess.* (1608–9.) Qq. N.D., 1629, 1634, 1656,
   1665. F. 1679. F.
4. *The Woman's Prize.* (1604 >.) Ff. 1647, 1679. F.
5. *Philaster.* (> 1610.) Qq. 1620, 1622, 1628, 1634, 1639, 1652,
   1652, N.D. [? 1663.] F. 1679. B + F.
6. *The Coxcomb.* (1608–10.) Ff. 1647, 1679. B + F.
7. *The Maid's Tragedy.* (> 1611.) Qq. 1619, 1622, 1630, 1638,
   1641, 1650, 1661. F. 1679. B + F.
8. *A King and No King.* (1611.) Qq. 1619, 1625, 1631, 1639, 1655,
   1661, 1676. F. 1679. B + F.
9. *Four Plays in One.* (? 1608–1612.) Ff. 1647, 1679. B + F.
10. *Cupid's Revenge.* (> 1612.) Qq. 1615, 1630, 1635. F. 1679.
    B + F.
11. *The Captain.* (1609–12.) Ff. 1647, 1679. F + M ? Rowley?
12. *Wit at Several Weapons.* (? 1609 10–?) Ff. 1647, 1679. F + B ?
    Middleton ? Rowley ?
13. *King Henry VIII.* (1613.) F. 1623 (Shakespeare). Not in Ff.
    1647, 1679. F + M ? + Shakespeare.
14. *Two Noble Kinsmen.* (1613.) Q. 1634. F. 1679. F + B ? M ?
    Shakespeare ?
15. *The Honest Man's Fortune.* (1613.) Ms. Dyce. 9. Ff. 1647,
    1679. F + M + B ? Field ? Daborne ? Tourneur ? Cart-
    wright ?
16. *Bonduca.* (1609–14.) Ff. 1647, 1679. F.
17. *Monsieur Thomas.* (1610–16) Qq. 1639, N.D. [c. 1661]. F.
    1679. F.
18. *Valentinian.* (1610–14.) Ff. 1647, 1679. F.
19. *The Faithful Friends.* (c. 1614.) MS. Dyce. 10. Not in Ff. 1647,
    1679. F ? + B ? M ? Daborne ? Field ? Shirley ?
20. *Wit Without Money.* (c. 1614.) Qq. 1639, 1661. F. 1679. F.
21. *The Scornful Lady.* (1613–17.) Qq. 1616, 1625, 1630, 1635, 1639,
    1651, 1677. F. 1679. B + F + M ?
22. *Thierry and Theodoret.* (> 1621.) Qq. 1621, 1648, 1649 (re-
    issue). F. 1679. F + M + Field ? Daborne ? Beaumont ?

23. *The Nightwalker* (?–?.) Qq. 1640, 1661. F. 1679. F + Shirley.
24. *Love's Cure.* (? 1621–?.) Ff. 1647, 1679. M + B ? F ?
25. *The Loyal Subject.* (1618.) Ff. 1647, 1679. F.
26. *The Queen of Corinth.* (> 1618/19.) Ff. 1647, 1679. F +
      M + ?
27. *The Mad Lover.* (c. 1618.) Ff. 1647, 1679. F.
28. *The Knight of Malta.* (> 1619.) Ff. 1647, 1679. F + M +
      Field ?
29. *The Humourous Lieutenant.* (1619–23.) MS. (Crane) 1625. Ff.
      1647, 1679. F.
30. *Women Pleased.* (1620 ?) Ff. 1647, 1679. F.
31. *The Island Princess.* (> 1621.) Ff. 1647, 1679. F.
32. *The Pilgrim.* (> 1621.) Ff. 1647, 1679. F.
33. *The Wild-Goose-Chase.* (> 1621.) F. 1652. F. 1679. F.
34. *Love's Pilgrimage.* Ff. 1647, 1679. F + Shirley ? + B. J. (bor-
      rowing).
35. *Beggars Bush.* (1615 ?–22.) Q. 1661. Ff. 1647, 1679. F + M.
36. *The Double Marriage.* (1619–22.) Ff. 1647–79. F + M.
37. *Sir John Van Olden Barnavelt.* (1619.) Not in Ff. 1647, 1679.
      Bullen. *Old English Plays* ii. 1883. F + M.
38. *The False One.* (1619–22.) Ff. 1647, 1679. F + M.
39. *The Little French Lawyer.* (1619–22.) Ff. 1647, 1679. F + M.
40. *The Custom of the Country.* (1619–22.) Ff. 1647, 1679. F + M.
41. *The Laws of Candy.* (1619–22.) Ff. 1647, 1679. M + F ?
42. *The Spanish Curate.* (1622.) Ff. 1647, 1679. F + M.
43. *The Prophetess.* (1622.) Ff. 1647, 1679. F + M.
44. *The Sea Voyage.* (1622.) Ff. 1647, 1679. F + M ? + ?
45. *The Maid in the Mill.* (> 1623.) Ff. 1647, 1679. F + W. Rowley.
46. *A Wife for a Month.* (1624.) Ff. 1647, 1679. F.
47. *Rule a Wife and Have a Wife.* (> 1624.) Q. 1640. F. 1679. F.
48. *The Chances.* (1615 ?–1627 ?) Ff. 1647, 1679. F + ?
49. *The Lover's Progress.* (1623 ?–1634.) Ff. 1647, 1679. F + M
      (rev.)
50. *The Nice Valour.* (> 1634.) Ff. 1647, 1679. F ? + Rowley ?
51. *The Bloody Brother.* (1624 >.) Qq. 1639, 1640. F. 1679.
      M + F + Jonson + Field.
52. *The Elder Brother.* (1625 >.) Qq. 1637, 1637, 1651, 1661, 1678.
      F. 1679. F + M.
53. *The Faire Maide of the Inne.* (> 1626.) Ff. 1647, 1679. M + ?
54. *The Noble Gentleman.* (> 1636.) Ff. 1647, 1679. F ? + ?
55. *The Coronation.* (?.) Q. 1640. F. 1679. Shirley.

[Nos. 13. 19 and 37 are not in Ff. 1647, 1679, but have subsequently
been attributed in part at least to Fletcher. Nos. 41, 53, 55 are in
F. 1679, but are not now generally attributed to Fletcher. No. 33
(*The Wild-Goose-Chase*) is the only play omitted from F. 1647 which
had not previously appeared in Q. The reason for this is explained
by the publishers of F. 1647 ; the play was then missing. It was
recovered and published separately in folio in 1652 and, of course,
included in F. 1679.]

Later editions are :
  A. Glover and A. R. Waller, *The Works of Francis Beaumont and
    John Fletcher.* 10 vols. (Cambridge English Classics), which
    follows the text of F. 1679 with collations from the texts of
    F. 1647 and the Quartos. (1905–12.)
  A. H. Bullen, *The Works of Francis Beaumont and John Fletcher* (in
    progress, 4 vols. issued) which bases its text on Dyce (1843–6,
    11 vols. ; 1852, 2 vols.) with editions of separate plays by various
    editors. (1904–12.)

Critical and Biographical

John Fletcher. (*T.L.S.*) Aug. 20, 1925.
The Hungry Knave in the B. & F. plays. Baldwin Maxwell. (*P.Q.*)
    Oct. 1926.
Italian Influence in Fletcher's 'Faithful Shepherdess'. V. M. Jeffery.
    (*M.L.R.*) April 1926.
A Probable Source of B. & F.'s 'Philaster'. T. P. Harrison. (*P.M.L.A.*)
    June 1926.
B. & F. on the Restoration Stage. A. C. Sprague. O.U.P. 1926.
The Plays of Beaumont and Fletcher. E. H. C. Oliphant. O.U.P.
    1927.
The Influence of B. & F. on Restoration Drama. J. H. Wilson. The
    Ohio State University Press. 1928.
Marlowe, Beaumont, and 'Julius Caesar'. T. M. Parrott. (*M.L.N.*)
    Feb. 1929.
Allusions to James I and his Court in Beaumont's 'Woman Hater'.
    A. W. Upton. (*P.M.L.A.*) Dec. 1929.
A hitherto unpublished John Fletcher Autograph. S. A. Tannenbaum.
    (*J.E.G.P.*) Jan. 1929.
A Question of Plus or Minus. W. W. Greg. (*R.E.S.*) July 1930.
Plays of B. and F. : Some Additional Notes. E. H. C. Oliphant.
    (*P.Q.*) Jan. 1930.
The Authorship of 'The Woman-Hater'. A. W. Upton. (*P.Q.*)
    Jan. 1930.
The John Fletcher Holograph. S. A. Tannenbaum. (*P.Q.*) Oct. 1934.
On Six Plays in 'Beaumont and Fletcher, 1679'. R. W. Bond.
    (*R.E.S.*) July, 1935.
The High Design of 'A King and No King'. A. Mizener. (*Mod. Phil.*)
    Nov. 1940.
Studies in Beaumont, Fletcher, and Massinger. Baldwin Maxwell.
    Univ. of North Carolina Press and O.U.P. 1940.
*A Note on the Stage History of Beaumont and Fletcher's 'Love's Pil-
    grimage' and 'The Chances'.* W. C. Powell. (*M.L.N.*) Feb.
    1941.
Characterisation in John Fletcher's Tragi-comedies. E. M. Waith.
    (*R.E.S.*) 1943.

Textual and Bibliographical

Bibliographical Studies in the Beaumont and Fletcher Folio of 1647.
    R. C. Bald. O.U.P. 1937.

332　THE JACOBEAN DRAMA

Standard Modern Edition
A. Glover and A. R. Waller. C.U.P. (10 vols.) 1906–12.

10. FORD
Early Editions
[See introductory note to book-list for Middleton.]
The Witch of Edmonton. (1621.) Q. 1658. (With Rowley and Dekker.)
The Sun's Darling. (1624.) Qq. 1656, 1657. (With Dekker.)
The Lover's Melancholy. (1628.) Q. 1629.
'Tis Pity She's a Whore. (1628–32.) Q. 1633.
The Broken Heart. (1628–32.) Q. 1633.
Love's Sacrifice. (1628–32.) Q. 1633.
Perkin Warbeck. (> 1634.) Q. 1634.
The Fancies, Chast and Noble. (1637 ?) Q. 1638.
The Lady's Trial. (1638.) Q. 1639.
The Queene (?). Q. 1653.

Editions : Single Works
Annabella. (Trans. and adapted by Maurice Maeterlinck.) 1895.
Perkin Warbeck, ed. J. P. Pickburn and J. le G. Brereton. 1896.
The Broken Heart, ed. O. M. Smeaton. 1906.
The Queene, ed. W. Bang. (*Materialen*, XIII.) 1906.
'Tis Pity, ed. S. P. Sherman. (*Belles Lettres.*) Boston 1916.
The Broken Heart, ed. S. P. Sherman. (*Belles Lettres.*) Boston 1916.
Le Sacrifice d'amour. (Trans. Georges Pillement.) (*La Renaissance du Livre.*) Paris. 1925.
Dommage qu'elle soit une prostituée. [Ibid., same volume.]
Perkin Warbeck. A critical edition. M. C. Struble. 1926.

Editions : Collected
(Nineteenth century editions by : H. Weber (1811), W. Gifford (1827), H. Coleridge (1846), A. Dyce (1869), H. Ellis (1888), (Mermaid, selection), H. Bullen (1895).)
The Dramatic Works of John Ford. Vol. II, ed. Henry de Vocht. (Materials for the study of the Old English Drama. New Series. Vol. I.) Louvain. 1927. (The continuation of Bang's *Materialen* from 1906.)

Critical and General
(The outstanding studies of the late nineteenth century are : A. C. Swinburne's *Essays and Studies*, 1888 ; Marcel Schwob's *Annabella et Giovanni*, 1894, and Emil Koeppel's, *Quellen Studien*, in *Quellen und Forschungen*, LXXXII, 1897.)
John Forde und Parthenios von Nikaia. W. Bang. (*Engl. Stud.*, XXXVI.) 1906.
A New Play by Ford. S. P. Sherman. (*M.L.N.*) 1908–9.
The Sources of Ford's 'Perkin Warbeck'. J. le G. Brereton. (*Angl.*, XXXIV.) 1911.

Ford's Posthumous Play : '*The Queen*'. H. D. Sykes. (*N. and Q.*) 1920.

The Authorship of 'The Witch of Edmonton'. H. D. Sykes. (*N. and Q.*) 1926.

Ford and 'The Phoenix'. D. MacCarthy. (*New Statesman.*) 1923.

Elegy on Randolph's Finger, ed. G. C. Moore Smith. Oxford, 1923.

John Ford the author of 'The Spanish Gipsey'. H. D. Sykes. (*M.L.R.*, XIX.) 1934.

An Inedited MS. of Ford's 'Fame's Memoriall'. Bertram Lloyd. *R.E.S.*, I.). 1925.

The Indebtedness of Ford's 'Perkin Warbeck' to Gainsford. M. C. Struble. (*Angl.*) 1925.

Keep the Widow Waking. C. J. Sisson. (*Library*, VIII.). 1927.

The Dedication of 'The City Madam'. A. K. MacIlwrath. (*Bodleian Quarterly Record*, V.) 1928.

Patmore and Ford. Clifford Bax. (*T.L.S.*) May 12, 1932.

John Ford at the Middle Temple. M. J. Sargeaunt. (*R.D.S.*, VIII.) Jan. 1932.

Bequests to John Ford. M. J. Sargeaunt. (*R.E.S.*, IX,) Oct. 1933.

Writings ascribed to John Ford by Joseph Hunter in 'Chorus Vatum'. M. J. Sargeaunt. (*R.E.S.*, X.) April 1934.

John Ford. M. J. Sargeaunt. Blackwell. 1935.

Burton's Influence on Ford's 'The Lover's Melancholy'. G. F. Sensabaugh. (*S. in Ph.*) 1936.

Abnormal Psychology on John Ford's 'Perkin Warbeck'. L. Babb. (*M.L.N.*) 1936.

Textual and Bibliographical

The Bakings of Betsy. W. W. Greg. (*Library*, 3rd ser.) No. 7, Vol. II, July 1911.

A Note on John Ford. T. M. Parrott. (*M.L.N.*). 1943.

Standard Modern Edition

W. Bang, *Materialen*, N.S. i., ed. H. de Vocht. (In progress.)

INDEX

(to Chaps. I–XIV)

335

JARROLD AND SONS, LTD., THE EMPIRE PRESS, NORWICH